T0313816

BEYOND BANKS

Beyond Banks

Technology, Regulation, and the Future of Money

Dan Awrey

PRINCETON UNIVERSITY PRESS

PRINCETON AND OXFORD

Copyright © 2024 by Princeton University Press

Princeton University Press is committed to the protection of copyright and the intellectual property our authors entrust to us. Copyright promotes the progress and integrity of knowledge. Thank you for supporting free speech and the global exchange of ideas by purchasing an authorized edition of this book. If you wish to reproduce or distribute any part of it in any form, please obtain permission.

Requests for permission to reproduce material from this work should be sent to permissions@press.princeton.edu

Published by Princeton University Press

41 William Street, Princeton, New Jersey 08540
99 Banbury Road, Oxford OX2 6JX
press.princeton.edu

All Rights Reserved

ISBN 978-0-691-24542-3
ISBN (e-book) 978-0-691-24547-8

British Library Cataloging-in-Publication Data is available

Editorial: Joe Jackson and Emma Wagh
Production Editorial: Jill Harris
Jacket Design: Karl Spurzem
Production: Danielle Amatucci
Publicity: James Schneider and Kate Farquhar-Thomson

This book has been composed in Adobe Text and Gotham

Printed in the United States of America

10 9 8 7 6 5 4 3 2 1

CONTENTS

ACKNOWLEDGMENTS

This book is the product of a six-year research project that was born out of a desire to fill what I felt were the many and significant gaps in my understanding of the law and institutions at the heart of our intricately intertwined systems of banking, money, and payments. I have spent my entire adult life in finance: first in information technology, then as a lawyer and adviser to financial services firms, and now for the past fourteen years as a scholar of banking and financial regulation. Over this period, I have frequently come across laws, institutions, and industry practices that piqued my curiosity: How on earth did we end up *here*? Sometimes my curiosity was driven by my deep admiration for how policymakers, lawyers, and financial engineers had successfully tackled a particular challenge. Yet, more often than not, it was driven by my intense frustration with our collective inability to harness the enormous human, economic, and technological resources at our disposal to solve pressing social problems. In this spirit, this book is my attempt to understand why the United States was able to send twenty-four men to the moon, but seems chronically incapable of delivering a cheap, fast, secure, and universally accessible system of money and payments.

This book is also a product of extreme good fortune. The first stroke of good luck was that I found myself writing in the thick of a period of rapid technological and institutional change. These changes have inspired entrepreneurs all over the world to undertake a myriad of new experiments in money and payments. These experiments have then forced policymakers to rediscover, rethink, and increasingly reformulate the laws and institutions at the heart of the current monetary order. The long overdue, but ultimately very welcome, result has been an explosion in conversations, debates, conferences, research, writing, and policy proposals exploring the past, present, and future of money and payments. While keeping up to speed with these developments has often been an overwhelming task, it is difficult to imagine a more inspiring, energizing, or intellectually stimulating environment in which to explore a subject that most people, most of the time, never even think about.

The second stroke of good luck began in Oxford in the fall of 2008. It was there, in the shadows of the dreaming spires, that I met the two people who have had the greatest impact on my development as a scholar. The first is my doctoral thesis supervisor and longtime colleague, Professor John Armour. John is a true scholar's scholar: with a precise and open mind, a truly inclusive approach to teaching and research, and a deep belief in the value of knowledge and its importance in an open society. The second is my colleague and erstwhile partner in crime, Professor Kristin van Zwieten. Kristin is without a doubt the smartest person in every room she has ever entered. She is also the kindest, funniest, and most empathetic. I try—and fail—every day to live up to the extraordinary example that John and Kristin have set.

In the course of writing this book, I have also greatly benefited from conversations, feedback, and advice from many other people. This includes some of the superstars of monetary economics, history, and law: scholars like Professors Christine Desan, Darrell Duffie, David Fox, Anna Gelpern, Ben Geva, Lev Menand, Alistair Milne, Katharina Pistor, Morgan Ricks, and George Selgin. It also includes a truly incredible group of financial regulation scholars who, like myself, were forged in the fires of the global financial crisis: in particular, Professors Peter Conti-Brown, Kate Judge, Saule Omarova, Rory Van Loo, Yesha Yadav, and David Zaring. Last but not least, the analysis and ideas set out in this book have been greatly influenced and sharpened by my more recent collaborations with Howell Jackson, Tim Massad, Aaron Klein, Josh Macey, and Jeff Zhang. I am incredibly grateful for your time, your honest and detailed comments, your insightful and probing questions, and in general to be part of such a talented and committed community of scholars and policymakers. I am also grateful to Joe Jackson and the editors at Princeton University Press who were willing to take a chance on a how-to book about financial plumbing.

Finally, I would like to thank my wonderful wife, Diana, our dog, Parkin, and our extended family for all their encouragement and support. Being the spouse, parent, child, or pet of an absent-minded, chronically jet-lagged, and frequently stressed-out academic is not easy at the best of times—and there were many moments in the process of writing this book that were definitely not the best of times. Your unfailing love and support mean everything to me, even if I cannot always find the words or deeds to express it. Sorry, thank you, sorry.

Ithaca, New York
June 2024

BEYOND BANKS

Introduction

WE NEED TO TALK ABOUT MONEY

> When I was young I thought that money was the most important thing
> in life. Now that I am old, I know it is.
> —OSCAR WILDE

We want it. We need it. We work ourselves to the bone for it. We scrimp and
we save it, use it to buy our groceries, pay our bills, put our kids through
school, and save for our retirements. Whether we have any of it or not,
money plays a profoundly important role in all our lives—both as a central
institution of modern society and as something we experience on a unique
and deeply personal level each and every day. Yet, for something so fundamental to the fabric of our lives and society, most of us spend remarkably
little time thinking about what money is, where it comes from, and why we
use *this* as money but not *that* as money.

The fact that we ask so few questions about the nature, sources, or design
of our money is not simply a product of apathy, time constraints, or an aver-
sion to complex, highly technical subjects. Our parents didn't talk to us about
monetary institutions at the dinner table. We didn't miss that day at school.
Believe it or not, the fact that most of us do not think about the institutional
design of money is itself more or less *by design*. In fact, our money is legally
engineered so that we can go about our daily lives without caring two cents
about what makes our two cents worth two cents.

Today, the vast majority of the money in circulation in virtually all
advanced economies exists in the form of bank deposits. These deposits
represent the liabilities—the contractually enforceable *promises*—of your

bank to accept, transfer, and return your money to you in accordance with your instructions. In the United States, these demand, time, savings, and other deposits account for roughly 85 percent of the total money supply—over $21 trillion.[1] This figure dwarfs the value of all the other sources of money combined, including paper notes and coins ($2.3 trillion) and retail "money market" funds ($1.4 trillion).[2] And the United States is not alone. From the United Kingdom to Canada, Singapore to Australia, one of the defining features of the financial systems in most developed countries is their overwhelming reliance on bank deposits as a source of money. Accordingly, while the iconography of money often depicts it as a physical object printed, forged, and stamped by the machinery of the state, the reality is that most of our money consists of fundamentally intangible, electronically recorded IOUs made by what are, in theory at least, private firms.

So why do we trust these private firms with so much of our hard-earned money? The answer is that banks are not just any private firms. Nor are bank deposits just any contracts. In fact, banks and bank depositors benefit from some of the most sophisticated legal engineering the world has ever seen. Most importantly, the law provides banks with a public safety net not generally available to other types of private firms. This safety net includes access to central bank emergency lending facilities and special resolution frameworks for struggling banks. In almost 150 countries, banks and their depositors also benefit from deposit insurance schemes designed to ensure that banks can continue to honor their promises to depositors even during periods of severe financial distress—under conditions where most other firms would be forced to shut their doors and declare bankruptcy.[3] Collectively, these privileges and protections give banks an enormous comparative advantage in the creation of the promises that we call money. They also place banks at the center of a vast and sprawling electronic payment network in which this money constantly flows between households, businesses, and governments.

1. See Federal Reserve Bank of St. Louis, Money Stock Measures—H.6 (July 2023), reporting bank M2 (deposits minus currency in circulation) of $18.445 trillion and total reserve balances of $3.178 trillion.

2. Federal Reserve Bank of St. Louis, Money Stock Measures; see also Investment Company Institute, "Money Market Fund Assets" (September 28, 2023), https://www.ici.org/research/stats/mmf.

3. International Association of Deposit Insurers, "Deposit Insurance Systems Worldwide" (October 2, 2023), https://www.iadi.org/en/about-iadi/deposit-insurance-systems/dis-worldwide/.

Yet this system is in the process of undergoing an important and potentially destabilizing period of technological disruption. New technology is rapidly expanding the frontier of what is possible in the realm of money and payments. Spurred by a dramatic leap forward in computer storage capacity and processing power, along with the emergence and widespread adoption of the internet, social media platforms, and smartphones, entrepreneurs all over the world have sought to harness new technology to challenge the long-entrenched position of banks at the apex of our systems of money and payments. These efforts have already yielded popular payment platforms such as PayPal, Venmo, and Wise, China's Alipay and WeChat Pay, and Kenya's M-PESA. They have also yielded a variety of new and still relatively untested payment instruments, such as Tether, USDC, and other so-called stablecoins. And on the horizon, it is probably only a matter of time before we see Amazon, Google, and other big tech platforms officially enter the race for our wallets. While the technological diversity of these new institutions, platforms, and instruments can be overwhelming, the defining feature of this emerging "shadow" monetary system is that it seeks to compete with banks in the lucrative markets for money and payments while remaining *outside* the perimeter of the public safety net that has historically served to protect banks and their depositors.

The emergence of the shadow monetary system is by no means a recent development. Varieties of shadow money—e.g., bills of exchange, commercial paper, repurchase agreements, and other wholesale money market instruments—have been around as long as the business of banking. This shadow monetary system has been at the root of many of the most destructive episodes in financial history: from the 19th century crises chronicled in Walter Bagehot's *Lombard Street*,[4] to the Panic of 1907 that spurred the creation of the Federal Reserve System,[5] to the global financial crisis.[6] Yet, historically, this shadow monetary system has almost always been the domain of banks, broker-dealers, investment funds, and other sophisticated

---

4. See Walter Bagehot, *Lombard Street: A Description of the Money Market* (1873).

5. See Roger Lowenstein, *America's Bank: The Epic Struggle to Create the Federal Reserve* (2015); Hugh Rockoff, "It Is Always the Shadow Banks: The Regulatory Status of the Banks That Failed and Ignited America's Greatest Financial Panics," in Rockoff & Suto (eds.), *Coping with Financial Crises: Some Lessons from Economic History* (2018); Robert Bruner & Sean Carr, *The Panic of 1907: Lessons Learned from the Market's Perfect Storm* (2007); US National Monetary Commission, *Reports of the National Monetary Commission* (1909–1912), https://fraser.stlouisfed.org/series/publications-national-monetary-commission-series-1493.

6. See Morgan Ricks, *The Money Problem: Rethinking Financial Regulation* (2016); Gary Gorton & Andrew Metrick, *Slapped by the Invisible Hand: The Panic of 2007* (2010).

financial institutions.[7] Reflecting this sophistication, these institutions have often taken advantage of a wide variety of legal strategies—from contract and property, to corporate law and trusts—explicitly designed to replicate the safety and liquidity of conventional bank deposits.[8] They have also successfully lobbied lawmakers from Washington, DC, to Beijing to enact laws that support their ability to enforce their contractual, property, and other legal rights in the event of their counterparty's default, thus avoiding the harsh strictures of general corporate bankruptcy law. The end result is a system in which these sophisticated players are able to functionally re-create—at least to a point—the core legal privileges and protections enjoyed by banks and their depositors.

Understandably, these more sophisticated wholesale varieties of shadow money have long dominated academic and policy debates. Yet arguably the most important, promising, and yet frankly troubling feature of the emerging shadow monetary system of PayPal, Venmo, Alipay, and Tether is that new technology has enabled the sudden and dramatic expansion of this system to an entirely new universe of potential players: *the rest of us*. This raises a trillion-dollar question: Can we really trust these new financial institutions and platforms with our money? Do they take advantage of the same legal strategies that have long enabled more sophisticated players to sidestep the constraints of corporate bankruptcy law? If not, are they subject to regulatory frameworks that insulate their customers from the risks of contractual default and bankruptcy? And are the customers themselves even asking these important questions before making decisions about what to do with their money? As we shall see, the answer to all of these questions is very often a clear and resounding *no*.

There is a second trillion-dollar question that too often gets lost in the increasingly high-stakes debates over the future of money. That question is whether we can continue to trust banks with our payments. Given the comparative advantages that banks enjoy in the realm of money, it is something of a puzzle that they have not always been at the cutting edge of technological

---

7. A notable modern exception being US money market funds, which emerged in the high inflation environment of the 1970s to cater to retail and other investors frustrated by the imposition of caps on the amount of interest that banks could pay their depositors; see Alton Gilbert, "Requiem for Regulation Q: What It Did and Why It Passed Away," 68 Federal Reserve Bank of St. Louis Review 22 (1986).

8. For foundational work on how law is used to construct money and other "safe assets," see Anna Gelpern & Erik Gerding, "Inside Safe Assets," 33 Yale Journal on Regulation 365 (2016). For a detailed treatment of how private law strategies are used as the basic code of capitalism, see Katharina Pistor, *The Code of Capital: How the Law Creates Wealth and Inequality* (2019).

advances in the realm of payments. Nor have banks in many countries been quick to adopt the new and potentially transformative payment technologies currently being developed outside the conventional banking system. In a world where banks typically own, control, or enjoy exclusive access to incumbent financial market infrastructure—the pipes through which payments flow—this raises the prospect that ongoing technological disruption may ultimately fail to yield meaningful benefits for customers looking to make cheap, fast, secure, convenient, and accessible payments.

This book is about the rapidly unfolding collision between money's past, present, and future: between the money of our parents and the money of our children. It is about the legal privileges enjoyed by conventional deposit-taking banks, and the significant barriers to entry they erect for potential new entrants. It is about the economic and technological forces driving the emergence of the new shadow monetary system, and the potential risks this system poses to customers, to incumbent banks, and to financial stability. It is about the comparative advantages of public policymakers and private enterprises in governing this system, and in providing both a stable medium of exchange and a fast, secure, convenient, and accessible means of payment. And, most importantly, it is about how the law should thread the incredibly difficult needle between promoting ongoing technological experimentation, competition, and innovation in payments and protecting the safety and stability of our core monetary institutions.

The story of the shadow monetary system will take us all over the world. This story begins in Continental Europe, the United Kingdom, and the United States, where centuries of legal and institutional experimentation gave birth to the banks, clearinghouses, and other financial market infrastructure at the heart of our conventional systems of money and payments. From there the story fast-forwards to the present day, where it expands to encompass the new generation of monetary experiments currently under way across the globe: from China, India, and Japan to Silicon Valley, Kenya, and Brazil. Accordingly, while this book is not strictly comparative in nature, its jurisdictional and temporal scope are specifically designed to draw out the potential insights these new experiments might hold for the future of money and payments. These insights are particularly salient for countries—like the United States—that, having once been at the forefront of the legal and institutional experiments that yielded the conventional banking system, now increasingly find themselves behind the technological and regulatory curve.

Before moving forward, it is also important to briefly explain what this book is *not* about. First, this book is not about the increasingly fraught politics of money. There is no doubt that monetary design is an inherently political project. Scholars, politicians, and economists from Aristotle to William Jennings Bryan to John Maynard Keynes have illuminated this essential truth. More recently, a rich vein of scholarship, including Christine Desan's *Making Money: Coin, Currency, and the Coming of Capitalism* (2015) and Stefan Eich's *The Currency of Politics: A Political Theory of Money from Aristotle to Keynes* (2022), has shed new light on the political choices underpinning our core monetary institutions.[9] Nevertheless, even the most honorable political intentions—whether they be to "democratize" finance, promote greater financial inclusion, or address the "too-big-to-fail" problem—will inevitably fail to yield the desired results if they are not built on solid legal and institutional foundations. This book seeks to rediscover these foundations, and to use them as a basis for designing new monetary institutions that meet the unique challenges and opportunities of the digital age. Accordingly, while monetary design is inevitably an exercise in social and political engineering, this book focuses more narrowly on the legal and institutional engineering of money and payments.

Second, this book is not about international payment flows or the foreign exchange market. Once again, there is no doubt that the global macroeconomic, international trade, and geopolitical dimensions of money are extremely important. There is also an enormous and ever-growing literature exploring these dimensions[10]—one that has only grown since Russia's invasion of Ukraine in March 2022 and the subsequent imposition of economic sanctions designed to cut off Russia's access to the global payment system.[11] This book sidesteps the international and geopolitical dimensions of money to focus squarely on the microeconomic and legal foundations of monetary design. While "good money" and a "strong currency" often go hand in hand, they are ultimately two very different things.

Third, this book is not about crypto—although it does draw on some of the lessons stemming from the recent failure of several high-profile crypto intermediaries. While writing a book about bitcoin (BTC) and other digital

---

9. See also Jakob Feinig, *Moral Economies of Money: Politics and the Monetary Constitution of Society* (2022).

10. See, e.g., Eswar Prasad, *The Dollar Trap: How the U.S. Dollar Tightened Its Grip on Global Finance* (2015); Barry Eichengreen, *Exorbitant Privilege: The Rise and Fall of the Dollar and the Future of the International Monetary System* (2011) and *Globalizing Capital: A History of the International Monetary System* (1998).

11. For an excellent recent book on the interplay between economic sanctions and the structure of the global payment system, see Daniel McDowell, *Bucking the Buck: U.S. Financial Sanctions and the International Backlash against the Dollar* (2023).

assets would have probably sold more copies, the reality is that most of these assets—including BTC—currently bear few of the essential hallmarks of money. Nor are these assets widely used as a means of payment for goods and services outside the crypto ecosystem. This is not to say that so-called stablecoins or the distributed ledger technology on which they are built might not *someday* drive important improvements to our systems of money and payments.[12] Indeed, one of the central themes of this book is that this type of experimentation can be extremely valuable—if the risks are effectively managed. By the same token, this book is entirely agnostic about which extant or future technologies will eventually emerge to provide the foundations for the next generation of money and payments. What is more important for our purposes is that there inevitably will be a next generation, and that our laws and institutions should be designed to both nurture and support the resulting opportunities and effectively address the potential risks.

Finally, at the other end of the spectrum, this book is not about central bank digital currencies, or CBDCs. In the current policy environment, in which over one hundred countries have announced that they are exploring the prospect of developing a CBDC, this may seem like a curious choice.[13] It is grounded in two intertwined observations. The first is that the development of CBDCs raises important consumer privacy and other concerns that have yet to be fully addressed and may ultimately serve to make them politically unpalatable. Second, and in part because of these concerns, the vast majority of CBDC models currently under consideration would be intermediated through the conventional banking system.[14] As we shall see, these intermediated models blur the distinction between CBDCs, bank deposits, stablecoins, and other monetary IOUs. This makes the decision of whether or not to call something a "CBDC" more a question of marketing than fundamental design. In the end, the name on the tin matters far less than what's inside.

This chapter introduces the conceptual building blocks that drive the rest of the book. It begins with Gresham's law, the distinction between "good" and "bad" money, and the role of informationally insensitive debt contracts at the

12. Although there are a number of technical obstacles that would seem to undermine the potential for permissionless distributed ledgers to supplant our existing systems of money and payments; see, e.g., Frederic Boissay, Giulio Cornelli, Sebastian Doerr, & Jon Frost, "Blockchain Scalability and the Fragmentation of Crypto," Bank for International Settlements Bulletin No. 56 (June 7, 2022).

13. See, e.g., Atlantic Council, Central Bank Digital Currency Tracker (March 2023), https://www.atlanticcouncil.org/cbdctracker/.

14. Atlantic Council, CBDC Tracker.

heart of our current monetary system. It explains how the core features of general corporate bankruptcy law can destroy the function and value of these contracts, along with how conventional bank regulation and specifically the financial safety net serves to neutralize the application and destructive impact of bankruptcy law. The chapter also draws out the critical, yet often undertheorized, distinction between money and payments. This distinction then provides the springboard for articulating Gresham's *new* law: the observation that the technological advances that deliver faster, cheaper, and safer payments often far outpace the changes to our laws and institutions that deliver sound money. This in turn frames the fundamental policy challenge motivating this book: how to create a level legal playing field that encourages greater technological experimentation, competition, and innovation in the realm of payments, without simultaneously creating new threats to customer protection, to the safety and soundness of financial institutions, or to the stability of the wider monetary and financial system. The chapter concludes by laying out a more detailed road map for the book.

Gresham's Law

Sir Thomas Gresham was a Renaissance man. Born into a prominent English commercial family in the early sixteenth century, the Cambridge-educated Gresham was a lawyer, statesman, smuggler, and spy.[15] Perhaps most importantly, Gresham was a shrewd foreign currency trader, arbitraging geographic and temporal differences in foreign exchange rates and advising a succession of kings and queens on matters of international finance. Armed with the profits and connections he acquired from these endeavors, Gresham would go on to found the Royal Exchange in London, which received a royal proclamation in 1571. Yet, for all his achievements, Gresham's legacy will forever be associated with a single and wholly unoriginal observation that he made to Queen Elizabeth I shortly after her accession to the English throne in 1558.

In Gresham's time, the bulk of the money circulating in England consisted of gold and silver coins. Two of Queen Elizabeth's predecessors, Henry VIII and Edward VI, had together overseen what has since come to be known as the Great Debasement.[16] Designed to increase the revenue

15. See John William Burgon, *The Life and Times of Thomas Gresham* (1839).
16. See J. D. Gould, *The Great Debasement: Currency and the Economy in Mid-Tudor England* (1970).

generated by the Crown by reducing the cost of minting coins, the Great Debasement involved a gradual but significant reduction in the gold and silver content of English coinage. Nevertheless, by the time of Queen Elizabeth's accession, this debasement had eroded the real value of the government's other—nominally fixed—revenue sources, triggering a decline in the value of English coinage in foreign exchange markets and, predictably, undermining public confidence and trust in the currency of the realm.[17] In a letter explaining to Queen Elizabeth why Her Majesty's coinage had thus descended into an "unexampled state of badness," Gresham observed that these debasements were the reason "that all your ffine goold was convayd ought of this your realm."[18]

Gresham's statement has subsequently been interpreted in a variety of ways. Some argue that Gresham was criticizing so-called bimetallism—the use of both gold and silver coins as legal tender—as fundamentally unsustainable.[19] Others have marshaled Gresham's law as an argument against private mints,[20] and in favor of replacing metallic coins with convertible paper currency.[21] Still others have framed Gresham's law as a testament to the "unintended consequence of legislation"—namely, legal tender laws—"the intention of which is to force people to treat a money they view as inferior as if it were not so."[22] But what we today know as Gresham's law is actually a reformulation of Gresham's original observation advanced by Henry Dunning Macleod almost three hundred years later, in 1858. In Macleod's view, the essence of Gresham's statement, and his enduring contribution to the field of monetary economics, was that "good and bad money cannot circulate together."[23] Over time, this reformulation has been further recast into the prosaic yet inscrutable aphorism that *bad money drives out good*.

So what exactly does this mean? One of the obvious properties of metallic coins is that they are subject to wear and tear, intentional shaving or

17. George Selgin, "Salvaging Gresham's Law: The Good, the Bad, and the Illegal," 28:4 Journal of Money, Credit and Banking 637, 644 (1996); Frank Fetter, "Some Neglected Aspects of Gresham's Law," 46:3 Quarterly Journal of Economics, 480–481 (1932), citing F. A. Froud, *History of England from the Fall of Wolsey to the Defeat of the Spanish Armada*, 471–472 (1870).

18. Letter from Gresham to Queen Elizabeth, headed "Information of Sir Thomas Gresham, Mercer, towching the fall of the exchaunge, MDLVIII," reproduced in Burgon, *Life and Times of Thomas Gresham*, 483–486.

19. See, e.g., Henry Dunning Macleod, *The Theory of Credit*, 421 et seq. (2nd ed., 1894).

20. See, e.g., Stanley Jevons, *Money and the Mechanism of Exchange*, 64, 82 (1875).

21. See discussion in George Selgin, "Gresham's Law," in Robert Whaples (ed.), EH.Net Encyclopedia (June 9, 2003), http://eh.net/encyclopedia/greshams-law/.

22. Selgin, "Gresham's Law."

23. Macleod, *The Elements of Political Economy*, 476–478 (1858).

"clipping," and other forms of physical debasement. With the passage of time, we would therefore expect to observe a divergence in the amount of metal contained in otherwise identical coins. At least as measured by the *market price* of the underlying metal—as opposed to the *face value* of the coins themselves—the result is that the coins with a higher metallic content will be more valuable than those with a lower metallic content. Importantly, where coins of both high and low metallic content are treated equally for the purposes of legal tender laws, thus requiring people and businesses to accept both at face value, this fixed equivalence can generate powerful incentive effects. Specifically, it compels holders to *hoard* the coins with a higher metallic content and *use* the coins with a lower metallic content to buy goods and services and pay their debts. It also encourages holders to export coins with higher metallic content to other countries in which they can engage in transactions that enable them to capture the higher intrinsic value of these coins (hence Gresham's explanation to Queen Elizabeth about where all Her Majesty's gold had gone). The result can be an equilibrium in which the universally preferred means of payment are coins with a lower metallic content and intrinsic value, which thereby come to dominate the money in circulation. Hence, bad money drives out good.

Over the decades, Gresham's law has been debated, refined, and qualified. As economists Arthur Rolnick and Warren Weber rightly point out, once we take into account the transaction costs of actually using money—e.g., differences in storage, transportation, search, or verification costs—good money may very well drive out bad.[24] Consistent with this observation, there have been several historical episodes that on the surface appear to contradict the predictions of Gresham's law, including the competing private mints that emerged during the California gold rush of 1848–1855.[25] Likewise, Nobel laureate Robert Mundell has observed that "strong" currencies tend to drive out "weak" ones in the context of international trade.[26] Yet it is worth noting that these observations tend to be drawn from historical episodes and contexts characterized by the absence of strict legal tender laws enforcing the fixed equivalence of good and bad money.[27] More importantly, these observations ultimately reinforce the fundamental insight at the heart of

24. Rolnick & Weber, "Gresham's Law or Gresham's Fallacy?," 94:1 Journal of Political Economy 185 (1986).

25. Brian Summers, "Private Coinage in America," 26:7 Freeman 436 (1976).

26. Robert Mundell, "Uses and Abuses of Gresham's Law in the History of Money," 2:2 Zagreb Journal of Economics 3 (1998).

27. See Selgin, "Salvaging Gresham's Law," 640–642.

Gresham's law: not all money is created equal, and differences in the quality, convenience, and, therefore, value of money can drive the patterns of how it is used in the real world.

Money, Good and Bad

Today, coins make up only a small fraction of the money supply in the United States, United Kingdom, European Union, and other advanced economies. Moreover, most of the coins that remain in circulation are no longer made of precious metals like gold or silver, but rather of highly engineered alloys of copper, nickel, and other less precious metals. But these changes in the economic importance and material composition of our coinage have not debased the relevance of Gresham's law in the twenty-first century. They simply demand that we further refine our understanding of the fundamental characteristics of "moneyness,"[28] and of the all-important distinction between good and bad money.

The standard textbook definition of money revolves around three core properties. As explained by economist Greg Mankiw in his influential textbook, "Money has three functions in the economy: It is a medium of exchange, a unit of account, and a store of value. The three functions together distinguish money from other assets."[29] Within this framework, an asset is a reliable *unit of account* if it can be used as a standardized benchmark—a yardstick for measuring the relative value of goods and services. As more artfully described by J. P. Koning, "The unit of account function of money refers to the fact that our economic conversations and calculations are couched in terms of a given monetary unit, whether that be the $, ¥, or £."[30] Yet, in theory, literally any asset that can be counted can function as a unit of account: everything from apples to zebras. The reason we don't use apples or zebras as money is that their perishability presents us with a clear and obvious problem—the deterioration in their value over time. This points us toward the second core property of money: its function as a *store of value*. An asset is a reliable store of value if a given quantity of it can be used to buy

28. See Milton Friedman & Anna Schwartz, *Monetary Statistics of the United States: Estimates, Sources, Methods, and Data*, 151–152 (1970); John Hicks, *Value and Capital*, 163 (2nd ed., 1946) (both utilizing the term *moneyness* in relation to assets that are viewed as a reliable store of nominal value).

29. Mankiw, *Macroeconomics*, 314 (1998).

30. Koning, "A Simpler and More Accurate Way to Teach Money to Students," American Institute for Economic Research (December 10, 2020), https://www.aier.org/article/a-simpler-and-more-accurate-way-to-teach-money-to-students/.

a roughly equivalent bundle of goods and services today, tomorrow, next week, and next year. Yet, once again, there are a great many assets—from real estate to diamonds to Birkin bags—that hold their relative value over time but that we do not generally use to buy food, make rent, or pay our taxes. This takes us to the third and final property of money. Specifically, an asset is a reliable *medium of exchange* if it is widely accepted within a society as an instrument for both buying goods and services and discharging debts.

This textbook definition of money has always been highly suspect. Perhaps most importantly, it's fairly clear that two of these three properties—the functions of money as a unit of account and a store of value—are neither necessary nor sufficient conditions for an asset to qualify as money. The citizens of Weimar Germany, who experienced triple-digit inflation *per month* in the early 1920s, continued to use Papiermarks in domestic transactions long after they ceased to represent a reliable store of value.[31] There have also been several episodes—including Brazil in the early 1990s and Chile today—where the official unit of account in which many goods and services are priced does not actually circulate as a medium of exchange.[32] In fact, as monetary economist George Selgin has observed, even William Stanley Jevons, the nineteenth-century economist who first advanced the standard tripartite definition of money, did not view these three functions as standing on equal terms.[33] Instead, Jevons saw money, first and foremost, as an asset "esteemed by all persons . . . and which, therefore, every person desires to have by him in a greater or lesser quantity, in order that he may have the means of procuring the necessities of life at any time."[34] Put simply, the defining property of money is that it is widely embraced as a medium of exchange.

This insight enables us to focus more squarely on the properties of money that make it more or less desirable for this very specific purpose. Two properties stand out. First, money should have a stable *nominal* value. The standard textbook definition of money hinges on whether an asset is a reliable store of real value; i.e., whether that asset is able to maintain its purchasing

---

31. For a detailed history of this episode, see Gerald Feldman, *The Great Disorder: Politics, Economics and Society in the German Inflation, 1914–1924* (1997).

32. For a detailed description of the design and uses of these "indexed units of account," see Robert Shiller, "Indexed Units of Account: Theory and Assessment of Historical Experience," National Bureau of Economic Research Working Paper No. 6356 (January 1998).

33. See George Selgin, "A Three-Pronged Blunder, or, What Money Is, and What It Isn't," Alt-M blog (October 27, 2021), https://www.cato.org/blog/three-pronged-blunder-or-what-money-what-it-isnt (as Selgin notes, Jevons's original taxonomy actually identified four functions of money).

34. Jevons, *Money and the Mechanism of Exchange*, 13.

power over time. In contrast, a stable nominal value means that when you go to spend one dollar, euro, or peso, it is accepted as representing that precise value and not, for example, 95 cents. Thus, when you order an espresso at Sant' Eustachio Il Caffe in Rome and the menu lists the price as €3.50, you can be confident that the three one-euro notes and 50c in your pocket will be sufficient to secure your caffeine fix for the day.

Paradoxically, the fundamental importance of this property is illuminated by proposals that envision a world in which new technology enables us to use assets with a floating nominal (and real) value to conduct day-to-day purchases.[35] As economist John Cochrane explains: "With today's technology, you could buy a cup of coffee by swiping a card or tapping a cell phone, selling two dollars and fifty cents of an S&P 500 fund, and crediting the coffee seller's two dollars and fifty cents to a mortgage-backed security fund."[36] Putting aside the fact that the sale of the S&P 500 fund would trigger a taxable event every time you purchased an espresso, the real problem with this proposal stems from the fact the most of us face fairly strict budget constraints. Specifically, we get paid a fixed amount of money each paycheck, which we must then use to buy food, clothing, and Jevons's other "necessities of life." Importantly, we also use this money to pay nominally fixed debts like our rent, mortgage, utilities, and student loans.

In the presence of these nominally fixed budget constraints, holding an asset that exposes us to the volatility of something like the S&P 500 index— which tracks the prices of a basket of 500 publicly traded US stocks—leaves us vulnerable to short-term declines in this asset's value. When this asset is then also used as a medium of exchange, these short-term declines leave us with less money in real terms and thus at risk of being unable to purchase the things we need to live or to meet our ongoing financial obligations. This risk is especially acute for those living paycheck to paycheck, who by definition lack the financial reserves needed to weather this type of volatility. Viewed from this perspective, ensuring that money has a stable nominal value is desirable because it means that households and businesses will be less likely to encounter short-term liquidity or solvency problems, while simultaneously putting them in a better position to engage in longer-term financial planning.

---

35. See John Cochrane, "Toward a Run-Free Financial System," in Martin Baily & John Taylor (eds.), *Across the Great Divide: New Perspectives on the Financial Crisis* (2014).

36. Cochrane, 199.

The second core property of money is that users should be able to quickly, easily, and securely use it within a relatively large network of individuals, households, businesses, and governments. This property—the role of money as a *means of payment*—exists on a multidimensional scale that incorporates variables such as cost, speed, convenience, security, accessibility, and the size of the relevant network. Almost inevitably, this property also depends greatly on context. While your euro notes and coins were useful at Sant' Eustachio Il Caffe, they are completely useless when shopping for a new coffeemaker on Amazon. Importantly, where a given monetary system or instrument resides on this scale depends on a range of different factors: including the legal frameworks supporting money and payments, the prevailing technological environment, and the level of social acceptance enjoyed by core monetary institutions. Together, these factors combine to determine what Keynes described as the "liquidity-premium" of money: the confidence that users have in the ability to immediately, and without question, use an asset to purchase goods and services and discharge their debts.[37] This confidence is the essence of money's moneyness.

This second property highlights the critically important, and yet often neglected, relationship between money and payments. It also frames how the two core properties of money as a medium of exchange serve to reinforce one another. Ultimately, the reason we want money to represent a reliable store of nominal value is because we use it every day to purchase the things we need. At the same time, the fact that we use money every day helps explain why we want it to have a fixed nominal value. As a consequence, a reliable store of nominal value that cannot easily be used to make everyday payments (like the Big Maple Leaf, a 220-pound, $1 million coin issued by the Royal Canadian Mint) is of no more use than a technologically advanced payment system that can only be used to transfer unreliable stores of nominal value (like BTC). Over the long term, these twin properties thus play a pivotal role in shaping what society views as good and bad money.

Today, we tend to take both of these properties for granted. As we shall see, this complacency reflects the legally engineered homogeneity at the root of our current systems of money and payments. But as the very existence of Gresham's law suggests, our ancestors would have been all too familiar with the acute problems created by pervasive heterogeneity in the quality of

---

37. John Maynard Keynes, *The General Theory of Employment, Interest and Money*, 142–144 (1936).

money as both a store of nominal value and a means of payment. This has an important upshot. As the rise of the shadow monetary system continues to reinject a significant and rapidly growing degree of diversity into our monetary system, we must rediscover the importance of these properties, how to use them to distinguish between good and bad money and, ultimately, how to design laws and institutions that can support this diversity without undermining confidence in our monetary system.

Money as a Promise

We have already observed that our money supply is no longer made up of gold and silver coins. Indeed, both logic and experience suggest that this type of "commodity" money poses unique challenges—especially in a dynamic and fast-growing economy. Most of these challenges stem from the natural supply constraints on the raw materials needed to mint this commodity money, and the fact that both the timing and quantity of the discovery and extraction of new supplies may not closely match the demand for money in the economy. Where the value of money is fixed relative to a specific commodity like gold or silver, this mismatch forces any changes in the prevailing supply and demand conditions for these commodities to be reflected in the prices of the goods and services we consume.[38] The net effect of this relationship is to tether the general rate of inflation to the rate at which these commodities can be found and extracted. Over the long term, where an economy is growing faster than these commodities can be discovered, mined, refined, and minted into money, the resulting imbalance between supply and demand can lead to economically damaging deflation as households, businesses, and governments hoard money rather than use it to purchase goods or services or make longer-term investments.

Further complicating matters, in a system based solely on commodity money, short-term constraints on the supply of these commodities can handcuff the ability of central banks and fiscal policymakers to expand the money supply in response to deflationary spirals, banking crises, or other macroeconomic shocks.[39] Thus, for example, the scale of the monetary and fiscal policy response to something like the COVID-19 pandemic would be dictated by the

38. See Ben Bernanke, "Origins and Mission of the Federal Reserve—the Gold Standard" (March 2012), https://www.federalreserve.gov/aboutthefed/educational-tools/lecture-series -origins-and-mission.htm.

39. See Barry Eichengreen, *Gold Fetters: The Gold Standard and the Great Depression* (1992); Liaquat Ahamed, *Lords of Finance: The Bankers Who Broke the World* (2009).

amount of gold, silver, or other monetary commodities locked away in central bank vaults. Some view these "hard money" constraints as a feature rather than a bug—a natural check on inflation, expansionary monetary policy, and moral hazard. Yet, as the experience of the US under the gold standard during the late nineteenth and early twentieth centuries arguably demonstrates, the use of commodity money can contribute to relatively high volatility in both inflation and economic growth, along with an increase in the number and severity of banking crises.[40] Adding insult to injury, the inherent inelasticity of commodity money has also frequently led policymakers to abandon it—sometimes temporarily, other times permanently—in response to severe economic and financial shocks.[41]

Predictably, as both domestic and international economies have grown more dynamic, the gold standard and other systems based on commodity money have gradually been supplanted by more flexible and elastic systems of credit-based money. As this name implies, these systems are based on the issuance of *debt contracts*—monetary IOUs—that can be used as both a nominal store of value and a means of payment. Today, the most familiar and ubiquitous form of credit-based money is the bank deposit contract. Bank deposits represent the contractually enforceable promises of your bank to accept your money, credit it to your account, transfer these credits in accordance with your instructions, and return an equivalent amount of money to you within the time frame specified in the contract. These promises are created whenever you deposit money into your bank account. Importantly, they are also created whenever your bank makes a

---

40. See Stephen Cecchetti & Kermit Schoenholtz, "Why a Gold Standard Is a Very Bad Idea," Money & Banking blog (December 19, 2016), https://www.moneyandbanking.com/commentary /2016/12/14/why-a-gold-standard-is-a-very-bad-idea (comparing the average and standard deviation of consumer price inflation and gross national product growth between 1882 and 1932 versus 1973 and 2016). For a competing view that both challenges the causal relationship between these variables and the gold standard and highlights the role of bad policy in contributing to the instability during this period, see George Selgin, "Ten Things Every Economist Should Know about the Gold Standard," Alt-M blog (June 4, 2015), https://www.alt-m.org/2015/06/04/ten-things-every -economist-should-know-about-the-gold-standard-2/#gold-supply-shocks.

41. For example, as described in greater detail in chapter 2, the government of the United Kingdom repeatedly suspended the gold standard—as operationalized by the Bank Charter Act of 1844—in response to a succession of financial crises between 1847 and 1866; see Mike Anson, David Bholat, Miao Kang, & Ryland Thomas, "The Bank of England as Lender of Last Resort: New Historical Evidence from Daily Transaction Data," Bank of England Staff Working Paper No. 691 (2017); Vincent Bignon, Marc Flandreau, & Stefano Ugolini, "Bagehot for Beginners: The Making of Lender-of-Last-Resort Operations in the Mid-Nineteenth Century," 65 Economic History Review 580 (2012).

new loan, with the proceeds taking the form of new deposits credited to the borrower's account.[42]

The widespread use of credit-based money poses profound challenges for monetary design. Unlike commodity money, bank deposits and other monetary IOUs have little or no intrinsic value. Instead, their value is a function of the expectation that the promises embodied in these contracts will be honored by the promisor—whether it be your bank, PayPal, M-PESA, or your cousin Greg. In theory, this means that the *identity* and *credibility* of the people or institutions making these promises should matter a great deal: with differences in risk appetite, wealth, revenue sources, debt levels, and overall creditworthiness all reflected in the value of monetary IOUs issued by different promisors. Intuitively, it also means that there should be some promisors that are so fundamentally lacking in credibility and creditworthiness that it would be foolish to accept their promises as representing either a reliable store of nominal value or an effective means of payment. As the late great Hyman Minsky once quipped, "Everyone can create money; the problem is to get it accepted."[43]

The challenges posed by the widespread use of credit-based money are compounded by the omnipresent threat of *bankruptcy*. In a nutshell, bankruptcy is a legal process whereby the assets and liabilities of firms that find themselves balance sheet insolvent, or otherwise unable to pay their debts as they fall due, are either restructured or wound down.[44] The substantive and procedural requirements of corporate bankruptcy law vary from jurisdiction to jurisdiction. However, once a firm enters into bankruptcy, bankruptcy law in most jurisdictions envisions the application of two foundational rules that dramatically interfere with the firm's ability to honor its outstanding contractual commitments, including its monetary IOUs. The first rule is a procedural requirement—an *automatic stay*—that suspends any enforcement action against the assets of the bankrupt firm by its creditors until the conclusion of the bankruptcy process. The second rule is a substantive requirement—the *pari passu rule*—that forces unsecured creditors to share

---

42. For a more detailed description of this process, see Michael McLeay, Amar Radia, & Ryland Thomas, "Money Creation in the Modern Economy," Bank of England Quarterly Bulletin (Q1: 2014).

43. Minsky, *Stabilizing an Unstable Economy*, 228 (1986).

44. For a detailed description of the logic of corporate bankruptcy law, see Thomas Jackson, *Logic and Limits of Bankruptcy Law* (1986); Thomas Jackson & Douglas Baird, "Corporate Reorganizations and the Treatment of Diverse Ownership Interests: A Comment on Adequate Protection of Secured Creditors in Bankruptcy," 51 University of Chicago Law Review 97 (1984).

in any distribution of the bankrupt firm's assets on a pro rata basis. In effect, the application of the pari passu rule means that each claim made by an unsecured creditor against the bankrupt firm will be pooled together with those of all its other unsecured creditors, with each creditor then eventually paid on a proportionate basis out of any assets that remain after other, more senior, creditors have been fully repaid.

Together, these rules undermine the credibility of monetary IOUs in two critical ways. First, the automatic stay prevents any party holding these IOUs from transferring or withdrawing their money for the duration of the bankruptcy process. In a world where this process may last several years, the practical effect is to "freeze" this money within the estate of the bankrupt firm—thereby suspending its use and value as a means of payment. Second, insofar as the holders of these monetary IOUs are unsecured creditors, the pari passu rule may ultimately force them to write down the value of their contractual claims against the bankrupt firm. Indeed, in some cases, these holders may only get back pennies on the dollar—and perhaps even nothing at all. The fact that these creditors are exposed to potentially enormous losses is fundamentally inconsistent with the expectation that these IOUs represent a reliable store of nominal value. Viewed in this light, the automatic stay and pari passu rule are the kryptonite of credit-based money—robbing monetary IOUs of their essential moneyness.

The Paradox of Good Money

Given the challenges posed by the widespread use of credit-based money in the shadow of bankruptcy, one might reasonably ask why depositors don't spend more time worrying about the creditworthiness of their banks. Indeed, we might ask why depositors entrust banks with their money, but typically not their local supermarket, hairstylist, or car dealership.[45] As a preliminary matter, bankruptcy law in countries like the United States explicitly exempts banks from the application of general corporate bankruptcy law, including the automatic stay and pari passu rule.[46] Bankruptcy law is then replaced with tailor-made bank resolution frameworks specifically designed

---

45. Although, in the absence of banks, other retail establishments have occasionally stepped into the breach. For example, in the thick of an industrial dispute that closed the Republic of Ireland's banks for several months in 1970, local pubs kept the nation's money and check clearing system afloat; see Antoin Murphy, "Money in an Economy without Banks: The Case of Ireland," 46:1 Manchester School 41 (1978).

46. Bankruptcy Act of 1978, § 109.

to reduce the risk that depositors will have their money frozen or be forced to write down the value of their monetary IOUs. These frameworks work in tandem with deposit insurance schemes that enable the government to step into the shoes of a failing bank and honor its contractual commitments to return depositors' money. And even before banks find themselves on the brink of failure, central bank emergency lending—or "lender of last resort"— facilities permit banks to borrow money against their illiquid loans and other assets; money that can then be used to keep their promises to depositors and other creditors. This public safety net ensures that a bank's monetary IOUs continue to serve as a reliable store of nominal value and means of payment even during periods of severe institutional stress—thus reengineering otherwise risky deposit contracts into paragons of good money.

The practical effect of this legal engineering is to transform bank deposits into what economists Bengt Holmstrom, Gary Gorton, and others have labeled "informationally insensitive" debt contracts.[47] In a world dominated by the twenty-four-hour financial news cycle, the concept of an informationally insensitive debt contract may seem somewhat counterintuitive. Indeed, we would normally expect the value of bonds, loans, and other debt contracts to fluctuate in response to changes in the business prospects and creditworthiness of the issuer, prevailing macroeconomic conditions, market interest rates, and any other variables that have an impact on the opportunity cost of money or the probability that a lender will eventually get paid back. In an informationally efficient market, we would then expect the process of price discovery to ensure that these changes in value were rapidly incorporated into the market price of these contracts.[48] The prices of many publicly traded bonds, for example, rise and fall on a daily basis in response to new information. The prospect of acquiring and trading on this information *first*—and thus reaping the profits from any subsequent price changes—is ultimately what drives investors to undertake due diligence into the value of these contracts.

---

47. See, e.g., Holmstrom, "Understanding the Role of Debt in the Financial System," Bank for International Settlements Working Paper No. 479 (January 2015); Gorton & George Pennacchi, "Financial Intermediaries and Liquidity Creation," 45(1) Journal of Finance 49 (1990); Gorton, Chase Ross, & Sharon Ross, "Making Money," National Bureau of Economic Research Working Paper No. 29710 (January 2022). For older work drawing on similar themes, see also Armen Alchian, "Why Money?," 9:1 Journal of Money, Credit and Banking 133 (1977).

48. See Eugene Fama, "Efficient Capital Markets: A Review of Theory and Empirical Work," 25 Journal of Finance 383 (1970). For a survey of the empirical literature testing Fama's efficient market hypothesis, see Burton Malkiel, "The Efficient Market Hypothesis and Its Critics," 17 Journal of Economic Perspectives 59 (2003), and "The Efficient-Market Hypothesis and the Financial Crisis," in Blinder et al. (eds.), *Rethinking the Financial Crisis*, 75 (2012).

Informationally insensitive debt contracts stand this paradigm on its head. The defining feature of these contracts is that they are specifically designed to eliminate any incentive to undertake this type of costly due diligence. This is typically achieved by overcollateralizing the relevant debt: either by backing it with other assets that exceed the face value of the IOU, or by obtaining a guarantee from an institution—like the government—that is not subject to bankruptcy or liquidity constraints. By making buyers and sellers of this debt indifferent to the creditworthiness of the promisor, this overcollateralization is designed to serve as a substitute for costly investments in the acquisition of new information about the probability that they will get paid back. The net effect is what Holmstrom describes as a "blissful state of symmetric ignorance" between buyers and sellers.[49]

This symmetric ignorance serves two important and self-reinforcing functions. First, it gives buyers and sellers confidence that, when engaging in transactions involving this debt, they will not be vulnerable to exploitation by counterparties who possess superior information. Second, by eliminating the process of price discovery, it ensures that the price of this debt will remain stable in every potential future state of the world. The net result is that both buyers and sellers are readily willing to accept this debt "no questions asked,"[50] without worrying about the identity or creditworthiness of the promisor. In theory, these traits combine to make informationally insensitive debt contracts an ideal species of monetary IOU.

In reality, of course, informationally insensitive debt contracts exist on a spectrum. Some monetary IOUs—like insured bank deposits—remain almost completely insensitive to new information in virtually all states of the world. But a great many others are exposed to the risk that, in some particularly volatile and uncertain states, their holders will start to question whether the promisor can continue to meet its contractual obligations. At this critical inflection point, the holders of these IOUs face a stark choice: either conduct the costly due diligence necessary to evaluate the probability and impact of the promisor's default or simply head for the exits. Where a critical mass of holders chooses the second option, this can trigger a chain reaction whereby the resulting liquidity pressure on the promisor can undermine its solvency, and where the threat of insolvency can undermine the credibility and stability of its monetary IOUs. Inevitably, this risk of instability depends on features specific to each IOU: including the holder's contractual and other

---

49. Holmstrom, "Understanding the Role of Debt," 6.
50. Gorton, Ross, & Ross, "Making Money," 2.

legal rights, the quantity and quality of any posted collateral, the correlation between the value of the collateral and the credit risk of the promisor, and the credibility and creditworthiness of any third-party guarantor. Understanding the variance in these features across different monetary IOUs is thus extremely important to successfully differentiating between good and bad money.

This presents us with something of a paradox. On the one hand, informationally insensitive debt contracts are designed to work in a world of symmetric ignorance—one in which neither buyers nor sellers undertake due diligence into the idiosyncratic features, credibility, or potential instability of monetary IOUs. On the other hand, this type of due diligence is precisely what is necessary to determine whether and to what extent a given monetary IOU is in fact informationally insensitive in each and every potential future state of the world, and thus whether the holders of these IOUs should view them as good money. After all, how else can we distinguish between good and bad money? Ultimately, *somebody* needs to ask these questions, or we are all very unlikely to be happy with the answers.

This paradox arguably presents few challenges in a world of completely static and homogeneous money. For well over a century, banks have been the dominant source of monetary IOUs in the United States, United Kingdom, Continental Europe, and many other jurisdictions. Over this span, financial policymakers and regulators have gradually developed and refined a variety of mechanisms for ensuring the credibility of bank deposits. These mechanisms include the various components of the financial safety net, along with sophisticated frameworks of prudential regulation and supervision.[51] Whether by accident or design, the result has been the creation of a monetary system and regulatory apparatus built around Mark Twain's famous advice to "put all your eggs in the one basket and WATCH THAT BASKET."[52] While this system and apparatus are far from perfect, they have nevertheless engendered a relatively high degree of public confidence in the idea—tested in the fires of thousands of bank failures—that we can accept and hold bank deposits, no questions asked.[53]

51. See Lev Menand, "Why Supervise Banks? The Foundations of the American Monetary Settlement," 74 Vanderbilt Law Review 951 (2021).

52. Mark Twain, "Pudd'nhead Wilson," *Century Magazine* (April 1894).

53. See, e.g., Agustin Carstens, Stijn Claessens, Fernando Restoy, & Hyun Song Shin, "Regulating Big Techs in Finance," Bank for International Settlements Bulletin No. 45, 6 (August 2, 2021) (reporting the results of a consumer survey in which respondents reported far higher levels of trust in banks and other conventional financial institutions than either big tech platforms or governments).

Importantly, the challenges presented by this paradox become far more evident and acute in a world of heterogeneous and fast-moving money. In particular, where there exists a diverse range of monetary IOUs, and where the universe of monetary IOUs is constantly expanding, policymakers face the herculean task of attempting to watch a thousand eggs in a thousand different baskets. Compounding matters, the general public—unaccustomed to asking questions about the design and credibility of its money—may fail to identify or fully comprehend the unique features of different monetary IOUs. In this more complex and dynamic world, Gresham's law takes on newfound importance as both policymakers and the public struggle to distinguish between good money and bad.

Good Money versus Good Payments

One could be forgiven for thinking of money and payments as inextricably intertwined. Not only are payments baked into the very definition of money, this tightly bundled relationship is reinforced by our everyday experience. The paper notes and coins in our wallets and purses are both money and their own built-in payment system—with physical delivery of the object itself sufficient to transfer its ownership and value from one person to another. Banks similarly play a dual role as both the dominant source of monetary IOUs and the principal architects and custodians of the technological infrastructure through which these IOUs are electronically transferred between individuals, households, businesses, and governments. As a result, we can both hold and transfer money around the world without it ever leaving the balance sheets and computer servers of the conventional banking system. Yet, in both theory and practice, money and payments are ultimately two very different things. Whereas money is a representation of *value*, payment systems are *how this value is transferred* in satisfaction of our financial obligations. If money is the liquid that lubricates the machinery of economic life, payment systems are the pipes through which this liquid flows.

This distinction introduces a new and important dichotomy into our framework: one between good money and good payments. This distinction can be observed across at least three dimensions. The first dimension is purely definitional: whereas money is an asset (stock), a payment is a transaction (flow) (see figure I.1). The second dimension reflects their key determinants—what drives them. Whereas good money is primarily a product of laws and institutions that establish and maintain the credibility of monetary commitments, good payments are the product of decisions about the design, application, and governance of the technology at the heart

FIGURE I.1. Good Money versus Good Payments

Objective	Principal drivers	Key benchmarks
Good money	• Law • Institutions	• Stable nominal value • Widely accepted as a means of payment
Good payments	• Technology • Network design • Network governance	• Cost • Speed • Security • Convenience • Accessibility • Interoperability

of financial networks. The third dimension represents the benchmarks by which we measure their success. The question of whether an asset qualifies as good money is ultimately measured against whether it's a reliable store of nominal value and widely used as a means of payment. In contrast, whether a transaction qualifies as a good payment is a function of considerations like cost, speed, security, convenience, accessibility, and interoperability.

In recent decades, we have witnessed a growing disconnect between good money and good payments. It started innocently enough with money transmitters, like Western Union and MoneyGram, that enabled customers to send and receive money by telegraphic wire transfer rapidly and across vast distances. While these money transmitters were not banks, their customers were generally not concerned about the credibility and creditworthiness of their monetary IOUs because they existed for such a brief period of time—typically only as long as it took for the intended recipient to get to the nearest branch. The invention and popularization of the internet, followed by the development and proliferation of smartphones, then gave birth to peer-to-peer (P2P) platforms like PayPal and WeChat Pay. These P2P payment platforms offered customers benefits like greater speed, convenience, and the ability to send and receive money electronically without sharing their bank details and other confidential information with complete strangers. In notable contrast with earlier money transmitters, these web-based payment platforms have also evolved to hold tens of billions of dollars in customer funds for lengthy, and potentially indefinite, periods of time.[54] And then,

54. For example, as of December 31, 2023, PayPal reported holding "funds payable and amounts due to customers" totaling $41.9 billion; PayPal Inc., Annual Report, page 58 (December 31, 2023): https://investor.pypl.com/financials/annual-reports/default.aspx. While reliable data is scarce, the customer balances held by the biggest Chinese platforms—WeChat Pay and Alipay—are thought to be considerably larger.

almost overnight, Tether, USDC, and other stablecoins emerged to support the growing crypto ecosystem. Between January 2019 and September 2023, these stablecoins collectively attracted over $100 billion in new customer funds.[55] While these figures are still a drop in the bucket compared to the outstanding stock of conventional bank deposits, the spectacular growth of these new monetary IOUs over such a short period of time has quite rightly made policymakers stand up and take notice.

This book explores whether these and other new monetary experiments should be viewed as good money. In many cases, it argues that they are not. Simultaneously, it is increasingly hard to deny that many of these new institutions and platforms hold out significant advantages over the incumbent bank-based payment systems they seek to compete with and, perhaps one day, supplant. Some offer greater speed or enhanced privacy. Others offer more convenience, like the ability to quickly and easily split a restaurant bill between friends. Still others offer greater interoperability, including the ability to cheaply and instantly send money overseas or connect to the rapidly expanding crypto ecosystem. And, last but not least, some provide basic access to an electronic payment network where both the government and conventional banking system have failed to build and maintain the necessary infrastructure. Accordingly, regardless of whether we think these new monetary IOUs are good money, it is increasingly hard to deny that they often represent very attractive ways to make good payments.

Clearly, the overarching policy objective should be to promote the development of financial institutions, platforms, and networks that combine good money and good payments. Some countries, like India, Sweden, and Australia, have taken great strides toward achieving this objective in partnership with the conventional banking industry. Others, like China and Brazil, have done so with far less initial support from incumbent banks. Yet for a great many countries—including the United States—the reality is a large and growing divergence between the sources of good money and good payments. The result is an equilibrium in which good and bad money increasingly circulate alongside one another, and where bad money enjoys a growing

---

55. See Gordon Liao & John Caramichael, "Stablecoins: Growth Potential and Impact on Banking," Federal Reserve Board of Governors, International Finance Discussion Paper No. 1334, 3 (January 2022) (reporting the growth in stablecoins between 2019 and 2021). For the current market capitalization of major stablecoins, see https://coinmarketcap.com/(reporting a market capitalization of over $110 billion for the two largest stablecoins, Tether, USDC, and DAI, as of January 2024).

comparative advantage in terms of fast, secure, convenient, accessible, and interoperable payments.

Shining a spotlight on this disconnect yields three important payoffs. The first is for consumer behavior. During periods of relative stability, we should expect consumers to shift toward the use of monetary IOUs that offer the cheapest, fastest, most convenient, and most accessible means of payment. The reason for this should be obvious: while customers experience the benefits of good payments *today*, the risk that the value of their monetary IOUs will be destroyed in bankruptcy is highly contingent, mind-numbingly technical, and thus extremely difficult to accurately predict. What's more, if this risk materializes at all, it will only do so at some indeterminate point in the *future*. Just as the paradox of good money suggests, consumers may therefore not even factor these risks into the equation when making important decisions about what to do with their money. At best, the result of this time inconsistency problem is a world in which consumers heavily discount the prospect that their money may one day no longer function as a reliable store of nominal value or means of payment—driving them to value good payments over good money. Over time, these collective decisions should then be reflected in the gradual expansion of the shadow monetary system, which is of course exactly what we are observing today.

The second payoff is for the nature and importance of the resulting policy challenge. If the problem was simply the emergence of bad money, the obvious solution would be to expand the perimeter of conventional bank regulation, along with the public safety net, to encompass the emerging shadow monetary system. Policymakers could also simply ban it: relegating this system to the dustbin of monetary history. Yet the problem is made significantly more complex by virtue of the fact that this system has yielded real benefits—benefits that the conventional banking system, despite all the advantages of incumbency, has often failed to deliver. This raises the prospect that forcing the shadow monetary system into the exquisitely tailored straitjacket of conventional bank regulation, ostensibly in order to promote good money, may ultimately come at the expense of good payments. Viewed in this light, the challenge for policymakers becomes how to ensure the safety and stability of the monetary system while simultaneously promoting ongoing experimentation, competition, and innovation in the realm of payments.

The final payoff is for the potential roles of both the public and private sectors in rising to meet this challenge. Scholars have long debated ontological questions around the nature of money: including whether it should be viewed as an inherently public or private institution. Some view money as a spontaneous, market-driven response to the frictions of bartering and the so-called double coincidence of wants problem.[56] Others view money as a creature of the state—with its importance and value derived from its status as legal tender and the fact that it is accepted by the government in satisfaction of taxes and other public debts.[57]

Yet by illuminating the fundamental distinction between good money and good payments, we can start to see that both accounts are woefully incomplete and that the hotly contested metaphysics of money are often less than helpful from a policy perspective. In reality, public and private actors often possess very different strengths when it comes to money and payments. Specifically, whereas the state often enjoys a unique comparative advantage in the legal and institutional construction of good money, private enterprise—by virtue of its collective expertise, powerful incentives, and the sheer number of experiments it is capable of conducting—often excels in the development of the new technology driving cheaper, faster, and more convenient payments. Similarly, while the state can play an important role in identifying emerging problems and challenges and in coordinating the subsequent policy response, private enterprise often possesses the technical knowledge, expertise, and other resources needed to design and implement effective solutions. As we shall see, these comparative advantages are far from universal. Nevertheless, they suggest that the best solutions are likely to be found when the public and private sectors work together, creatively and pragmatically, to deliver both good money and good payments.

Gresham's *New* Law

We now have all the pieces we need to reframe Gresham's law for the digital age. The foundations of Gresham's *new* law are built on three observations. First, we live in a world of increasingly heterogeneous money. Gone are the days when banks were the only game in town. Today, even though banks still typically reside at the apex of our systems of money and payments, they are facing mounting competitive pressure from technology-driven financial institutions and platforms that have emerged as part of the rapidly expanding and evolving "fintech" ecosystem. Second, for a variety of reasons, these new

56. See, e.g., Karl Menger, "On the Origin of Money," 2:6 Economic Journal 239 (1892); Jevons, *Money and the Mechanism of Exchange.*

57. See, e.g., Georg Knapp, *The State Theory of Money* (1905); John Maynard Keynes, *A Treatise on Money* (1930); Minsky, *Stabilizing an Unstable Economy.*

institutions and platforms are often better positioned to invest in the development and application of new technology designed to improve the cost, speed, security, convenience, interoperability, and accessibility of payments. Third, despite the technological superiority of these new institutions and platforms, the public safety net and other unique privileges enjoyed by conventional deposit-taking banks continue to give them an enormous competitive edge in the creation of monetary IOUs that serve as both a reliable store of nominal value and a means of payment. The result is a monetary system in which good money increasingly circulates alongside bad, but where the harbingers of bad money are very often the catalysts of cheaper, faster, more secure, more convenient, and more inclusive payments.

Together, these observations take us back to the growing disconnect between good money and good payments. At the root of this disconnect is a mounting tension between the design of our laws and institutions and the seemingly relentless advance of new technology. Today, laws and institutions like the financial safety net play a central role in promoting the stability and credibility of monetary IOUs. Yet, at present, these laws and institutions often evolve far more slowly than the technology that drives good payments. Further complicating matters, the financial institutions and platforms that are best positioned to develop and apply this technology typically do not enjoy the privileges and protections afforded by the financial safety net. Accordingly, the financial institutions that issue the most credible monetary IOUs—banks—are generally not at the forefront of technological advances in payments, while the institutions and platforms at the cutting edge of payments—the shadow monetary system—struggle to establish and maintain the credibility of their monetary commitments. The upshot is a monetary system in which people and businesses are often forced to choose between good money and good payments and, ultimately, between good and bad money.

This disconnect is compounded by a time inconsistency problem: while people and businesses value cheaper, faster, and more convenient payments in good times, they also value stable and credible monetary IOUs during periods of heightened uncertainty and instability. When combined with the growing disconnect between good money and good payments, this time inconsistency problem enables us to make two tentative yet important predictions. First, during periods of institutional and systemic stability, where consumers are more sensitive to the benefits of good payments, *bad money will drive out good.* Second, during periods of institutional and systemic instability, where consumers are more sensitive to the benefits of good money, the resulting flight to safety means that *good money will drive out bad.*

These predictions are the essence of Gresham's new law. Like Gresham's (old) law, they are grounded in the observation that differences in the quality of money determine the patterns of how it is used in the real world. The key difference reflects changes in the nature of money itself. In Gresham's time, the intrinsic value of English coinage was linked to its gold or silver content, along with the prices that the holder could obtain for it at domestic and foreign mints. Crucially, this intrinsic value was also what determined whether a particular coin was widely used as a means of payment: after all, this is why bad money drove out good. Today, the determinants of good money have fundamentally changed. Reflecting the ubiquity of credit-based monetary IOUs, laws and institutions like the financial safety net are what now give our money a stable nominal, if not strictly intrinsic, value. Moreover, these laws and institutions are entirely separate from the technology-driven financial networks that enable us to use these IOUs as a cheap, fast, secure, and convenient means of payment. This book is an attempt to update Gresham's old law for our credit-based, digital, and networked age, and to explore the complex and evolving relationship between law, institutions, and technology at the heart of our monetary system.

Like the design of money itself, the predictions of Gresham's new law have profound implications for individuals, for the economy, and for the fabric of our institutions and society. On an individual level, the expansion of the shadow monetary system as bad money drives out good increases the risk of financial ruin for households and businesses as the IOUs they thought were sound money turn into empty promises during periods of institutional and broader systemic instability. On a macroeconomic level, while it is perhaps difficult to imagine today, the shadow monetary system may one day grow to rival the conventional banking system in size and systemic importance. If this eventually happens, it would raise the troubling prospect that the correlated and uncoordinated bankruptcy of the institutions and platforms at the heart of this system could precipitate a severe contraction in the money supply, leading to damaging deflation, a reduction in investment and commercial activity, and undermining economic growth. While we might then expect policymakers to take extraordinary measures to prevent the resulting economic devastation, planning on these types of ad hoc and ex post bailouts of the shadow monetary system would itself represent a critical policy failure. And lastly, at the societal level, either the breakdown or bailout of the shadow monetary system could potentially trigger a broader crisis of confidence in our monetary institutions—one that could spread beyond this system to banks, central banks, and even governments.

But it's not all doom and gloom. Gresham's new law also highlights the incredible opportunity that lies before us. The emerging problem of bad money is ultimately a by-product of the development of new technology that holds out the promise of a more efficient, effective, and equitable payment system. If this technology can be harnessed within a legal and institutional framework that delivers universally good money, the result would be a safer, more convenient, and more dynamic system of money and payments. Almost five hundred years ago, the young Queen Elizabeth I understood that tackling the malaise afflicting the English economy demanded that she fix the nation's money. This book describes the malaise afflicting our own monetary system and lays out a blueprint for how to fix it.

A Road Map for the Book

Every story has a beginning, and ours begins with a group of enterprising seventeenth-century London goldsmiths. Chapter 1 chronicles the emergence and evolution of a single, hearty, and rather peculiar species of financial institution—banks—on their winding path toward becoming both the dominant sources of money in the global economy and the gatekeepers of the modern payment system. It begins by tracing the historical development of banks in Europe and North America, the evolving legal treatment of their contractual promises to their depositors, and the increasing use of these promises as a form of money. It then traces the emergence, development, and functions of the specialized financial market infrastructure—*clearinghouses*—that banks established in order to ensure the safe, secure, and timely clearing and settlement of payments between banks. This chapter traces almost two centuries of sometimes radical experimentation, spanning changes in the common law, statutory reforms, and the development of entirely new public and private institutions. It also demonstrates how embedded banks have become within our systems of money and payments and, accordingly, why we cannot even begin to talk about the rise of the shadow monetary system without first understanding the important and fundamentally intertwined economic roles that banks currently play.

The story of how banks became so deeply entrenched at the heart of our systems of money and payments is long, complicated and, in many ways, still being written. It is a story about war, politics, economics, entrepreneurship, technology, and path dependence. Importantly, it is also a story about the law. Chapter 2 describes the unique privileges and protections that the law currently bestows on conventional deposit-taking banks. Collectively, these privileges and protections create a comprehensive public backstop: a financial safety net that includes access to central bank lender-of-last-resort facilities, deposit insurance schemes, and special resolution regimes for struggling banks. This safety net gives banks a comparative advantage in the creation of monetary IOUs—transforming otherwise risky deposits into good money. In order to address the resulting moral hazard problems, banks are then subject to sophisticated frameworks of prudential regulation and supervision. Compliance with these frameworks is also often a legal precondition for obtaining access to the clearinghouses and other financial plumbing through which the vast majority of payments currently flow. In many countries, this gives banks—and *only* banks—direct access to our basic financial infrastructure. Viewed in this light, the law plays a number of critical, and yet critically understudied, roles in promoting the tight institutional bundling of banking, money, and payments. Chapter 3 explores how this bundling entrenches banks at the apex of the financial system, thereby erecting significant barriers to entry, undercutting competition, and slowing technological innovation and adoption in the markets for money and payments. It also identifies the risks that this bundling creates for customer protection, for microprudential safety and soundness and, ultimately, for financial stability.

The historical, legal, and institutional developments chronicled in the first three chapters will be familiar to most students of banks and bank regulation. The *real* story—the story at the heart of this book—is what happened next. Despite the legally entrenched bundling of banking, money, and payments, recent years have witnessed an explosion in the number and variety of new financial institutions and platforms seeking to compete with banks in the increasingly lucrative markets for money and payments. Chapter 4 describes the emergence, evolution, and staggering growth of this shadow monetary system and the collective process of unbundling it has already started to unleash. This chapter is structured around four case studies— P2P payment platforms, mobile money, cryptocurrency exchanges, and stablecoins—each designed to illuminate the various ways in which these new entrants are responding to the pent-up demand for cheap, fast, secure, convenient, interoperable, and accessible payments.

The common thread connecting these case studies is that they all involve technology-driven financial institutions and platforms that seek to issue monetary IOUs *outside* the perimeter of conventional bank regulation.

As a consequence, these institutions and platforms do not enjoy the same legal privileges and protections as conventional deposit-taking banks. Among other important differences, this means that these new entrants are generally subject to the strict procedural and substantive requirements of general corporate bankruptcy law. Compounding matters, the business models of these new entrants, and the way they use customer funds, often contribute to the risk of bankruptcy. Chapter 5 explains how the bankruptcy process fundamentally undermines the ability of these new entrants to make credible monetary commitments. It also demonstrates how even the threat of bankruptcy can make these aspiring monetary institutions vulnerable to destabilizing customer runs. Accordingly, while the monetary IOUs of these new entrants may initially seem like close functional substitutes for good old-fashioned bank deposits, the reality is that many are an important and growing source of bad money.

In theory, these new entrants can enhance the credibility of their monetary IOUs through the thoughtful use of various legal strategies. These strategies include collateralization, structural subordination, and trusts. Yet in practice, with a few notable exceptions, the use of these strategies within the shadow monetary system is exceedingly rare. Chapter 6 begins by illuminating the inevitable commercial pressures and trade-offs that explain this failure and why, ultimately, we should not expect profit-seeking firms to voluntarily adopt these effective but costly strategies.

If we can't trust these new entrants to voluntarily adopt legal strategies designed to enhance the credibility of their monetary commitments, the burden inevitably falls to public law and regulation to address the resulting risks. At present, the shadow monetary system is governed by a loose patchwork of heterogeneous regulatory frameworks that vary greatly from jurisdiction to jurisdiction and from framework to framework. While some of these frameworks have, at least in theory, been designed for the digital age, many—especially in the United States—are antiquated and inadequate rulebooks left over from the age of the telegraph. Chapter 6 concludes by surveying the core regulatory frameworks that currently govern the shadow monetary system in the United States, European Union, China, and other key jurisdictions. It then explains why many of these frameworks fail to transform the risky, bankruptcy-prone IOUs of the shadow monetary system into good money.

The final chapter confronts the fundamental policy challenge: how to promote ongoing technological experimentation, competition, and innovation in payments without posing new threats to monetary and financial stability. Conventional wisdom suggests that policymakers seeking to answer this question inevitably confront an intractable set of trade-offs. On the one hand, if policymakers roll back the public safety net for banks, they risk undermining public confidence in our money and, with it, the stability of the conventional banking system. On the other hand, if they expand the public safety net and access to basic financial market infrastructure to include the shadow monetary system, they risk fomenting moral hazard and—once again—instability.

Further compounding matters, designing regulatory frameworks that are both functionally equivalent to conventional bank regulation and yet specifically tailored to the unique business models of these new institutions and platforms poses a host of thorny technocratic challenges. These challenges help explain why policymakers have often been reluctant to fundamentally reimagine the regulatory frameworks that support and entrench our current bundled system of banking, money, and payments. If policymakers get it wrong, they risk not only squandering the inherent promise of new technology but also—and far worse—undermining public confidence in the money supply, the stability of the financial system, and perhaps even the longer-term trajectory of the broader economy.

On its face, this challenge is made even more daunting by the fact that unleashing the potential of new payments technologies will in many cases demand that we rethink, and perhaps even rebuild, our existing financial market infrastructure. Over the long term, this process of building, dismantling, and rebuilding is all but inevitable. As part of this process, policymakers should not simply settle for capturing the efficiency gains at the edge of today's technological frontier. Instead, they should ensure that the markets in which this technology is developed and finds its applications remain fundamentally contestable, so that the forces of competition can continue to drive innovation and push the boundaries of this frontier tomorrow and beyond.

These challenges are significant, but they are not insurmountable. The problems of new money simply demand new thinking—along with a better appreciation for the very different drivers of good money versus good payments. Chapter 7 concludes by laying out a more detailed blueprint for legal and institutional reform. This blueprint is built on three pillars. The first is a new payments charter that draws a clear legal distinction between conventional deposit-taking banks and the diverse range of other financial institutions and platforms that issue monetary IOUs. While banks would still be permitted to engage in financial intermediation, these other institutions and platforms would be subject to a strict "no intermediation" rule that would prohibit them from making loans or other long-term, risky investments. These new entrants would then be subject to far less intrusive regulation and supervision designed to reflect their far more narrow business models and risks. Second, having obtained a payments charter, these new entrants would benefit from open access and interoperability rules, making them eligible for direct access to existing financial market infrastructure and, where necessary, protecting them from discriminatory pricing or other anticompetitive conduct on the part of incumbent players. Third, this blueprint envisions the creation of a new governance framework for the payment system. This framework would be designed to harness the comparative advantages of public and private sector stakeholders, better coordinate ongoing decisions about the development and adoption of new payments technology and, ultimately, ensure that these decisions are made in the public interest.

This blueprint would level the legal and institutional playing field: promoting greater experimentation, competition, and innovation in pursuit of better payments. Simultaneously, it would help protect consumers, financial institutions, and the stability of the monetary system when, inevitably, some of these experiments go wrong. Finally, it would strengthen and improve the often neglected governance of the payment system, thereby ensuring that our laws and institutions keep pace with new technology and reflect, first and foremost, the public interest. In the end, the implementation of this blueprint—or something like it—may ultimately be the only thing standing between us and the destructive dynamics at the heart of Gresham's new law.

1

The Goldsmiths' Experiment

Money doesn't grow on trees. The real story is way more crazy
than that.

—UNKNOWN

There is an apocryphal story about the famous bank robber "Slick" Willie
Sutton. Shortly before Sutton was captured in February 1952, a reporter for
the *Saturday Evening Standard* asked him why he robbed banks. Sutton's
response, which both he and the arresting officer would later deny, has
become perhaps the most famous quote in the history of grand larceny:
"because that's where the money is."[1] Today, we take it for granted that
banks are where the money is. Indeed, for many of us, opening our first bank
account was an important rite of passage—a symbol of our growing legal
and economic autonomy and the fact that we were on the verge of becoming full-fledged members of society. But banks have not always played this
role. Nor should we blithely assume that they will continue to play this role
in the future. Accordingly, in order to better understand where we are, how
we got here, and where we might be going, it is helpful to first understand
something about where we have been.

1. Lorena Mongelli, "Former Cop Recalls NYPD Arrest of Willie Sutton 60 Years Later,"
New York Post (February 12, 2012).

The nature and sources of money have always varied across time, place, culture, and circumstance.[2] The first reliable written records documenting the use of money date back to ancient Mesopotamia (3500–800 BC), where the administrators of Sumerian temples used a basic accounting system to record financial obligations (debits) and the corresponding rights (credits), and to calculate outstanding rents, loans, and various administrative fees.[3] Sumerian merchants and tradespeople would also record debits and credits on clay and metal tablets that could then be transferred from hand to hand.[4] While most of these ancient records and tablets have long since been lost to time, this basic architecture—built on a dual system of bookkeepers' records and negotiable instruments—will be familiar to any student of modern banking. Indeed, if you open your wallet right now, you are likely to find both a plastic card enabling you to access the money in your bank account and a random collection of paper bills and coins.

Yet history rarely travels in a straight line. The Sumerian monetary system was dismantled by Alexander the Great, who replaced it with one based on plundered gold and silver that he then had minted into coins.[5] This *commodity*-based monetary system differed from the Sumerian *credit*-based system in several important respects. Most importantly, rather than basing money on the debts—monetary IOUs—that borrowers owed to their creditors, the Alexandrian system was anchored by physical commodities that were deemed to have intrinsic value beyond their use as a widely accepted medium of exchange.[6] Around the same period, other commodity money systems based on gold, silver, bronze, and copper coins, disks, spades, or

2. For a sweeping (if sometimes oversimplified) overview of the variety of credit, commodity-based, and hybrid monetary systems that have existed over the course of human history, see David Graeber, *Debt: The First 5,000 Years*, chapters 8–12 (2011).

3. This system was denominated in units—known as shekels—that were based on quantities of barley and ultimately backed by ingots of silver. For a more detailed description, see Michael Hudson, "Reconstructing the Origins of Interest-Bearing Debt and the Logic of Clean Slates," in Hudson & Van de Mieroop (eds.), *Debt & Economic Renewal in the Ancient Near East* (2002). This system also foreshadowed the emergence of a number of credit-based monetary systems that were tied in various ways to the value of underlying commodities.

4. See Mitchell Innes, "What Is Money?," Banking Law Journal (May 1913) (describing the key features of these "shuhati" tablets and how they changed hands).

5. See Peter Green, *Alexander to Actium: The Historical Evolution of the Hellenistic Age* (1993) (describing how Alexander emptied the gold and silver reserves in conquered territories and then minted the bullion into coins in order to pay his soldiers and other creditors).

6. See Lawrence White, *The Theory of Monetary Institutions*, 26 (1999) (describing the features of commodity money).

other physical objects also emerged in northwest India,[7] northern China,[8] and the eastern Mediterranean—including the Roman Empire (625 BC–AD 476).[9] Over the next millennium, the decline and fall of these civilizations was then accompanied by a return to rudimentary credit-based monetary systems, often under the aegis of local religious institutions.[10]

Fueled by the discovery of the New World and its plentiful sources of gold and silver, the pendulum in Europe would swing back toward the widespread use of commodity money beginning in the fifteenth century.[11] Remarkably, this same period would also witness important and enduring innovations in credit-based monetary systems, including the emergence of the Lombard and Medici banking families in northern Italy, the Fugger and other merchant banking groups in Germany, and early public banks such as the Bank of Amsterdam.[12] In Europe, Asia, and the Americas, this dual system of credit and commodity-based money would survive in various countries, at various times, and in various forms for most of the next five centuries, until the abandonment of the gold exchange standard in the early 1970s finally broke the golden fetters.[13] The historical record thus reveals a pattern of periodic oscillation between credit and commodity-based monetary systems, with many systems characterized by the simultaneous use of both credit and commodity money.[14]

So how did we end up with the monetary system we have today? This chapter explores the historical origins and basic structure of our current bundled system of banking, money, and payments. It describes the emergence and evolution of conventional deposit-taking banks, along with the clearinghouses that these banks created to clear and settle their financial obligations toward one another. It also describes some of the core legal

7. See Madhukar Dhavalikar, "The Beginning of Coinage in India," 6:3 World Archeology 330 (1975), and Satya Prakash & Rajendra Singh, *Coinage in Ancient India* (1968).

8. See David Schaps, "The Invention of Coin in Lydia, in India, and in China," XIV International Economic History Congress (2006).

9. See Walter Scheidel, "The Monetary Systems of the Han and Roman Empires," Princeton-Stanford Working Papers on Classics No. 110505 (February 2008).

10. See Graeber, *Debt*, chapter 10.

11. With much of this gold and silver ultimately finding its way east, reflecting the burgeoning European trade with India and China; see Kenneth Pomeranz, *The Great Divergence: China, Europe and the Making of the Modern World Economy* (2000).

12. See generally Charles Kindleberger, *A Financial History of Western Europe*, chapter 3 (1984) (describing the Italian banking families, German merchant banks, and early public banks).

13. For a detailed history of the gold standard, see Barry Eichengreen & Marc Flandreau, *The Gold Standard in Theory and History* (1997).

14. See Graeber, *Debt*, 420. ("What we see is a broad alternation between periods dominated by credit money and periods in which gold and silver come to dominate.")

engineering that was necessary to establish and maintain the credibility of this once innovative, now aging, and always controversial system of money and payments. As we shall see, two themes stand out. The first is that the emergence, development, decay, and reimagining of our monetary institutions are part of a complex, iterative, and experimental process that has spanned well over a millennium—a process that continues to this day. The second is the central role of both public and private law in this process as important building blocks in the legal and institutional foundations of good money.

Banking before Banks

The origins of our modern system of banking, money, and payments can be traced at least as far back as the Italian banking system of the early thirteenth century.[15] Genovese notarial records dating from the year 1200 describe the process by which local bankers would allow their wealthy clients to make payments by means of book transfers on the accounts of the bank.[16] In the simplest terms, a book transfer involves two sequential entries on a ledger: the first *debiting* the account of the payor, the second *crediting* the account of the payee. Using this book transfer process, merchants could thus make payment for goods or services by directing their bank to debit their account and credit that of their agents, suppliers, or other creditors— provided, of course, that these creditors held an account at the same bank. These notarial records also suggest the existence of relatively informal *interbank* arrangements that were used to make payments between accounts held by and at different banks.[17] This same basic system of ledgers, book transfers, and informal interbank payment arrangements was subsequently adopted by the Venetian banking system of the thirteenth through fifteenth centuries[18] and eventually spread throughout much of Western Europe.[19]

---

15. See Benjamin Geva, *The Payment Order of Antiquity and the Middle Ages: A Legal History*, 354 (2011); Robert Lopez, "The Dawn of Medieval Banking," in Centre for Medieval and Renaissance Studies, UCLA (ed.), *The Dawn of Medieval Banking* (1979). At the same time, there is a strong case to be made that these practices may have been imported from the Middle East and Asia.

16. See Robert Reynolds, "A Business Affair in Genoa in the Year 1200: Banking, Bookkeeping, a Broker and a Lawsuit," in Besta (ed.), *Studi di Storia e Diritto in Onore di Enrico Besta per il xi anno del suo Insegnamento* (1938).

17. Reynolds, "Business Affair in Genoa"; see also Geva, *Payment Order of Antiquity*, 359.

18. See Reinhold Mueller, "The Role of Bank Money in Venice, 1300–1500," 3 Studi Veneziani 47 (1979), and *The Venetian Money Market: Banks, Panics, and the Public Debt, 1200–1500* (1997).

19. Geva, *Payment Order of Antiquity*, 359.

In reality, of course, the institutions of medieval European finance were not generally known as "banks." Nor in many cases did these institutions perform all the functions that we today associate with the business of banking. Instead, medieval financiers fell broadly into two categories: merchant bankers and money changers.[20] Merchant bankers were initially large commodity merchants, first of Italian and later German origin, with extensive trading and correspondent networks throughout Western Europe.[21] Among their many important functions, these bankers combined long-distance lending and money remittance: extending credit in one geographic location and currency—e.g., Venice and lira—with the understanding that it would be repaid in another location and currency—e.g., Paris and livres.[22]

The principal financial instrument through which these lending and remittance services were provided was the *cambium*, or letter of payment. A letter of payment was a written acknowledgment by a borrower of money received, and a corresponding direction to the borrower's foreign agent to repay this money to the lender's foreign agent at a specified time, location, and currency. The borrowed money was typically used by the borrower to purchase goods locally that were then destined for export and sale by the borrower's foreign agent at the location stated in the letter of payment. Upon receipt, the lender's foreign agent would present the letter to the borrower's foreign agent for acceptance and, once due, repayment.[23] The borrower's agent would then discharge the repayment obligation out of the proceeds generated from the sale of the goods.

Thus, for example, a merchant could obtain a lira-denominated loan from a lender in Venice, which they would then use to purchase silk or spices for export to the markets of northern France. Once the goods had been sold by the borrower's agent at market, the livre-denominated proceeds would be used to repay the Venetian lender via their French agent. The lender's agent could then remit the money back to the lender by entering into a "reverse" letter of payment with a French merchant looking to purchase goods for export to Venice. Among other benefits, these letters of credit thus

---

20. Geva, 355. Geva also notes a third category—pawnbrokers—that played little or no role in the payment system. In practice, these categories were not mutually exclusive, with many institutions acting as both money changers and merchant banks.

21. See Jean-Francois Bergier, "From the Fifteenth Century in Italy to the Sixteenth Century in Germany: A New Banking Concept?," in Centre for Medieval and Renaissance Studies, UCLA (ed.), *The Dawn of Medieval Banking* (1979).

22. Geva, *Payment Order of Antiquity*, 356.

23. Geva, 379–380.

greatly reduced the need for merchants to carry large quantities of physical currency—e.g., gold and silver coins—as they made their way across the long and treacherous trade routes of medieval Europe.

Merchant bankers and their clients could also settle outstanding obligations at "exchange" fairs that were often held in conjunction with the annual Champagne and other regional commercial fairs at which agricultural goods, spices, leather, textiles, and other products were bought and sold. In time, many merchant bankers would also establish a more permanent presence in major commercial centers such as Florence, Bruges, Geneva, and London.[24] In effect, medieval merchant bankers combined trade financing, foreign exchange trading, and payment services.[25] In this and other important respects, they were the forerunners of modern investment banks.[26] As we shall see, the institutional arrangements through which merchant banks provided these services—namely, letters of payment and exchange fairs—were also the precursors of modern bills of exchange and more formal interbank clearing and settlement systems.[27]

The other principal category of monetary institutions in medieval Europe were money changers. Money changers accepted deposits of gold and silver coins and other forms of currency from customers, which they would then use to make loans and other investments.[28] As part of the deposit-taking process, money changers would assess the authenticity, weight, and metal content of deposited coins and then credit the deposit holder's account with an amount based on their assessment of its intrinsic value.[29] Money changers then enabled deposit holders to execute book transfers from their accounts to those of other deposit holders.[30] They also facilitated book transfers between deposit holders that had accounts with different money changers, which were settled through informal networks of correspondent accounts that money changers held with each other.[31]

---

24. Geva, 382.

25. Geva, 356.

26. For a detailed description of how these medieval institutions evolved into modern-day investment banks, see Alan Morrison & Bill Wilhelm, *Investment Banking: Institutions, Politics, and Law* (2007).

27. See Geva, *Payment Order of Antiquity*, 387–417, for a more in-depth discussion of the historical development and legal issues surrounding both letters of payment and bills of exchange.

28. Geva, 356.

29. See Mueller, "Bank Money in Venice," 48.

30. For this reason, money changers were often called "transfer bankers"; Geva, *Payment Order of Antiquity*, 356.

31. Geva, 359–361.

Medieval money changers thus performed an important role as both custodians and transfer agents in an age when coins and other physical payment instruments were difficult to transport in large quantities and vulnerable to loss, theft, destruction, counterfeiting, and debasement.

Following several high-profile scandals in the sixteenth century, public confidence in these money changers began to ebb, and authorities in many European countries took matters into their own hands.[32] In many cases, this state intervention involved the creation of a public bank to provide deposit and other payment services. One of the first such public banks was the Bank of Amsterdam, created in 1609 with a public guarantee from the City of Amsterdam.[33] Coins and bullion deposited in the bank were credited to the account of the depositor in *banco florin*—a unit of account representing the value of a standardized light coin. The bank would then execute book transfers between florin-denominated accounts, with settlement taking place daily and on a multilateral—or "net"—basis. Notably, the creation of the Bank of Amsterdam was accompanied by a prohibition against private money changers. While this prohibition was subsequently lifted, money changers were thereafter required to obtain a license and maintain accounts with the bank. Similar public banks were established throughout Western Europe during the sixteenth and seventeenth centuries, gradually squeezing many private money changers out of the marketplace.[34] These public banks would continue to play an important role in the Continental payment system until the end of the eighteenth century, before eventually being supplanted by a series of legal and institutional innovations that would together lay the foundations for our modern systems of money and payments.

Enter the Goldsmiths

If Continental Europe is the birthplace of the business of banking, the United Kingdom is the birthplace of the modern bank. The origins of modern banks can be traced back to the activities of a small community of goldsmiths that operated on and around Lombard Street in the City of London. Historically,

32. See Raymond de Roover, "New Interpretations of the History of Banking," in Kirshner (ed.), *Business, Banking and Economic Thought in Late Medieval and Early Modern Europe: Selected Case Studies of Raymond de Roover*, 219 (1974). Public authorities also intervened out of concerns that the deposit-taking activities of money changers threatened the integrity of ducal mints and coins; Geva, *Payment Order of Antiquity*, 365.

33. For a more detailed description of the Bank of Amsterdam and its operations, see Geva, *Payment Order of Antiquity*, 364–367.

34. de Roover, "New Interpretations," 223.

the business of these goldsmiths consisted mainly of the production of gold and silver plates and jewelry, along with the purchase and sale of diamonds and other precious jewels. As part of this business, goldsmiths were also frequently called upon to assess the purity of gold and silver coins.[35] Following the outbreak of the English Civil War (1642–51), these goldsmiths saw an opportunity to expand this business by permitting wealthy customers to store their gold and silver coins in the goldsmiths' vaults, thus protecting them from loss, theft, seizure, or destruction amid the chaos of the escalating conflict.[36] Eventually, this safekeeping role evolved into one in which the goldsmiths enjoyed full legal authority to use these coins to make loans to individuals, businesses, and governments. These goldsmiths had thus stumbled upon the "fractional reserve" model that would eventually become synonymous with the business of banking: combining the acceptance of short-term deposits with the extension of longer-term loans and other forms of credit.

Strictly speaking, the goldsmiths did not invent modern banking. In Europe, that honor arguably falls to the Genoese, the Venetians, and the Lombards. There is also a strong case that many of the techniques that we today associate with modern banking were originally imported to Europe from the ancient Middle East and Asia. Yet the goldsmiths' model did combine three elements that continue to define our intertwined systems of banking, money, and payments. First, as described above, the goldsmiths accepted *deposits* of gold and silver coins. These deposits would then be credited to accounts held in the name of the goldsmiths' customers. Second, goldsmiths would issue receipts—or *notes*—as documentary evidence of these deposits.[37] These notes, which represented the goldsmiths' promise to repay deposited funds on demand when presented with the receipt, were typically payable to either the designated payee or the "bearer"—i.e., the person in possession—of the receipt.[38] Over time, these notes came to

---

35. See J. Milnes Holden, *The History of Negotiable Instruments in English Law*, 71 (1955); Geva, *Payment Order of Antiquity*, 473.

36. See James Rogers, *The Early History of the Law of Bills and Notes: A Study of the Origins of Anglo-American Commercial Law*, 119 (1995); Geva, *Payment Order of Antiquity*, 474.

37. The goldsmiths appear to have borrowed this element from the Bank of Amsterdam, which issued paper receipts that were often worth more than the equivalent denomination of metal coins because they were not vulnerable to clipping. I am grateful to Professor Lev Menand for pointing out this connection.

38. Geva, *Payment Order of Antiquity*, 475. The oldest surviving description of the goldsmiths' model, along with the notes they issued, is a remarkable letter from 1676 entitled "Mystery of the New Fashioned Goldsmiths or Bankers: Their Rise, Growth, State and Decay"; see "The New-Fashioned Goldsmiths," 2:2 Quarterly Journal of Economics 251 (1888). Two of the oldest surviving notes, both issued by Field Whorwood in 1654, make it clear that the goldsmith undertook

possess a relatively high degree of transferability, thus enabling the holder to "settle a great variety of tradesman's bills, to pay fees and taxes, to provide ready cash, and to purchase shares, lottery tickets, and tallies."[39] That is, these receipts could themselves be used as *money*.[40] Third, depositors could request drafts in any amount up to the full value of their deposit made payable to either the bearer of the draft or a specified third party. These drafts were the precursors of modern checks.[41]

The transformation of the goldsmiths' notes into widely accepted monetary IOUs did not take place overnight. In fact, it required almost two centuries of experimentation and evolution in common law jurisprudence, public law, and institutional design. At the outbreak of the English Civil War, the question of whether the goldsmiths enjoyed full legal authority to invest any gold or silver coins that had been deposited with them was still not entirely clear. Specifically, questions periodically arose around the circumstances in which depositors seeking to enforce their legal rights against a goldsmith who refused to return their money needed to sue for a common law writ of detinue or debt.[42] Whereas detinue recognized the rights of the depositor in the deposited property and therefore required the party holding it to return the exact same property, debt merely required the return of a sum of money equal in value to this property.

The distinction between detinue and debt was enormously important for the legality of the goldsmiths' emerging business model. In order to engage in fractional reserve banking, the goldsmiths needed deposits to be recognized as a *loan* to the bank, thereby establishing them as the legal owners of deposited property. Legal ownership then gave them the right to

---

to "repay" deposit funds "on demand"; see Frank Melton, "Goldsmiths' Notes, 1654–1655," 6:1 Journal of the Society of Archivists 30 (1978).

39. D. M. Mitchell, "Mr. Fowle Pray Pay the Washwoman: The Trade of a London Goldsmith-Banker, 1660–1692," 23(1) Business and Economic History 27, 35 (1994).

40. Final settlement would then take place when the seller of the goods and services, or a subsequent transferee, returned the note to the goldsmith—in effect demanding that it honor its promise to repay the deposited funds. Over time, these privately issued notes would be largely replaced by notes issued by the Bank of England; see Desan, *Making Money,* chapters 8–10.

41. Geva, *Payment Order of Antiquity*, 476–477; Holden, *History of Negotiable Instruments*, 206–210.

42. In some circumstances, those entitled to the return of money could also sue for an accounting. For a more detailed discussion of the case law parsing the distinction between the writs of detinue, debt, and accounting, see, e.g., Benjamin Geva, "Bank Money: The Rise, Fall and Metamorphosis of the Transferrable Deposit," in Fox & Ernst (eds.), *Money in the Western Legal Tradition: Middle Ages to Bretton Woods* (2016); Geva, *Bank Collections and Payment Transactions: A Comparative Study of Legal Aspects*, 76–77 (2001); David Fox, "Bona Fide Purchase and the Currency of Money," 55:3 Cambridge Law Journal 547 (1996); and Jongchul Kim, "How Modern Banking Originated: The London Goldsmith-Bankers' Institutionalisation of Trust," 53:6 Business History 939 (2011).

determine what to do with this property, including whether and on what terms to lend it out in search of profit. Yet this distinction also presented English courts with something of a conceptual problem: How should they distinguish between detinue and debt where the deposited property—gold and silver coins—was itself recognized as a form of money?

Historically, some English courts had argued that there was a distinction between money and other types of property on the grounds that the identity and value of one deposited coin was, from a practical perspective, indistinguishable from another.[43] However, other courts rejected the idea that money could not be distinguished or "earmarked" in the same way as other property.[44] Professor David Fox, a leading scholar on the history of English money, has suggested that the legal status of deposits as grounded in debt, rather than detinue, appears to have been established no later than 1660.[45] Nevertheless, questions surrounding the nature and scope of the goldsmiths' legal authority over deposited money would not be definitively settled until a series of cases in the early nineteenth century,[46] culminating in the landmark 1848 judgment of the House of Lords in *Foley v. Hill*.[47] As explained by Lord Cottenham in *Foley*: "Money, when paid into a bank, ceases altogether to be the money of the principal; it is then the money of the banker, who is bound to return an equivalent by paying a similar sum to that deposited with him when he is asking for it."[48]

Whatever legal uncertainty remained during the latter half of the seventeenth century, it certainly did not prevent the goldsmiths from investing the gold and silver coins stored within their vaults. Initially, the bulk of these deposits were invested in debt securities issued by the English government.[49] Accordingly, when Charles II repudiated England's debts in 1672—the infamous Stop of the Exchequer—the resulting crisis consumed

43. See *Bretton v. Barrett* 74 ER 918 (1598) ("for if a horse be delivered to be redelivered, there the property is not altered, and therefore a detinue lies, for they are goods known: but if money be delivered, it cannot be known, and therefore the property is altered, and therefore a debt will lie"; *Higgs v. Holiday* Cro. Eliz. 746 (1600) ("if a man delivers money to another, the property in the money is in the bailee, because it cannot be known").

44. See *Miller v. Race* 97 ER 398 (1758) ("It has been quaintly said, 'that the reason why money can not [sic] be followed, is because it has no earmark:' but this is not true.").

45. Fox, "Currency of Money," 556.

46. See, e.g., *Carr v. Carr* 35 ER 799 (1811); *Devaynes v. Noble* 35 ER 767 (1816); *Sims v. Bond* 110 ER 834 (1833) ("Sums which are paid to the credit of a customer with a banker, though usually called deposits, are, in truth, loans by the customer to the banker.").

47. *Foley v. Hill* 2 HL 28 (1848).

48. *Foley*, 38–39.

49. See Desan, *Making Money,* 389 (noting that it was only after 1720 that goldsmiths effectively lent to private businesses).

not only the government but also the goldsmiths that had lent it money. Facing potentially devastating losses, many goldsmiths found themselves unable to repay their depositors, leading to public opprobrium and allegations of incompetence, usury, and fraud.[50] Yet while the episode would tarnish the reputation of the goldsmiths for over a generation, the Stop of the Exchequer would also set in motion a series of legal and institutional reforms that would collectively remake the English monetary system. In time, these reforms would put the goldsmiths' heirs at the very heart of an increasingly vibrant and burgeoning London money market.

The primary impetus for these reforms was the then chronic problem of a lack of gold and silver coins. It has been estimated that on the eve of the Glorious Revolution (1688–89) somewhere between £10 million and £14.5 million in gold and silver coins was circulating in England.[51] With annual tax obligations to the Crown averaging approximately £4.5 million in the years that immediately followed, due in large part to the demands of financing England's war with France, this meant that a significant percentage of the overall money supply found its way into the government's coffers. While much of this money ultimately found its way back into circulation when the government purchased goods and services, the reality of fighting a foreign war meant that its route back into the domestic economy was often long, circuitous, and incomplete.[52] Together with the lingering aftereffects of the Stop of the Exchequer, the resulting lack of gold and silver coins made it increasingly difficult for the government to raise money through the issuance of new debt.[53]

The solution that the government eventually seized upon was for it to borrow money from a bank against *future* tax revenues. But rather than borrowing gold and silver coins, the proceeds of this loan were to be paid in notes issued by the bank itself.[54] The government would then use these bank notes to purchase goods and services and pay its outstanding debts, thereby promoting the use of these notes as a form of money.[55] Today, we know this bank as the

50. Desan, 302.

51. See Peter Lindert, "English Population, Wages, and Prices: 1541–1913," 15:4 Journal of Interdisciplinary History 609, 633–634 (1985); N. J. Mayhew, "Population, Money Supply, and the Velocity of Circulation in England, 1300–1700," 48:2 Economic History Review 238, 247 (1995).

52. Desan, *Making Money*, 297.

53. See William Killigrew, "A Proposal Shewing How This Nation May Be Vast Gainers by All the Sums of Money, Given to the Crown, without Lessening the Prerogative," 12 (1690).

54. Set forth in "An Act for Granting to Their Majesties Several Rates and Duties upon the Tonnage of Ships," more commonly known as the Bank of England Act (5 & 6 W & M c 20, 1694). The act contemplated that the Bank would be permitted to issue several types of instruments, including bills and notes. While the original intention was that it would be the Bank's bills that circulated as money, it was its notes that came to perform this role; see Desan, *Making Money*, 308–311.

55. See William Patterson, "A Brief Account of the Intended Bank of England," 2 (1694).

Bank of England. Established by statute in 1694, the Bank of England represented a departure from earlier public banks, such as the Bank of Amsterdam, in that it was designed from its inception not only to accept deposits of gold and silver coins but to actually create new—*paper*—money.[56]

Over the next century and a half, Parliament introduced a series of measures designed to enhance the attractiveness of Bank of England notes as monetary IOUs. Yet, as a matter of practice, the bank's notes were accepted in satisfaction of a holder's tax obligations almost from the beginning. As Professor Christine Desan explains, this made perfect sense: "Officials, having used Bank notes to pay those who serviced or supplied [the government], quite predictably felt compelled to take the notes back in payment of taxes."[57] Between 1698 and 1816, Parliament also passed a series of laws enshrining this practice, gradually expanding the use of the Bank's notes and other liabilities to pay taxes, fees, and other public debts.[58] In 1697, Parliament made the forgery of the Bank's notes punishable by death.[59] And in 1833, it officially recognized Bank of England notes as legal tender, thereby ensuring that they would be accepted in connection with commercial transactions and the repayment of private debts.[60]

Over this same span, the United Kingdom passed legislation that enhanced the attractiveness of the goldsmiths' notes. In 1704, for example, Parliament made goldsmiths' notes that were payable to either a specified party or the "bearer" legally assignable, thereby facilitating their transfer from hand to hand.[61] Yet even then the goldsmiths' notes initially struggled to compete with the increasingly popular notes issued by the Bank of England. Not only were the Bank's notes typically more creditworthy and convenient, but between 1708 and 1833 the Bank also enjoyed an effective monopoly over the business of joint-stock banking in the City of London.[62] Nevertheless, over the longer term, the relationship between the Bank, the burgeoning community of goldsmith bankers, and their ostensibly

---

56. See John Clapham, *The Bank of England: A History: Volume 1*, 2–4 (1944); David Richards, *The Early History of Banking in England*, 136 (1929); Desan, *Making Money*, 304.

57. Desan, *Making Money*, 312.

58. See, e.g., 9 Will 3 c 44, s. 79 (1697–1698); 10 Will 3 c 11, s. 13 (1698); 56 Geo 3 c 96, s. 4 (1816).

59. 8 & 9 Will 3 c 20, s. 36 (1696–1697).

60. 3 & 4 Will 4 c 98, s. 6 (1833).

61. 3 & 4 Ann c 9, s. 1 (1704).

62. 7 Ann c 30, s. 66 (1708); 3 & 4 Will 4 c. 98 (1933). In 1826, joint-stock banks operating outside a sixty-five-mile perimeter around the City of London were given permission to operate by virtue of the Country Bankers Act; 7 Geo IV c 46 (1826). While this monopoly technically only applied to note issuance, it was often understood as extending to deposit taking; see Walter Bagehot, *Lombard Street: A Description of the Money Market*, chapter 3 (1873).

competing monetary IOUs would become intricately intertwined and, in many ways, mutually reinforcing.

This symbiotic relationship between the Bank of England and the gold-smith bankers manifested itself in at least two important ways. First, reflecting strong demand for the new paper currency, the goldsmiths' loans were increasingly paid out in the Bank's notes instead of gold or silver coins. In exchange for these loans, borrowers would typically issue debt instruments, known as *bills of exchange*. Bills of exchange were a type of short-term commercial paper that enabled manufacturing firms, textile and commodity merchants, and other business enterprises to borrow money in exchange for a promise to repay it either on demand or at a specified future date.[63] The expectation was that the money needed to discharge the debt would then be generated by the sale of the goods and services that these enterprises produced.

While "its earliest history is still wrapped in obscurity,"[64] by the late eighteenth century bills of exchange were typically written and transferred to a specified party or the "bearer" on the promise of funds from a bank in London.[65] As Desan explains: "Endorsing the bill, the party receiving it could pass it on, also by endorsement, to another party. *This enabled the bills to travel hand to hand as money*."[66] In addition to extending loans, bankers also stood ready to both *guarantee* repayment of outstanding bills of exchange—through the issuance of so-called bankers' acceptances—and *purchase* bills for less than their stated face value—a practice known as *discounting*.[67] Together, bills of exchange, bankers acceptances, and discounting would become the key ingredients of London's thriving nineteenth-century money market. In turn, England's regional or "country" banks came to depend on the London money market as both a depository for their own reserves and as a source of market liquidity. In this way, demand for Bank of England notes

63. The legal treatment of bills of exchange has its own fascinating history and was pivotal in their journey toward becoming widely used as a form of money; see generally R. D. Richards, "The Evolution of Paper Money in England," 41:3 Quarterly Journal of Economics 361, 383–388 (1927); Keith Horsefield, "The Beginnings of Paper Money in England," 6:1 Journal of European Economic History 117, 119–120 (1977).

64. Richards, "Evolution of Paper Money," 383.

65. Desan, *Making Money*, 395.

66. Desan, 395 (emphasis added).

67. For a detailed description of these acceptance and discount markets, see Mike Anson, David Bholat, Miao Kang, & Ryland Thomas, "The Bank of England as Lender of Last Resort: New Historical Evidence from Daily Transaction Data," Bank of England Staff Working Paper No. 691, 8–11 (2017), and Vincent Bignon, Marc Flandreau, & Stefano Ugolini, "Bagehot for Beginners: The Making of Lender-of-Last-Resort Operations in the Mid-Nineteenth Century," 65 Economic History Review 580, 586–589 (2012).

provided the "anchor" not only for the extension of credit to businesses in the real economy, but also for a dramatic expansion in the nature, size, and liquidity of England's money supply.[68]

Second, reflecting its growing importance, the Bank of England would eventually come to play a critical role in supporting the liquidity and stability of the London money market. In much the same way that banks stood ready to discount bills of exchange—thereby enabling merchants to swap expected future revenue streams for cash on the barrelhead—the Bank of England was periodically compelled to lend money to banks against their illiquid loans and other assets. These loans enabled banks to continue to honor their promises to depositors and other creditors during periods of severe illiquidity in the London money market, where the demand for Bank of England notes exceeded available supply. The rationale and mechanics of the Bank's discount window lending and how it evolved into a modern "lender of last resort" are described in greater detail in chapter 2. The key takeaway at this stage is simply that the expectation that the Bank of England would stand behind a bank's promises served to enhance the credibility of the bank's notes and deposits as monetary IOUs. Perhaps more than any other single legal or institutional development during this period, this expectation transformed England's banks into "powerhouses of money creation,"[69] with bank deposits eventually supplanting both gold and silver coins and Bank of England notes as the dominant source of money. Today, retail and wholesale bank deposits represent almost 97 percent of the United Kingdom's money supply—vastly overshadowing the remaining stock of pound notes and coins.[70]

Coming to America

The goldsmiths' experiment would eventually be replicated across Western Europe. It was also exported—slowly and in pieces—to the New World. Elements of the goldsmiths' model first appeared in the American colonies as early as 1690.[71] These first protobanks experimented with the issuance of promissory notes to their depositors, typically secured against land or

68. Desan, *Making Money*, 378–381, 394–395.

69. Desan, 420.

70. See Bank of England, Bankstats Tables A2.2.1—Components of M4 (tables VRJX, VQKT, VRJV, VWDO; not seasonally adjusted, minus repo liabilities, as of May 22, 2022), https://www.bankofengland.co.uk/statistics/tables.

71. Serendipitously, that same year would witness the first experiments with paper currency issued by colonial governments as a form of legal tender; see Dror Goldberg, *Easy Money: American Puritans and the Invention of Modern Currency* (2023).

precious metals.[72] Mirroring their development in the United Kingdom, these notes would eventually come to possess a relatively high degree of transferability and thus circulate, often widely, as a form of paper money. The first conventional deposit-taking bank was likely the Bank of Pennsylvania, established in 1780 to raise capital to finance the American Revolutionary War (1775–83).[73] This was followed by the creation of the Bank of North America, which received the first federal bank charter in 1781.[74] Robert Morris, then United States superintendent of finance, supported the creation of the Bank of North America on the grounds that it would stimulate private investment and thereby expand government tax revenues.[75] Future treasury secretary Alexander Hamilton, meanwhile, saw the new bank as the linchpin of his plan to create what he described as "a sufficient medium" of exchange.[76] Put differently, Hamilton sought to develop a banking system in order to support the development of a more reliable system of money and payments.

The Founding Fathers were deeply divided over the role of the federal government in steering the economic, financial, and monetary affairs of the new nation.[77] The creation of a quasi-public bank in 1791, the First Bank of the United States, was one of the most hotly debated issues in the early Republic, pitting Federalists George Washington and Alexander Hamilton against Republicans Thomas Jefferson and James Madison.[78] Despite playing an important role in quelling the Panic of 1792, the Republican-led Senate narrowly voted not to reauthorize the First Bank's charter when it expired in 1811.[79] Almost immediately, however, shifting political and economic winds

72. See Goldberg, *Easy Money*; William Sumner, "A History of Banking in Leading Nations," 1 Journal of Commerce & Commercial Bulletin 4 (1896), citing James Trumbull, *Proceedings of the American Antiquarian Society* (1884); Richard Sylla, "Monetary Innovation in America," 42:1 Journal of Economic History 21 (1982).

73. Although, unlike modern banks, the Bank of Pennsylvania was incorporated with a limited life span; Sumner, "History of Banking," 14.

74. Sumner, "History of Banking," 17. Sumner refers to the Bank of North America as the first "specie paying, convertible bank note bank" in the US.

75. Sumner, 15.

76. See Hamilton, Alexander, "Letter to Robert Morris," 12 (April 30, 1781), https://founders.archives.gov/documents/Hamilton/01-02-02-1167.

77. See generally Bray Hammond, *Banks and Politics in America from the Revolution to the Civil War*, 89–14 (1957) (describing the disagreements among the Founding Fathers over the role the federal government should play in the banking system).

78. The compromise between Hamilton, Jefferson, and Madison that paved the way for the creation of the First Bank was subsequently immortalized in Lin Manuel Miranda's play *Hamilton*, where it provided the inspiration for the song "The Room Where It Happens."

79. Technically, the Senate's vote to reauthorize the First Bank resulted in a tie, with the casting vote going to Republican vice president George Clinton.

forced Congress to reconsider its decision, leading to the creation of the Second Bank of the United States in 1816.[80] Yet, over the next two decades, the Second Bank would become a casualty of the same dysfunctional political dynamics as its predecessor—suffering repeated and withering attacks by President Andrew Jackson before ultimately losing its quasi-public status upon the expiration of its federal charter in 1836.[81]

Following the expiration of the Second Bank's federal charter, responsibility for chartering and regulating US banks fell exclusively to the states. This ushered in a period of experimentation in bank business models and regulation known as the free banking era.[82] By 1836, the legislatures in many states had already adopted relatively strict licensing and prudential regulatory requirements. In New York, for example, legislation was passed in 1829 that required banks to contribute a small percentage of their capital to a state-managed fund created for the purpose of compensating the noteholders of failed banks.[83] In Massachusetts, the Suffolk Bank operated a private clearinghouse for notes issued by other New England banks.[84] In exchange for accepting the notes issued by these local and regional banks at face value, the Suffolk Bank required its members to maintain minimum deposits of gold and silver and subjected them to basic prudential supervision.[85] Several other states adopted banking statutes that contemplated

80. For a detailed description of the political dynamics leading to the establishment of the Second Bank, see generally Raymond Walters, Jr., "The Origins of the Second Bank of the United States," 53 Journal of Political Economy 115 (1945); Ralph Catterall, *The Second Bank of the United States* (1903).

81. See Hammond, *Banks and Politics,* 369–450 (describing the assault on the Second Bank and its eventual privatization).

82. For a detailed comparative assessment of the successes and failures of various free banking regimes in the US and elsewhere, see Lawrence White, *Free Banking in Britain: Theory, Experience and Debate 1800–1845* (2nd ed., 1995); White (ed.), *Free Banking, Volumes 1–3* (1993); and Kevin Dowd (ed.), *The Experience of Free Banking* (1992) (collectively describing experiments in free banking in Australia, Canada, Colombia, France, Ireland, Scotland, Switzerland, and the US).

83. For a detailed description, see Robert Chaddock, *The Safety Fund Banking System in New York, 1829–1866* (1910). While the New York safety fund system was originally designed to protect *all* creditors of a failed bank, the legislation was subsequently amended to limit protection to a bank's noteholders; John Holdsworth, "Lessons of State Banking before the Civil War," 30 Proceedings of the Academy of Political Science 23, 30–31 (1971).

84. For a detailed description, see George Trivoli, *The Suffolk Bank: Study of a Free-Enterprise Clearing System* (1979), and Charles Calomiris & Charles Kahn, "The Efficiency of Self-Regulated Payments Systems: Learning from the Suffolk System," 28 Journal of Money, Credit and Banking 766 (1996).

85. David Whitney, for example, documents several cases where the Suffolk Bank intervened to warn member banks that they were extending too much credit or issuing too much debt; Whitney, *The Suffolk Bank,* 35–38 (1878).

"free" entry into the business of banking, but on the stipulation that banks would be required to post government bonds as security against the issuance of new bank notes.[86]

There is some debate among scholars about whether the free banking era should be viewed as a triumph of free market capitalism or as a cautionary tale regarding the dangers of laissez faire monetary policy.[87] While there is no need for us to wade too deeply into this debate, there are several notable features of the free banking system that are relevant for our purposes—and about which scholars on both sides of the debate generally agree. The first is that the label *free banking* is fundamentally misleading. In reality, banks established in free banking states were often subject to costly regulatory constraints: including the requirement to post collateral against the bank notes they issued, contribute to default funds, and submit to basic prudential supervision. The second is that the era was characterized by an explosion in the number and variety of privately issued bank notes. While there exists no definitive record, as of February 1846, *Thompson's Bank Note Reporter* lists thousands of different species of private bank notes in circulation, issued by almost seven hundred state-chartered banks.[88] These notes typically took the form of perpetual, non-interest-bearing debt instruments that legally, if not always practically, entitled noteholders to redeem them on demand in exchange for gold or silver coins. Importantly, while these bank notes were all denominated in US dollars, their value in the hands of noteholders often varied depending on a number of specific characteristics.

86. States adopting free banking statutes included Michigan (1837), Georgia (1838), New Jersey (1850), Illinois (1851), Ohio (1851), Connecticut (1852), Indiana (1852), Minnesota (1858), and Pennsylvania (1860); Hugh Rockoff, "The Free Banking Era: A Reexamination," 6 Journal of Money, Credit and Banking 141, 150 (1974). While New York (1850) and Massachusetts (1851) also technically adopted free banking statutes, it would be incorrect to include them in this category given the existence of other public and private regulatory frameworks within these states—e.g., the New York safety fund system and the New England Suffolk banking system—that, strictly speaking, deviated from the free banking model.

87. See Rockoff, "Reexamination" (arguing that instability was endemic to many free banking systems). But see these articles by Arthur Rolnick and Warren Weber: "The Causes of Free Bank Failures: A Detailed Examination," 14 Journal of Monetary Economics 267 (1984) (arguing that free bank failures were attributable to falling asset prices); "Free Banking, Wildcat Banking and Shinplasters," 6 Federal Reserve Bank of Minneapolis Quarterly Review 10, 10 (1982) (arguing that bank failures in free banking states were due to broader recessions); "New Evidence on the Free Banking Era," 73 American Economic Review 1080 (1983) (arguing that empirical evidence regarding free bank failures is overstated). See also Rockoff, "New Evidence on Free Banking in the United States," 76 American Economic Review 866 (1985).

88. *Thompson's Bank Note Reporter*, 2–15 (February 19, 1846) (this figure excludes banks listed as either "closed" or "fraud").

The first characteristic was the potential *physical distance* between the holder of a bank note and the bank that originally issued it.[89] In a world dominated by a large number of relatively small and geographically dispersed banks, and without reliable and secure long-distance communication networks, noteholders would need to actually visit these banks in person in order to redeem their notes for gold or silver coins. Accordingly, the farther noteholders found themselves from the issuing bank, the higher the cost of redeeming the notes and the less valuable the notes were likely to be as a medium of exchange in their present location. Indeed, a small subset of these banks—known as wildcat banks—built their entire business models around establishing their offices in remote locations that made it difficult for noteholders to redeem their notes.[90]

Second, the value of a bank note would understandably depend on public perceptions of the *creditworthiness* of the issuing bank. Specifically, while notes issued by fundamentally solvent banks would trade at or very near their face value, the notes of weaker banks would often trade at a steep discount.[91] This in turn points to the important role played by publications such as *Thompson's Bank Note Reporter*, which published a monthly list of banks and their notes—identifying which banks were "broke," "closing" or "closed," or the subject of allegations of "fraud" (figure 1.1).[92] In effect, publications like *Thompson's* were necessary in order to help consumers and merchants differentiate between good and bad bank notes and thus to determine the value of the money in their pockets.

Finally, the value of bank notes depended on the *strength of the regulatory frameworks* that governed note-issuing banks. For example, notes issued by banks in New York or by members of New England's Suffolk banking system tended to change hands closer to their face value than those of banks located in states where the regulatory framework offered noteholders lower levels of protection against the default of the issuing bank.[93] Even among free

89. See Gary Gorton, "Pricing Free Bank Notes," 44 Journal of Monetary Economics 33 (1999) (describing the relevant transportation costs and the impact of new technology—i.e., railroads—on these costs and, correspondingly, on the discounts applied to different bank notes).

90. See Rockoff, "Reexamination," 141–42 (describing the defining features of wildcat banks).

91. See Gorton, "Pricing Free Bank Notes," 47–50. See also Matthew Jaremski, "Bank-Specific Default Risk in the Pricing of Bank Note Discounts," 71 Journal of Economic History 950 (2011) (reporting empirical findings of sensitivity to idiosyncratic credit risk in the secondary market for bank notes).

92. Other similar publications included *Van Court's Counterfeit Detector* and *Bank Note List*. As Gary Gorton has observed, it also helps explain the emergence of professional note brokers who served as middlemen in the market for bank notes; Gorton, "Pricing Free Bank Notes," 39.

93. See Rockoff, "Reexamination," 144, and Gorton, "Pricing Free Bank Notes," 42–43, 46 (both describing discounts on bank notes on a state-by-state basis). While noteholders in New

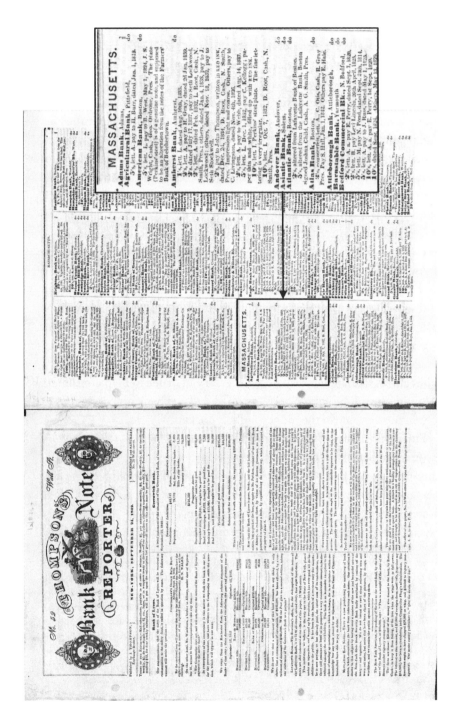

FIGURE 1.1. Extract from *Thompson's Bank Note Reporter* (September 1842)

banking states, the value of bank notes could differ on the basis of subtle but important differences in the legal requirements to post government bonds as security against the issuance of new bank notes. Economic historian Hugh Rockoff, for example, has documented how lax bond security requirements in states like Michigan, Indiana, and Minnesota were often associated with higher losses for noteholders.[94] In at least some cases, the expectation that noteholders were more likely to suffer losses appears to have then been reflected in the discounts applied to these notes relative to those applied to notes issued by banks in other states.[95]

These pricing dynamics drive home a stark reality: in a world characterized by an almost dizzying array of different types of money—and where the quality of this money depended on geography, technology, the creditworthiness of individual banks, and the regulatory frameworks that governed them—noteholders would have been required to invest significant time and energy conducting due diligence to determine the value of a bank's monetary IOUs. While our ancestors might not have thought about it precisely in these terms, this due diligence was necessitated by the existence of bank notes of variable quality circulating in the marketplace and the resulting imperative of distinguishing between good and bad money.

The free banking era would effectively come to an end with the enactment of the National Bank Acts of 1863–65.[96] The National Bank Acts were designed to establish a national banking system, raise much-needed finance for the Civil War, and prevent the further buildup of inflationary pressures stemming from the widespread issuance of state bank notes. They achieved the first objective by creating the federal Office of the Comptroller of the Currency (OCC) and giving it the authority to charter, regulate, and supervise national banks. They achieved the last two objectives by requiring these national banks to purchase government bonds, and by conditioning the ability of these banks to issue new notes on the size of their bond holdings. However, while Congress's

York suffered significant losses in the late 1830s, losses were reduced to close to zero following changes to the safety fund system designed to provide stronger protections to noteholders. See Gerald Dwyer, Jr., "Wildcat Banking, Banking Panics, and Free Banking in the United States," Federal Reserve Bank of Atlanta Economic Review 1, 7 (December 1996).

94. See Rockoff, "Reexamination," 145–47, 150 (describing differences in state-level bond security requirements, how these requirements may have incentivized wildcat banking and other practices, and state-level losses to noteholders).

95. See Rockoff, 144, and Gorton, "Pricing Free Bank Notes," 42–43, 46 (both describing discounts on bank notes on a state-by-state basis).

96. National Bank Act of 1863, 12 Stat 665, superseded by the National Bank Act of 1864 § 62, 13 Stat 99, 118; National Bank Act of 1864 § 16, 13 Stat at 104.

intention was to replace bank notes with a single national currency "licensed, manufactured, and guaranteed by the federal government,"[97] the practical, inadvertent, and enduring effect was to create the "dual system" of federal and state-chartered banks that survives in the United States to this day.[98]

The National Banking System had the effect of dividing the US money supply into two distinct and now familiar components.[99] The first is the one, five, ten, twenty, fifty, and one hundred dollar bills that are today printed by the US Treasury Department, together with the quarters, dimes, nickels, and pennies minted by the US Mint. The second component consists of the demand, savings, time, checking, and other deposit liabilities issued by federal and state-chartered banks. While the specific features of these deposit liabilities vary from contract to contract, they all reflect the same core bundle of rights and obligations. First, these contracts permit customers to *deposit* cash or other funds with the bank. These deposits are then credited to accounts in each customer's name recorded on the bank's books, thus creating a monetary IOU. Second, these monetary IOUs permit customers to *withdraw* funds of equivalent value, either on demand or upon the expiration of a specific term. Third, customers can instruct the bank to *transfer* these monetary IOUs to specified third parties in satisfaction of their financial obligations.

In their seminal treatise, *A Monetary History of the United States*, Milton Friedman and Anna Schwartz trace the growth and composition of the US money supply between 1867 and 1960.[100] One of the most striking elements of their findings is that the composition of the money supply has slowly but inexorably shifted since the enactment of the National Bank Acts. Friedman and Schwartz report that in 1867 the total stock of paper bills and coins in public circulation was less than $600 million. When compared against the total outstanding stock of bank deposits of approximately $729 million, this translated into a deposit-to-currency ratio of just over 1:1.[101] Yet less than one hundred years later, with the aggregate money supply having ballooned from

---

97. Calomiris & Kahn, "Self-Regulated Payment Systems," 780.

98. See National Bank Act of 1864, ch. 106, §§ 5, 8, 22, 13 Stat. 99, 100–01, 105–06 (superseding the National Currency Act of 1863, ch. 58, 12 Stat. 665). See also Act of March 3, 1865, ch. 78, § 6, 13 Stat. 469, 484 (as am.). For a more detailed description of the dual banking system as it exists today, see Michael Barr, Howell Jackson, & Margaret Tahyar, *Financial Regulation: Law & Policy*, 171–182 (2nd ed., 2018).

99. A third component—central bank reserve balances—would be introduced with the creation of the Federal Reserve System. In effect, these central bank reserve balances replaced the private, "pyramided" correspondent bank reserves that were a central feature of the National Banking System.

100. Friedman & Schwartz, *A Monetary History of the United States 1867–1960* (rev. ed., 1971).

101. Friedman & Schwartz, 704.

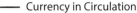 Demand Deposits: Total+Total Checkable Deposits+Other Checkable Deposits+
Total Savings Deposits at all Depository Institutions+Small Time Deposits - Total

─── Currency in Circulation

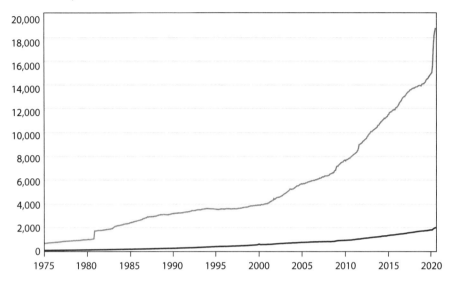

FIGURE 1.2. Monetary Liabilities of Depository Institutions versus Currency in
Circulation (1975–2020; $USD billions). The figure compares (1) the sum of total
demand deposits, total checkable deposits, other checkable deposits, total savings deposits at all depository institutions, and total small time deposits against
(2) currency in circulation. It also reports the total stock of deposits for all "depository institutions"—a category that includes banks, savings and loan associations,
credit unions, and industrial loan companies. Despite subtle differences in their
chartering and regulation, all of these institutions can essentially be understood
as conventional deposit-taking banks. *Source*: Board of Governors of the Federal
Reserve System (US). FRED® Graphs ©Federal Reserve Bank of St. Louis. 2023.
All rights reserved. All FRED® Graphs appear courtesy of Federal Reserve Bank
of St. Louis. http://fred.stlouis.org/.

under $2 billion to nearly $248 billion, this same ratio stood at 7.6:1—almost
eight dollars in bank deposits for every dollar in paper currency and coins.[102]
Perhaps even more remarkably, this shift has continued more or less unin-
terrupted to the present day, with the deposit-to-currency ratio currently
standing at just under 10:1.

Figure 1.2 compares the total stock of outstanding currency versus
demand, savings, time, and checking deposits from 1975 to 2020.[103] This
figure makes two things abundantly clear. First, banks are by far and away

102. Friedman & Schwartz, 722.
103. Comparison of "total monetary liabilities" and currency in circulation, Federal Reserve
Bank of St. Louis: FRED, https://fred.stlouisfed.org/.

the largest source of money in the United States. Second, the dominance of banks as engines of money creation appears only to be increasing over time. At least as measured against these yardsticks, there can be little doubt that the goldsmiths' experiment has been a resounding success.

Plumbers in Pinstripes

Given the central role that banks play in money *creation*, it is perhaps not surprising that they have also come to play a central role in the financial plumbing that facilitates the *transfer* of money between individuals, businesses, and governments. The fact that bank deposits represent the accounting liabilities of a bank to its customers makes it relatively easy to execute payments between customers at the same bank. With the proverbial stroke of the bookkeeper's pen, all a bank needs to do is debit the account of the payor and credit the account of the recipient payee. As we have already seen, the first evidence of these book transfers dates back to 1200, where Italian court records describe how Genoese bankers enabled their wealthy clients to make payments to each other on the accounts of the bank. This basic system of book transfers would eventually spread throughout Western Europe, where it was also adopted by our ambitious and resourceful London goldsmiths.[104]

The far bigger technical challenge was how to facilitate payments between customers at different banks. For the goldsmiths, the solution initially revolved around an informal network of correspondent relationships.[105] Within this network, banks would maintain a separate set of books recording the notes, checks, and other negotiable instruments drawn and cashed with every other bank.[106] Representatives of two banks, typically junior clerks, would then meet periodically on a bilateral basis to calculate and settle their accounts, with the net debtor paying the net creditor in paper currency or coins.[107] Among this system's many inefficiencies was therefore that it required these clerks to navigate London's crowded and dangerous streets and alleys carrying large quantities of money.[108]

104. Geva, *Payment Order of Antiquity*, 359.

105. See generally Stephen Quinn, "Balances and Goldsmith-Bankers: The Co-ordination and Control of Inter-banker Debt Clearing in the Seventeenth Century," in Mitchell (ed.), *Goldsmiths, Silversmiths, and Bankers*, 53–76 (1995).

106. Geva, *Payment Order of Antiquity*, 494.

107. See Phillip Matthews, *The Bankers' Clearing House: What It Is and What It Does*, 2 (1921).

108. Matthews, 6–7.

Over time, this system took on a more formal and secure institutional structure.[109] In the early 1770s, a number of large London banks rented a room at The Five Bells pub on Lombard Street, where their clerks would regularly meet to clear and settle payments—presumably followed by a nice warm pint. By 1775, clearing and settlement were taking place on Lombard Street on a daily basis.[110] A permanent rules committee was created in 1821, a new home on Lombard Street was erected in 1833, and in 1841 the bilateral settlement system was replaced with a multilateral one—with each bank's net obligations calculated on the basis of the negotiable instruments drawn and cashed with all the other banks in the network.[111] The institutionalization of this once informal network was completed in 1895, when member banks reorganized it as a private company: the Bankers Clearing House Limited.[112]

Echoing the emergence of the first protobanks in the American colonies over a century earlier, this new institutional innovation—the *clearinghouse*— would eventually take root in the United States.[113] The first clearinghouse was established in New York in 1853.[114] Within a little over a decade, clearinghouses had also sprung up in other major commercial centers, including Boston (1856), Philadelphia (1858), Baltimore (1858), and Chicago (1865).[115] By the end of the century, hundreds of regional and local clearinghouses "dotted the American banking landscape."[116] Like the Bankers Clearing House Limited, these early clearinghouses were almost invariably owned and operated by member banks. Once established, these clearinghouses imposed strict criteria governing the admission of new members. Member banks were also subject to basic capital and liquidity requirements, financial reporting and audit obligations, and restrictions on the interest rates they were permitted to offer their customers. While these admission criteria and ongoing membership requirements were designed to protect the

---

109. See William Lawson, *The History of Banking*, 215 (2nd ed., 1885); Matthews, *Bankers' Clearing House*, 3–19 (both providing a detailed description of the transition to a more formal institutional structure).

110. Geva, *Payment Order of Antiquity*, 495; Matthews, *Bankers' Clearinghouse*, 8.

111. Geva, 495; Matthews, 8.

112. Matthews, 14.

113. Once again, the goldsmiths did not invent the clearinghouse. The basic practice of merchants meeting periodically to calculate and settle net debts dates at least as far back as medieval European champagne fairs and was likely employed in parts of Asia far earlier.

114. See Gary Gorton, "Private Clearinghouses and the Origins of Central Banking," Federal Reserve Bank of Philadelphia Business Review 3, 4 (1985).

115. Gorton, 5.

116. Gorton, 5.

clearinghouse against member default, they also erected significant barriers to direct participation in this burgeoning new financial market infrastructure.

For those banks that enjoyed direct access to them, clearinghouses held out three important advantages. The first stemmed from the use of multi-lateral netting. Rather than periodically calculating and settling their net debts on a bilateral basis, multilateral netting enabled each member bank to settle its net debts with all other member banks with a single institution: the clearinghouse itself. To facilitate multilateral netting, the clearinghouse would first aggregate, calculate, and confirm the payments owed by or to each member bank. This process was known as clearing. It would then pay (or collect) the net amount owing to (or by) each member bank. This process was known as settlement. By clearing and settling payments on a multilateral basis, clearinghouses thus reduced the total number and size of payments, along with the exposure of the clearinghouse and each member bank to the default of its members.

The second advantage was that, having reduced the number and size of payments, clearinghouses greatly reduced the need for banks to keep large amounts of physical notes and coins on hand to settle their bilateral pay-ment obligations. Indeed, in theory, each bank needed only to keep enough cash on hand to settle its net obligations to the clearinghouse. In practice, however, clearinghouses would often issue certificates that served as cash substitutes for the expressly limited purpose of settling transactions between a clearinghouse and its member banks.[117] These certificates eliminated the transportation, security, and other costs of settling payments in cash.

Lastly, in the absence of a central bank, early American clearinghouses played an important role in crisis management.[118] Between 1853 and 1907, eight major banking panics roiled the American financial system.[119] Deposi-tors, understandably concerned about the prospect of bank failures, were often quick to withdraw their deposits at the first sign of trouble. And because banks did not typically hold all their deposits in cash or other highly liquid assets, they were often unable to meet the correlated demands from

117. See Gorton, 4–5. The certificates were themselves backed by gold deposited by one member bank with another designated member bank.

118. See Richard Timberlake, Jr., "The Central Banking Role of Clearinghouse Associations," 16 Journal of Money, Credit and Banking 1, 2 (1984); Gary Gorton, "Clearinghouses and the Origin of Central Banking in the United States," 45 Journal of Economic History 277 (1985).

119. See Charles Calomiris, Marc Flandreau, & Luc Laeven, "Political Foundations of the Lender of Last Resort: A Global Historical Narrative," 28 Journal of Financial Intermediation 48 (2016).

their depositors—thus triggering a self-fulfilling prophecy in the form of widespread bank runs.[120]

Clearinghouses provided a makeshift solution to the liquidity problem at the root of these periodic panics. In response to an incipient panic, member banks would submit bonds and other less liquid investments to the clearing-house as collateral.[121] In exchange, the clearinghouse would issue certificates that member banks could use to satisfy their outstanding obligations within the clearing network, thereby freeing up much-needed cash for the purpose of honoring their commitments to depositors and other creditors. Member banks were willing to accept these certificates not only because they were backed by collateral but also, and crucially, because they represented the *joint*, or mutual, obligations of other member banks. Where a clearing member defaulted and the posted collateral was insufficient to cover its outstanding obligations, surviving members would thus be required to cover the residual losses in proportion to their capital in the clearinghouse.[122]

Initially, these certificates were only issued in large denominations and circulated exclusively among member banks. However, by the closing decade of the nineteenth century, clearinghouses had begun issuing small-denomination certificates, many of which found their way into public circulation.[123] In effect, the issuance of these certificates enabled clearinghouses to expand the money supply during periods of widespread financial instability, thus providing much-needed liquidity to member banks and preventing a cascading series of bank failures.[124]

This last advantage had a rather sobering upshot: if a bank was *not* a member of a clearinghouse, the absence of a central bank meant that it would be left to fend for itself in the thick of an unfolding crisis. This is exactly what happened during the Panic of 1907. The epicenter of the panic was a group of New York City trust companies: state-chartered financial institutions

120. See Timberlake, "Clearinghouse Associations," and Gorton, "Private Clearinghouses." As described in greater detail in chapter 2, these runs were at least in part a by-product of the peculiar structure of the National Banking System.

121. See Timberlake, "Clearinghouse Associations," and Gorton, "Private Clearinghouses."

122. While defaulting banks were typically not permitted to fail during a panic, they were often expelled from the clearinghouse once the panic subsided. The threat of expulsion was thus viewed as a powerful enforcement mechanism. See Gorton, "Origin of Central Banking," 279.

123. During the Panic of 1893, for example, clearinghouses issued approximately $100 million in small-denomination certificates. During the Panic of 1907, this figure jumped to approximately $500 million; Gorton, "Origin of Central Banking," 282.

124. See Timberlake, "Clearinghouse Associations," 14; Gorton, "Origin of Central Banking," 280–81; James Cannon, *Clearing-House Methods and Practices* (1910) (each describing the use of loan certificates by clearinghouses).

that competed with banks for deposits, but which were not members of the New York Clearing House.[125] The proximate cause of the panic was a failed attempt to corner the stock of United Copper by two speculators, Augustus Heinze and Charles Morse. News that the speculators' strategy had failed triggered runs on several banks associated with Heinze and Morse. While the New York Clearing House issued clearinghouse loan certificates to support its own member banks, it denied all requests to extend emergency loans to the city's trust companies. This included Knickerbocker Trust Company, then one of the largest financial institutions in the United States, which was forced to suspend its operations on October 22, 1907.

While a more widespread financial crisis was ultimately averted following a private bailout orchestrated by John Pierpont Morgan, the Panic of 1907 would become one of the principal catalysts for the creation of a new central bank: the Federal Reserve System.[126] The creation of the Federal Reserve signaled the end of the historical role of clearinghouses as financial crisis firefighters. Yet clearinghouses would continue to perform a number of important functions at the heart of the US payment system.

Today, the architecture of the US payment system revolves around three core institutions. The first is the Federal Reserve System. This system—often known simply as "the Fed"—is best known for conducting monetary policy,[127] acting as "lender of last resort" during financial crises,[128] and, more recently, coordinating the economic response to the COVID-19 pandemic.[129] Less well known and understood is the role the Fed plays at the heart of the payment system. Most importantly, the regional Federal Reserve banks maintain a system of master accounts in the name of each participating member bank. These master accounts enable banks to settle their payment obligations to other banks using their deposit balances—known as *reserve*

125. See Hugh Rockoff, "It Is Always the Shadow Banks: The Regulatory Status of the Banks That Failed and Ignited America's Greatest Financial Panics," in Rockoff & Suto (eds.), *Coping with Financial Crises: Some Lessons from Economic History* (2018); Robert Bruner & Sean Carr, *The Panic of 1907: Lessons Learned from the Market's Perfect Storm*, 65–70 (2007).

126. For a detailed description of the economic and political developments leading up to the creation of the Federal Reserve System, see Roger Lowenstein, *America's Bank: The Epic Struggle to Create the Federal Reserve* (2015).

127. For a detailed history of the Federal Reserve and its role in monetary policy, see Allan Meltzer, *A History of the Federal Reserve, Volume 1: 1913–1951* (2004), *Volume 2:1: 1951–1969* (2014), and *Volume 2:2: 1969–1986* (2014).

128. The role of the Fed as lender of last resort is described in greater detail in chapter 2.

129. For a detailed overview of this response and an analysis of its legality, see Lev Menand, "Unappropriated Dollars: The Fed's Ad Hoc Lending Facilities and the Rules That Govern Them," Working Paper (May 22nd, 2020).

balances—on the books of the Federal Reserve. The monetary liabilities of the Fed to repay these reserve balances then represent the ultimate settlement asset within the domestic banking system. As explained by longtime Federal Reserve payments expert Bruce Summers, "The central bank is the logical final settlement authority because of its unique status as an institution that does not pose credit or liquidity risks to its accountholders."[130] Put simply, the fact that the Fed cannot go bankrupt makes its liabilities the first, best, and final source of monetary IOUs.

The second group of core institutions consists of a small network of public and private clearinghouses. Technological advances over the past several decades have resulted in a marked increase in the volume of electronic payments between banks.[131] As these payment volumes have increased, so too have the demands on the technological and operational infrastructure of both member banks and the Federal Reserve System. Reflecting their historical role, modern clearing networks have stepped into this breach, employing highly automated processes to clear the vast majority of interbank payments before routing these payments to the Federal Reserve for final settlement.[132] Yet, in stark contrast with the fragmented system of regional and local clearinghouses that prevailed during the nineteenth and early twentieth centuries, these modern clearing networks are now highly concentrated: with five national networks dominating the US payment market and a sixth, FedNow, launched in July 2023. Figure 1.3 lists these clearing networks and describes their ownership structure, membership, and other key features.

Last but not least, the architecture of the US payment system revolves around a large population of banks, many of which are connected to each other via their membership in one or more clearing networks. As of June 2023, the United States was home to over 4,500 licensed commercial banks, over 4,600 credit unions, and 574 thrift institutions.[133] Despite this

---

130. Bruce Summers, "The Payment System in a Market Economy," in Bruce Summers (ed.), *The Payment System: Design, Management, and Supervision*, 5 (1994). For a more detailed and critical assessment of the role of central banks at the apex of the payment system, see Jeffrey Lacker, "Payment Economics and the Role of Central Banks," speech at the Bank of England Conference on Payments (May 20, 2005), https://tinyurl.com/58c7skx4.

131. For annual payment statistics collected by the Committee on Payments and Market Infrastructure (CPMI), see Bank for International Settlements, Payment, Clearing, and Settlement Statistics, https://www.bis.org/statistics/payment_stats.htm?m=3|16|385.

132. In theory, banks can also settle these payments using private settlement agents or their correspondent accounts with other banks.

133. See Federal Deposit Insurance Corporation, Statistics at a Glance (June 30, 2023), https://www.fdic.gov/bank/statistical/stats/2023jun/industry.pdf National Credit Union

FIGURE 1.3. Major US Clearing Networks

Name	Est.	Ownership	Membership	Key features
Fedwire	1918	Public	Approximately 5,500 deposit-taking institutions	Large-value interbank clearing and settlement system Real-time gross settlement via member accounts at the Federal Reserve Operates 21.5 hours a day, business days only
CHIPS	1970	Private	48 member banks	Large-value interbank clearing and settlement system Deferred net settlement funded via transfers from Fedwire
ACH	1974	Private	Approximately 9,000 deposit-taking institutions	Small-value interbank clearing system Deferred net settlement via member accounts at the Federal Reserve
EPN	1981	Private	Approximately 450 deposit-taking institutions	Small-value interbank clearing system Deferred net settlement via member accounts at the Federal Reserve
RTP	2017	Private	Approximately 350 deposit-taking institutions	Small-value interbank clearing and settlement system Real-time gross settlement via a joint account held by members at the Federal Reserve Operates 24 hours a day, 7 days a week
FedNow	2023	Public	Approximately 100 deposit-taking institutions	Small-value interbank clearing system Real-time gross settlement via member accounts at the Federal Reserve

extremely high level of industry fragmentation, the vast majority of payments are cleared and settled through a relatively small number of very large banks. For example, research conducted by the Federal Reserve in 2006 found that just 66 banks—less than 1 percent of all licensed deposit-taking institutions—accounted for roughly 75 percent of the total volume of payments between banks.[134] Using techniques from network topology, the same researchers then mapped the dense thicket of bilateral payment relationships between all the banks within the US payment network. They found

---

Administration, Quarterly Credit Union Data Summary Q2-2023 (June 30, 2023), https://www.ncua.gov/files/publications/analysis/quarterly-data-summary-2023-Q2.pdf.

134. See Kimmo Soramäki, Morten Bech, Jeffrey Arnold, Robert Glass, & Walter Beyeler, "The Topology of Interbank Payment Flows," Federal Reserve Bank of New York Staff Report No. 243 (March 2006) (figures reported by dollar value).

that, while almost 50 percent of banks had less than four direct payment connections with other banks, the largest banks averaged more than two thousand connections.[135] While new research is almost certainly needed to update this topography, the picture we have is one of a large, diffuse network of relatively small banks surrounding a tightly knit core of large and highly interconnected money center banks.[136]

So what exactly does the flow of money look like within the current US payment system? Figure 1.4 depicts the stylized sequence of events in a typical "push" payment.[137] The process begins when the payee, who holds an account at Bank B, issues an invoice requesting payment in the amount of $100 from the payor (step 1). Upon receipt of this invoice, the payor then instructs its bank, Bank A, to transfer $100 from her account to the payee's account at Bank B (step 2). Bank A then transmits the details of this and any other transactions to the relevant clearinghouse, which, after sorting, calculating, reconciling, and confirming payments owed by or to each bank (step 3), communicates the net payment obligations between Bank A and B to the Federal Reserve (step 4). Final settlement then takes place on the books of the Fed, with $100 transferred from the master account of Bank A to the master account of Bank B (step 5).[138] If Bank B has not already done so, it will then credit $100 to the payee's account.

What this description makes clear is that banks are deeply embedded at virtually every stage of the payment process. Banks are the interface through which most people make and receive electronic payments. Banks are also members—and often owners—of the clearing networks that process the vast majority of payments. And, perhaps most importantly, banks have access to the Federal Reserve master accounts that represent the fastest, most convenient, and most reliable means of final settlement. On its own, the centrality of banks within the US payment system is not necessarily problematic. Yet, as we shall see, this centrality can generate significant distortions where the law *privileges* the monetary IOUs of banks, grants them *exclusive access* to our basic financial infrastructure, and provides a range of

---

135. Soramäki et al., 5. See also Adam Copeland & Rodney Garratt, "Nonlinear Pricing and the Market for Settling Payments," 51:1 Journal of Money, Credit and Banking 195, 207 (2019) (reporting that 50 percent of banks processed less than 148 payments per month via Fedwire, whereas the top 0.5 percent of banks processed over 1,483,387 payments per month).

136. Soramäki et al., "Topology of Interbank Payment Flows."

137. This form of payment can be contrasted with "pull" payments initiated by the payee. For the purpose of figure 1.4, the only difference between the two is the reversal of steps 1 and 2.

138. For the sake of simplicity, we assume here that the $100 is the only payment between accountholders at Bank A and Bank B over the relevant period.

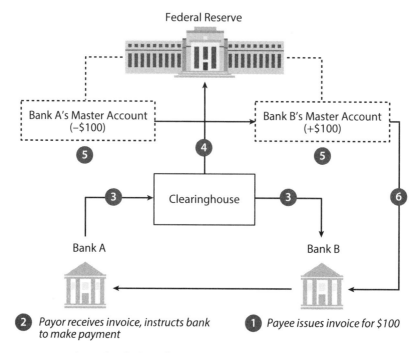

Federal Reserve

Bank A's Master Account
(–$100)

Bank B's Master Account
(+$100)

⑤

④

⑤

③ → Clearinghouse → ③

⑥

Bank A

Bank B

② *Payor receives invoice, instructs bank to make payment*

① *Payee issues invoice for $100*

FIGURE 1.4. The Stylized Flow of Money within the US Payment System

regulatory protections that entrench the existing bundled system of banking, money, and payments.

Banking's Empire

The United States, United Kingdom, and Continental Europe are not the only places where the seeds of modern banking and payment systems were planted, grown, and cultivated. In China, for example, a credit-based, long-distance remittance system intermediated through *piaohoa*, or "draft banks," was developed by Shanxi merchants during the last century of the Qing dynasty (1636–1912).[139] This system enabled merchants to deposit gold or silver coins at one branch of a piaohoa, receive a receipt evidencing this deposit, and then present the receipt at another branch, in another part of the country, where they were entitled to exchange it for cash. These piaohoa operated alongside small money shops, known as *qianzhuang*, that engaged

139. See Andrea McElderry, *Shanghai Old-Style Banks 1800–1935: A Traditional Institution in a Changing Society* (1976); Linsun Cheng, *Banking in Modern China: Entrepreneurs, Professional Managers and the Development of Chinese Banks, 1897–1937*, 10–16 (2003).

in currency exchange, deposit taking, note issuance, and the discounting of bills of exchange for local merchants.[140] In Japan, protobanks known as exchange houses operated at the heart of an organized and regulated money market dating back to at least 1662.[141] And in India, local bankers known as *shroffs* played an important role at almost every level of society "from time immemorial."[142] Yet while each of these local systems shared important parallels with the goldsmiths' model, none of them appears to have combined all the key features that we today associate with fractional reserve banking or the business of conventional deposit-taking banks.

Reflecting the rise of Western Europe and later the United States as international financial powerhouses during the nineteenth and early twentieth centuries, these local banking systems eventually came under increasing competitive pressure from foreign banks. In India, the first joint-stock bank, the Bank of Bengal, was chartered by the East India Company in 1809.[143] By the mid-eighteenth century, the subcontinent had developed a relatively sophisticated money market—albeit one that generally only catered to European merchants.[144] In China, the first foreign banks entered around the same period to serve the expanding number of trading firms from the United Kingdom and Continental Europe. Banks such as Deutsch-Asiatische Bank, founded by the venerable German banking giant Deutsche Bank, would go on to play an important role in financing China's international trade and the development of its domestic financial system.[145] These foreign banks also introduced a system of clearinghouses that, by 1896, could be "compared, in excellence, to the system prevailing at the clearing-houses of London, New York, and other great commercial centers."[146] Over time, these foreign banks were grafted onto local banking systems and practices, with the resulting combinations taking on their own distinctive characteristics. Nevertheless, by the dawn of the twentieth century, the results of the goldsmiths' experiment

140. See McElderry, *Shanghai Old-Style Banks*; Cheng, *Banking in Modern China*, 10–16.

141. See Sydney Crawcour, "The Development of a Credit System in Seventeenth-Century Japan," 21:2 Journal of Economic History 342 (1961). These exchange houses even used their own monetary IOUs (*Furisashi gami*) that were exclusively used to discharge obligations with other exchange houses. A less organized system of money changers (*ryogae*), wholesale merchants (*tonya* or *toiya*), and financial agents (*kakeya*) emerged even earlier.

142. C. N. Cooke, *The Rise, Progress, and Present Condition of Banking in India*, 11 (1863).

143. See Amiya Kumar Bagchi, "Transition from Indian to British Indian Systems of Money and Banking, 1800–1850," 19:3 Modern Asian Studies 501, 507 (1985). See also Cooke, *Condition of Banking in India*.

144. Bagchi, 511–519.

145. See Ghassan Moazzin, *Foreign Banks and Global Finance in Modern China* (2022).

146. Sumner, "History of Banking in Leading Nations," 560.

FIGURE 1.5. Banks around the World. *Source*: IMF Financial Access Survey (2021). Used with the permission of the IMF.

could be observed far beyond its humble origins in the crowded shops and offices of London's Lombard Street.

Today, the forces of globalization have made banks a ubiquitous feature of the financial landscape in almost every country on the planet (see figure 1.5). Of course, there are still significant differences between banks and banking systems across countries. Some banks and banking systems are large, economically important, and internationally focused, while others leave a more modest footprint and cater exclusively to domestic depositors, borrowers, and other customers. Some banks are privately owned and controlled, while others are, to varying degrees, state-sponsored institutions. Some play an important role in extending loans and other forms of credit to private individuals and firms, while others perform more narrow (e.g., state financing) or specialized (e.g., custodial) functions. Yet one thing that has remained remarkably constant across countries—until very recently—has been the role of banks at the apex of their systems of money and payments.

The Test Results

There is little doubt that the goldsmiths' experiment will go down as one of the most important developments in the history of finance. Not only did the shift from a commodity-based monetary system to one dominated by monetary IOUs pave the way for a dramatic expansion in the money supply, but banks themselves became increasingly important vehicles for channeling investment into the real economy—driving greater economic growth and prosperity. Yet this experiment did have one critical and very troubling side effect. The combination of short-term deposit financing with the business of making longer-term loans and other investments inevitably introduced a degree of fragility into the business of banking. This fragility was on full display throughout the nineteenth and early twentieth centuries, with the banking systems in the United Kingdom, the United States, and elsewhere frequently struck by bouts of paralyzing illiquidity, destabilizing bank runs, and widespread bank failures that often wreaked havoc on both the financial system and the wider economy.

Indeed, the goldsmiths' experiment may have turned out very differently had it not been for what happened *next*: how policymakers responded to this fragility. For having stumbled upon the business of fractional reserve banking, and observed its game-changing benefits as a catalyst for monetary expansion and economic growth, policymakers now had to solve the problem of how to make banks safe. This would eventually force them to embark on a second, more complex, and far more ambitious phase of the experiment: building the financial safety net. The story of how and why this safety net was built, how it transformed bank deposits into good money, and its enduring impact on competition and innovation in the realm of money and payments is the subject of the next two chapters.

2

Making Banks Safe

> It needs no prophet to tell you that when the people find that they can get their money—that they can get it when they want it for all legitimate purposes—the phantom of fear will soon be laid. People will again be glad to have their money where it will be safely taken care of and where they can use it conveniently at any time. I can assure you that it is safer to keep your money in a reopened bank than under the mattress.
>
> —FRANKLIN DELANO ROOSEVELT, FIRESIDE CHAT
>   ON THE BANKING CRISIS, MARCH 12, 1933

If you've ever made a baking soda volcano for an elementary school science fair, then you already know the most important thing about experiments: they have a tendency to explode. By the dawn of the twentieth century, banks in the United Kingdom, the United States, and around the world were well on their way to solidifying their position at the apex of our monetary and financial systems. But policymakers had yet to come to grips with one of the unwanted by-products of fractional reserve banking: *fragility*. The fragility of banks reflects their peculiar business model. The business of banking is based on leverage, with banks obtaining a significant percentage of their financing through the issuance of deposits and other short-term debt instruments. For example, as of March 2022, over 83 percent of the total financing obtained by banks insured by the US Federal Deposit Insurance Corporation (FDIC) took the form of demand, savings, time, and other deposits.[1] Banks then combine this short-term debt financing with invest-ments in longer-term loans and other assets. The mismatch created by this combination of short-term, highly liquid monetary IOUs and longer-term, risky, and illiquid investments is ultimately an important part of what makes banks vulnerable to destabilizing depositor runs.

In a nutshell, a bank run takes place when a critical mass of a bank's depositors seek to withdraw their money within a relatively short span of time. Where the vast majority of a bank's assets are invested in long-term loans, real estate, mortgages, or other illiquid private debt instruments, these correlated withdrawals can put enormous pressure on a bank's balance sheet. This pressure can force the bank to draw down its liquid reserves and, potentially, sell its other less liquid assets rapidly and at discounted—or "fire sale"—prices in order to repay depositors and other short-term creditors.[2] This in turn can trigger a pernicious negative feedback loop, with mounting depositor withdrawals eroding a bank's liquidity and solvency, the erosion of its liquidity and solvency undermining public confidence, and the evapo-ration of public confidence encouraging even more depositors to head for the exits.[3]

The vulnerability of banks to destabilizing runs has been obvious almost from their inception, with banking experts like Walter Bagehot and relative neophytes like President Roosevelt both instinctively understanding their inherent fragility.[4] Similarly, economists like Irving Fisher, Milton Friedman, Anna Schwartz, and Robert Merton have long sought to explain how the individually rational behavior of depositors to withdraw their money can collectively lead to a bank run.[5] Nevertheless, these complex behavioral dynamics are today typically explained using one of three basic frameworks. The first, and in many respects most intuitive, framework views bank runs as a response to the revelation of negative information about a bank's financial

1. See FDIC, Quarterly Bank Profile: First Quarter, Table II-A (2022), https://www.fdic.gov/analysis/quarterly-banking-profile/qbp/2022mar.

2. For a review of the literature on these fire sale dynamics, see Andrei Shleifer & Robert Vishny, "Fire Sales in Finance and Macroeconomics," 25 Journal of Economic Perspectives, 35–43 (2011).

3. Shleifer & Vishny, "Fire Sales," 35–36.

4. Several important monetary economists, including perhaps most notably Lawrence White and George Selgin, have argued that there is nothing "inherent" about bank fragility; rather, it is a question of their institutional design and regulation. While none of the analysis in this book hinges on this question, one might counter that their unique institutional design and regulation are themselves inherent features of banks.

5. See, e.g., Irving Fisher, *The Purchasing Power of Money* (1911); Robert Merton, *Social Theory and Social Structure* (1949).

health and future prospects.[6] The dynamics of these "information-based" runs are relatively straightforward. First, new information is revealed that has a negative impact on a bank's creditworthiness and, in theory, the value of its monetary IOUs. Second, responding to this news, depositors withdraw their money in order to reduce or eliminate their exposure to the creditworthiness of the struggling bank. Finally, news of these withdrawals further compounds these dynamics, exacerbating the run and ultimately leading to the failure of the bank.

The second framework, made famous by economists Douglas Diamond and Philip Dybvig, views runs as a coordination problem among a bank's many dispersed depositors.[7] In this framework, the threat of a bank run is a function of the collective demands by depositors for *liquidity*—i.e., for the option to withdraw their money at any time.[8] In most states of the world, we would expect these liquidity demands to be relatively uncorrelated, as depositors withdraw or transfer funds in response to their own idiosyncratic needs. However, where these liquidity demands become highly correlated— whether because of suspected solvency problems at the bank, wider liquidity problems within the financial system, or otherwise—the mismatch between a bank's short-term (liquid) deposit liabilities and long-term (illiquid) assets means that it may not have a large enough stock of cash and other reserves to honor all immediate withdrawal requests. These correlated demands can then force banks to prematurely liquidate their illiquid assets, potentially at a steep discount.

As famously (if not entirely accurately) portrayed in the movie *It's a Wonderful Life*, this prospect can result in a "first come, first served" dynamic in

---

6. See Fisher, *Purchasing Power*; Charles Jackin & Sudipto Bhattacharya, "Distinguishing Panics from Information-Based Bank Runs: Welfare and Policy Implications," 96:3 Journal of Political Economy 568 (1998).

7. Diamond & Dybvig, "Bank Runs, Deposit Insurance, and Liquidity," 91 Journal of Political Economy 401, 401–2 (1983). For a critique of this account, see generally Kevin Dowd, "Models of Banking Instability: A Partial Review of the Literature," 6 Journal of Economic Surveys 107 (2002). Morgan Ricks has advanced a subtly but materially different model. Like Diamond and Dybvig, Ricks's model views bank runs as reflecting a coordination problem among a bank's dispersed depositors. However, unlike Diamond and Dybvig, Ricks places the role of banks in the creation of monetary IOUs front and center in his account; see Ricks, *The Money Problem: Rethinking Financial Regulation*, 63–70 (2016).

8. Economists Markus Brunnermeier and Lasse Pedersen refer to this type of liquidity, which essentially reflects the immediacy with which a creditor can exercise this option, as *funding* liquidity. This is distinct from *market* liquidity, which measures the speed with which a financial asset can be bought and, more importantly, sold without impacting its price; Brunnermeier & Pedersen, "Market Liquidity and Funding Liquidity," 22 Review of Financial Studies 2201 (2009).

which depositors rush to withdraw their money before the bank is forced to close its doors.[9] More specifically, anticipating that other depositors may seek to withdraw their money, depositors may decide that the rational thing to do is to withdraw their money as well—and ideally first. Where enough depositors display this type of decision making, the mere threat of a run can result in a self-fulfilling prophecy that, in theory, can destabilize even otherwise healthy banks.

The third framework starts with the observation that bank deposits are a type of informationally insensitive debt contract.[10] We have already seen that these contracts are designed to eliminate the incentives of creditors to conduct due diligence into the identity and creditworthiness of the promisor, the quantity and quality of any posted collateral, and other factors bearing on the probability that the creditor will be repaid on time and in full. We have also seen that bank deposits—like other monetary IOUs—are designed to perform precisely this function, enhancing their use and value as a medium of exchange. But what happens when a bank's depositors realize that the IOUs they previously believed to possess a high degree of moneyness turn out, at least in certain states of the world, to be sensitive to the revelation of new information about the bank and its prospects? At this point, depositors face a stark choice. First, they can undertake time-consuming and costly due diligence to determine whether the bank's monetary IOUs are, in fact, good money. Second, they can simply exercise their option to withdraw the money from their account. Where a sufficient number of depositors, holding a sufficiently large stock of deposits, choose to withdraw first and ask questions later, the cumulative effect of these individual decisions is a bank run.

Regardless of what we think causes bank runs, their crystallization poses two principal risks. The first—*microprudential*—risk encompasses the potential impact of idiosyncratic bank runs on a failing bank's depositors, creditors, employees, customers, and other stakeholders.[11] These risks include

---

9. The depiction of a bank run in *It's a Wonderful Life* has long been a thorn in the side of banking scholars because the institution in question, the Bailey Savings & Loan, was—as its name suggests—not actually a *bank* but a "savings and loan" or *thrift* institution. At the time the movie takes place, the business model of thrifts did not typically involve offering demand deposit accounts to customers.

10. See, e.g., Bengt Holmstrom, "Understanding the Role of Debt in the Financial System," Bank for International Settlements Working Paper No. 479 (January 2015); Gary Gorton & Andrew Metrick, *Slapped by the Invisible Hand: The Panic of 2007* (2010).

11. Ricks, *Money Problem*, 36–37.

the potential loss of money (for creditors), the loss of access to credit (for borrowers), and the loss of income and employment (for the bank's employees). The second—*macroprudential*—risk reflects the prospect that idiosyncratic bank runs can, and sometimes do, metastasize into more widespread and destructive banking panics.[12] Among other problems, these panics can lead to an economy-wide contraction in the money supply, a reduction in bank lending, potential disruption to the payment system, and broader financial instability.

Over the course of more than a century, policymakers have developed, tested, and refined three key policy tools to address these risks. The first suite of tools are central bank emergency lending facilities. These lender-of-last-resort facilities enable banks facing an incipient run to obtain loans collateralized by their illiquid assets, the proceeds of which can then be used to pay depositors and other creditors. In many cases, they also enable banks to sell illiquid or distressed assets directly to the central bank. The second tool is deposit insurance. Deposit insurance schemes envision that the government will step into the shoes of a failing bank, honoring its contractual commitments to return depositors' money on demand. The money to meet these obligations can then come from either general tax revenues or dedicated deposit insurance funds. And, last but not least, banks are subject to special bankruptcy or "resolution" regimes. These regimes are designed to restructure a failing bank's assets and liabilities on an expedited basis, thereby enabling them to recapitalize and live to lend another day. Together, these three tools comprise a unique public safety net designed to protect banks, their depositors, and, indirectly, the wider financial system.

This public safety net has dramatically reduced the fragility of banks and greatly bolstered the stability of the conventional banking system. Importantly, by effectively circumventing general corporate bankruptcy law, this safety net has also given banks an enormous competitive advantage in the creation of monetary IOUs. Yet one firm's entrenched competitive advantage is almost inevitably another firm's insurmountable barrier to entry. This chapter describes how the public safety net enhances the credibility, value, and use of bank deposits as monetary IOUs. Chapter 3 then explores how this safety net has entrenched banks at the apex of our intertwined systems of money and payments, too often leaving them as the only game in town.

12. Ricks, 41–43. See also John Armour, Dan Awrey, Paul Davies, Luca Enriques, Jeff Gordon, Colin Mayer, & Jennifer Payne, *Principles of Financial Regulation*, chapter 19 (2016).

The Most Mischievous Doctrine

Today, central bank lender-of-last-resort (LOLR) facilities are often viewed as the last line of defense before governments are forced to resort to costly, taxpayer-funded bank bailouts. But the role that central banks play as lenders of last resort was actually the first pillar of the modern financial safety net to emerge and take shape. The origins of modern LOLR facilities can be traced back to the periodic and largely improvised interventions of the Bank of England in support of the nineteenth-century London money market. Importantly, Parliament did not originally envision these interventions as part of the Bank of England's mandate. Instead, only slowly and with great reluctance did the Bank take up the mantle of this new role.

Between 1825 and 1839, the United Kingdom was struck by a series of major financial crises. These crises followed what would become a familiar pattern: a rapid expansion in the outstanding stock of Bank of England notes, bank deposits, and other monetary IOUs, followed by the flow of capital into speculative investments, and inevitably ending in a stock market crash and bank runs throughout the United Kingdom.[13] Historically, the Bank's response to widespread bank runs was to ration credit at its discount window, restricting the types of borrowers and collateral against which it would lend.[14] This response reflected the unforgiving logic and mechanics of the then prevailing gold standard. Specifically, the funds received by a borrower at the Bank's discount window were typically credited to the borrower's account with the Bank. These deposits could then be withdrawn in the form of Bank of England notes, which entitled the bearer to hand them straight back to the Bank in exchange for gold. Since the aggregate value of the deposits held with the Bank vastly exceeded its reserves of Bank notes and gold, there was the ever-present threat that correlated liquidity demands could jeopardize the Bank's solvency. In the shadow of this threat, rationing access to credit at the discount window enabled the Bank to protect its own balance sheet against the risks of a destabilizing run.[15]

---

13. See Denis O'Brien, "The Lender-of-Last-Resort Concept in Britain," 35 History of Political Economy 1 (2003). See also Frank Fetter, *Development of British Monetary Orthodoxy, 1797–1875* (1965); Ralph Hawtrey, *The Art of Central Banking* (1932); John Clapham, *The Bank of England: A History: Volume 1* (1944).

14. See Francis Baring, *Observations on the Establishment of the Bank of England and on the Paper Circulation in the Country* (1797).

15. Notably, the ability of the Bank to use interest rate policy to increase the attractiveness of its deposits, thereby slowing the flight of note and bullion reserves, was constrained by applicable usury laws until 1833.

Initially, the Bank's response to the Panic of 1825 followed this conservative script. However, in the face of dwindling reserves and a still escalating panic, the Bank eventually and rather abruptly reversed course—lending freely to a wide range of banks and other counterparties on the basis of an even wider range of collateral. As described by Jeremiah Harman, then one of the Bank's directors:

> We . . . lent money by every possible means, and in modes which we had never adopted before; we took in stock on security, we purchased Exchequer Bills, we made advances on Exchequer Bills, we not only discounted outright, but we made advances on deposits of bills of Exchange to an immense amount—in short, by every possible means consistent with the safety of the Bank . . . Seeing the dreadful state in which the public were, we rendered every assistance in our power.[16]

The Bank's unprecedented intervention promptly halted the panic.[17] In the eyes of many subsequent commentators, this decision—signaling the Bank's willingness to do whatever it took to restore confidence in the banking system—stands out as a turning point in its development into a modern lender of last resort.[18] Following the expansion of its emergency lending powers under the Bank Charter Act of 1833,[19] the Bank would subsequently mount successful interventions in response to the Panics of 1836–37 and 1839.[20] Yet, once again, history would not travel in a straight line.

Despite its success in quelling these panics, the Bank's interventions proved extremely controversial. Several observers, including many of the Bank's own directors, objected to the idea that the Bank should ever act as a lender of last resort.[21] Their argument, which is still frequently advanced today, was that the widespread expectation that a central bank would lend freely during a crisis would inevitably undercut the incentives of banks to act prudently by, for example, holding a sufficient stock of Bank notes, gold, or other liquid reserves. Where banks responded to these incentives, the net

---

16. Walter Bagehot, *Lombard Street: A Description of the Money Market*, 48, 158 (1873).

17. See W.T.C. King, *History of the London Discount Market*, 35–70 (1936) (although bankruptcies of banks and other firms continued into 1826).

18. See Hawtrey, *Art of Central Banking*, 122; O'Brien, "Lender-of-Last-Resort Concept," 5–6; Fetter, *British Monetary Orthodoxy*, 116.

19. 3 & 4 Will. 4 c. 98 (the 1833 act).

20. Clapham, *Bank of England*, 152–70. Perhaps most importantly, the 1833 act exempted the Bank's discount window business from applicable usury laws, giving it considerably more flexibility in its emergency lending operations.

21. See O'Brien, "Lender-of-Last-Resort Concept," 11–12.

effect would then be to increase, rather than decrease, the probability and severity of future banking crises.[22] This argument slowly gained momentum over the course of the early 1840s, and eventually became one of the key rationales for what is perhaps the single most important piece of legislation in the history of English central banking.

The objective of the Bank Charter Act of 1844[23] was to curb the monetary expansion and speculative excesses associated with the widespread use of Bank of England notes as a form of money.[24] As described by prime minister Sir Robert Peel, the act was designed to "inspire just confidence in the medium of exchange . . . put a check on improvident speculation, and . . . ensure, as far as legislation can ensure, the just reward of industry, and the legitimate profit of commercial enterprise, conducted with integrity and controlled by provident calculation."[25]

The most important feature of the 1844 act was the strict, mechanical relationship it established between the amount of gold in the Bank's vaults and its legal authority to issue new Bank notes. Beyond a £14 million "fiduciary" issue, the ability of the Bank to issue new notes was strictly limited by the size of its existing stock of reserves and, in theory, its ability to acquire additional bullion on the open market. This requirement was designed to constrain the growth of the *public* money supply, along with what were seen as the inevitable booms and busts generated by rapid monetary expansion and contraction. By the same token, the 1844 act did absolutely nothing to constrain *private* money creation. More importantly, strict adherence to the 1844 act would prevent the Bank from using its discount window and other lending facilities—the practical effect of which would inevitably be to expand the money supply—to support the London money market in times of crisis. To its credit, Parliament was well aware of this trade-off. MPs Thomas Tooke, John Fullarton, and Henry Bosanquet, among others, warned the government that placing strict legal constraints on note issuance would undermine the Bank's ability to provide liquidity to the market during a crisis.[26] Even Prime Minister Peel himself was rumored to have conceded

---

22. O'Brien, 11–12.

23. 7 & 8 Vict. c. 32 (the 1844 act).

24. John Wood, "Bagehot's Lender of Last Resort: A Hollow Hallowed Tradition," 7 Independent Review 343, 344 (2003).

25. See James Wilson, *Capital, Currency, and Banking*, 107 (1847) (quoting Peel).

26. See Richard Grossman & Hugh Rockoff, "Fighting the Last War: Economists on the Lender of Last Resort," National Bureau of Economic Research Working Paper No. 20,832 (2015); Wood, "Hollow Hallowed Tradition," 344–45; Fetter, *British Monetary Orthodoxy*, 187–91.

in private that it might be necessary to suspend the 1844 act in response to widespread financial instability.[27]

Between 1844 and 1866, Parliament's resolve would be tested in the fire of three separate crises. It spectacularly failed all three tests. Widespread crop failures and the collapse of the railway boom of the 1840s triggered a crisis in 1847.[28] While the Bank expanded lending via its discount window, at least on shorter-term government debt securities, the result was the rapid depletion of the Bank's reserves and a sharp spike in long-term interest rates.[29] With the crisis pushing many financial and commercial firms to the brink of insolvency, the government was eventually forced to introduce legislation permitting the Bank to issue new notes in excess of the strict limits imposed under the 1844 act.[30] In the event, knowledge that the Bank was authorized to issue these new notes was sufficient to stem the panic, and the Bank was never required to exercise this temporary authority.

In September 1857, another railway boom gone spectacularly bust— this time in the United States—threw the United Kingdom into crisis. As in 1847, the Bank's initial response was to throw open its discount window. Reflecting the severity of the crisis, this resulted in the rapid depletion of the Bank's reserves, which by November stood at a meagre £581,000—down nearly 90 percent from their precrisis levels.[31] With the screws rapidly tightening, the prime minister and chancellor of the exchequer were compelled to write to the Bank, informing it of the government's intention to once again suspend the 1844 act.[32] Unlike 1847, however, the announcement that the government planned to authorize the Bank to expand the supply of notes did not immediately halt the panic, and the Bank was actually forced to issue £928,000 of new and technically illegal notes.[33] On December 4, the government finally tabled a bill indemnifying the Bank for breaching the 1844 act.

27. Grossman & Rockoff, "Fighting the Last War," 11.

28. Wood, "Hollow Hallowed Tradition," 344.

29. See Vincent Bignon, Marc Flandreau, & Stefano Ugolini, "Bagehot for Beginners: The Making of Lender-of-Last-Resort Operations in the Mid-Nineteenth Century," 65 Economic History Review 580, 589–96 (2012).

30. See *Times of London*, "Important Resolution of the Bank of England" (October 16, 1847).

31. See Neumann, "The Nightmare before Christmas," Bank Underground blog (December 20, 2016), https://bankunderground.co.uk/2016/12/20/the-nightmare-before-christmas-1857-financial-crises-go-global/.

32. See Charles Grey, "Letter from the Prime Minister and Chancellor to the Governor of the Bank of England" (November 12, 1857), Bank of England Archives G6/397.

33. See J.R.T. Hughes, "The Commercial Crisis of 1957," 8 Oxford Economic Papers 194, 216 (1956).

This bill was passed on December 11 and the crisis—at least in the United Kingdom—was essentially over by Christmas Eve.[34]

Less than a decade later, the United Kingdom would be struck by a third major financial crisis.[35] The failure of discount house Overend Gurney & Co. on May 10, 1866, triggered widespread panic, with depositors lining up in the streets to withdraw their money from London's banks.[36] The *Bankers' Magazine* described the "terror and anxiety"[37] that gripped the city. The *Times of London* reported that the police had to be called to Overend Gurney's offices on Lombard Street in order to restore order.[38] Predictably, as London's money market ground to a halt, the Bank was swamped with requests for emergency loans—reducing the Bank's reserves from more than £5.75 million to £3 million in a single day.[39] Fearing that the Bank's remaining reserves would soon be exhausted, the Bank's governor, Henry Lancelot Holland, wrote to the chancellor of the exchequer requesting the suspension of the 1844 act.[40] The chancellor agreed[41] and, as it had in 1847, the expectation that the Bank would provide unlimited liquidity support to the London money market was sufficient to put an end to the panic.

It is against the backdrop of the 1844 act, and the crises of 1847, 1857, and 1866, that Walter Bagehot wrote his seminal treatise, *Lombard Street*, describing the operations of the London money market and the role of the Bank of England as a lender of last resort. Bagehot's argument was not simply that the Bank *should* act as a lender of last resort. That argument had already been forcefully made by several others, most notably Henry Thornton.[42] Rather, Bagehot's key insight was that—despite the constraints imposed by the 1844 act—the Bank's response to the succession of financial crises

34. Neumann, "Nightmare before Christmas."

35. Following the crisis of 1857, the Bank adopted strict rules around lending to bill brokers and discount houses. These rules, known collectively as the Rule of 1858, would have profound implications in terms of the Bank's response to the next crisis; see Marc Flandreau & Stefano Ugolini, "Where It All Began: Lending of Last Resort and the Bank of England during the Overend-Gurney Panic of 1866," Norges Bank Working Paper No. 2011-03 (2011).

36. See *Times of London*, "The Panic" (May 12, 1866).

37. Lewis, "Overend Gurney Goes Bust" (describing the *Bankers' Magazine* article from August 1866).

38. *Times of London*, "The Panic."

39. See Lewis, "Overend Gurney Goes Bust."

40. Lewis, "Overend Gurney Goes Bust."

41. Lewis, "Overend Gurney Goes Bust" (citing a letter from the chancellor to the governor, May 11, 1866).

42. See Thornton, *An Enquiry into the Nature and Effects of the Paper Credit of Great Britain* (1802).

that engulfed the United Kingdom during the nineteenth century demonstrated that it was clearly already performing a critical role in supporting the London money market, and by extension the banking system, during periods of financial instability.[43] This observation was eventually reframed as "Bagehot's rule": during times of widespread panic, central banks should lend freely, against good collateral, and at a penalty rate of interest, to illiquid but fundamentally solvent banks.[44] Yet Bagehot's argument was never strictly prescriptive. His argument was simply that this was how the London money market actually worked, and that denying it served little purpose other than undermining the credibility of both the British government and its central bank.

At the time, Bagehot's argument was vehemently rejected by the Bank itself. Thomson Hankey, one of the Bank's directors and the author of a leading textbook on banking, referred to Bagehot's rule as "the most mischievous doctrine ever broached in the monetary or banking world,"[45] arguing that even just acknowledging its existence would encourage socially excessive risk taking.[46] In Bagehot's view, what Hankey and his many followers failed to grasp was that the most important question was not whether a central bank should act as a lender of last resort, but whether it could ever credibly commit *not* to perform this role in the thick of an escalating crisis.[47] In the cut and thrust of the exchange between Bagehot and Hankey we can thus see the genesis of contemporary debates around the function and design of LOLR facilities.[48] On one side are those, echoing Hankey, who view central bank emergency lending as contributing to the buildup of moral hazard and potential systemic risks—thus necessitating strict legal constraints on central banks. On the other side are those who view these constraints as fundamentally lacking credibility in the face of financial Armageddon.

---

43. See Bignon, Flandreau, & Ugolini, "Bagehot for Beginners," 2–3; Mike Anson, David Bholat, Miao Kang, & Ryland Thomas, "The Bank of England as Lender of Last Resort: New Historical Evidence from Daily Transaction Data," Bank of England Staff Working Paper No. 691, 6 (2017).

44. The components of Bagehot's rule, which were never sewn together by Bagehot himself, have been the subject of significant debate. For a synthesis of this debate, see Dan Awrey, "The Puzzling Divergence of the Lender of Last Resort Regimes in the US and UK," 45:3 Journal of Corporation Law 597 (2020).

45. Thomson Hankey, *The Principles of Banking, Its Utility and Economy; with Remarks on the Working and Management of the Bank of England*, 25 (1867).

46. Hankey, 25–38; Bagehot, *Lombard Street*, 169.

47. Bagehot, *Lombard Street*, 171.

48. See Bignon, Flandreau, & Ugolini, "Bagehot for Beginners," 3.

In the event, neither side could claim a clear victory.[49] While the Bank subsequently played a central role in orchestrating the bailout of Barings Bank in 1890, this intervention did not fit the mold of earlier LOLR operations.[50] The same can be said of the Bank's response to both the so-called secondary banking crisis of 1973–75 and the small banks crisis of the early 1990s.[51] Proponents of central bank emergency lending could point to the relative stability over this period as evidence of both the Bank's acceptance of its role as lender of last resort and, importantly, that banks had come to expect it to lend freely during both idiosyncratic and marketwide liquidity shocks.[52] Critics, meanwhile, could point to the dramatic increase in the size and systemic importance of financial markets and institutions over this same period as evidence that this expectation had generated rampant moral hazard. In the end, it would take a crisis of truly global proportions to reveal the true influence of Bagehot's thinking on the Bank of England's approach to financial crisis management.

America Gets a (Not So) Central Bank

While the Bank of England was reluctantly finding its footing as a lender of last resort, the United States was operating without a fully fledged central bank. After the Second Bank of the United States lost its quasi-public status in 1836, the US found itself without a public bulwark against financial panics. The resulting fragility was compounded by the National Banking System

49. In at least one important respect, Bagehot can claim victory, with subsequent empirical research conclusively demonstrating that the Bank acted as a lender of last resort during the crises of 1825, 1847, 1857, and 1866; see Michael Collins, "The Bank of England as Lender of Last Resort, 1857–1878," 45 Economic History Review 145 (1992); Anson, Bholat, Kang, & Thomas, "Bank of England as Lender of Last Resort"; Bignon, Flandreau, & Ugolini, "Bagehot for Beginners."

50. See Grossman & Rockoff, "Fighting the Last War," 45. In the case of Barings, the Bank actually refused the government's offer to suspend the 1844 act and instead coordinated the creation of a guarantee fund contemplating the mutualization of losses between the Bank (in a senior position) and private creditors (in a junior position). Eventually, Barings was split into a "good" bank and a "bad" bank, with the latter managed and eventually sold by the Bank itself; see Eugene White, "Rescuing a SIFI, Halting a Panic: The Barings Crisis of 1890," Bank of England, Bank Underground blog (February 10, 2016), https://bankunderground.co.uk/2016/02/10/rescuing-a-sifi-halting-a-panic-the-barings-crisis-of-1890/.

51. The latter crisis was precipitated by a real estate crash that threatened to bankrupt a number of smaller "secondary" lenders. As it had in the case of Barings, the Bank coordinated a rescue package involving private sector participation.

52. However, as John Wood observes, "It is conceivable that the market came to rely on the Bank to behave as Bagehot had advised, but any such confidence was not put to a test."; Wood, "Hollow Hallowed Tradition," 348.

established under the National Bank Acts of 1863–65. The National Banking System envisioned a three-tiered structure: with central reserve city—or "money center"—banks in New York (and later Chicago and St. Louis) at the apex, followed by "reserve city" banks in other major metropolitan areas, and then a large number of relatively small "country" banks. Importantly, both reserve city banks and country banks were permitted to hold a proportion of their required reserves in the form of deposits with banks higher up in the system.[53] The resulting "pyramiding" meant that reserves tended to gravitate toward New York, where money center banks would, among other things, use them to finance call loans to investors purchasing shares and other securities on margin.[54]

The fragility of the National Banking System was a function of two intertwined dynamics. First, many parts of the United States that were reliant on agriculture experienced predictable spikes in loan and currency demand during the spring planting and fall harvest seasons. This localized seasonal demand periodically translated into withdrawals by country banks from the accounts they held with reserve city banks higher up in the system. These correlated withdrawals would then force reserve city banks to call in loans or withdraw deposits from other banks, thereby amplifying and transmitting shocks throughout the system and potentially triggering more widespread banking crises. Second, where this dynamic reached money center banks in New York, the resulting liquidity demands could force these banks to call in margin loans, necessitating the sale of borrowed securities and putting downward pressure on stock prices.[55]

As described in chapter 1, in the absence of a central bank, clearinghouses often played an important role in managing these periodic banking panics. Nevertheless, they did little to address the underlying fragility of the US

53. Reserve city banks could hold up to 50 percent of their reserves as demand deposits in money center banks. Country banks, meanwhile, could hold up to 60 percent of their reserves as deposits in either reserve city or money center banks. At the time, holding reserves in the form of demand deposits was an attractive option: while vault cash did not bear any interest, banks could earn as much as 2 percent on reserves held in the form of demand deposits.

54. O. M. Sprague, "History of Crises under the National Banking System," in *The National Banking System*, 5–35 (1910).

55. Sprague, 5–35 (describing the spread of crises under the National Banking System). See also Asaf Bernstein, Eric Hughson, & Marc Weidenmier, "Identifying the Effects of a Lender of Last Resort on Financial Markets: Lessons from the Founding of the Fed," 98 Journal of Financial Economics 40, 42 (2010) (describing the drivers of demand during the spring planting and fall harvest seasons); Jeffrey Miron, "Financial Panics, the Seasonality of the Nominal Interest Rate, and the Founding of the Fed," 76 American Economic Review 125 (1986) (describing the relationship between seasonal demand spikes and financial panics).

banking system. Indeed, in the fifty years after the establishment of the New York Clearing House, the United States experienced no less than eight major banking crises—an average of one just over every six years.[56] Ultimately, it was the Panic of 1907, in which J. P. Morgan organized an ad hoc consortium to bail out profligate New York trust companies, that finally spurred Congress to take financial crisis management into its own hands.

Congress's initial response was the Aldrich-Vreeland Act of 1908, establishing a National Monetary Commission (NMC) to study the US banking system, compare it with the systems in the United Kingdom, Canada, and Continental Europe, and advance a proposal for monetary reform.[57] The NMC performed this role with exceptional diligence, producing a series of detailed country reports and other analysis. This analysis identified three principal defects in the structure of the US banking system. First, unlike the United Kingdom, the United States did not benefit from a fully developed and well-functioning money market. As a result, there was no market mechanism by which the excess reserves of one bank could easily be redistributed to another bank in need of short-term liquidity. Second, the highly fragmented US banking system—then home to more than ten thousand banks—made it difficult to marshal reserves in response to an incipient panic. Paul Warburg, an early advocate for the creation of the Federal Reserve System, likened the system to providing each citizen with a few buckets of water instead of establishing a local fire department.[58] Third, and most importantly, the NMC observed that the US money supply was particularly "inelastic."[59]

The inelasticity of the US money supply was a function of the National Banking System, which required federally chartered banks to purchase government bonds as collateral against the issuance of new bank notes. During a widespread panic, banks were understandably reluctant to use their remaining reserves to purchase additional bonds, thereby limiting the ability of the banking system to expand the money supply in response to a crisis. Collectively, these defects rendered the US banking system particularly vulnerable

56. These crises took place in 1857, 1861, 1873, 1884, 1890, 1893, 1896, and 1907; see Charles Calomiris, Marc Flandreau, & Luc Laeven, "Political Foundations of the Lender of Last Resort: A Global Historical Narrative," 28 Journal of Financial Intermediation 48, 55 (2016).

57. Aldrich-Vreeland Act of 1908, Pub. L. 60–169, 35 Stat. 546 (1908). The complete collection of the commission's publications is available from the Federal Reserve Bank of St. Louis, *Publications of the National Monetary Commission Series*, https://fraser.stlouisfed.org/series/1493.

58. Warburg, "The Discount System in Europe: Report for the National Monetary Commission," S. Doc. No. 402, 33 (1910).

59. Warburg, 31–41.

to bouts of paralyzing illiquidity and the resulting contractions in the supply of both money and credit. The NMC's findings would ultimately provide the blueprint for the Federal Reserve Act of 1913 and the creation of the Federal Reserve System.[60]

Economist and historian Allan Meltzer has argued that the architects of the Federal Reserve System were highly influenced by the theory and practices developed by the Bank of England.[61] While this is almost certainly true, the structure and mandate of the Fed was also heavily influenced by domestic political considerations, including long-standing concerns about the concentration of political and economic power within the agencies and organs of the federal government.[62] These considerations explain why the United States has a "Federal Reserve System" instead of a central bank. They also explain this system's highly decentralized structure, with power split between a seven-member Federal Reserve Board in Washington, DC, and twelve regional reserve banks. And, last but not least, they explain why, unlike the Bank of England, the Fed was given a clear statutory mandate from its inception to "furnish an elastic currency"[63] and thereby act as a lender of last resort.[64]

The Federal Reserve Act gave the newly created Fed two principal powers in support of this mandate. First, pursuant to what is now Section 10B, the act authorized each regional reserve bank to lend to commercial banks through their discount windows.[65] As originally drafted, reserve banks were only permitted to make these loans against "notes, drafts, and bills of exchange arising out of actual commercial transactions" that had been "issued or drawn for agricultural, industrial or commercial purposes."[66] Today, these

60. Federal Reserve Act, 12 U.S.C. §§ 221–522 (1913).

61. Warburg, Senator Nelson Aldrich, and Harvard professor Piatt Andrew had made a first-hand study of the Bank of England and other European central banks on behalf of the NMC; Meltzer, *A History of the Federal Reserve, Volume 1: 1913–1951,* 19 (2004).

62. See Roger Lowenstein, *America's Bank: The Epic Struggle to Create the Federal Reserve* (2015) (describing the myriad political dynamics and trade-offs that ultimately led to the enactment of the Federal Reserve Act).

63. Federal Reserve Act, preamble. That the Fed acknowledged this crisis management role from the outset is evident from its first annual report, which states that "its duty plainly is not to await emergencies but by anticipation to do what it can to prevent them"; Annual Report of the Federal Reserve System 17 (1914).

64. Gary Gorton & Andrew Metrick, "The Federal Reserve and Panic Protection: The Roles of Financial Regulation and Lender of Last Resort," 27 Journal of Economic Perspectives 45, 47 (2013).

65. Federal Reserve Act, §§ 10B, 13(2), and 13A.

66. Federal Reserve Act, § 13(2). The original text of this section also excluded from discounting any notes, drafts, or bills covering "merely investments or issued or drawn for the purpose of carrying or trading in stocks, bonds, or other investment securities."

loans—known as *advances*—need only be secured to the satisfaction of the relevant reserve bank.[67] Second, pursuant to Section 14, the Federal Reserve Board was authorized to purchase or sell gold and US treasury securities on the open market, along with any cable transfers, bankers' acceptances, or bills of exchange eligible for discounting under Section 10B.[68] While discount window lending under Section 10B was restricted to banks that were members of the Federal Reserve System, Section 14 permitted the Fed to engage in open market operations (OMOs) with "banks, firms, corporations or individuals."[69]

By most accounts, the creation of the Federal Reserve System had an almost immediate impact on the stability of the US banking system. The years following the Fed's creation were characterized by a significant reduction in the seasonal volatility of both interest rates and stock prices, thus eliminating the destabilizing feedback loops that had plagued the National Banking System.[70] Yet, just like the Bank of England, the Federal Reserve would spectacularly fail its first real test as a lender of last resort.

The Fed's response to the Great Depression has been euphemistically described as one of "direct pressure."[71] With a few notable exceptions, this pressure was imposed through tight restrictions on discount window lending to the member banks that Fed officials believed were responsible for the speculative credit expansion at the root of the boom and subsequent bust.[72] The results were calamitous. Between December 1929 and the end of 1933, the number of banks in the United States fell from 24,633 to 15,015—a whopping 39 percent decrease.[73] While the banks that failed tended to be smaller banks, many of which were not members of the Federal

67. Federal Reserve Act, § 10B. The current version of Section 10B imposes a number of limitations on advances to "undercapitalized" or "critically undercapitalized" depository institutions.

68. Federal Reserve Act, § 14.

69. Federal Reserve Act, § 14.

70. Bernstein, Hughson, & Weidenmier, "Lessons from the Founding," 40; Gorton & Metrick, "Federal Reserve and Panic Protection," 45. See also A. Steven Holland & Mark Toma, "The Role of the Federal Reserve as 'Lender of Last Resort' and the Seasonal Fluctuation of Interest Rates," 23 Journal of Money, Credit and Banking 659 (1991) (measuring the reduction in seasonal fluctuations in interest rates following the creation of the Fed).

71. A. C. Miller, "Responsibility for Federal Reserve Policies: 1927–1929," 25 American Economic Review 442, 454 (1935).

72. Miller, 454. See also Thomas Humphrey, "Lender of Last Resort: What It Is, Whence It Came, and Why the Fed Isn't It," 30 Cato Journal 333, 353–54 (2010). As documented by Gorton and Metrick, the Fed's policy of discouraging banks from borrowing at the discount window could be observed as early as the mid-1920s; Gorton & Metrick, *Panic Protection*, 47.

73. Federal Reserve Board, Banking and Monetary Statistics: 1914–1941, 16 (1943).

Reserve System, the losses to depositors still amounted to approximately $1.3 billion[74]—roughly $27 billion in today's terms.[75] Even more striking, the resulting loss of confidence in the US banking system was associated with a sharp reduction in the money supply: with Milton Friedman and Anna Schwartz estimating a contraction of 33 percent between 1929 and 1933.[76] While the causal impact of this contraction has been hotly debated, there is little doubt that it contributed to the marked decline in prices, investment, and economic output that drove the Great Depression.[77] Ultimately, the tide of bank failures would only begin to turn following the imposition of a national bank holiday, announced by President Roosevelt in his first fireside chat on March 12, 1933.[78]

In the decades following World War II, the United States experienced low and stable real interest rates, relatively few bank failures, and no widespread banking panics. This environment would change dramatically during the commodity and interest rate–fueled turbulence of the 1970s and early 1980s (see figure 2.1). In June 1970, the Fed threw open its discount window, engaged in significant open market operations, and suspended interest rate ceilings on bank deposits in order to prevent the breakdown of the commercial paper market following the bankruptcy of Penn Central Railroad.[79] This included actively encouraging member banks to borrow at the Fed's discount window for the purpose of extending loans to any of their customers that relied on the commercial paper market as a source of short-term financing.[80] In 1974, the Fed provided more conventional emergency lending to Franklin National Bank and eventually purchased the struggling

---

74. Federal Reserve Board, 16.

75. See Inflation Calculator, https://www.officialdata.org/1933-dollars-in-2022.

76. Friedman & Schwartz, *A Monetary History of the United States 1867–1960*, 15–17 (rev. ed., 1971).

77. For a relatively recent contribution to this debate, see Christina Romer & David Romer, "The Missing Transmission Mechanism in the Monetary Explanation of the Great Depression," 103 American Economic Review 66 (2013).

78. A bank holiday involves closing banks, inspecting their books, and then only permitting fundamentally solvent banks to reopen their doors to the public.

79. See Charles Calomiris, "Is the Discount Window Necessary? A Penn Central Perspective," 76:3 Federal Reserve Bank of St. Louis Review 31 (1994).

80. Calomiris, 41–42. While the Fed did not release a statement to this effect, the *Wall Street Journal* reported that a Fed official had indicated "that the circumstances imply a liberal stance towards any banks finding it necessary to borrow temporarily from a district Reserve Bank"; see *Wall Street Journal*, "Reserve Suspends Interest Limits on Some Big Deposit Certificates" (June 24, 1970).

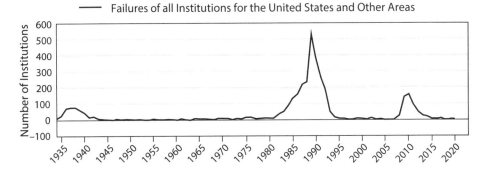

FIGURE 2.1. Bank Failures in the United States (1934–2020). This figure includes over a thousand savings and loans or "thrift" institutions that failed in the late 1980s and early 1990s. At the time, these institutions were not under the oversight of the Federal Reserve System and therefore were technically not eligible to access the Fed's LOLR facilities. *Source*: Federal Deposit Insurance Corporation. FRED® Graphs ©Federal Reserve Bank of St. Louis. 2023. All rights reserved. All FRED® Graphs appear courtesy of Federal Reserve Bank of St. Louis. http://fred.stlouis.org/.

bank's foreign exchange positions.[81] And in 1984, the Fed agreed to provide emergency liquidity support in connection with the rescue of Continental Illinois, then the country's eighth largest bank.[82] Yet, while these targeted interventions arguably demonstrated that the Fed had learned its lesson from the Great Depression, their scale and scope would ultimately pale in comparison to the Fed's response to the global financial crisis.

No Hankeys in a Foxhole

The decision would have scandalized Thomson Hankey, the nineteenth-century Bank director and Bagehot's erstwhile sparring partner. On September 14, 2007, the Bank of England extended an emergency loan to struggling mortgage lender Northern Rock. News of this loan was leaked by the press, sparking a run by the bank's retail depositors.[83] The size and timing of the loan reflected Northern Rock's heavy reliance on both wholesale money and mortgage securitization markets, thus exposing it to the widespread

81. See Mark Carlson & David Wheelock, "The Lender of Last Resort: Lessons from the Fed's First 100 Years," Federal Reserve Bank of St. Louis Working Paper No. 202-056B, 23–25 (2013).

82. Carlson & Wheelock, 23–25.

83. See UK Treasury Committee, "The Run on the Rock," 2007–8 HC 56-I, 5 (2007).

breakdown of these markets in the summer of 2007.[84] As the crisis in these markets deepened in the autumn of 2007 and into early 2008, the Bank introduced a series of ad hoc LOLR mechanisms designed to provide liquidity support to the domestic banking system.[85] These mechanisms included the Special Liquidity Scheme (SLS), which enabled banks to swap a wide range of collateral—including whole loans and mortgages—for highly liquid government securities that could be sold into the market in exchange for much-needed cash. Introduced in April 2008, the SLS was explicitly designed to provide temporary liquidity support for a period of no more than six months.[86] As it turned out, the failure of Lehman Brothers in September 2008 forced the Bank of England to extend this six-month deadline. The Bank was also forced to provide targeted liquidity support to two of the country's largest banks: Halifax Bank of Scotland (HBOS) and Royal Bank of Scotland (RBS). At its peak, the Bank's liquidity support under the SLS reached approximately £185 billion,[87] with another £61.5 billion provided directly to HBOS and RBS.[88] In the case of HBOS and RBS, this support was accompanied by large-scale recapitalization packages that effectively nationalized the besieged lenders.

In the United States, the global financial crisis was not primarily a banking crisis. Indeed, the crisis will forever be remembered for the rescue or failure of *nonbank* financial institutions, such as the investment banks Bear Stearns and Lehman Brothers, global insurance giant AIG, along with the alphabet soup of emergency lending facilities that Congress and the Fed introduced to support the so-called shadow banking system.[89] Nevertheless, the crisis represented exactly the type of widespread liquidity squeeze that the Fed's traditional

84. UK Treasury Committee, 19.

85. Andrew Hauser, "Lender of Last Resort Operations during the Financial Crisis: Seven Practical Lessons from the United Kingdom," Bank for International Settlements Working Paper No. 79, 84–85 (2014); Kaleb Nygaard, "The United Kingdom's Special Liquidity Scheme (SLS) (U.K. GFC)," 2:3 Journal of Financial Crises 504 (2020).

86. Bank of England, "Special Liquidity Scheme," press release (April 21, 2008), https://www.bankofengland.co.uk/-/media/boe/files/news/2008/april/special-liquidity-scheme.

87. Ian Plenderleith, "Review of the Bank of England's Provision of Emergency Liquidity Assistance in 2008–09," *Plenderleith Review*, 7–18 (2012).

88. Plenderleith, 48.

89. For a description of this shadow banking system, see Zoltan Pozsar, Tobias Adrian, Adam Ashcraft, & Hayley Boesky, "Shadow Banking," 19 Federal Reserve Bank of New York Economic Policy Review 1 (2013). For a description of the alphabet soup of lending facilities created during the crisis to support this system, see Dietrich Domanski, Richhild Moessner, & William Nelson, "Central Banks as Lender of Last Resort: Experiences during the 2007–2010 Crisis and Lessons for the Future," Federal Reserve Board Working Paper No. 2014-110 (2014).

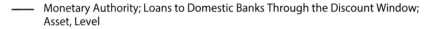

—— Monetary Authority; Loans to Domestic Banks Through the Discount Window; Asset, Level

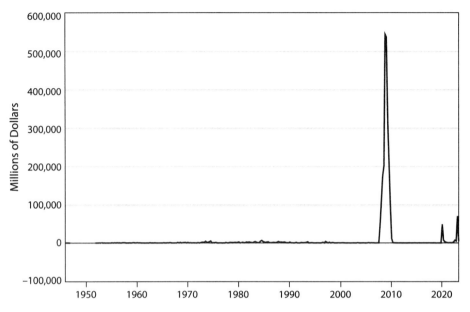

FIGURE 2.2. Federal Reserve Discount Window Lending (1946–2022). *Source*: Board of Governors of the Federal Reserve System (US). FRED® Graphs ©Federal Reserve Bank of St. Louis. 2023. All rights reserved. All FRED® Graphs appear courtesy of Federal Reserve Bank of St. Louis. http://fred.stlouis.org/.

LOLR facilities were designed to address. Over a decade later, we still do not yet know the identity of all the banks that borrowed from the Fed during the financial crisis. But we do know that the volume of discount window lending increased exponentially: from a total of $202 million in the second quarter of 2007 to over $544 *billion* in the fourth quarter of 2008 (figure 2.2). At the height of the crisis, the Fed also lent over $400 billion to banks via two newly created programs: the Term Auction Facility and the Primary Credit Facility.[90] In all, it has been estimated that the Fed extended over $1.2 trillion in emergency loans to domestic and foreign banks: as two Bloomberg reporters observed, enough to fill 539 Olympic-size swimming pools with $1 bills.[91] The fact that this unprecedented intervention flew largely under the

90. See Federal Reserve Board of Governors, "Factors Affecting Reserve Balances, Federal Reserve," statistical release H.4.1 (July 4, 2007–December 29, 2010).

91. Bradley Keoun & Phil Kuntz, "Wall Street Aristocracy Got 1.2 Trillion in Secret Loans," *Bloomberg News* (August 21, 2011).

radar—attracting little of the attention or controversy associated with the Fed's support for the shadow banking system—speaks volumes about the extent to which the Fed's role as lender of last resort to the conventional banking system had been normalized within the bank policy community, financial media, and perhaps even the general public.

This is not to suggest that the use of these emergency lending facilities did not come without a reckoning. In the United Kingdom, the actions of the Bank of England were subsequently the target of not one but two separate independent reviews,[92] followed by the reform and—for the very first time—publication of the Bank's framework governing the future use of its emergency lending powers.[93] In the United States, Congress tightened the restrictions on the Fed's ability to lend to financial institutions other than banks and introduced new disclosure obligations requiring it to reveal—going forward and with a two-year lag—the recipients of discount window loans.[94]

The global financial crisis also highlighted the prevalence of LOLR facilities around the world: with the central banks of China, Hong Kong, Germany, France, the Netherlands, Canada, and a host of other countries intervening to support their domestic banking systems. In the wake of the crisis, many of these countries have also taken concrete measures to modernize their emergency lending facilities. These LOLR facilities vary, often dramatically, from jurisdiction to jurisdiction. While some are enshrined in statute, others are shrouded in secrecy or left entirely to the discretion of central banks. While some only permit emergency lending to conventional deposit-taking banks, others envision lending to a wide range of other financial institutions. And naturally, the legal frameworks, eligible collateral, interest rates, and institutional mechanics of emergency loans vary greatly from country to country, facility to facility. Yet the very existence of these LOLR facilities, combined with their widespread use during the financial crisis, drives home the expectation that central banks will do whatever it takes to support banks, and the wider banking system, during periods of extreme institutional and systemic stress. It turns out that Bagehot was right after all: the role of banks at the apex of our monetary and financial systems

92. Plenderleith, "Bank of England's Provision." Bill Winters, "Review of the Bank of England's Framework for Providing Liquidity to the Banking System" (2012).

93. Bank of England, *The Bank of England's Sterling Monetary Framework* (2015). While several of these reforms had actually been proposed just prior to the crisis, the crisis ultimately gave impetus to their subsequent adoption.

94. See Dodd-Frank Act, §§ 716 and 1101.

means that governments simply cannot credibly commit not to extend them a lifeline in times of crisis. There are no Hankeys in a foxhole.

Confidence Game

LOLR facilities are today rarely used by banks, outside of systemwide liquidity crises of the variety encountered during the global financial crisis. One of the reasons for this is the perceived stigma—the risk that news of a bank's decision to borrow money at a central bank's discount window, rather than in the wholesale money market, will be interpreted by the marketplace as a sign of financial weakness and potential instability.[95] A second and perhaps more important reason has been the development of two additional components of the financial safety net. Together, these components provide a more targeted and effective approach toward both the *prevention* of idiosyncratic bank failures and, when banks do fail, ensuring that their *resolution* is coordinated in a way that limits the associated costs for the bank's depositors and other creditors.

The first component is deposit insurance. The unprecedented wave of bank failures during the Great Depression wiped out billions of dollars in bank deposits, representing the accumulated savings of millions of Americans. In the shadow of President Roosevelt's national bank holiday, Congress set to work creating a comprehensive deposit insurance scheme under the oversight of a new federal regulator, the Federal Deposit Insurance Corporation, or FDIC. Notably, this was not the first attempt to establish a deposit insurance scheme in the United States. Several states, including New York, Michigan, and Ohio, adopted relatively sophisticated insurance schemes for both bank notes and deposits between 1829 and 1858.[96] However, these state-level insurance programs were all abandoned within a year of the creation of the National Banking System.[97] Between 1908 and 1917, a small handful of states, mostly in the Midwest, would again experiment with the introduction of deposit insurance. Yet these small and generally underfunded schemes were quickly decimated, and eventually

95. See generally Huberto Ennis & David Price, "Understanding Discount Window Stigma," Federal Reserve Bank of Richmond Economic Brief No. 20-04 (April 2020).

96. For a more detailed history and description of these state-level deposit guarantee schemes, see FDIC, "A Brief History of Deposit Insurance in the United States," 1–11 (1998), https://www.fdic.gov/bank/historical/brief/brhist.pdf.

97. FDIC, 5.

dismantled, following the economic turmoil and resulting bank failures of the early 1920s.[98]

The first federal deposit insurance scheme was introduced as part of the far-reaching financial sector reforms ushered in under the Banking Act of 1933, more commonly known as the Glass-Steagall Act.[99] The Glass-Steagall Act created the FDIC and established a guarantee that depositors of any bank supervised by the FDIC would receive compensation of up to $2,500 in the event of that bank's failure.[100] A temporary scheme was put in place as of January 1, 1934, with the permanent scheme scheduled to go into effect on July 1 of that same year.[101] The impact of the scheme, together with the national bank holiday and other temporary stabilization measures, could be observed almost immediately: with bank failures falling from an average of over two thousand per year between 1930 and 1933 to a total of just nine in 1934.[102] The year 1934 also saw a net inflow of deposits totaling $7.2 billion—an increase of 22 percent over the previous year and equivalent to roughly half of the deposits that had taken flight over the previous three years.[103] As President Roosevelt had predicted during his fireside chat, rebuilding public confidence was the key to stabilizing the US banking system.

Nevertheless, at least initially, the introduction of federal deposit insurance was extremely controversial. Many thought that letting bank shareholders and managers off the hook for their mistakes would incentivize poor management.[104] The chorus of critics included President Roosevelt himself, who thought that deposit insurance would prove unduly expensive and benefit poorly managed banks.[105] It also initially included Senator Carter Glass, the cosponsor of the Glass-Steagall Act, who had long opposed the introduction of deposit insurance before switching sides shortly before the act was

---

98. FDIC, 12–17.

99. Banking Act of 1933, Pub. L. No. 73-66, § 8, 48 Stat. 162, 168. This scheme supplanted the then existing system of double liability for shareholders of national banks; see Jonathan Macey & Geoffrey Miller, "Double Liability of Bank Shareholders: History and Implications," 27 Wake Forest Law Review 31, 38–39 (1992).

100. Banking Act of 1933, § 8. This cap was quickly changed to a maximum of $5,000 for most banks.

101. The introduction of the permanent scheme was eventually delayed to July 1, 1935.

102. FDIC, "Brief History," 1.

103. FDIC, 31.

104. See Helen Burns, *The American Banking Community and the New Deal Banking Reforms, 1933–1935* (1974).

105. FDIC, "Brief History," 1.

passed.[106] Indeed, even the banking industry itself viewed deposit insurance with some skepticism, with the president of the American Bankers Association labeling it "unsound, unscientific and dangerous."[107] For a time, it looked like deposit insurance might die in conference, with the House and Senate split over the introduction of the temporary scheme and who would pay for any losses.[108] But in the end, overwhelming public support for deposit insurance won the day, and the Glass-Steagall Act was signed into law by President Roosevelt on June 16, 1933.[109]

Today, the FDIC insures 100 percent of covered deposits up to a maximum of $250,000 per depositor per bank.[110] The FDIC thus effectively steps into the shoes of a failed bank, honoring its contractual commitment to return depositors' money. In order to make this commitment more credible, this compensation is paid out from a dedicated deposit insurance fund that, in the normal course of business, is financed by ex ante contributions from banks and other insured depository institutions.[111] Crucially, the FDIC also commits to compensate depositors of failed banks within an extremely short time frame—typically in as little as one business day.[112]

FDIC deposit insurance was originally conceived as an ex post consumer protection mechanism—i.e., a way of compensating the depositors of failed banks.[113] But most modern thinking around the role of deposit insurance frames it as an ex ante prophylactic against the threat of destabilizing bank runs. Viewed through the lens of the Diamond and Dybvig coordination problem framework, the FDIC's guarantee that insured depositors will be fully compensated up to $250,000 makes the vast majority of depositors

106. See Mark Flood, "The Great Deposit Insurance Debate," in Papadimitriou (ed.), *Stability in the Financial System* 35 (1996).

107. See *New York Times*, "Wires Banks to Urge Veto of Glass Bill" (June 16, 1933).

108. FDIC, "Brief History," 26–27.

109. See *Business Week*, "Deposit Insurance" (April 12, 1933). ("It became perfectly apparent that the voters wanted the guarantee, and that no bill which did not contain such a provision would be satisfactory to Congress or the public. Washington does not remember any issue on which the sentiment of the country has been so undivided or so emphatically expressed as upon this.")

110. See Dodd-Frank Act, § 335(a) (making permanent the increase of FDIC insurance coverage to $250,000).

111. See Federal Deposit Insurance Act, 12 U.S.C. §§ 1817 and 1821.

112. See FDIC, "Common Misconceptions about FDIC Insurance . . . and the Real Facts," *FDIC Consumer News* (December 22, 2014), https://www.fdic.gov/consumers/consumer/news /cnfall14/misconceptions.html.

113. Charles Calomiris & Eugene White, "The Origins of Federal Deposit Insurance," in Goldin & Libecap (eds.), *The Regulated Economy: A Historical Approach to Political Economy*, 145 (1994).

more or less indifferent to the prospect of a bank's failure.[114] This in turn reduces the pernicious "first come, first served" dynamic—essentially by guaranteeing that all insured depositors will ultimately get served. Viewed through the lens of the Gorton and Holmstrom informationally insensitive debt framework, the fact that the vast majority of insured depositors will be repaid extremely rapidly and in full makes FDIC insurance claims very close substitutes for bank deposits. This substitutability reduces both the incentives of depositors to undertake costly due diligence and, ultimately, the perceived benefits of preemptively withdrawing their deposits from a struggling bank. Either way, the existence of the FDIC's deposit insurance scheme can thus be viewed as engineering something of a confidence game: with the reduction in the impact of bank failure on depositors reducing their incentives to run, and the resulting reduction in the threat of runs reducing the probability of bank failure.

Intuitively, we would expect the success of this confidence game to hinge on the legal and institutional design of a given deposit insurance scheme. If depositors do not believe they will get paid rapidly and in full, they will not view bank deposits and deposit insurance claims as close functional substitutes, and the incentives for them to run will remain intact. This intuition finds support in the design of the United Kingdom's deposit insurance scheme on the eve of the global financial crisis. This scheme had several notable features: including a relatively low cap on insured deposits, a 10 percent deductible payable by depositors on insured deposits over £2,000, and a payout policy that contemplated that depositors would only be repaid at the conclusion of a potentially lengthy bankruptcy process.[115] As a result, a depositor with £10,000 in a UK bank would only be entitled to £9,200 in the event of its failure. Compounding matters, she would only receive this money after a lengthy legal proceeding that, conservatively, would likely take more than a year—leaving her in the interim to answer important and frightening questions about how to pay her mortgage, put food on the table, and pay her bills. Given these design flaws, it is hardly surprising that the retail depositors of Northern Rock ran for the exits after the news broke that the beleaguered lender was about to receive an emergency loan from the Bank of England.[116] In the end, the government was forced to announce a blanket

114. Diamond & Dybvig, "Bank Runs," 413.

115. Armour et al., *Principles of Financial Regulation*, 335.

116. Armour et al., 335.

guarantee covering all the bank's deposits.[117] Before the crisis was over, the UK's Financial Services Authority would also announce a complete overhaul of its deposit insurance scheme.[118]

The introduction of FDIC deposit insurance in 1934 was not immediately followed by a global rush to adopt deposit insurance schemes. Nevertheless, momentum would eventually begin to build during the turbulence of the 1970s and early 1980s. Between 1975 and 2022, the number of countries adopting deposit insurance schemes increased from a relatively modest 8 to an impressive 146, with another 24 schemes under development.[119] Like LOLR facilities, these schemes vary across several dimensions, including their statutory mandates, institutional and account coverage, insurance caps, funding models, and the role of the deposit insurance administrator in bank regulation and supervision.[120] Yet, despite these differences, the core function of these schemes remains remarkably similar across jurisdictions: protecting depositors from some or all of the consequences of bank failure, thereby reducing both the probability and potential impact of destabilizing depositor runs. Like lender-of-last-resort facilities, deposit insurance schemes have thus become an important part of the legal and institutional superstructure that turns bank deposits into good money.

Catch Them if They Fall

In reality, of course, even a well-designed deposit insurance scheme will not completely eliminate the risk of bank runs. As a preliminary matter, the majority of bank runs are not the product of correlated withdrawals by retail depositors, but rather the withdrawal of short-term funding by uninsured institutional creditors within the wholesale money market. At the same time, almost inevitably, some banks will simply make bad investments, find themselves in financial distress, and ultimately fail. When they do, the aftermath can impose significant costs on the failed bank's employees, customers, uninsured depositors, and other creditors. In at least some cases, it can also have destabilizing knock-on effects within the wider financial system, with direct

117. See Alistair Darling, "Statement of the Chancellor of the Exchequer on Financial Markets" (September 17, 2007).

118. See UK Financial Services Authority, "FSA Announces FSCS Reforms to Ensure Faster Payouts and Boost Consumer Confidence" (July 24, 2009).

119. See International Association of Deposit Insurers, "IADI Annual Survey" (2021), https://www.iadi.org/en/research/data-warehouse/deposit-insurance-surveys/.

120. International Association of Deposit Insurers, "IADI Annual Survey."

counterparty exposures, the fire sale of a failed bank's illiquid assets, and correlated business models each creating potential channels of contagion between the failed bank and other banks and financial institutions. These costs are often advanced as one of the principal justifications for the third and final component of the financial safety net: a special bankruptcy or "resolution" framework for failed banks.[121]

The first dedicated bank resolution framework was introduced in the United States as part of the same New Deal reforms that created the FDIC and introduced federal deposit insurance.[122] Prior to these reforms, the standard practice in bankruptcy proceedings was to treat the depositors of a failed bank as simply another class of unsecured creditors.[123] As a result, depositors would have to wait until the conclusion of the bankruptcy process before getting their money back—a process that, on average, took upwards of six years from start to finish.[124] Even then, where the sale or liquidation of a failed bank did not generate enough cash to fully repay its creditors, depositors would often receive only a small fraction of what they were originally owed. For example, between 1921 and 1930, the United States experienced over 1,200 bank failures, the vast majority of which resulted in the liquidation of the failed bank's assets. Following liquidation, depositors of state-chartered banks recovered an average of 62 percent of their money, while depositors of federally chartered banks received only 58 percent.[125] Understandably, these bleak recovery rates— and the fact that depositors would typically have to wait several years to recover anything at all—only reinforced their incentives to run at the first sign of trouble.

The Banking Act of 1933 circumvented this standard bankruptcy process by requiring the appointment of the FDIC as the receiver for all national banks. Today, the FDIC is also the receiver for the state-chartered banks, thrifts, and other depository institutions for which it provides deposit

121. John Armour, "Making Bank Resolution Credible," in Moloney et al. (eds.), *The Oxford Handbook of Financial Regulation*, 453 (2015).

122. See Banking Act of 1933, § 8 (describing the role of the FDIC in the event that "any member or nonmember bank shall be declared insolvent").

123. See FDIC, *Resolutions Handbook*, 24–25 (2014), https://www.fdic.gov/bank/historical /reshandbook/resolutions_handbook.pdf. Indeed, in many respects, bank receivership was even less favorable to depositors and other unsecured creditors than normal corporate bankruptcy processes; see Stephen Lubben, *The Law of Failure: A Tour through the Wilds of American Business Insolvency Law*, 103–4 (2018).

124. FDIC, *Resolutions Handbook*, 24.

125. FDIC, 24–25.

insurance.[126] In this capacity, once a bank fails, the FDIC has a duty to maximize the value of its remaining assets, while simultaneously minimizing any compensation that must be paid from the deposit insurance fund.[127] The FDIC has been given several legal tools to pursue these objectives: including the ability to write down a bank's uninsured liabilities, convert its outstanding debt into equity, repudiate its contracts, and transfer its assets to either a private sector purchaser or a public sector bridge bank.[128] Armed with these tools, the expectation is typically that the FDIC will trigger the resolution process after the close of business on Friday afternoon, with the newly acquired or restructured bank able to open its doors for business as usual first thing on Monday morning.

As of August 2022, more than four thousand banks and other insured depository institutions have gone through the process of FDIC receivership.[129] In most cases, the FDIC's preferred strategy for resolving these institutions is a process known as *purchase and assumption* (P&A). The starting point for P&A involves the FDIC identifying one or more healthy banks that are willing and able to purchase some or all of the failed bank's assets and assume some or all of its liabilities.[130] In a "clean" P&A, the acquiring bank typically purchases the failed bank's cash, reserve balances, and other high-quality liquid assets, and assumes only its insured deposit liabilities. The assets and liabilities of the failed bank that are not purchased and assumed by the acquiring bank then remain in the failed bank during the receivership process. Where the liabilities assumed by the acquiring bank exceed the value of the assets it purchases, the FDIC will also in many cases provide financial support equivalent to the shortfall.

The vast majority of the resolution transactions overseen by the FDIC between 1934 and 1980 were clean P&As.[131] However, spurred first by the

126. See FDIC, "About FDIC: What We Do" (May 15, 2020), https://www.fdic.gov/about/what-we-do/index.html.

127. See Federal Deposit Insurance Act, § 2; 12 U.S.C. § 1821(d)(13)(E) (requiring the FDIC to maximize the net present value, or minimize any loss, from the sale of a failed bank's assets); 12 C.F.R. § 360.1 (2021) (requiring the FDIC to pursue the resolution option that would impose the lowest costs on the deposit insurance fund).

128. See Federal Deposit Insurance Act, 12 U.S.C. §§ 1818, 1819, and 1821(c) (describing in full the FDIC's powers as receiver).

129. See FDIC, "Bank Failures and Assistance Data" (2022), https://banks.data.fdic.gov/explore/failures.

130. Where there are multiple potential acquirers interested in a failed bank's assets and/or liabilities, the FDIC typically conducts an auction.

131. For a more detailed overview of the development and use of P&A transactions, see FDIC, "Bank Resolutions and Receiverships," in FDIC, *Crisis and Response: An FDIC History, 2008–2013* (2013).

savings and loan crisis of the 1980s, and then by the global financial crisis, the FDIC has more recently experimented with two other variants of the P&A model: "whole bank" and "loss sharing" P&As.[132] As the name implies, whole bank P&A involves the acquiring bank purchasing all the assets, and assuming all the liabilities, of a failed bank. This variant has the benefit of greatly streamlining the resolution process, resulting in faster and less complicated resolutions that can be more easily communicated to the failed bank's depositors and other stakeholders. In contrast, loss sharing P&A envisions that the acquiring bank will purchase all the assets of the failed bank, but that the FDIC will absorb an agreed-upon percentage of any future losses stemming from the deterioration in the value of these assets. This loss sharing is explicitly designed to increase the attractiveness of the failed bank's assets from the perspective of potential purchasers.[133] Simultaneously, of course, it also effectively transfers some of the risk associated with any future decline in the value of these assets to the deposit insurance fund, and from there to surviving banks and, ultimately, to the US government.

In the absence of strong demand for a failed bank's assets and liabilities, the FDIC can also create a so-called bridge bank. Similar to a clean P&A, bridge bank transactions typically involve a newly chartered bank purchasing the failed bank's cash, reserve balances, and high-quality liquid assets and assuming its insured deposits and secured liabilities. The key difference is that the FDIC itself then takes full ownership and control of the bridge bank, attempts to stabilize its operations, and seeks to preserve its value as a going concern.[134] As explained by the FDIC, the benefits of using a bridge bank stem from the ability to bridge the temporal gap between the moment of bank failure—where prevailing financial and macroeconomic conditions may generate strong headwinds for both asset values and interest from potential acquirers—and the optimal time frame for realizing the full value of the failed bank and its assets.[135] Bridge banks can also be useful in the resolution of larger, more complex banks, where the size, scope, and sophistication of

---

132. FDIC, "Bank Resolutions and Receiverships."

133. FDIC, 175. Loss sharing P&A was introduced by the FDIC in response to the exigencies of the global financial crisis and technically phased out in 2013 (195–96). However, the FDIC reintroduced limited loss sharing in connection with the P&A of First Republic Bank by JPMorgan Chase in May 2023.

134. Michael Barr, Howell Jackson, & Margaret Tahyar, *Financial Regulation: Law & Policy*, 971–72 (2nd ed., 2018).

135. FDIC, *Crisis and Response*, 184.

a failed bank's business, combined with the smaller universe of potential acquirers, often makes P&A a less realistic option.[136]

While these bank resolution strategies can vary greatly in their design and execution, they all share one crucial feature: they are not bankruptcy. Conventional corporate bankruptcy law includes a variety of procedural mechanisms—like the automatic stay—that are designed to buy *time*. This time is often necessary for the bankruptcy court or administrator to identify the firm's outstanding assets and liabilities, determine how best to preserve its value, and ensure that payouts are ultimately made to creditors in accordance with their priorities.[137] In many cases, time is also necessary to carve out space for negotiation among a bankrupt firm's creditors. Importantly, the use of these procedural mechanisms reflects the assumption that the passage of time will not, in and of itself, result in a significant deterioration in the value of a firm's assets and liabilities. Yet, as we have already seen, this assumption stands in jarring contrast to the unique and harsh reality confronting struggling banks, their depositors, and other short-term creditors. Indeed, faced with the prospect of being deprived of access to their money for an uncertain and potentially lengthy period of time, the threat of bankruptcy would only strengthen the incentives of depositors to run. The heightened threat of a run, followed by the strict application of conventional corporate bankruptcy law, could also undermine public confidence in a bank, making it more difficult to retain—let alone attract—business partners, creditors, employees, and customers. Viewed from this perspective, the speed and certainty of the resolution process are critical to the preservation of public confidence in a failed bank and its monetary IOUs. By circumventing the relatively slow and deliberate procedural mechanisms accompanying conventional corporate bankruptcy law, strategies such as P&A and bridge banks enable the FDIC to resolve a troubled bank before most of its stakeholders even know there's a problem.

The global financial crisis taught policymakers a valuable lesson about the limits of P&A and other conventional resolution strategies in connection with the failure of large, complex banks—especially during periods of wider financial instability.[138] And, as recently driven home by the collapse

---

136. Barr, Jackson, & Tahyar, *Law & Policy*, 972 (noting that between 1987 and 1994, while bridge banks were used for only 10 percent of all FDIC resolutions, these resolutions accounted for 45 percent of all failed bank assets).

137. Armour, "Making Bank Resolution Credible," 454.

138. In response to the crisis, the US adopted a new resolution framework, known as the Orderly Liquidation Authority, designed to facilitate the orderly resolution of systemically

and subsequent bailout of Silicon Valley Bank in March 2023, policymakers are sometimes reluctant to use these strategies to resolve far smaller and simpler banks. Nevertheless, in the wake of the crisis, the FDIC bank resolution framework has become a template for other jurisdictions. Following the failure of Northern Rock, the United Kingdom adopted a Special Resolution Regime (SRR) modeled closely on FDIC receivership.[139] In the European Union, policymakers would subsequently base their own new resolution framework largely on the SRR.[140] And, at the international level, the FDIC's framework also heavily influenced the "Key Attributes of Effective Resolution Regimes for Financial Institutions," published by the Financial Stability Board (FSB) in 2011. As of writing, at least twenty-three FSB member states have or are in the process of implementing domestic bank resolution frameworks reflecting some or all of these principles.[141] Accordingly, while a great deal of work remains to be done, struggling banks around the world increasingly benefit from special legal treatment exempting them from the application of conventional corporate bankruptcy law, thereby insulating both a bank's stakeholders and the wider financial system from the otherwise potentially devastating impact of their failure. This special treatment is designed, often explicitly, to promote public confidence in banks as a source of good money.

The Money Shot

The medieval and Renaissance bankers of Lombardy, Amsterdam, and London deserve the lion's share of the credit for pioneering the system of banking, money, and payments that we enjoy today. Yet, over the longer arc of history, it seems unlikely that this system would have survived—let alone thrived—had we not successfully addressed the problem of bank fragility. To be sure, the modern financial safety net is not the only way to solve this problem—a fact that we return to in chapters 6 and 7. Nevertheless, the three components of the financial safety net work in tandem to make banks safe. Central bank LOLR facilities provide fundamentally solvent banks with a

---

important bank holding companies and other specified financial institutions; see Dodd-Frank Act, Title II.

139. UK Banking Act 2009, c. 1; see also Armour, "Making Bank Resolution Credible," 461 (observing the influence of FDIC receivership on the design of the SRR).

140. European Union Bank Recovery and Resolution Directive, 2014/59/EU (May 15, 2014).

141. See Financial Stability Board, "2021 Resolution Report: Glass Half-Full or Still Half-Empty?" (December 7, 2021), Annex 1.

valuable option to borrow money against their illiquid assets for the purpose of honoring their contractual commitments to depositors and other creditors. Deposit insurance makes depositors indifferent to the risks of bank failure, thereby reducing the probability and impact of destabilizing runs. And, for those banks that do fail, special resolution frameworks reduce the destructive impact on the bank's creditors, employees, customers, and other stakeholders.

Together, the components of the financial safety net have greatly bolstered the creditworthiness of the promises that banks make to their depositors—thus paving the way for their ubiquitous use as monetary IOUs. Yet, because the components of this safety net were specifically designed to address the business model and risks associated with fractional reserve banking, its unique privileges and protections are generally only available to conventional deposit-taking banks. As we explore in the next chapter, the resulting legal and institutional path dependency has had an enormous impact on both the structure of our financial system and, as a direct result, the prevailing levels of experimentation, competition, and innovation in the increasingly high-stakes markets for money and payments.

3

The Only Game in Town

The Bank never "goes broke." If the Bank runs out of money, the Banker may issue as much more as needed by writing on any ordinary paper.

—THE INSTRUCTIONS TO MONOPOLY

If you've ever played the board game Monopoly, you know that the Bank enjoys certain privileges. The Bank is the only source of money. The Bank holds the title deeds to all property, railroads, and utilities before they are purchased by the players, and it is the only institution that can sell property or underwrite mortgages. And it is the Bank that collects all taxes, fines, and bail money from players who, through nothing more than the roll of the dice, land themselves in jail. Ironically, Monopoly is based on an earlier board game—The Landlord's Game—released in 1906 at the height of the "trust busting" era in the United States. Created by writer Lizzie Magie, the game was designed to teach children about the dangers of concentrated ownership and production.[1] Yet right smack dab in the middle stands a single all-powerful bank, endowed by the rules with an uncontested monopoly over money, payments, loans, real estate sales, and tax collection—*the only game in town.*

1. For a history of the game, see Philip Orbanes, *Monopoly: The World's Most Famous Game—and How It Got That Way* (2006).

For many of us, it's hard to imagine a world in which banks are not at the center of our financial universe. Not only do we keep the vast majority of our savings in the form of bank deposits, but banks often play a key supporting role in many of our most important financial milestones—whether it be buying a car, getting a student loan, or purchasing a home. Today, even many relatively small banks provide a wide range of other financial products and services, such as stock trading, asset management, and insurance. And, in the background, banks continue to perform their long-standing role as the owners and custodians of the clearinghouses and other financial market infrastructure that move money and other financial assets across the economy. Perhaps Lizzie Magie was not that far off the mark.

By now, at least one important reason why banks have risen to the apex of our financial system should be abundantly clear. In theory, almost anyone can create their own money: witness the erstwhile popularity of Ithaca HOURS, Brixton Pounds, Canadian Tire money, and thousands of other small-scale monetary IOUs that have emerged, flourished, and disappeared throughout history.[2] During periods of financial stability, when public confidence is high, and when the institutions that create these monetary IOUs are fundamentally solvent, these private monies can create the illusion of being close substitutes for bank deposits.[3] Yet during periods of financial instability, when confidence evaporates, and when the threat of bankruptcy looms over these would-be monetary institutions, the critical role of the public safety net comes squarely into view. For it is precisely at this moment that access to the three components of the safety net—central bank LOLR facilities, deposit guarantee schemes, and special resolution frameworks—separate the wheat from the chaff, good money from bad. Ultimately, it is their legally privileged access to this safety net that gives banks such an enormous comparative advantage in the creation of the IOUs that we call money.

2. See Paul Glover, "Creating Community Economics with Local Currency," Ithaca HOURS Online (December 11, 2006), http://www.lightlink.com/hours/ithacahours/intro.html (denominated in US dollars, Ithaca HOURS could be earned by providing services for Ithaca residents, which could then be used to purchase services within the community); Brixton Pound, https://brixtonpound.org/(Brixton Pounds are a local, complementary currency that circulates alongside the British pound in the London district of Brixton); Harold Don Allen, "Canadian Tire Scrip," Numismatist 63, 63–64 (2006) (Canadian Tire Money was a form of coupon that could be redeemed for products and services at Canadian Tire stores).

3. Even then, the small network footprint of these private monies—i.e., that they can only be used in specific locations or establishments—often makes them less useful than more widely accepted forms of money; see George Selgin, "Friday Flashback: The Folly That Is 'Local' Currency," Alt-M (January 6, 2017), https://www.alt-m.org/2017/01/06/the-folly-that-is-local-currency/.

But the modern financial safety net is not the *only* reason why banks reside at the apex of our systems of money and payments. In fact, the financial safety net has evolved in parallel with—and, in many respects, given rise to—the construction of a far larger and more elaborate legal and institutional superstructure. Reflecting the moral hazard concerns of Thomson Hankey, President Roosevelt, and a great many others, the first column of this superstructure is a sophisticated framework of prudential regulation and supervision. This framework includes comprehensive rule books governing how much banks can borrow, what type of investments they can make, the quantity and quality of required reserves, and whether they can engage in activities other than the business of banking. These rule books are designed to constrain bank risk taking, thereby limiting potential recourse to the financial safety net. In the process, however, these rulebooks introduce a high degree of legal path dependency and institutional homogeneity into the design of our monetary institutions. They also erect significant barriers to entry for novel and potentially more efficient financial institutions and platforms, the business models of which do not fit perfectly into the well-worn mold of conventional deposit-taking banks.

The second pillar of this legal superstructure is built on the first. Ongoing compliance with bank regulation and supervision—simply *being* a bank—typically comes with an important perk: eligibility to open a central bank reserve account. As described in chapter 1, central bank reserve accounts are one of the central nodes of modern payment networks, enabling banks to discharge their obligations toward one another using the central bank's own monetary IOUs—known as reserve balances—as the final settlement asset. Accordingly, just as opening your first bank account represented an important step on your journey to adulthood, opening a reserve account is an essential step toward full participation in the modern payment system. Where central banks limit the types of financial institutions and platforms that can open these accounts, they are effectively dictating the competitive structure of this system—creating a significant and growing regulatory bottleneck and giving banks yet another edge in the increasingly lucrative market for moving our money.

Eligibility to open a central bank reserve account becomes even more critical once we consider that access to these accounts is typically a legal and operational precondition for direct membership in the clearinghouses through which the vast majority of payments are routed before final settlement. Without direct access, financial institutions and platforms other than banks are effectively forced to rely on banks—in many cases their principal competitors—for indirect access to this basic infrastructure. In addition to compounding existing bottleneck problems, the lack of direct access also leaves these institutions and platforms on the outside looking in as clearinghouses and their member banks make pivotal decisions about the development and adoption of new payments technology. Crucially, these decisions relate not only to things like network speed and security, but also to important technical specifications regarding network design, integration, and interoperability. These technical specifications can have enormous implications on prevailing barriers to entry, competition, and the trajectory and pace of future network innovation.

To be clear, this legal superstructure was constructed to perform a very specific and extremely important function: each pillar working in tandem with the others to protect the stability and integrity of the payment system. But that does not mean that this superstructure does not simultaneously generate significant anticompetitive, and potentially destabilizing, effects. This chapter explains how the financial safety net, bank regulation and supervision, and restrictions on infrastructure access distort competition in the markets for money and payments. It also explains how these competitive distortions can create significant risks for customer protection, for the microprudential safety and soundness of banks and other financial institutions, and for the stability of the wider financial system.

An Exquisitely Tailored Straitjacket

Bank deposits are the quintessential monetary IOUs: a contractually enforceable promise made by a bank to its depositors that serves as both a nominal store of value and a means of payment. While we often take it for granted, this makes each and every depositor a *creditor* of their bank. Yet most depositors have never flipped through the pages of their deposit contract, let alone read their bank's financial statements or attended its annual general meeting to ask the CEO about its net interest margin, nonperforming loans, or prospects for the future. As we have seen, this otherwise appalling lack of due diligence reflects the role of the financial safety net in rendering depositors more or less indifferent to the risk of bank failure.

Yet insured depositors are not the only creditors of a bank that benefit from the financial safety net. Indeed, to the extent that LOLR facilities and bank resolution frameworks enable a struggling bank to escape the harsh strictures of general corporate bankruptcy law, these components of the financial safety net also serve to insulate the bank's *other* creditors from at least some of the consequences of bank failure. This is most clearly evident in the case of whole bank P&A, where the acquiring bank agrees to assume all the liabilities of the failed bank, thus stepping into its shoes as the promisor of all its outstanding debt obligations—not only to depositors but also to bondholders, derivatives and repo counterparties, and commercial trade creditors. The same is true of government-orchestrated bank bailouts, where the principal beneficiaries of public funds are ultimately the creditors of the failed bank. Where the expectation that creditors will not be forced to absorb the full costs of bank failure is sufficiently ingrained, we might therefore expect the financial safety net to significantly reduce the incentives of these creditors to closely and continuously monitor bank risk taking.[4]

In theory, the resulting lack of creditor discipline can give rise to an acute moral hazard problem, with a lack of oversight giving bank managers free rein to take socially excessive risks. This moral hazard problem is compounded by the fact that bank managers are often compensated on the basis of their bank's return on equity (ROE). All other things being equal, the easiest and most effective way for a manager to increase a bank's ROE is to maximize the use of debt financing, or *leverage*. Maximizing the use of leverage—and thereby minimizing the use of equity—mechanically increases a bank's ROE because the profits generated from the bank's operations will ultimately be divided among a smaller stock of outstanding shares.[5]

Normally, any increase in a firm's leverage translates into a corresponding increase in the probability of balance sheet insolvency and, ultimately, bankruptcy. For this reason, the financial creditors of most firms take a very close interest in the amount of leverage that these enterprises employ. They also often demand contractual restrictions on the ability of these firms to take on new debt. Yet, in the case of banks, it is precisely these incentives that are diluted by the financial safety net. This gives rise to a peculiar governance model in which both the managers of a bank and its diversified shareholders are driven to boost ROE by maximizing leverage, but where many of the creditors that would otherwise face the heightened credit and bankruptcy risks posed by higher leverage are not strongly incentivized to

---

4. While not technically reliant on the financial safety net, a bank's repo and derivatives creditors face a similar set of incentives due to statutory carveouts from the automatic stay; see chapter 5.

5. A simple numerical example may help illustrate this point. Imagine a bank with $100 of assets yielding $5 in income per year. Where these assets are financed using $10 of equity and $90 of deposits and other debt, the bank's ROE equals 50 percent ($5/$10). Where the bank finances the assets with $5 of equity and $95 of debt, the bank's ROE is 100 percent ($5/$5).

push back.[6] Left unchecked, we might expect this lack of creditor discipline to result in higher leverage, greater risk taking, more potential bank failures, and increased reliance on the financial safety net.

Modern bank regulation seeks to address this moral hazard problem in three principal ways. The first is liquidity regulation. Banks have always held reserves of vault cash or central bank reserve balances as a form of self-insurance against potential runs. Yet the opportunity costs of holding these reserves rather than using them to make more profitable investments also raise the prospect that banks may not select the socially optimal level of reserves in all states of the world. Reflecting this prospect, the oldest and most ubiquitous form of liquidity regulation consists of reserve ratios designed to ensure that banks hold a minimum threshold level of vault cash and other reserves relative to their stock of outstanding deposits.[7] More recently, these simple reserve ratios have been supplemented or replaced by more sophisticated mechanisms, like the Basel III liquidity coverage ratio, which is designed to ensure that banks hold enough cash, reserve balances, and other high-quality liquid assets to survive a hypothetical thirty-day stress test scenario.[8] In effect, this liquidity regulation is designed to ensure that banks purchase a sturdy umbrella before the storm hits, thereby reducing ex post reliance on LOLR facilities and other components of the financial safety net for protection from the elements.

The second way that bank regulation seeks to address this problem is through the imposition of equity capital requirements. These requirements demand that banks finance their loans and other investments using a minimum amount of retained earnings, common equity, and other loss-absorbing capital. Reflecting the position of shareholders as subordinated or "residual" claimants whose shares only have value where the bank is able to honor its commitments to all its creditors, the use of equity capital enables a bank to absorb losses without triggering balance sheet insolvency.[9] Accordingly,

---

6. See John Armour & Jeffrey Gordon, "Systemic Harms and Shareholder Value," 6:1 Journal of Legal Analysis 35 (2014).

7. The Federal Reserve's current reserve ratio requirements are published at https://www.federalreserve.gov/monetarypolicy/reservereq.htm. As of writing, the basic reserve ratio is set at zero.

8. For a detailed description of the rationale and design of the liquidity coverage ratio, see Basel Committee on Banking Supervision, "Basel III: The Liquidity Coverage Ratio and Risk Monitoring Tools" (2013), https://www.bis.org/publ/bcbs238.htm.

9. For a detailed explanation of why common equity in particular is capable of absorbing losses without triggering balance sheet insolvency, see Anat Admati & Martin Hellwig, *The Bankers' New Clothes: What's Wrong with Banking and What to Do about It*, 81–99 (2013).

the more equity capital a bank "holds"[10] against its assets, the more losses on those assets it will be able to withstand before triggering bank resolution or necessitating recourse to a deposit insurance scheme.

In the United States, banks are currently subject to a minimum capital requirement of 8 percent of their risk-weighted assets.[11] This minimum capital requirement is then subject to a potential increase on the basis of a bank's idiosyncratic risk profile, systemic importance, prevailing macroeconomic conditions, and other factors. Many larger banks are also subject to a non-risk-weighted supplementary leverage ratio that measures a bank's retained earnings and common equity (CET1) capital against a "leverage exposure" that includes both its on-balance-sheet assets and certain off-balance-sheet exposures.[12] As of May 2023, the average CET1 capital ratio of the largest US banks stood at approximately 12 percent.[13] Whereas liquidity requirements impose constraints on the ability of bank managers to operate a bank with an insufficient stock of liquid reserves, minimum capital requirements constrain their ability to maximize leverage as a means of increasing a bank's ROE.

Finally, in order to ensure ongoing compliance with the capital, liquidity, and myriad other regulatory requirements to which they are subject, banks are typically required to submit to intensive prudential supervision.[14] The basic building blocks of bank supervision in the US include comprehensive reporting requirements, onsite examinations by bank supervisors, and a composite rating process designed to evaluate the safety and soundness of individual banks.[15] In the aftermath of the global financial crisis, banks in many jurisdictions have also been subjected to periodic "stress testing"

10. The linguistic convention of saying that banks "hold" equity capital is a long-standing source of confusion, suggesting that this capital is somehow set aside for the purpose of offsetting potential future losses. In reality, equity capital is simply a means of financing a bank's assets, not an asset in and of itself. This is reflected in the fact that owners' equity, or capital, is reported on the same side of a bank's balance sheet as its deposits and other liabilities.

11. For a detailed description of the various components of minimum capital requirements, see John Armour, Dan Awrey, Paul Davies, Luca Enriques, Jeff Gordon, Colin Mayer, & Jennifer Payne, *Principles of Financial Regulation*, chapter 14 (2016) (describing the definition of capital, the basic requirements, and various mandatory and discretionary capital buffers).

12. Armour et al., chapter 14.

13. See Federal Reserve Board of Governors, *Financial Stability Report*, 27 (October 2023), file:///Users/aja288/Desktop/financial-stability-report-20231020.pdf.

14. For a detailed description of the evolution of bank supervision in the US, see Peter Conti-Brown & Sean Vanetta, *The Bankers' Thumb: A History of Bank Supervision in America* (forthcoming).

15. For a more detailed overview of the key pillars of banking supervision in the US today, including the so-called CAMELS rating process, see Barr, Jackson, & Tahyar, *Law & Policy*, 898–903.

designed to evaluate the resilience of their balance sheets in the face of a hypothetical set of adverse financial and macroeconomic shocks.[16] The results of these stress tests are then fed back into the supervisory process, helping supervisors identify and address potential weaknesses in a bank's capital or liquidity positions. Where these stress tests reveal material weaknesses, banks may then be prohibited from making distributions to managers or shareholders, or required to raise additional capital. Together, these supervisory and stress testing processes are designed to buttress the microprudential safety and soundness of individual banks, further reducing the risk of bank failure and its associated burdens on the financial safety net.

These key pillars of bank regulation and supervision are just the tip of the spear of a highly sophisticated and complex regulatory framework. The most recent edition of the international standards governing bank capital—the so-called Basel framework—runs 616 pages.[17] The regulations implementing this framework in the US weigh in at over a thousand pages.[18] Using techniques from computer programming, economist Andrew Lo and his coauthors have found that Title 12 of the US code, which governs banks and banking, is second only to the tax code in its complexity.[19] Perhaps not surprisingly, compliance with this framework is also extremely costly, demanding significant investments in both compliance personnel and technology. While reliable data is scarce, it has been estimated that the largest banks can each spend over $1 billion per year on regulatory compliance.[20] At the other end of the spectrum, compliance also represents a significant component of the total operating costs for smaller community banks. For example, a 2016

16. From 2011 to 2020, the stress tests conducted by the Federal Reserve involved two separate but complementary processes: the Dodd-Frank Act–mandated stress test (DFAST) and the Comprehensive Capital Analysis and Review (CCAR). The results of the 2022 DFAST are available at https://www.federalreserve.gov/publications/files/2022-dfast-results-20220623.pdf. The 2020 CCAR results are available at https://www.federalreserve.gov/supervisionreg/ccar-2020-archive.htm. In 2020, the Federal Reserve replaced the quantitative CCAR evaluation with the stress capital buffer.

17. See Basel Committee on Banking Supervision, "Basel III: A Global Framework for More Resilient Banks and Banking Systems" (2011), https://www.bis.org/publ/bcbs189.pdf, and "Basel III: Finalising Post-Crisis Reforms" (2017), https://www.bis.org/bcbs/publ/d424.pdf (articulating the Basel capital rules).

18. See 12 C.F.R. 208, 217, and 225 (containing many of the rules governing the minimum capital of US banks).

19. See William Li, Pablo Azar, David Larochelle, Phil Hill, & Andrew Lo, "Law Is Code: A Software Engineering Approach Analyzing the United States Code," 10 Journal of Business and Technology Law 297 (2015).

20. See Peter Farley, "Spotlight on Compliance Costs as Banks Get Down to Business with AI," *International Banker* (July 4, 2017).

survey conducted by the Federal Reserve Bank of St. Louis found that, on average, 8.7 percent of the noninterest expenses of banks with assets under $100 million go toward regulatory compliance.[21]

From our perspective, the critical if mind-numbing details of bank regulation and supervision are far less important than their impact on experimentation, competition, and innovation within the markets for money and payments. This impact can be felt in a variety of ways. As a preliminary matter, the economic rationale for policy tools like reserve requirements, minimum capital rules, and intensive prudential supervision reflects the unique risks posed by the combination of *money issuance* with *financial intermediation*. In effect, these policy tools are designed for firms that rely on monetary IOUs in order to finance their investments in long-term, risky, and illiquid assets. As we have seen, these tools also serve as a counterweight to the potential moral hazard problems generated by the financial safety net. These observations have an important upshot. Specifically, where financial institutions and platforms that operate outside this safety net issue monetary IOUs but do not engage in meaningful financial intermediation, the reflexive imposition of these tools can impose significant and unnecessary costs. Compounding matters, the enormous costs of ongoing compliance with bank regulation and supervision can represent a formidable barrier to entry—especially for smaller, technology-driven firms that we might expect to serve as important catalysts of innovation. The resulting regulatory path dependence and institutional homogeneity warps the markets for both money and payments, forcing novel new entrants to choose between the exquisitely tailored straitjacket of bank regulation and supervision or forgoing the unique competitive advantages enjoyed by conventional deposit-taking banks.

Membership Has Its Privileges

To this point, the spotlight has been squarely focused on how the financial safety net gives banks a unique comparative advantage in the creation of good money. But regulation also gives banks an important and far too often overlooked advantage in the realm of payments. Payment systems are classic "network" goods. The defining feature of these goods is that their utility, and therefore attractiveness, to prospective *new* users is largely a function

---

21. See Drew Dahl, Andrew Meyer, & Michelle Clark Neeley, "Scale Matters: Community Banks and Compliance Costs," Federal Reserve Bank of St. Louis (July 14, 2016).

of the number of *existing* users.[22] Hence, for much the same reason that an unpopular social media platform is unlikely to survive, an electronic payment network that only enables you to send and receive payments within a relatively small community of people and businesses is unlikely to deliver good payments. Put somewhat differently, all other things being equal, people would prefer to use payment networks that give them the ability to transact with the largest possible number of people. These network effects are often compounded by pronounced economies of scale, with the relatively high initial fixed costs of designing and building a network eventually giving way to the relatively low marginal costs of connecting each additional new user.[23] Together, these economies of scale and network effects combine to make the size of payment networks extremely important—effectively giving larger and more established networks an inherent advantage over their smaller, newer rivals.

These economies of scale and network effects also make the question of who enjoys direct access to payment networks absolutely pivotal from the perspective of industry competition. In the United States and many other countries, the answer to this question is remarkably simple: banks. Pursuant to Section 13(1) of the Federal Reserve Act, the Fed's regional reserve banks are only permitted to accept deposits from "member banks," "other depository institutions," or, for a limited range of purposes, any "nonmember bank or trust company."[24] As reflected in the Fed's operating rules and guidance, the practical effect of Section 13(1) is therefore to restrict eligibility to open Federal Reserve master accounts to commercial banks, mutual and federal

22. See Paul Klemperer, "Network Goods (Theory)," in Steven Durlauf & Lawrence Blume (eds.), *The New Palgrave Dictionary of Economics*, 915 (2nd ed., 2008). For research examining network effects in payment systems, see Sujit Chakravorti & Roberto Roson, "Platform Competition in Two-Sided Markets: The Case of Payment Networks," 5:1 Review of Network Economics 118 (2006); Alistair Milne, "What Is in It for Us? Network Effects and Bank Payment Innovation," 30:6 Journal of Banking and Finance 1613 (2006); James McAndrews, "Network Issues and Payment Systems," Federal Reserve Bank of Philadelphia Business Review 15 (November/ December 1997).

23. Thus enabling larger networks to amortize their initial fixed costs across a larger number of users. For research examining economies of scale in payment systems, see Christine Beijnen & Wilco Bolt, "Size Matters: Economies of Scale in European Payments Processing," 33 Journal of Banking and Finance 203 (2009); Wilco Bolt & David Humphrey, "Payment Network Scale Economies, SEPA, and Cash Replacement," 6 Review of Network Economics 453 (2007); Robert Adams, Paul Bauer, & Robin Sickles, "Scope and Scale Economies in Federal Reserve Payment Processing," Federal Reserve Bank of Cleveland Working Paper No. 02-13 (November 2002).

24. 12 U.S. Code §§ 342, 461, 1813. A limited number of public institutions, including the US Treasury Department, are also expressly permitted to open Fed master accounts.

savings banks, savings and loan associations, and credit unions.[25] As we have seen, these master accounts enable banks to make payments to each other using the ultimate risk-free settlement asset: central bank reserve balances. Whereas banks can settle their obligations directly on the balance sheet of the Federal Reserve, the rest of us are forced to transact through banks as the gatekeepers of the modern payment system.

In reality, even eligible banks have sometimes encountered obstacles when applying to open a Federal Reserve master account.[26] A recent case in point is the application of TNB USA Inc.[27] TNB—which stands for the narrow bank—is a state-chartered bank created to provide large institutional investors with a safe place to park their money at attractive interest rates. Rather than using deposits to make loans or other investments, TNB's plan was to hold the vast majority of its assets in the form of reserve balances in a Federal Reserve master account. When TNB submitted its application to open a master account in August 2017, these reserve balances were then paying an annualized interest rate of 1.25 percent—far higher than the rate that conventional banks were paying their retail and commercial depositors.[28] It was at this point that the Federal Reserve Bank of New York (FRBNY) threw a wrench into TNB's plan. After waiting more than six months, the FRBNY informed TNB that it had "policy concerns" about its application.[29] In August 2018, TNB then filed a complaint in the Southern District of New York seeking declaratory judgment and injunctive relief requiring the

25. See Federal Reserve Board, "Federal Reserve Banks Operating Circular 1: Account Relationships" (2013), https://www.frbservices.org/assets/resources/rules-regulations/020113 -operating-circular-1.pdf, and "Guidelines for Evaluating Account and Service Requests" (August 15, 2022), https://www.federalreserve.gov/newsevents/pressreleases/files/other20220815a1.pdf.

26. There is something of a debate among legal scholars regarding the ability of the Fed to deny an application made by an eligible institution. For a flavor of this evolving debate, see Julie Hill, "From Cannabis to Crypto: Federal Reserve Discretion in Payments," 109 Iowa Law Review 117 (2023) and "Bank Access to Federal Reserve Accounts and Payment Systems," Yale Journal on Regulation (forthcoming) (arguing that the Fed retains discretion to reject an application by a legally eligible institution); Peter Conti-Brown, "The Fed Wants to Veto State Banking Authorities—but Is That Legal?," Brookings Center on Regulation on Markets (November 14, 2018) (arguing that the Fed does not have the legal authority to deny an application from an otherwise eligible institution).

27. See TNB, "About Us," https://www.tnbusa.com/about/.

28. Federal Reserve Bank of St. Louis, Interest Rate on Required Reserves (IORR), (July 28, 2021), https://fred.stlouisfed.org/series/IORR, and Interest Rate on Excess Reserves (IOER), (July 28, 2021), https://fred.stlouisfed.org/series/IOER.

29. Complaint, *TNB USA Inc. v. Federal Reserve Bank of New York*, Case 1:18-cv-07978 (S.D.N.Y.), *3 (filed August 31, 2018).

FRBNY to open a master account in TNB's name.[30] This complaint was subsequently dismissed on standing and ripeness grounds in March 2020.[31] More than six years after submitting its initial application, TNB's application was finally rejected in December 2023.

An even more timely and controversial case involves the recently launched crypto bank Custodia. Custodia is a Wyoming-chartered special purpose depository institution (SPDI), a species of "narrow bank" prohibited by law from making loans or other long-term investments.[32] Custodia was created to serve as a bridge between digital assets like BTC and the conventional US dollar payment system—an interoperable node standing between two otherwise technologically incompatible networks. Like TNB, this makes access to a Federal Reserve master account vital to Custodia's business model. Custodia submitted an application to the Federal Reserve Bank of Kansas City in October 2020, completing the standard one-page form that states that applicants should receive a decision within five to seven business days.[33] Almost six hundred business days later, Custodia sued the Federal Reserve Board, along with the Kansas City Fed, arguing that they had engaged in a "patently unlawful delay" in processing its application.[34]

One of the things Custodia alleged in its lawsuit is that the Fed's process for making decisions about whether to grant master account applications is extremely opaque.[35] In an attempt to head off this criticism, the Federal Reserve Board has recently published guidance regarding the factors that regional reserve banks use to evaluate applications from eligible banks.[36] These guidelines divide banks into three tiers: federally chartered insured depository institutions (tier 1), state-chartered institutions subject to prudential supervision at the federal level (tier 2), and state-chartered institutions not subject to federal oversight (tier 3).[37] These tiers are then used to determine the level of scrutiny that the relevant regional Federal Reserve bank will apply in evaluating an application, with tier 1 institutions subject

---

30. Complaint, *TNB USA v. Federal Reserve of New York.*

31. *TNB USA Inc. v. Federal Reserve Bank of New York,* 2020 WL 1445806 (S.D.N.Y.), *10 (March 25, 2020).

32. Wyoming Special Purpose Depository Institutions Act, Wyo. Stat. § 13-12-101 et seq.

33. Complaint, *Custodia Bank, Inc. v. Federal Reserve Board of Governors and the Federal Reserve Bank of Kansas City,* Case 1:22-cv-00125-SWS (filed June 7, 2022).

34. Complaint, *Custodia Bank, Inc. v. Federal Reserve Board.* The case was dismissed in early 2024 and is being appealed by Custodia.

35. Complaint, 1.

36. Federal Reserve Board, "Guidelines for Evaluating Account and Service Requests."

37. Federal Reserve Board, "Guidelines," Section 2.

to the lightest review and tier 3 institutions the most stringent. In processing an application, regional reserve banks must then take into consideration factors such as the credit, operational, settlement, and cyber risks associated with a given institution, and the impact of these risks on the Fed, the payment system, the stability of the US financial system, and the broader economy.[38] A regional reserve bank can also deny an application if granting it would adversely affect the Fed's ability to implement monetary policy.[39] In a very narrow sense, these new guidelines have introduced an unprecedented level of transparency into the application process. Yet from the perspective of novel tier 3 institutions, like TNB and Custodia, the clearest message the Fed is sending is that it retains enormous discretion to deny master account applications from otherwise legally eligible institutions that, nevertheless, simply do not fit neatly into the mold of conventional deposit-taking banks.[40]

The Fed's conservative approach toward granting master account applications becomes even more critical once we expand our frame to encompass the central operational role that these accounts play within the US payment system. As described in chapter 1, the operational frameworks of each of the six major US clearing networks contemplate final settlement of all net payments through Federal Reserve master accounts. In the case of Fedwire, CHIPS, FedACH, EPN, and FedNow, these net payments settle on the master accounts of individual member banks.[41] In the case of RTP, net payments settle within a single master account held jointly for the benefit of the network's member banks.[42] Given this central operational role, a Federal Reserve master account is understandably a threshold condition for membership in each of these six clearing networks. The Rules and Administrative Procedures governing CHIPS, for example, restrict direct participation

38. Federal Reserve, Section 3.

39. Federal Reserve, Section 3.

40. This is not to suggest that the Fed does not have potentially valid reasons for denying both the TNB and Custodia applications. In the case of TNB, the Fed's principal policy concerns likely revolved around monetary policy implementation. In the case of Custodia, there are legitimate concerns about the ability to apply anti-money-laundering laws within decentralized payment networks.

41. See, e.g., The Clearing House, CHIPS Rules and Administrative Procedures 16–23 (2020), https://www.theclearinghouse.org/-/media/new/tch/documents/payment-systems/chips_rules _and_ administrative_procedures_2020_effective_04-01-2020.pdf. Typically, the clearing network itself will also have a (pre-funded) master account for the purpose of making (receiving) payments to (from) member banks.

42. The Clearing House, RTP System Operating Rules 7 (2020) (defining Prefunded Balance Account), https://www.theclearinghouse.org/payment-systems/rtp/-/media /86DC139B68A143AD9 CC2FE367E6D2429.ashx.

to depository institutions that "have an account on the books of a Federal Reserve Bank."[43] The Participation Rules for RTP likewise restrict direct participation to depository institutions that have "an account with a Federal Reserve Bank."[44] Together with the narrow eligibility requirements under Section 13(1), along with the Fed's conservative approach toward granting master account applications submitted by novel institutions, the practical effect of these operational requirements is to bar all financial institutions other than banks from direct participation in the US payment system.

In chapter 6, we explore how policymakers in a small number of jurisdictions have already started to experiment with the expansion of access to core financial market infrastructure. For the moment, the key takeaway is simply that, in countries like the United States, current law, regulation, and policy guidance all continue to tightly restrict access to central bank reserve accounts. And because these reserve accounts are a universal threshold condition for full membership in the major clearing networks, the practical effect of these access restrictions is to prevent new financial institutions and platforms from direct participation in the conventional payment system. Clearly, if the ability of these institutions and platforms to compete with banks is a function of their access to the largest payment networks, then the legal frameworks in countries like the United States have their boot firmly planted on one side of the scale.

Plugs and Sockets

Together, strong economies of scale and network effects mean that the largest and most successful networks also tend to be the most efficient. In theory, this can lead to natural monopolies in which the most efficient industry structure is one characterized by a very small number of networks—and perhaps even just one—that supply the entire marketplace.[45] Yet in practice, it is not uncommon to encounter highly fragmented network structures, with multiple technologically incompatible networks providing otherwise substitutable products and services. Take electrical plugs and sockets, for

---

43. The Clearing House, CHIPS Rules and Administrative Procedures, 29. CHIPS rules also contemplate direct access for foreign banks and Edge Act or agreement corporations with an account at a Federal Reserve Bank. While CHIPS rules also contemplate indirect participation, indirect participants must still be depository institutions.

44. The Clearing House, RTP Participation Rules, Rule 1.B (2019), https://www .theclearinghouse.org/payment-systems/rtp//media/3E5DAF36BB29436BAAC61C08D11 48B6F.ashx.

45. See Alfred Kahn, *The Economics of Regulation*, 11 (1988).

example. As every seasoned traveler knows, the plugs and sockets used in the United States are different from those used in the United Kingdom, which are themselves different from those used in Continental Europe and elsewhere. In fact, despite valiant efforts to promote international standardization, there are no less than fifteen different types of plug and socket designs currently in use around the world.[46]

The reasons for this fragmentation vary from network to network. In the case of electrical plugs and sockets, they include the technological path dependency associated with the use of different voltages and the staggered adoption of electrical power networks by different countries over time, and thus at different stages of technological development. For example, as an early adopter, the United States invested heavily in network infrastructure based on the 110-volt power systems developed by Thomas Edison, George Westinghouse, and Nikola Tesla.[47] While many European countries adopted electrical power systems far later, the resulting delay enabled them to capture the efficiency gains associated with the subsequent development of 220-volt systems.[48] Capturing these efficiency gains then required the adoption of technical features that made European plugs and sockets incompatible with those used in the United States.

As these networks became more established, this incompatibility was reinforced by the emergence of differences in domestic industry safety standards, along with the predictable sunk cost, coordination problems, and "battle of the sexes" problems that so often prevent convergence around the most efficient standards.[49] Whatever the combination of underlying reasons, the end result is the erection of technological barriers to network compatibility that make it more costly, and in some cases impossible, for the users of one network to access the products and services available on other networks. Everybody loses—except, of course, the manufacturers of electric power adapters.

Another important reason for entrenched network fragmentation in industries characterized by pronounced economies of scale and network

---

46. See Theordore Kury, "Why Do Different Countries Have Different Electrical Plugs?," *The Conversation* (December 21, 2020), https://theconversation.com/why-do-different-countries-have-different-electric-outlet-plugs-151192.

47. Kury, "Different Countries."

48. Kury, "Different Countries."

49. For a description of these problems in the context of the adoption of international financial standards, see Chris Brummer, "How International Financial Law Works (and How It Doesn't)," 99 Georgetown Law Journal 257 (2011).

effects stems from the powerful incentives of the players that own and control these networks. Almost by definition, developing a successful network demands that these players make significant investments in the design and implementation of technological, operational, and other network infrastructure. Having built this infrastructure and attracted a critical mass of network users, these players understandably want to protect the economic value of these investments. One potentially effective strategy for doing so is the introduction of technological features that are specifically designed to limit compatibility with rival products and networks.[50] Thus, for example, an incumbent electric vehicle maker like Tesla can invest in a large network of charging stations that include features—like unique plugs and sockets—that prevent the owners of other vehicle brands from using them.[51] Similarly, Apple, the designer of the highly popular iPod, was alleged to have introduced software updates that prevented the device from playing music files downloaded from competing digital media players.[52] Especially where these incumbent players already enjoy a dominant market position, this strategy can be used to construct a "competitive moat" around their products and services, thereby protecting the economic value of their previous investments in network infrastructure and reinforcing the advantages of incumbency.

Importantly, this strategy can often be embedded in what might otherwise seem like benign and highly technical decisions about network design. The narrow and relatively slow adoption of application programming interfaces (APIs) in the world of banking and payments offers an illustrative case in point. At its most basic level, an API represents a structured data sharing protocol: a set of common data standards, messaging formats, rules, and procedures that enable the information systems of network participants to communicate and share information with one another.[53]

---

50. For detailed antitrust analysis around these types of product design decisions, see, e.g., Phillip Areeda & Herbert Hovenkamp, *Antitrust Law: An Analysis of Antitrust Principles and Their Application*, ¶ 776a (2017); Thibault Schrepel, "Predatory Innovation: The Definite Need for Legal Recognition," 21 SMU Science & Technology Law Review 19 (2017); John Newman, "Anticompetitive Product Design in the New Economy," 39 Florida State University Law Review 681 (2012).

51. See Shannon Osaka, "Elon Musk Agrees to Open Parts of Tesla's Charging Network to Everyone," *Washington Post* (February 15, 2023), https://www.washingtonpost.com/climate-environment/2023/02/15/tesla-supercharger-network-locked/.

52. See Apple iPod iTunes Antitrust Litigation, 796 F. Supp. 2d 1137 (N.D. Cal 2011).

53. See Daniel Jacobson, Greg Brail, & Dan Woods, *APIs: A Strategy Guide* (2012) (describing APIs as "a way for two computer applications to talk to each other over a network using a common language that they both understand").

In effect, APIs are the language, grammar, and syntax that enable information systems to describe the kind of data that can be requested and retrieved, how to request and retrieve it, and the format in which this data will be provided to the recipient. By specifying these inputs and outputs ex ante and enshrining them in executable computer code, APIs can thus facilitate the rapid and automated transfer of an enormous volume of information between participants across a very large network. In theory, this makes APIs an extremely useful tool for the banks and clearinghouses responsible for processing millions of payments, representing trillions of dollars, each and every business day.

Historically, virtually all bank-based electronic payment systems have been classic "hub-and-spoke" networks. These networks are characterized by the fact that the information systems of each bank are indirectly connected to those of other banks by a centralized, and typically proprietary, electronic interface developed and maintained by the relevant clearinghouse (see figure 3.1). In physical terms, the structure of these networks is perhaps best exemplified by the existence of central nodes or junctions like the Culpeper switch—a high-security facility in rural Virginia that was once home to Fedwire and the Federal Reserve's communications and records center.[54] Within these networks, a bank that wants to initiate a transaction must send an electronic payment message in the prescribed format to the relevant interface via a secure, and often dedicated, network connection. The clearinghouse that manages this interface must then authenticate the payment message, check its formatting and syntax and, if everything is correct, route the message into an automated queue for processing. Once the payment has been successfully processed, the clearinghouse then sends a confirmation to both the sending and recipient banks via the same network connection.

At least initially, this highly centralized network structure was largely dictated by prevailing technological limitations. Until relatively recently, the information systems of banks needed to be housed in computer servers connected to each other via telegraphic, ethernet, or fiber optic cables. Building, maintaining, and upgrading this physical infrastructure made connecting to a single, centralized interface like the Culpeper Switch far more cost-effective than directly connecting each bank in the network. Simultaneously, the limits of early computer processing power imposed a natural constraint on the speed with which payments could be processed.

54. See Federal Reserve System, *The Culpeper Switch* (1975).

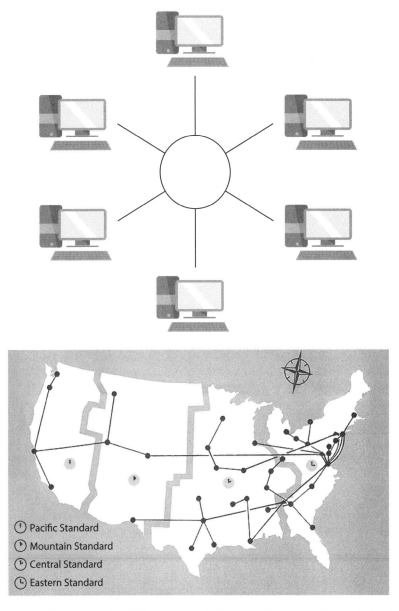

FIGURE 3.1. Two Centralized "Hub-and-Spoke" Payment Networks. *Source*: Federal Reserve System.

The resulting delays exposed banks to credit risk, which made mechanisms like multilateral netting, loss mutualization, and the coordinated unwinding of failed transactions under the auspices of a clearinghouse more attractive to network participants.

Yet these highly centralized payment networks also have potentially significant shortcomings. To begin with, centralization increases the probability and impact of widespread network failure. Reflecting this risk, the Culpeper Switch not only had its own security force but was actually built to withstand a nuclear attack. Centralization can also increase the risk of network congestion as the volume of payments increases over time. But most importantly for our purposes, centralization makes it relatively easy for the owners of a clearinghouse—typically member banks—to tightly control who has access to the network and on what terms.

The internet changed everything—and yet also very little. In theory, the development and widespread adoption of the internet dramatically expanded the universe of ways in which these interfaces could be designed, thus paving the way for modern web-based APIs. There are essentially three types of APIs: closed, partner, and open. Whereas *closed APIs* are designed to eliminate internal information silos within a single firm, *partner APIs* enable the creation of closed networks that facilitate information sharing across multiple firms.[55] Both closed and partner APIs were in widespread use prior to the development of the internet, including by many larger banks and clearinghouses. It was the prospect of developing open—web-based—APIs that was the real game changer. Unlike closed and partner APIs, *open APIs* are based on publicly available protocols that technically enable anyone to look them up, follow the relevant instructions, and thereby obtain access to and share information within a given network.[56] These protocols allow network participants to access and share information directly with each other, without this information flowing through a centralized hub (see figure 3.2). Viewed from this perspective, the key feature of open APIs is that they allow prospective new entrants to simply "plug and play," thus wresting control over network access from a centralized institution controlled by incumbent players.

The development of modern web-based APIs has revolutionized a wide range of industries: from manufacturing, to retail sales, to advertising, media,

55. See Basel Committee on Banking Supervision, "Report on Open Banking and Application Programming Interfaces," 19 (November 2019) (defining a partner API as "an API created with one or two strategic partners who will create applications, add-ons, or integrations with the API").

56. Basel Committee on Banking Supervision, "Report on Open Banking," 19 (defining an open API as "an interface that provides a means of accessing data based on a public standard").

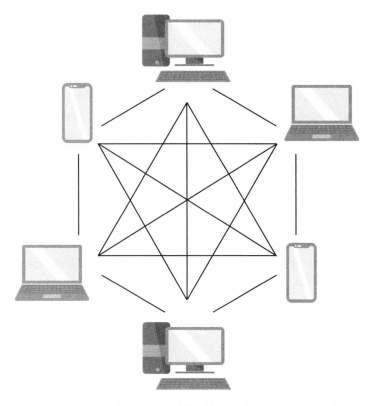

FIGURE 3.2. A Fully Connected "Web"-Based Payment Network

and entertainment. Yet one industry where open APIs hold out enormous promise, but where API development and adoption remain at stubbornly low levels, is conventional banking and payments. This is particularly true in the United States. More than twenty years after the emergence of the first commercial web-based APIs, a 2022 survey of US banks revealed that more than half had yet to make *any* investments in API development, adoption, or use whatsoever.[57] Indeed, even in 2023, in the wake of the pronounced shift toward digital banking triggered by the COVID-19 pandemic, *American Banker* reported that most banks were putting investments in API development and integration "on the back burner."[58] While bank-owned clearing-houses have arguably been somewhat more proactive, they have also—and

57. See "APIs to Drive Banking-as-a-Service Growth in 2022," pymnts.com (February 8, 2022), https://www.pymnts.com/api/2022/apis-to-drive-banking-as-a-service-growth-in-2022/.

58. Michael Moeser, "Is Your Tech Agenda Set for Safety or Standout Growth?," *American Banker* (February 27, 2023).

predictably—invested primarily in the development of partner, rather than open, APIs.

As with electrical power systems, at least part of the reason for the glacial pace of API development and adoption reflects the path dependency and high switching costs associated with earlier rounds of technological investment, innovation, and integration. This is especially the case for many larger banks that have grown through mergers and acquisitions, which have often been forced to grapple with the enormous complexity and costs of managing a patchwork of legacy information systems.[59] Conversely, many smaller but well-established community banks simply do not have the financial, operational, or human resources needed to migrate their antiquated information systems to new, internet-compatible platforms.[60] Yet it is hard to deny that the industry's collective decision not to invest in APIs serves to protect its privileged access to core financial market infrastructure, thereby insulating it from the threat of competition from aspiring new entrants eager to use this very technology to disrupt the markets for banking, money, and payments.

This analysis yields two key insights. First, even in the presence of strong economies of scale and network effects, the players that control incumbent payment networks often have powerful incentives to restrict network access in order to forestall the emergence of new and potentially more efficient competitors. This can result in inefficient network fragmentation. Second, the governance and highly centralized structure of incumbent payment networks often put these players in a unique position to make decisions about the direction and pace of technological innovation—the choice between different plugs and sockets. These decisions can have a significant impact on network access, interoperability and, ultimately, competition. Where these dynamics are combined with legal restrictions on network access, the almost inevitable result is to hand incumbent players the keys to the network, along with a permit to dig a deep and potentially unassailable competitive moat.

---

59. For example, it was recently revealed that Citigroup has been forced to allocate more than 30,000 staff members to addressing IT integration issues; see David Benoit, "Federal Reserve Wants Citigroup to Move Faster to Fix Problems with Its Risk Systems," *Wall Street Journal* (September 15, 2022).

60. As one chief financial officer of a community bank put it, "The challenge with legacy [technology] cores is that so many are written in ancient language that makes them hard to change and lengthens the timelines to innovate"; Miriam Cross, "Community Banks Find Right Fit with Smaller Core Providers," *American Banker* (August 17, 2022).

The Impact on Competition

Despite the seemingly relentless pace of financial and technological innovation, it is hard to deny that many parts of the financial services industry have long suffered from a serious competition problem. This problem is illuminated by empirical evidence that suggests that the efficiency of the financial services industry in many developed countries has almost completely stagnated over the past century.[61] Economist Thomas Philippon, for example, has measured the efficiency of the US financial services industry by comparing the total stock of assets held by financial institutions against the spreads, charges, and other fee income generated on these assets. Strikingly, Philippon finds that the resulting intermediation ratio—effectively comparing the scale of the financial services industry with the costs of using its products and services—has remained relatively constant over the past 130 years, at between 1.5 and 2 percent.[62] Employing essentially the same methodology, Guillaume Bazot has found a similar torpor in the United Kingdom, Germany, and France.[63]

These and other findings point to a stark and counterintuitive conclusion. They suggest that the financial services industries in some of the world's largest and most dynamic economies failed to generate any tangible efficiency gains over the course of a century that saw the invention of the computer, fiber optic telephony, and communications satellites, as well as dramatic advances in data storage and processing power and the emergence and widespread adoption of the internet, social media platforms, and smartphones.[64]

61. For empirical research exploring the potential existence, nature, and extent of this competition problem, see, e.g., Patrick Bolton, Tano Santos, & Jose Scheinkman, "Cream Skimming in Financial Markets," 71:2 Journal of Finance 709 (2016); Nicola Gennaioli, Andrei Shleifer, & Robert Vishny, "Money Doctors," 70:1 Journal of Finance 91 (2015); Robin Greenwood & David Scharfstein, "The Growth of Modern Finance," 27:2 Journal of Economic Perspectives 3 (2013).

62. Philippon, "Has the U.S. Finance Industry Become Less Efficient? On the Theory and Measurement of Financial Intermediation," 105:4 American Economic Review 1408 (2015), and "The Fintech Opportunity," National Bureau of Economic Research Working Paper No. 22476 (August 2016), http://www.nber.org/papers/w22476.

63. Bazot, "Financial Consumption and the Cost of Finance: Measuring Financial Efficiency in Europe (1950–2007)," 16:1 Journal of the European Economic Association 123 (2018).

64. Consistent with these findings, there is also empirical and anecdotal evidence pointing to a lack of competition within specific segments of the financial services industry, including banking, payments, and even the burgeoning fintech market; see, e.g., Carin van der Cruijsen & Maaike Diepstraten, "Banking Products: You Can Take Them with You, So Why Don't You?," 52 Journal of Financial Services Research 123 (2017); Lawrence Ausubel, "The Failure of Competition in the Credit Card Market," 81 American Economic Review 50 (1991); Victor Stango, "Pricing with Consumer Switching Costs: Evidence from the Credit Card Market," 50 Journal

Perhaps most importantly, they suggest that the seemingly endless parade of technological advances over this period did nothing to drive down the costs that consumers pay for financial products and services.[65] As Philippon observes, "Financial services remain expensive and financial innovations have not delivered significant benefits to consumers. The point is not that finance does not innovate. It does. But these innovations have not improved the overall efficiency of the system."[66]

The dynamics of competition within the financial services industry vary from country to country. They also vary across different markets. As we have already seen, the competitive distortions in the markets for money and payments stem from two principal sources—both grounded in law and regulation. The first is the exquisitely tailored straitjacket of conventional bank regulation and supervision, together with the unique legal privileges and protections afforded by the financial safety net. The second is the pronounced bottleneck problem created by the fact that banks are often the only firms that enjoy direct access to the vital network infrastructure used to send, receive, and process electronic payment instructions (clearinghouses) and to settle the corresponding payments (central bank reserve accounts). Together, these legally entrenched privileges erect extremely high barriers to entry, giving banks a huge comparative advantage in the delivery of both good money and good payments.

Measuring the real-world impact of these competitive distortions is extremely difficult. Among a host of empirical, methodological, and other challenges, it requires us to construct a counterfactual world in which new entrants compete with incumbent banks on a level legal playing field. Beyond the law, there are also a wide range of other factors at play, including the path dependence, pronounced economies of scale, and network effects stemming from the tight institutional bundling of banking, money, and payments. Nevertheless, there are a variety of ways that we can attempt to gain a better understanding of the true nature and scale of the problem—at least on a relative basis.

---

of Industrial Economics 475 (2002); Rory Van Loo, "Making Innovation More Competitive," 65 UCLA Law Review 232 (2018).

65. Of course, these costs need to be adjusted to reflect improvements in the quality of financial products and services over this same period. Yet this begs a series of other questions: Where do these improvements come from? Who controls the direction and pace of the technological innovation that yields them? Are these improvements available to everyone or only to a privileged group of financial institutions and consumers? Ultimately, the answers are highly salient to understanding the dynamics of competition within the financial services industry.

66. Philippon, "Fintech Opportunity," 9.

The first involves looking at the *fees* people and businesses pay for basic payment services in different countries. As of 2022, the average interchange fee paid by a US merchant in connection with a $40 debit card transaction at a bricks-and-mortar retail store was somewhere between twenty-two and fifty cents. Yet the same transaction in the EU, United Kingdom, Norway, or Australia would be under ten cents—more than 50 percent lower than the cheapest US payment option. In fact, US merchants currently pay higher interchange fees than their counterparts in countries like Malaysia, South Africa, Serbia, Belarus, and Bosnia and Herzegovina.[67] While fee regulation in the EU and elsewhere helps explain some of this difference, it is striking that US businesses and consumers pay so much more for their payments.

A second way to measure these competitive distortions is by looking at the speed of *technological development and adoption*. Once again, the United States provides an illuminating, if unflattering, basis for comparison. Over the past several decades, the US banking industry has been relatively slow to roll out a variety of new payment technologies: including the development and application of APIs,[68] mobile banking,[69] EMV security chips,[70] contactless payments,[71] and real-time settlement.[72] Although their use has declined significantly in recent years, the United States is also the only developed country in the world that still relies heavily on costly, inconvenient,

---

67. Fumiko Hayashi & Sam Baird, "Credit and Debit Card Interchange Fees in Various Countries," Federal Reserve Bank of Kansas City 5 (August 2022).

68. Susan Pandy, "Developments in Open Banking and APIs: Where Does the U.S. Stand?," Federal Reserve Bank of Boston Brief, 2–4 (March 17, 2020) (describing the status of open banking initiatives in the US relative to Singapore, Hong Kong, China, Japan, Australia, and New Zealand).

69. Compare FDIC, "How America Banks: Household Use of Banking and Financial Services," 4 (2019) (reporting that 34 percent of survey respondents in the US use mobile banking), with Statista, "Online Banking Penetration in Great Britain from 2007 to 2020" (August 2020), (reporting that 73 percent of households in the UK use mobile banking); as of 2019.

70. See Kathleen Elkins, "Why It Took the US So Long to Adopt the Credit Card Technology Europe Has Used for Years," *Business Insider* (September 27, 2015).

71. See "Is the US on the Verge of a Contactless Surge?," pymnts.com (June 6, 2019) (noting that the US has lagged behind other developed countries in the adoption of contactless payments).

72. See US Department of the Treasury, "*A Financial System That Creates Economic Opportunities: Nonbank Financials, Fintech, and Innovation*," 156 (2018) ("Many jurisdictions around the world have embarked on initiatives to increase the speed of payments. In many cases, the progress towards faster payments abroad has outpaced progress in the United States"); Morten Bech, Yuuki Shimizu, & Paul Wong, "The Quest for Speed in Payments," in Bank for International Settlements (ed.), *BIS Quarterly Review: International Banking and Financial Market Developments*, 57, 59–60 (2017) (describing country-level developments in real-time payment systems, notably excluding any mention of the US).

unsecure, and environmentally harmful paper checks.[73] Viewed from this perspective, the problem is not that new and better payment technologies do not presently exist. Indeed, in many cases, American financial institutions and technology firms have played an important role in their development.[74] Rather, the problem is that American banks have been relatively slow to invest in the adoption of these new technologies. Accordingly, while the United States is often held up as a global leader in both finance and technology, the benefits of this leadership have not always been immediately or fully shared with the customers of US banks.

Lastly, we can attempt to measure these problems using the benchmark of *financial inclusion*. While the United States has undoubtedly made significant strides in recent years, the stark reality is that many American households still do not have access to a basic bank account. The FDIC's most recent survey on household use of banking and financial services estimates that over 5 percent of all households—7.1 million in all—did not have any members with an active checking or savings account.[75] The rates of these "unbanked" households were even higher for lower-income households, households with lower levels of educational attainment, and households including African Americans, Hispanics, Native Americans, and people with disabilities.[76] Of the unbanked households that took part in the survey, over 34 percent identified high fees as one of the reasons for not having a bank account, almost 20 percent identified a lack of products and services that met their needs, and almost half identified insufficient funds to meet minimum balance requirements imposed by banks.[77] Asked what their principal reason was for not having a bank account, 29 percent responded that they were not able to meet minimum balance requirements, 7.3 percent said high fees, and just under 2 percent said that banks did not offer the right products and services.[78] For these households, the inability to access a basic bank account almost inevitably translates into a decidedly limited range of relatively expensive options for making and receiving payments.

73. See Katie Robertson, "Why Can't Americans Ditch Checks?," *Bloomberg Business* (July 26, 2017).

74. EMV security chips, for example, were first developed by US-based Visa and Mastercard, together with the European company Europay (hence the acronym EMV—Europay, Mastercard, Visa). See Robin Saks Frankel, "When Were Credit Cards Invented: The History of Credit Cards," *Forbes* (July 27, 2021).

75. FDIC, "How America Banks," 1 (2019).

76. FDIC, 46.

77. FDIC, 3.

78. FDIC, 3.

While these statistics are part of a far larger and more complex set of economic and social problems, they are also consistent with the observation that the markets for money and payments in the US have not been subject to the type of vigorous competition that might have otherwise driven banks to reduce interchange and other fees, harness efficiency-enhancing technologies, or offer new and better products and services to the broadest possible range of potential customers. At the very least, it suggests that a little more competition from outside the conventional banking industry might yield some meaningful progress toward these important objectives.

The Bigger Picture

The impact of the financial safety net, bank regulation and supervision, and access restrictions on competition should not be underestimated. But evaluating the full impact of these competitive distortions demands that we also explore the risks they pose for customer protection, for microprudential safety and soundness, and ultimately for the stability of the financial system.

To understand these bigger-picture problems, we first need to understand in more detail the stark and unpalatable choices that new institutions and platforms looking to offer money and payments currently face. The first option is to make the substantial technological, operational, and other investments needed to build their own stand-alone financial market infrastructure. In theory, building this infrastructure from scratch enables them to leverage any technological superiority to compete with incumbent banks and payment networks on the basis of cost, speed, security, convenience, and other payment features. Yet in practice, it also demands that they somehow overcome the pronounced path dependency, economies of scale, and network effects enjoyed by incumbent networks. And even where these aspiring new entrants can effectively compete with incumbents in the delivery of good payments, they still find themselves at an obvious disadvantage insofar as their monetary IOUs would not benefit from the unique privileges and protections of the financial safety net.

The second option is for these institutions and platforms to slip on the exquisitely tailored straitjacket of conventional bank regulation. Yet, while obtaining a bank charter would help transform their monetary IOUs into good money, the initial and ongoing compliance costs would often be prohibitive—especially for many smaller, technology-driven firms. Making this option even less attractive, many of these costs would be essentially unnecessary insofar as their business models did not envision significant levels of financial intermediation. In the United States, there would also be the risk that institutions and platforms seeking to pursue novel business models or technologies would—like TNB and Custodia—be denied access to a Federal Reserve master account, thereby depriving them of one of the most important privileges of membership.

The third option is to do what everyone else does when they need access to the modern payment system: open a bank account. This option—effectively a form of correspondent banking—has the obvious and immediate advantage of giving these institutions and platforms indirect access to major clearing networks, thereby expanding their reach to the broadest possible universe of potential customers. Yet the resulting bottleneck problem also serves to compound existing competitive distortions. As a preliminary matter, this option makes these institutions and platforms extremely reliant on their principal competitors for access to the financial market infrastructure they need to provide basic payment services to their customers. Correspondent banks can then use their position as legally entrenched gatekeepers to extract valuable insights about their competitors' payment volumes, growth rates, and other strategic information—all of which can be used to gain a competitive edge.[79] Importantly, they can also use this position as leverage to set prices and other terms in ways designed to limit a competitor's profitability, growth potential, and returns from scale.[80] In many cases, the logical solution to this holdup problem is for banks to acquire these new entrants—thus effectively eliminating a potentially promising source of competition.[81]

Over the longer term, none of these three options bodes well for either competition or the trajectory and pace of technological innovation. Where these new institutions and platforms decide to obtain a bank charter, this will frequently amount to forcing square pegs into round holes—erecting unnecessary barriers to experimentation with new and potentially more efficient business models and technologies. Conversely, where a large number of new entrants simultaneously clamor to create payment infrastructure outside the conventional banking system, the resulting network fragmentation can lead to overinvestment and the failure of novel and potentially more

79. Conversely, banks can block or limit a new entrant's access to valuable customer data; see Van Loo, "Making Innovation More Competitive," 242–43.

80. See Oliver Williamson, "Transaction-Cost Economics: The Governance of Contractual Relations," 22(2) Journal of Law and Economics 233 (1979) (describing holdup problems).

81. For an example of this type of "buy to kill" strategy in the tech context, see generally Lina Khan, "Amazon's Antitrust Paradox," 126 Yale Law Journal 710 (2017); Colleen Cunningham, Florian Ederer, & Song Ma, "Killer Acquisitions," 129 Journal of Political Economy 649 (2021).

efficient institutions and platforms to attract a critical mass of new customers. Finally, where new entrants partner with banks, we would expect these banks to work cooperatively with them right up to the point at which their own business models come under threat.

At present, the question of whether these new entrants might have more attractive options depends entirely on the perimeter of domestic regulatory frameworks. As described in chapter 6, several jurisdictions have already embarked on the creation of bespoke regulatory frameworks tailored to their specific business models, technologies, and risks. In many cases, these frameworks contemplate some type of access to central bank reserve accounts and other financial market infrastructure. While these frameworks are often far from perfect, they at least offer potential new entrants an option that does not compound the significant competitive disadvantages they already face. This stands in stark contrast with jurisdictions like the United States, where federal policymakers have yet to either carve out any clear regulatory space for these new institutions and platforms or systematically update the antiquated and inadequate regulatory frameworks that currently govern them.

It is here that we encounter three intertwined problems. The first problem stems from the prospect of regulatory arbitrage and the resulting impact on *consumer protection*. Faced with a decidedly limited range of options, new institutions and platforms have rationally sought shelter in the regulatory frameworks that impose the least onerous licensing requirements, the fewest restrictions on their activities, and the lowest compliance costs. In the United States, the regulatory frameworks of choice have been a collection of highly fragmented and heterogeneous state laws that were first introduced in the 1930s to regulate telegraphic wire transfer services, such as Western Union. As described in greater detail in chapter 6, these state money transmitter licenses often permit these institutions and platforms to invest in a wide range of risky investments—everything from publicly traded stocks and bonds to mortgage-backed securities and opaque and illiquid intragroup debt.

In theory, customers holding the monetary IOUs issued by these institutions and platforms are not directly exposed to any volatility in the price of these assets. In practice, however, they are exposed to the corresponding risk that this volatility could generate losses sufficient to push these institutions and platforms into bankruptcy. Amplifying this risk, the ability to combine the issuance of monetary liabilities with investments in a diverse range of risky assets only heightens their vulnerability to destabilizing customer runs. Once in bankruptcy, customers almost inevitably find themselves exposed to the destructive application of the automatic stay and the pari passu rule (see chapter 5). By exploiting antiquated and inadequate state laws, these new entrants have thus become a significant and growing source of bad money.

The second problem reflects the risks to *microprudential safety and soundness* created when these new institutions and platforms are forced to use correspondent banking relationships to gain indirect access to basic financial market infrastructure. Importantly, these relationships often mean that platforms like PayPal, Venmo, and Circle deposit a large fraction of their customers' funds with a small handful of major banks. Equally important, the large size of these deposits means that they are typically uninsured.[82] The result is an intricate intertwining of balance sheets, with banks issuing monetary IOUs to these companies and the companies issuing monetary IOUs to their customers. This intertwining creates two distinct risks. The first—*downstream*—risk materializes when the failure of the correspondent bank imposes losses on platforms and institutions that then jeopardize their own ability to honor their obligations to customers. The second—*upstream*—risk materializes when large customer withdrawals force these institutions and platforms to make large and potentially destabilizing withdrawals from their correspondent banks. Indeed, under pressure, we might expect these institutions and platforms to withdraw money from their correspondent bank *first*; i.e., before selling risky and more profitable investments. In theory, these large and lumpy withdrawals could then spark doubts about the bank's own liquidity and solvency, thus potentially triggering a run on the bank itself.

The third and final problem is *macroprudential instability*. Specifically, by hardwiring the role of banks at the heart of our monetary and financial systems, the financial safety net and restrictions on infrastructure access exacerbate the too-big-to-fail problem. As described by the FSB, the global oversight body for macroprudential risk, the too-big-to-fail problem reflects the widespread view that some banks—due to their size, complexity, interconnectedness, geographic footprint, or lack of available substitutes—are too important to the financial system and real economy

---

82. While these platforms can theoretically obtain pass-through deposit insurance by holding customer funds in a "for-benefit-of" (or FBO) account, the compliance and other costs associated with this option typically make it unattractive. And even where it exists, this pass-through deposit insurance would only protect customers from the failure of the bank, not the bankruptcy of the relevant platform itself.

to simply let fail.[83] Not surprisingly, these are the same banks for which conventional resolution strategies like P&A are likely to be the least effective. This raises the prospect that policymakers would be compelled to use public funds to bail out these banks in the thick of a crisis rather than face the potential consequences.[84]

Ultimately, the too-big-to-fail problem is a product of our reliance on banks as critical sources of financing, money, and payments.[85] This reliance is an important part of the rationale for the financial safety net. Yet it also creates the widespread expectation that these banks will receive extraordinary state support above and beyond the financial safety net. This expectation can be observed empirically in the form of lower financing costs for banks that are viewed as protected by this second, implicit, and more controversial public backstop.[86] In effect, if the creditors of these banks expect the government to bail them out whenever they get into trouble, the corresponding reduction in credit risk should mean that they will be willing to lend money to these banks at lower interest rates. Viewed in this light, the too-big-to-fail problem is yet another source of competitive distortions: giving the banks that benefit from it access to an important resource—capital—at a lower price than their smaller, more simple, and less interconnected competitors.

As reflected in the FSB's description, one of the root causes of the too-big-to-fail problem is a lack of *substitutability*.[87] Put simply, where a socially useful financial product (such as money) or service (such as payments) is only offered by a relatively small number or single type of financial institution, the failure of these institutions introduces the risk that the supply of these products or services may not meet existing demand from people,

---

83. Financial Stability Board, "Evaluation of Too Big to Fail Reforms," ¶ 2 (May 23, 2019), https://www.fsb.org/wp-content/uploads/P230519.pdf.

84. See Ben Bernanke, "Statement before the Financial Crisis Inquiry Commission," 20 (September 2, 2010), http://www.federalreserve.gov/newsevents/testimony/bernanke20100902a.

85. See generally Lee Davison, "Continental Illinois and 'Too Big to Fail,'" in FDIC (ed.), *History of the Eighties—Lessons for the Future: An Examination of the Banking Crises of the 1980s and Early 1990s*, 235 (1997) (describing the origins of the term *too big to fail*).

86. For recent empirical work documenting this phenomenon, see generally Viral Acharya, Deniz Anginer, & Joseph Warburton, "The End of Market Discipline?: Investor Expectations of Implicit Government Guarantees" (May 1, 2016) (unpublished), https://papers.ssrn.com/sol3/papers.cfm?abstract_id=1961656; Priyank Gandhi & Hanno Lustig, "Size Anomalies in U.S. Bank Stock Returns," 70 Journal of Finance 733 (2015).

87. The importance of substitutability is also reflected in the Basel III capital rules, where it represents one of the key variables for identifying and calculating the capital surcharge for systemically important banks.

businesses, and governments. This lack of substitutability can have devastating economic effects. Perhaps most famously, the widespread bank failures at the height of the Great Depression led to severe contractions in the US money supply, commercial lending, and other financial services.[88] Ultimately, it is the threat of these types of destabilizing contractions that compel policymakers to intervene—using bailouts as an administratively expedient, if politically toxic, strategy for ensuring that the supply of these vital products and services keeps flowing.

Against this backdrop, the financial safety net and restrictions on infrastructure access make it extremely difficult for institutions and platforms other than banks to provide truly substitutable money and payments. This in turn only serves to further entrench our reliance on banks for arguably the two most critical products and services in the entire economy, thereby reinforcing the too-big-to-fail problem.

The Payoff

The financial safety net, bank regulation and supervision, and restrictions on access to basic financial market infrastructure play an important and often unheralded role in protecting our intertwined systems of money and payments. Yet they also give banks unique privileges and protections that cement them at the apex of our financial system—too often making them the only game in town. These privileges and protections create competitive distortions that can have an enormous impact on the emergence and adoption of new institutions, platforms, and technologies—impeding precisely the type of experimentation that gave birth to the goldsmiths' model. With the emergence of the shadow monetary system, these distortions also pose significant and growing risks to customers, to microprudential safety and soundness, and to the stability of the wider financial system.

Together, these competitive distortions, along with the bigger-picture problems they create, provide us with a useful starting point for evaluating three important questions. First, what role should law and public policy play in promoting greater experimentation, competition, and innovation in the rapidly evolving markets for money and payments? Second, what challenges and trade-offs does this role potentially pose for monetary and

---

88. See Ben Bernanke, "Nonmonetary Effects of the Financial Crisis in the Propagation of the Great Depression," 73 American Economic Review 257 (1983); see generally Milton Friedman & Anna Schwartz, *A Monetary History of the United States 1867–1960*, 299–420 (rev. ed., 1971).

financial stability? And third, are there policy alternatives that strike a better balance between these often competing objectives than the current bundled system of banking, money, and payments? There are effectively two ways to approach these questions. The first is to view the rise of the shadow monetary system and the emergence of Gresham's new law as a problem to be solved and, ideally, eliminated. The second is to acknowledge the attendant challenges and trade-offs, but to view these developments as simultaneously holding out the promise of a safer, more competitive, and more dynamic system of money and payments. To this end, the next chapter chronicles some of the new experiments in money and payments that are already under way.

4

New Experiments in Money and Payments

Payments are a problem rooted in code, not finance.
—STRIPE, INC.

There is a good chance you've never heard of Stripe—but you've almost certainly trusted it to move your money. Founded in 2010 by brothers John and Patrick Collison, Stripe is one of a growing number of firms that, despite their relatively low profile, are fast revolutionizing the world of payments. Yet Stripe is not a bank. In fact, in many ways, it's not even a financial institution. It's a *software* company. Stripe's core product is an application programming interface—an open API—that software developers can simply drop into their own code when building the technological backbone for web-based businesses. This API, and others like it, enable these businesses to do something that, while almost unimaginable only a generation ago, we now almost completely take for granted: sending and receiving payments over the internet. So if you've ever purchased your Christmas presents on Amazon, bought groceries on Instacart, hailed an Uber, or ordered takeout from DoorDash, you already know exactly how critical firms like Stripe are to the modern payment system and economy.

The emergence, success, and expanding footprint of firms like Stripe reflect an important yet often neglected truth: money is *information*.[1] This

---

1. See Joseph Ostroy & Ross Starr, "The Transactions Role of Money," in Benjamin Friedman & Frank Hahn (eds.), *Handbook of Monetary Economics*, 3 (1990) (describing money as a

is especially true of the credit-based money upon which the modern financial system and economy are built. Fundamentally, the Sumerian accounting system, together with the clay and metal tablets, used in ancient Mesopotamia were just a written record of who owed what to whom. The same is true of the vellum and paper ledgers used by early Genoese and Venetian bankers to record the account balances of their wealthy merchant clients. Similarly, today's bank deposits are little more than a digital record of the monetary IOUs that banks have issued to their depositors—a vast collection of ones and zeros stored in thousands of electronic databases, representing the accumulated savings of billions of people and trillions of dollars in financial wealth. While it's a sobering thought, the destruction of these records—and the valuable information they contain—would be tantamount to the destruction of money itself.

If money is information, then payments are the process by which changes in this information are initiated, approved, and recorded for posterity. For much of human history, this process revolved around either physical delivery of a payment instrument or the stroke of a bookkeeper's pen. Yet over the course of the past two centuries, a series of technological advances has radically transformed how we make payments. Many of these advances are built on general-purpose innovations in telecommunications, like the telegraph, telephone, modern computers, fiber optic cables, and, most recently, the internet. These advances include payment-specific hardware, like debit and credit cards, magnetic stripe technology, chip-and-PIN security, near field communications, and the payment dongle.[2] They also include the ongoing development of new APIs and other software that today enable us to make fast, reliable, convenient, and secure payments to almost anyone, almost anywhere in the world. Framed against the background of this broader historical arc, the story of payments is, and always has been, inextricably intertwined with the story of advances in information technology.[3]

---

recordkeeping device); Robert Townsend, "Economic Organization with Limited Communication," 77 American Economic Review 954 (1987) (describing money as a communication device).

    2. For a narrative history of many of these innovations, see Gottfried Leibrandt & Natasha de Teran, *The Payoff: How Changing the Way We Pay Changes Everything* (2021).

    3. Indeed, long before the emergence and widespread adoption of the internet, debates about the impact of technological disruption were a common theme in the economic literature examining payment systems; see, e.g., Morten Bech & Bart Hobjin, "Technology Diffusion within Central Banking: The Case of Real Time Gross Settlement," 3 International Journal of Central Banking 147 (2007); Mark Flannery, "Technology and Payments: Déjà vu All Over Again?," 28:4 Journal of Money, Credit and Banking 965 (1996); Mark Flannery, *The Economic Implications of*

Given the important functions that banks perform at the heart of the conventional payment system, one might assume that they have played a starring role in this story. Indeed, one can imagine an alternate universe in which banks used their privileged legal position and unparalleled financial resources to continuously invest in the development and adoption of new technology and, ultimately, deliver both good money and good payments. Yet, sadly, that is not the universe in which we live. In fact, one of the most remarkable parts of this story is how diverse the wellsprings of payment innovation have been, and how little initial support they received from banks. Before being popularized by Visa, the magnetic stripe technology long used in debit and credit cards was invented by an IBM employee trying to make ID badges for the Central Intelligence Agency.[4] The chip-and-PIN technology that is now replacing magnetic stripes in many parts of the world was invented by Roland Moreno, a French engineer, inventor, journalist, and humorist.[5] And the first APIs that allowed merchants to accept so-called "card not present" payments over the internet were pioneered by technology firms like PayPal, Plaid, and Stripe. While banks have since—and often begrudgingly—incorporated these innovations into their own product offerings, it is telling that banks played little or no role in their initial development.

To some, this observation may seem like an unfair indictment. After all, banks are not technology firms. Nor did the vast majority of bankers train as engineers, computer scientists, or software developers—although that may soon change. But this is precisely the point. For all their legally entrenched comparative advantages in the creation of good money, there is very little reason that we should expect to find banks at the cutting edge of technology-driven businesses like payments. In fact, there are many compelling reasons—from their conservative management, to their enormous scale, to their antiquated patchwork of legacy technology systems—for thinking that incumbent banks may be particularly slow in responding to the opportunities and challenges presented by rapid technological change. Given these comparative *dis*advantages, it should hardly come as a surprise

an Electronic Money Transfer System (1973); "The Giro, the Computer, and Checkless Banking," Federal Reserve Bank of Richmond Monthly Review 2 (April 1966).

4. See Dag Spicer, "Oral History of Jerome Svigals," Computer History Museum (June 19, 2007), http://archive.computerhistory.org/resources/access/text/2012/04/102658148-05-01 -acc.pdf.

5. See Marijke De Soete, "Smart Card," Encyclopedia of Cryptography and Security, 1224 (2011).

that it has generally been firms from outside the regulated banking industry that have pushed the technological frontier in an effort to offer customers cheaper, faster, more secure, more convenient, more interoperable, and more accessible payments.

This chapter shines a spotlight on some of these new experiments in money and payments. It revolves around four case studies, each reflecting a different starting point, employing a different business model, and driven by a different underlying rationale. The first case study encompasses peer-to-peer (P2P) payment platforms like PayPal, Wise, WeChat Pay, and Alipay. These platforms enable people and businesses to send money to each other over the internet, typically without having to provide the intended recipients with sensitive personal information like the sender's name, address, or bank details. The second case study is mobile money. As the name suggests, mobile money platforms piggyback off the existing telecommunications networks owned and operated by mobile phone carriers, thereby providing their customers with access to a basic electronic payment network in countries where both central banks and the conventional banking system have failed to build the necessary infrastructure.

The final two case studies are drawn from the much-hyped, jargon-filled, and increasingly controversial world of so-called digital assets—more commonly known as *crypto*. At present, the blockchain technology at the heart of the crypto ecosystem is largely incompatible with the information systems used by most banks, clearinghouses, and other conventional financial market infrastructure.[6] The resulting need for a technological bridge between these two systems—i.e., for greater interoperability—has helped spur the rise of two new species of financial institutions and platforms. The first species are stablecoin issuers like Tether, Circle's USDC, and Paxos's BUSD. These stablecoins are the de facto currency of the digital realm, enabling people to buy and sell other digital assets like BTC, Ethereum (ETH), and Ripple's XRP. In theory, they might also one day be used for making everyday payments. The second species includes cryptocurrency exchanges like Binance, Coinbase, and Kraken. These exchanges are the supermarkets of the crypto world, offering customers the ability to hold digital assets, trade them in an online marketplace, and use them as collateral for crypto lending and

---

6. Although there are a growing number of initiatives currently under way designed to address these compatibility issues, often contemplating the transition of legacy financial market infrastructure to distributed ledger technology; see, e.g., Ghiath Shabsigh, Tanai Khiaonarong, & Harry Leinonen, "Distributed Ledger Technology Experiments in Payments and Settlements," International Monetary Fund FinTech Notes 20/01 (June 2020).

borrowing. Perhaps not surprisingly, many of these exchanges also issue their own stablecoins. For better or worse, these new institutions and platforms have rapidly risen to become the central hubs of the rapidly evolving crypto ecosystem.

These case studies vary across a number of important dimensions—from the technology underpinning their products and services, to how they make money, to the potential benefits they hold out for consumers. Nevertheless, all of them share three important things in common. First, and most obviously, they all use new technology to solve often age-old payment problems that the conventional banking system has thus far been unable, or unwilling, to tackle. Second, they all operate outside the perimeter of conventional bank regulation and, accordingly, have not historically enjoyed the unique privileges and protections of the financial safety net.

Ultimately, of course, the fact that these new experiments are taking place outside the conventional banking system might not matter very much if the laboratories in which they are conducted are just technology firms that never actually touch people's money. After all, bank regulation and the financial safety net are designed to enhance the credibility of a bank's *monetary IOUs*—promoting good money, not good payments. This takes us to the third and arguably most important thing that each of these case studies share in common. The promise of these new platforms and institutions stems from the development and application of new (and sometimes not so new) technologies in order to deliver cheaper, faster, safer, and more convenient payments. It is only in the process of harnessing this technology to deliver better payments that many of them have also come to issue new and exotic types of monetary IOUs. As we shall see, in several cases, this technology has moved far faster than the laws and institutions that might be used to transform these monetary IOUs into good money. Accordingly, while these institutions and platforms are using code to solve important problems in payments, they are often creating new problems for the safety and stability of our monetary system.

This chapter explores how these new institutions and platforms are delivering on the technological promise of better payments. Chapters 5 and 6 then explore the all-important question of whether they are simultaneously able to issue monetary IOUs that can be viewed as close economic substitutes for conventional bank deposits—IOUs that the public can trust as good money. Together, these three chapters illuminate the core dynamics of Gresham's new law and the growing disconnect between good money and good payments. They also provide important insights into how we might strike a better balance between inherent dangers of Gresham's new law and its tantalizing opportunities.

The Real Magic Internet Money

For almost the entire twentieth century, people and businesses looking to make payments had three basic and often unappealing options. The first was to pay in cash. However, while cash was often convenient for small, local payments, it was highly impractical for large-value payments, along with payments where the payor and payee were separated by time or space. The second option was to pay by check. Checks allowed payors to transfer money to payees at specific, predetermined times; e.g., to pay rent on the first of every month. They were also far less expensive to transport than cash, making them more convenient for long-distance payments. The catch was that payors needed to provide payees with sensitive personal information, like their name, address, and bank account number—all written right there on the face of the check. The third option was for the payor to ask their bank to arrange for a telegraphic wire transfer. Like checks, wire transfers made it relatively easy to send money across long distances. While expensive, they were also typically more secure and faster than other existing forms of payment. Yet wire transfers almost inevitably required payees to provide payment instructions to payors that, once again, included their name, bank details, and other sensitive personal information. Viewed in this light, each of these three options presented consumers with important trade-offs between cost, speed, security, and convenience.

The internet has dramatically expanded the payments universe beyond these three basic options. Perhaps most importantly, it has given birth to a wide variety of P2P payment platforms. These platforms enable customers to open an account, link their bank or credit card details, and then instantly send and receive money over the internet. These payments are processed using APIs that enable the platform to first confirm that the payor has the necessary funds, and then to send payment instructions to their bank or credit card company for processing and, ultimately, payment. Importantly, because these platforms already have each party's payment details, the only information that payors typically need to initiate a transfer is the payee's email address, telephone number, or some other type of unique identifier or alias.

The advantages of early P2P payment platforms are best understood in the context of online auction or e-commerce websites like eBay or Etsy. Sellers on these websites are typically private individuals or small firms looking to sell specific goods—e.g., an old sofa, unloved musical instrument, Star Wars collectibles, or handmade arts and crafts. For these small sellers, the costs of obtaining merchant banking services that would enable them to accept credit or debit card payments are often prohibitively high.[7] Sellers are also understandably reluctant to provide sensitive financial information that would enable buyers to arrange for a wire transfer. Accordingly, as Ronald Mann explains, "Purchasers in the early days of eBay had to use cashier's checks or money orders. Typically, sellers waited to ship products until they received the paper-based payment device in the mail."[8] Thus, while the internet may move at the speed of light, payment for goods and services still generally moved at the speed of the US Postal Service.

The development of early P2P payment platforms simultaneously solved each of these problems: offering a fast, easy, affordable, and secure way of making payments between anonymous buyers and sellers. In the US and Europe, by far the most well-known and widely used P2P payment platform is PayPal. PayPal customers can make payments using their debit or credit cards or via electronic fund transfer from their bank. Importantly, they can also pay using any positive balance in their PayPal account. As of December 2023, these customer balances totaled just under $42 billion.[9] If PayPal was a bank, this healthy deposit base would make it the forty-fifth largest in the United States.[10]

PayPal's rise is closely linked with its partnership with eBay, which eventually purchased it in 2002 as a replacement for its own, far less popular, P2P payment platform. In July 2015, eBay then spun off PayPal into an independent, publicly traded company. At the end of 2022, PayPal reported

---

7. These costs include so-called interchange fees that are paid by merchants accepting credit or debit card payments from consumers. In the US, these fees average between 1.5 and 2.0 percent for credit card transactions and around 0.5–1.0 percent for debit card transactions; see Angelo Duarte, Jon Frost, Leonardo Gambacorta, Priscilla Koo Wilkens, & Hyun Song Shin, "Central Banks, the Monetary System, and Public Payment Infrastructures: Lessons from Brazil's Pix," Bank for International Settlements Bulletin No. 52 (March 23, 2022).

8. Mann, "Regulating Internet Payment Intermediaries," 82 Texas Law Review 681, 683–84 (2003).

9. PayPal, Inc., Annual Report, page 58 (December 31, 2023): https://investor.pypl.com/financials/annual-reports/default.aspx

10. Putting PayPal ($38.8 billion) just ahead of New York Community Bank ($32.6 billion) and behind E*TRADE Bank ($54.7 billion).

having 426 million active customer accounts across its various products, supporting payments in twenty-five different currencies.[11] The total volume of payments processed through these accounts was approximately $1.25 trillion—or roughly $39,000 per second.[12] While these figures still pale in comparison to those of the conventional banking system, they are nevertheless impressive—especially given that banks have an almost two-hundred-year head start.

Beyond greater speed and enhanced privacy, P2P payment platforms have leveraged their APIs to offer customers a variety of more convenient features than conventional bank-based payment systems. PayPal's sister platform, Venmo, is an illustrative example. Like PayPal, Venmo enables customers to send and receive payments instantly and to hold received funds in their Venmo account. Venmo also includes an integrated calculator, along with the ability to simultaneously send multiple requests for payment to other Venmo customers. This combination of features makes it incredibly easy to use Venmo for so-called social payments, like splitting a restaurant check between friends or dividing up a utility bill among roommates. In the US, these features have helped make the platform synonymous with internet-based payments, with the word *Venmo* recently being added to the Urban Dictionary as a verb meaning "to send money."

Yet Venmo is far from the only P2P platform using new technology to solve age-old payment problems. This includes the complex, opaque, and inefficient world of cross-border payments. For centuries, the architecture of the cross-border payment system has mirrored the structure of domestic banking systems, with the vast majority of transactions cleared and settled through a tight-knit network of large, internationally active correspondent banks.[13] In recent decades, this system has been buttressed by the emergence of institutions like the Society for Worldwide Interbank Financial Telecommunication (Swift), developer of the eponymous and widely used payment messaging system, and Continuous Linked Settlement (CLS),

---

11. PayPal, Inc., Annual Report, 2 (December 31, 2022), https://s201.q4cdn.com/231198771 /files/doc_financials/2022/ar/PayPal-Holdings-Inc.-2022-Combined-Proxy-Statement-and -Annual-Report.pdf.

12. PayPal, Annual Report, 3.

13. For a description of the historical antecedents of today's cross-border payment system, see Henry Harfield, "Elements of Foreign Exchange Practice," 64(3) Harvard Law Review 436 (1951), and Raymond de Roover, "Early Accounting Problems of Foreign Exchange," 19:4 Accounting Review 381 (1944). For a more detailed description of the modern cross-border correspondent banking system, see Committee on Payments and Market Infrastructures, "Correspondent Banking," Bank for International Settlements (July 2016), https://www.bis.org/cpmi/publ/d147.pdf.

a clearinghouse for foreign exchange transactions.[14] Nevertheless, this system has been plagued by challenges, ranging from fragmented data standards and inconsistent regulatory compliance frameworks, to long settlement chains, outdated legacy technology systems, and a lack of competition.[15] As recently observed by the FSB, "Cross-border payments sit at the heart of international trade and economic activity. However, for too long cross-border payments have faced four particular challenges: high costs, low speed, limited access and insufficient transparency."[16]

Enter P2P payment platforms like Wise. Formerly known as Transfer-Wise, Wise is a web-based platform that gives its customers the ability to send money overseas—currently to more than fifty countries and in dozens of different currencies. The majority of the payments executed on the platform take less than one business day, with many payments arriving in the recipient's bank account in a matter of seconds. The price for sending these payments is completely transparent to the customer up front, and is typically only a small fraction of the price of sending a cross-border payment using the conventional banking system. The speed and cost of using the platform is even more remarkable given that Wise effectively piggybacks off the incumbent payment system. Not only do all funds begin and end in customer bank accounts, but the payments themselves flow through Wise's own network of correspondent accounts that it holds with banks all over the world. In effect, Wise sits on top of the current cross-border payment system, providing a technological layer that enables it to engineer a degree of interoperability that the fragmented legacy banking system has long been unable to achieve. This technological interoperability gives Wise a comparative advantage in the delivery of faster and cheaper cross-border payments.

In China, meanwhile, P2P payment platforms have taken the quest for greater interoperability to an entirely new level. Until very recently, the Chinese financial system was dominated by a handful of extremely large,

---

14. For a detailed description of Swift, its origins, and role, see Susan Scott & Markos Zachariadis, *The Society for Worldwide Interbank Financial Telecommunication: Cooperative Governance for Network Innovation, Standards, and Community* (2014); for a detailed description of CLS, see John Armour, Dan Awrey, Paul Davies, Luca Enriques, Jeff Gordon, Colin Mayer, & Jennifer Payne, *Principles of Financial Regulation*, 398–400.

15. For a comprehensive overview of these challenges, see Ulrich Bindseil & George Pantelopoulos, "Toward the Holy Grail of Cross-Border Payments," European Central Bank Working Paper No. 2693 (August 2022).

16. Financial Stability Board, "Cross-Border Payments" (March 2023), https://www.fsb.org /work-of-the-fsb/financial- innovation-and-structural-change/cross-border-payments/.

state-controlled banks. These banks were connected to one another by a single financial market utility, UnionPay, that was itself jointly owned by these state-controlled banks and the Chinese central bank, the People's Bank of China (PBOC). This highly concentrated, state-run system contributed to a high level of financial repression: with banks offering uncompetitive interest rates on deposits, small businesses struggling to obtain conventional bank loans, and relatively few Chinese consumers enjoying access to credit cards or other consumer credit products.[17] The use of debit cards was also remarkably low—perhaps not surprising given that they were typically not accepted at stores, could not be used for making purchases over the internet, and only allowed cardholders to withdraw cash from ATMs operated by their own bank.

By the dawn of the new century, the Chinese payment system was clearly ripe for technological disruption. And, predictably, the harbingers of disruption would eventually come from outside the conventional banking system.[18] The first harbinger was Alipay. Launched in 2004, Alipay is a P2P payment platform, originally created to foster trust between anonymous buyers and sellers transacting for the delivery of physical goods on Taobao, the Amazon-like online shopping platform owned by Alipay's parent company, Alibaba. Following Alibaba's lead was Tencent, a social media, gaming, and entertainment conglomerate. Tencent needed to find an efficient way to make "micropayments" for the digital goods—e.g., video games, movies, and music—sold on its various online platforms. The quest to solve this problem would eventually lead to the development of WeChat Pay, introduced in 2013.

The low levels of credit and debit card penetration in China meant that Alipay and WeChat Pay—unlike PayPal, Venmo, or Wise—could not simply build their new payment platforms on top of existing financial market infrastructure.[19] This eventually forced both platforms to make two fateful and, as

17. For a more detailed description of financial repression in China prior to the emergence of Tencent and Alipay, see Yiping Huang & Tingting Ge, "Assessing China's Financial Reform: Changing Roles of the Repressive Financial Policies," 39:1 Cato Journal 65 (Winter 2019). At the same time, this repression resulted in the emergence of a vibrant shadow financial system; see Dan Awrey, "Law and Finance in the Chinese Shadow Banking System," 48:1 Cornell International Law Journal 1 (2015).

18. For a deep dive into the rise of fintech in China and how it disrupted the domestic banking and payment systems, see Martin Chorzempa, *The Cashless Revolution: China's Reinvention of Money and the End of America's Domination of Finance and Technology* (2022).

19. Chorzempa, *Cashless Revolution*, 21.

it turned out, fortuitous decisions.[20] The first was to design and build mobile-first payment apps for use by China's then rapidly expanding population of Apple iOS and Android smartphone users. This included the integration of quick response (QR) code technology that enabled customers to make instant and anonymous offline payments. The second was to create digital wallets that enabled customers to make and receive payments across Tencent's and Alibaba's various platforms. The positive balances in these wallets represented credits in each customer's name—credits that could be held as a nominal store of value in anticipation of making future payments. In the course of solving their distinctly different payments problems, WeChat Pay and Alipay had thus both become the issuers of a new and fledgling species of monetary IOU.

Having initially built these P2P payment platforms from scratch in order to help grow their existing businesses, Tencent and Alibaba would go on to use them as the technological foundations for an almost unprecedented period of strategic expansion. Today, both platforms offer a broad range of financial services: everything from payments, to retail and commercial lending, to insurance and investments.[21] This includes Alipay's Yu'E Bao, the world's largest money market fund, which many Chinese consumers now use instead of a conventional bank account. The WeChat and Alipay "super-apps" have also expanded into a wide variety of nonfinancial businesses, including ride hailing, food delivery, and travel. Martin Chorzempa explains:

> The super-apps are in many ways more like operating systems than regular apps. Just as developers create apps for Google's Android and Apple's iOS, China's large tech firms signed on partners, from big retailers to small start-ups, to create new services and products distributed through the super-apps. Each super-app thus became an immense, unbeatable bundle of services.[22]

As one might expect, this seamless interoperability has helped turbocharge consumer demand and, ultimately, platform adoption. As of September 2022, both WeChat Pay and Alipay had over 900 million active

---

20. Both Tencent and Alipay experimented with several business models before arriving at these decisions. Tencent introduced its QQ Coin in 2005 before running into regulatory problems stemming from its use in illicit transactions. Alipay initially attempted to build its payment platform on top of the conventional banking system.

21. While both Tencent and Alipay would eventually expand into conventional banking, neither uses banks as the foundation of their deposit-taking or payments businesses.

22. Chorzempa, *Cashless Revolution*, 72.

customers worldwide—with Alipay's 1.3 billion active users easily outpacing Apple's 507 million and PayPal's 426 million.[23] Within a few short years, these platforms have enabled smartphones to replace cash at the heart of the Chinese payment system. In the process, they have also enabled China to leapfrog the United States and many other developed countries in the race to offer cheap, fast, convenient, interoperable, and accessible payments.

Together, WeChat Pay and Alipay offer a window into how new technology is revolutionizing the world of payments—and what the future might hold for those countries that follow in China's footsteps. Yet China's experience is also a cautionary tale about the potential dangers of rapid technological change to an institution so fundamental to our lives and society. These dangers include the growing threat of cyber fraud, digital discrimination, the inefficient concentration of economic power, and the weaponization of the payment system as an instrument for social control. In chapter 6, we look at how Chinese policymakers have responded to one of these potential dangers—the problem of bad money.

Finance on your Phone

China is not the only country where banks have a poor historical track record when it comes to building the infrastructure necessary to ensure that people and businesses enjoy a convenient and widely accessible system of money and payments. In large parts of sub-Saharan Africa and South Asia, the lack of financial market infrastructure has long been a significant driver of high levels of financial exclusion. As recently as 2010, a survey of 148 countries conducted by the World Bank found that only 33 percent of adults in South Asia, and just 24 percent in sub-Saharan Africa, had opened an account at a regulated financial institution.[24] This exclusion forces many—especially poorer—households to rely on cash as a vehicle for both accumulating savings and making and receiving payments. The heavy reliance on cash increases transaction costs for these households, exposes them to the heightened risk of loss, theft, and destruction, and

---

23. "AliPay Is the Most Popular Digital Wallet in the World in 2022," *Fintech News* (September 26, 2022), https://www.fintechnews.org/alipay-is-the-most-popular-digital-wallet-in-the-world-in-2022/.

24. See Asli Demirguc-Kunt & Leora Klapper, "Measuring Financial Inclusion: The Global Financial Inclusion Indicators," World Bank Policy Research Working Paper No. 6025 (2012).

limits valuable opportunities for both risk sharing and pooling and allocating capital for investment.[25]

In the absence of effective financial market infrastructure, many countries have sought to capitalize on the emergence, development, and rapid adoption of an entirely different type of infrastructure: mobile phone networks. The first payment using a mobile phone was conducted in Helsinki in 1997 when Coca-Cola introduced a vending machine that enabled users to pay for soft drinks using a short message service (SMS) text message. That same year Finland also became home to the world's first mobile banking service.[26] But it would be in Africa where the use of mobile phones as payment devices would really take off. Between 2002 and 2012, the number of mobile phone users in Africa increased from 34 million to 710 million—from roughly 3 percent of the continent's total population to more than half over the course of a single decade.[27] This sharp increase in mobile connectivity provided the technological foundations for an entirely new system of money and payments.

The early poster child for what would become known as "mobile money" was Kenya. At the dawn of the new millennium, Kenya had well under a thousand physical bank branches and an anemic ATM network supporting a population of almost 32 million, spread out over a land mass covering 224,961 square miles (roughly the size of Texas). Beyond hand-to-hand exchanges, the most common way of sending money was an informal, unsecure, and often unreliable network of bus and taxi companies that connected rural communities with urban populations in cities like Nairobi and Mombasa.[28] Perhaps even more than China, Kenya's retail payment system was thus ripe for technological disruption.

In 2007, Kenya's largest mobile phone company, Safaricom, launched a new mobile payment application called M-PESA. To use this application, Safaricom mobile customers simply register with an authorized retail agent,

---

25. See Dan Radcliffe & Rodger Vorhies, "A Digital Pathway to Financial Inclusion," Bill and Melinda Gates Foundation (December 2012), https://papers.ssrn.com/sol3/papers.cfm?abstract _id=2186926.

26. See Pengfei Han & Zhu Wang, "Technology Adoption and Leapfrogging: Racing for Mobile Payments," Federal Reserve Bank of Richmond Working Paper No. 21-5, 6 (August 30, 2022).

27. See Ignacio Mas & Dan Radcliffe, "Mobile Payments Go Viral: M-PESA in Kenya," 32 Capco Institute Journal of Financial Transformation 169, 172 (August 2011); Radcliffe & Vorhies, "Digital Pathway," 9.

28. While Kenya also had an established postal banking system, this system was "perceived by customers as costly, slow, and prone to liquidity shortages at rural outlets"; Mas & Radcliffe, "Mobile Payments Go Viral," 174.

using an official document like a national ID card as proof of identity. Safaricom then opens an electronic account—effectively, a digital wallet—linked to the customer's mobile phone number. Once registered, M-PESA users can deposit and withdraw cash from their account by visiting an authorized agent—typically a local shop, gas station, or post office. Having deposited cash, M-PESA users can then send money to their family and friends, pay their bills, or purchase goods and services via SMS text message. To make a payment, all M-PESA users need to do is open the app on their phone, enter the phone number of the intended recipient and the desired amount, and confirm their unique PIN. In effect, the phone's SIM card serves as both an authentication mechanism and point of sale (POS) terminal, enabling M-PESA payments to be processed in real time and without the need for agents to invest in costly hardware.[29] Safaricom customers can even use M-PESA to send money to the customers of other mobile phone networks.[30]

A study by economists William Jack and Tavneet Suri estimates that, within four years of its launch, 70 percent of Kenyan adults and more than 75 percent of unbanked households were using M-PESA.[31] Over this same period, Safaricom authorized over 39,000 retail agents—more than ten times the total number of bank branches, ATMs, and post office locations in Kenya *combined*.[32] A little more than a decade later, M-PESA has over fifty-one million customers across seven countries, more than 600,000 authorized agents, and processes over $314 billion in payments per year.[33] M-PESA and its partners have also branched out into other financial services, including savings products, personal and small business loans, wealth management, and insurance.

Since M-PESA's introduction, dozens of developing countries have sought to replicate its success. As of 2021, there were more than three hundred mobile money projects under way around the world, in almost one hundred countries, collectively serving over 1.3 billion customers.[34] Not

29. Mas & Radcliffe, "Mobile Payments Go Viral," 172.

30. Mas & Radcliffe, 172. In order to make payments to customers of other mobile phone networks, M-PESA debits money from the sender's account and sends a code by SMS that can then be used to claim the monetary value at any Safaricom-authorized retail agent.

31. See William Jack & Tavneet Suri, "Risk Sharing and Transaction Costs: Evidence from Kenya's Mobile Money Revolution," 104:1 American Economic Review 183 (2014); Jack, "M-PESA Extends Its Reach," GSMA Mobile for Development blog post (April 5, 2012), https://www.gsma .com/mobilefordevelopment/country/kenya/m-pesa-extends-its-reach/.

32. Radcliffe & Vorhies, "Digital Pathway," 11–12.

33. "About M-PESA," (December 2022), https://www.vodafone.com/about-vodafone/what -we-do/consumer-products-and-services/m-pesa.

34. Global System for Mobile Communications (GSMA), *State of the Industry Report*, 2 (2022), https://www.gsma.com/sotir/#download.

surprisingly, the majority of these projects are taking place in countries where the conventional banking system is either underdeveloped or has simply failed to invest in the infrastructure needed to offer an inexpensive, secure, reliable, and universally accessible alternative to cash. Today, most mobile money customers are concentrated in sub-Saharan Africa (45.6 percent) and South Asia (33.2 percent).[35] Yet, more recently, regions like the Middle East, North Africa, Latin America, and the South Pacific have also reported double-digit annual increases in mobile money projects, customers, and transaction volumes.[36]

For these regions, the introduction of mobile money holds out a number of potentially transformative benefits.[37] Often for the first time, mobile money promises people and communities access to a fast, safe, and reliable electronic payment network—bypassing the underdeveloped or nonexistent financial market infrastructure that for too long has forced them to rely on cash and informal institutions. The ability to send and receive money using a basic GSM mobile phone saves time, reduces cost, and makes it easier for individuals, households, and businesses to transact with one another: whether to buy goods and services, pay bills, or send their wages to family members on the other side of the country. Looking beyond payments, access to a basic digital wallet can make it easier for households to weather short-term financial shocks, like job loss, serious illness, or crop failure. These wallets also provide a conduit for aggregating and channeling capital into productive investments. Last but not least, by giving people and businesses a digital footprint, mobile money can provide a springboard for greater access to other financial products and services, such as consumer and small business loans, insurance, and investments.

A Bridge to Cryptoland

Over the past decade, few developments in the world of finance have captured the public's imagination, or courted more controversy, than the spectacular rise in popularity of BTC, ETH, and other digital assets.[38] These

---

35. Han & Wang, "Technology Adoption and Leapfrogging," 9.

36. GSMA, *2022 State of the Industry Report*, 10.

37. For a detailed discussion of these potential benefits, and the progress mobile money has made toward realizing them, see Jack & Suri, "Risk Sharing and Transaction Costs."

38. While now widely used, the term *digital asset* is highly unsatisfactory, given that the vast majority of financial assets are now "digital" in the sense that they are both recorded in electronic form and bought and sold on electronic trading platforms. As used here, the term exclusively refers to assets that are recorded and traded using blockchain or other distributed ledger technology.

digital assets are based on pairs of cryptographic keys: a "public" key that can be observed by anyone, and a "private" key known only to the owner of the digital asset. Together, these public and private keys enable the participants of a given network to authenticate the ownership of digital assets, and to transfer these assets from one network participant to another. The networks themselves are built on a type of decentralized database known as a blockchain. While the features of these blockchains vary from network to network, most contemplate some form of direct involvement by network participants in the clearing—often referred to as validation, or *mining*—of these transactions. They also typically record final settlement of transactions using a unique cryptographic signature, creating a publicly verifiable record of all changes to the database. In these critical respects, the use of blockchain technology reflects the desire to eliminate the centralization and opacity associated with banks, clearinghouses, and other financial market infrastructure at the heart of conventional payment networks.

Once the obsession of a small but passionate community of self-styled "cypherpunks," the crypto ecosystem has grown and evolved into a truly global phenomenon, with millions of people now trading thousands of different digital assets, 24 hours a day, 7 days a week, 365 days a year, on hundreds of online trading platforms. At the market's peak in October 2021, at least one estimate suggested that there were at least 419 online crypto trading platforms, supporting over 16,000 digital assets and over $100 billion in trading volume per day.[39]

This highly fragmented market structure presented early traders with both a tantalizing opportunity and a vexing problem. The opportunity arose from the fact that the prevailing market price of a digital asset would often diverge across different trading platforms, typically due to differences in platform fees, market liquidity, and other idiosyncratic features. In theory, these differences created highly profitable arbitrage opportunities that could be captured by buying the asset on the platform quoting the lower price and then selling it on the platform quoting the higher price. Predictably, however, these arbitrage opportunities were often fleeting—demanding that traders move money extremely quickly to exploit any price differences.

The problem was that the blockchain technology at the heart of crypto markets was and remains more or less incompatible with the technological

---

39. Grandview Research, "Cryptocurrency Exchange Platform Market Size, Share & Trends Analysis Report," cited in Yesha Yadav, "Toward a Public-Private Oversight Model of Crypto Markets," Vanderbilt Law Research Paper No. 22-26 (2022).

infrastructure of the conventional payment system. As a result, it could often take several days to transfer money from the buyer's bank account to their crypto wallet. Moreover, even where the buyer was purchasing a digital asset (e.g., BTC) using another digital asset (e.g., ETH), clearing and settling the transaction on the blockchain could still take days or even weeks—thus exposing both the buyer and seller to any volatility in the price of these assets over the intervening period. In effect, what traders needed was a blockchain-compatible monetary IOU that could be used as both a nominal store of value and a means of transferring it rapidly within the crypto ecosystem.

To this point, by far the most popular solution to this problem revolves around the issuance and use of so-called stablecoins. In a nutshell, a *stablecoin* is a digital asset, the value of which is anchored—or "pegged"—to the value of a specified reference asset—typically a fiat currency, like the US dollar, British pound, or Chinese yuan. Thus, for example, where a stablecoin is pegged to the US dollar, one unit of that stablecoin should always be redeemable for exactly one US dollar. In theory, these features—blockchain compatibility and an external peg—make stablecoins both a convenient technological on-ramp into the crypto ecosystem and a useful vehicle for "parking value" in advance of trading other digital assets.

In practice, of course, the value of a given stablecoin fundamentally depends on the credibility of the mechanisms used to anchor its value to the reference asset. At present, stablecoins typically seek to maintain their peg in one of two ways. The first involves collateralizing the stablecoin one-for-one with reserve assets like cash, bank deposits, government debt, or other low-risk money market instruments denominated in the reference asset.[40] The second involves the use of algorithms designed to automatically increase or decrease the supply of a stablecoin in response to changes in market demand, thereby theoretically ensuring that its value always remains pegged to that of the underlying reference asset.[41]

The monetary IOUs created by stablecoin issuers typically have two important features that distinguish them from conventional bank deposits, P2P payment platforms, and mobile money. First, stablecoin holders often possess relatively limited legal rights to redeem their holdings for the underlying reference asset. For example, Tether, the world's largest stablecoin, only permits direct redemptions for larger holders redeeming a minimum

---

40. See Christian Catalini & Jai Massari, "Stablecoins and the Future of Money," *Harvard Business Review* (August 10, 2021).

41. See Douglas Arner, Raphael Auer, & Jon Frost, "Stablecoins: Risks, Potential, and Regulation," Bank for International Settlements Working Paper No. 905, 6 (November 2020).

of $100,000.[42] Tether's rival, USDC, similarly only commits to one-to-one redemption into US dollars for its Type A partners—typically, large institutional customers.[43] The absence of direct redemption rights for most small stablecoin holders then gives rise to the second distinguishing feature: the fact that stablecoins are bought and sold on organized crypto trading platforms. This introduces the troubling prospect that—depending on prevailing supply and demand conditions—the market price of a stablecoin could become untethered from its peg. In this one narrow respect, stablecoins more closely resemble the bearer instruments of nineteenth-century English and money markets than they do conventional bank deposits.

The first stablecoins were launched in 2014 to very little fanfare and enjoyed limited commercial success. This relatively low public profile would change dramatically in June 2019, when Facebook announced the creation of the Libra Association and its intention to launch a global stablecoin to be known as Libra.[44] The original objective of the Libra Association— which initially included established payment industry players like PayPal, Stripe, Visa, and Mastercard—was to create a "global currency and financial infrastructure" designed to overcome the speed, cost, and interoperability problems that had long plagued international payment and remittance systems.[45] The Libra stablecoin was to be backed by a basket of fiat currencies and sovereign debt, accessed through a network of authorized trading platforms, and held in digital wallets developed by Facebook's subsidiary, Calibra. Once up and running, the vision was that units of Libra would be transferred instantaneously between user wallets via the Libra blockchain— thus combining the functionality of a stablecoin with the convenience of a more conventional P2P payment platform.

Not surprisingly, Facebook's global ambitions, unwieldy governance, and untested technology were met with considerable skepticism from financial regulators, many of whom viewed Libra as a potential threat to both individual privacy and national monetary sovereignty. After receiving significant pushback from regulators in several key jurisdictions, the Libra Association

42. See Tether Fee Schedule, https://tether.to/es/fees.

43. See USDC Terms, Section 2, https://www.circle.com/en/legal/usdc-terms.

44. See Libra Association, "Introducing Libra" (June 18, 2019), https://www.diem.com/en -us/updates/introducing-libra/; Mike Isaac & Nathaniel Popper, "Facebook Plans Global Financial System Based on Cryptocurrency," *New York Times* (June 18, 2019), https://www.nytimes.com /2019/06/18/technology/facebook-cryptocurrency-libra.html.

45. See Libra Association White Paper v1.0, 3 (June 18, 2019), https://www.diem.com/en -us/updates/introducing-libra/.

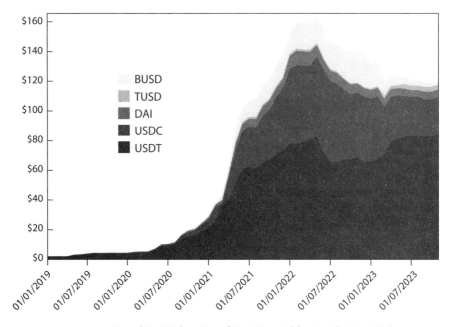

FIGURE 4.1. Growth in Market Cap of Top Five Stablecoins (2019–2023)

announced in April 2020 that it intended to pursue a more modest version of its proposal based on a series of single-currency stablecoins pegged to the US dollar, British pound, euro, and other major global currencies.[46] Shortly thereafter, Facebook rebranded the project from Libra to Diem. With each new twist and turn, the Libra project was thrust farther into the public spotlight—and with it the growing importance of stablecoins at the heart of the emerging crypto ecosystem.

The Libra project died ignominiously in January 2022. Yet, rather than signaling the end of the stablecoin boom, Libra's struggles and eventual demise coincided with a period of dramatic market growth. Between January 2021 and September 2022, the market capitalization of the three largest stablecoins—Tether, USDC, and BUSD—grew by almost 600 percent to over $110 billion (see figure 4.1). By the autumn of 2022, more than three-quarters of all transactions on crypto trading platforms involved at least one stablecoin.[47]

46. Libra Association, White Paper v2.0 (April 2020), https://wp.diem.com/en-US/wp-content/uploads/sites/23/2020/04/Libra_WhitePaperV2_April2020.pdf.

47. The Block, "Share of Trade Volume by Pair Denomination" (September 2022), https://www.theblock.co/data/crypto-markets/spot/share-of-trade-volume-by-pair-denomination.

For the time being, the use of stablecoins is limited to transactions within the still-embryonic crypto ecosystem. Yet, looking ahead, many see the potential for stablecoins to play a broader role as the technological backbone of a new and better system of money and payments. Christian Catalini and Jai Massari explain:

> The benefits of stablecoins include lower-cost, safe, real-time, and more competitive payments compared to what consumers and businesses experience today. They could rapidly make it cheaper for businesses to accept payments and easier for governments to run conditional cash transfer programs (including sending stimulus money). They could connect unbanked or underbanked segments of the population to the financial system.[48]

The potential for stablecoins to play this broader role has even received a measure of support from key global policymakers. The FSB has suggested that stablecoins, and the decentralized payment rails on which they run, could eventually be used to enhance the efficiency of cross-border payments, domestic wholesale payment systems, and securities clearing and settlement systems.[49] There are also those who see promise in combining stablecoins with so-called smart contracts to create programmable money that could be used to automate the payment process across a wide spectrum of transactions. These transactions theoretically include large-value transfers, like home purchases, where the money could be sent instantly from the buyer to the seller upon the completion of the inspection and any other conditions of sale.[50] They also include micropayments—e.g., for streaming content like movies, music, or magazine articles, to pay for parking or road tolls, or for making machine-to-machine payments as part of the emerging Internet of Things—that are simply too small to be economical for the incumbent bank-based payment system.[51] Whether this futuristic vision becomes a reality remains to be seen. Indeed, there are very good reasons to believe

48. Catalini & Massari, "Stablecoins and the Future of Money," *Harvard Business Review* (August 10, 2021).

49. See Financial Stability Board, "Decentralised Financial Technologies: Report on Financial Stability, Regulatory and Governance Implications" (June 6, 2019), https://www.fsb.org/wp -content/uploads/P060619.pdf.

50. Arner, Auer, & Frost, "Stablecoins: Risks, Potential, Regulation," 7.

51. See, e.g., Netta Korin, "Blockchain Technology Can Make Micropayments Finally Functional," *Cointelegraph* (October 31, 2021), https://cointelegraph.com/news/blockchain-technology -can-make-micropayments-finally-functional; Udo Milkau, "The Advent of Machine Payments: The Right Way to Pay?," 12:4 Journal of Payment Strategy and Systems 293 (Winter 2018–19).

that it ultimately may not live up to the hype. The important thing is that stablecoins are here, and that these and other experiments exploring their potential future applications are already well and truly under way.

Crypto Casino Chips

Reflecting the desire for greater decentralization, BTC, ETH, XRP, and other digital assets are designed to be held in *unhosted* digital wallets. These unhosted wallets include hardware devices (e.g., thumb drives) and software programs (e.g., Guarda or Electrum) that allow the owner of the wallet to store the cryptographic private keys that, together with the corresponding public keys, enable them to hold and transfer digital assets. Yet many crypto enthusiasts eschew this "self-custody" model in favor of the simplicity, cost-effectiveness, and convenience of holding digital assets in *hosted* wallets offered by financial intermediaries known, rather unhelpfully, as cryptocurrency "exchanges."[52] Indeed, while reliable data is scarce, some estimates suggest that perhaps as many as half of all crypto transactions involve at least one hosted wallet maintained by exchanges such as Binance, Coinbase, or Kraken.[53]

At their core, cryptocurrency exchanges are platforms: centralized marketplaces that bring together buyers and sellers of digital assets. By lowering search costs for traders, these platforms generate higher trading volumes, thereby enhancing market liquidity and improving price formation.[54] Yet, unlike conventional stock exchanges, cryptocurrency exchanges combine this basic market-making role with a variety of other financial products and services. As a preliminary matter, these exchanges provide traders with a highly accessible on-ramp into the crypto ecosystem, typically including sleek, user-friendly online interfaces that enable customers to transfer money into their digital wallets using a debit or credit card. Traders can then use these interfaces to execute buy and sell orders, with large exchanges like Binance, Coinbase, and Kraken typically supporting trading in several

---

52. For a detailed description of the business models of these exchanges, see Adam Levitin, "Not Your Keys, Not Your Coins: Unpriced Credit Risk in Cryptocurrency," 101 Texas Law Review 877 (2023); Kristin Johnson, "Decentralized Finance: Regulatory Cryptocurrency Exchanges," 62:6 William & Mary Law Review 1911 (2021); Yadav, "Toward a Public-Private Model."

53. Crystal Crypto, "Travel Rule Risk Mitigation: Hosted versus Unhosted Crypto Wallets" (November 6, 2022), https://crystalblockchain.com/articles/part-2-the-travel-rule-hosted-vs-unhosted-crypto-wallets/.

54. See Yadav, "Toward a Public-Private Model," 32–33.

hundred digital assets.[55] While these orders can be executed directly on the relevant blockchain, it is often faster and cheaper for exchanges to simply execute trades on their own internal accounts. Once traders have funded their wallets in order to buy or sell digital assets, exchanges also typically offer to hold these fiat currency and digital assets in custody for the benefit of their customers. And when traders ultimately want to cash out their crypto casino chips, exchanges also serve as the off-ramp back into the conventional banking system.

Having initially served as a gateway to the crypto ecosystem, exchanges have evolved to offer traders a variety of digital lending and borrowing products. Three in particular stand out. The first, known as *staking*, enables traders to pledge their digital assets to specific blockchain projects—in effect agreeing to lock them up in exchange for the right to generate interest or other rewards by validating transactions on the relevant blockchain. Closely linked to staking is *yield farming*, which enables traders to directly lend their digital assets to third parties—typically, liquidity pools created to support decentralized trading protocols—in exchange for a fee, ongoing interest payments, or other rewards. In both cases, cryptocurrency exchanges essentially act as middlemen, connecting traders searching for higher returns with projects and protocols where they can put their crypto to work.

Second, many exchanges offer *margin trading*. Margin trading allows traders to borrow money or digital assets from an exchange and then use them—along with any other assets in a trader's wallet—as collateral for the loan. Depending on how much an exchange is willing to lend against a given quantity and quality of collateral, margin lending can dramatically increase the amount of leverage that crypto traders can employ—thereby magnifying both their potential gains and losses. For example, as recently as 2022, the popular exchange BitMEX offered 100x margin trading on BTC.[56] That meant that for every $1 change in the value of BTC, a trader using the exchange's margin trading product would experience, depending on the direction of the change, either a $100 windfall or a $100 loss.

Last but not least, a number of cryptocurrency exchanges sponsor, issue, and trade their own stablecoins and other digital assets. Some of the best-known examples include KuCoin's KCS, Bitfinex's LEO, and FTT, issued

55. See Coinmarketcap.com, "Top Cryptocurrency Spot Exchanges," https://coinmarketcap .com/rankings/exchanges/(listing the number of supported coins for Binance (383), Coinbase (237), Kraken (219), and KuCoin (776) as of December 28, 2022).

56. CryptoVantage, "Top Crypto Margin Trading Exchanges (2022)" (September 30, 2022), https://www.cryptovantage.com/best-crypto-exchanges/best-exchanges-for-margin-trading/.

by the now defunct FTX. Exchanges issue and trade these digital assets for a wide variety of reasons—from financing the exchange and allocating rights to participate in its governance, to ensuring sufficient liquidity on its trading platform, to being able to offer traders incentives and rewards denominated in its own in-house unit of account. Exchanges may also issue and trade these assets in order to capitalize on their privileged position as market makers—competing against their own customers in search of profitable trading opportunities.

In a relatively short span of time, cryptocurrency exchanges have thus grown to provide an incredibly broad range of financial products and services. As observed by Professor Adam Levitin, within the conventional financial system, these products and services would typically be provided by several different and generally independent financial intermediaries: with exchanges making markets, broker-dealers executing trades and holding customer assets in custody, and clearinghouses coordinating the clearing and settlement of transactions.[57] Ultimately, the fact that cryptocurrency exchanges provide all these products and services, and often far more, under one fast and easy-to-use roof helps explain their popularity. In effect, these exchanges are rapidly becoming the supermarkets of cryptoland.

Importantly, this growing suite of crypto-related financial products and services can create a complex and difficult-to-navigate set of legal relationships between exchanges and their customers. Legally speaking, there are at least two different ways to view hosted wallets. The first is as a virtual safety deposit box: a secure place for customers to keep their fiat currency and digital assets. The second is as a set of accounts consisting of the customer's "assets" and the exchange's corresponding obligation—its liability or promise—to deliver these assets or their equivalent value to the customer upon demand. Whereas the first view effectively sees digital assets as the customer's *property* and cryptocurrency exchanges as *custodians*, the second sees the customer's claim as fundamentally *contractual* in nature and, therefore, exchanges as a new and still evolving species of *financial intermediary*.

As described in greater detail in chapter 5, which view should and will ultimately prevail depends on the legal and regulatory frameworks governing exchanges, together with the contractual documentation—the "terms and conditions"—that defines the rights and obligations of each exchange vis-à-vis its customers. Importantly, the answer can vary not only from jurisdiction to jurisdiction and from exchange to exchange but also, and

---

57. Levitin, "Not Your Keys, Not Your Coins," 14.

crucially, between products and services provided by the same exchange. In some cases, the law will treat a hosted wallet like a safety deposit box: giving customers clear and easily enforceable property rights over their digital assets. In other cases, however, customers will only be entitled to the legal remedies of an unsecured creditor: namely, the right to sue an exchange for the failure to live up to its contractual obligations. And other times still, the law will be manifestly unclear, necessitating costly ex post judicial intervention to define the nature and scope of the customer's legal rights. As we shall see, while these distinctions may seem relatively minor and highly technical, they can have absolutely enormous consequences for customers when the exchanges they entrust with their assets are forced into bankruptcy.

Of course, not all the obligations that cryptocurrency exchanges owe to their customers should be viewed as monetary IOUs. Indeed, the vast majority of the assets floating around in the ether of the crypto ecosystem are nowhere near becoming a reliable store of nominal value or widely used as a means of payment. Yet there are some assets that arguably do have a distinctly monetary flavor. These assets include fiat currency balances held by an exchange on behalf of its customers. They also include any stablecoins held in hosted customer wallets, whether issued by third parties or by the exchange itself. And if there was any remaining doubt, exchanges like Coinbase have recently started to run television and online advertisements touting their platforms as the future of money and payments.[58] Accordingly, while cryptocurrency exchanges in many respects defy conventional legal and economic classifications, one of the things they almost certainly *are* is a new breed of monetary institution.

Zebras of a Different Stripe

Each of these four case studies—P2P payment platforms, mobile money, stablecoins, and cryptocurrency exchanges—involve institutions and platforms that *combine* money and payments. After all, this is the essence of what makes them integral parts of the shadow monetary system. Yet it is worth briefly observing that a great deal of the experimentation currently taking place in the world of payments has been spearheaded by technology firms that process payments, but whose business models do not necessarily require them to hold

---

58. See Asa Hiken, "Coinbase Takes Aim at US Financial System in New Campaign," *AdAge* (March 9, 2023), https://adage.com/article/digital-marketing-ad-tech-news/coinbase-takes-aim-us-financial-system-new-campaign/2478871.

customer funds or, at most, to only hold them very briefly before routing them to the conventional banking system for final settlement. These firms include established payment processors like Visa and Mastercard. They also include a wide variety of specialist payment software developers, like Block, Shopify, Clover, and Stripe, which seek to integrate payments with sales, payroll, accounting, tax, treasury management, and other back-office processes.

The technology developed by these firms already plays a myriad of critical roles in the digital economy. To take just a few examples, this technology is what allows bricks-and-mortar businesses to accept electronic payments. It's also what enables online retailers to instantly and securely process card-not-present payments over the internet. And, behind the scenes, this technology is increasingly being used to help businesses of all shapes and sizes pay their employees faster; better integrate their sales, accounting, and tax records; and streamline their financial management. Yet, because this technology represents an entirely new layer of infrastructure built on top of existing payment networks, it can also introduce additional complexity and cost to what is already an unwieldy and expensive system of money and payments. Like everyone else, it also makes these firms extremely reliant on banks. Accordingly, while not technically part of the shadow monetary system, these firms often face similar bottleneck problems and other competitive disadvantages. Given their technology-driven business models, there is also often very little impetus for these firms to seek a conventional banking license.

The Upshot

Across the globe, new financial institutions and platforms are using their comparative technological advantages to unleash a revolution in money and payments. This chapter has explored just a tiny fraction of the new experiments this revolution has yielded to date. And if anything, the pace of experimentation has only increased in the few short years since PayPal, Alipay, M-PESA, and Tether first burst onto the scene. Some of these experiments have and will continue to generate tangible benefits for customers, and perhaps one day grow to rival or even supplant incumbent bank-based payment networks. Others will almost certainly prove to be little more than a flash in the pan—fool's gold for the digital age.[59] And even if many of these experi-

---

59. Martha Muir, "Case for Blockchain in Financial Services Dented by Failures," *Financial Times* (December 22, 2022), https://www.ft.com/content/cb606604-a89c-4746-9524-e1833cd4973.

ments do not pay dividends in the short run, the global tech industry has a long track record of turning today's apparent technological failures into the foundations of tomorrow's success stories.

Ultimately, failure is an inherent part of experimentation. The key policy problem is how to simultaneously harness the social benefits of successful experiments while limiting the harmful effects of the experiments that can and do go wrong. Importantly, these harmful effects are not generally a product of the core experiments in the development and adoption of new payments technology. Rather, they are typically the product of the parallel, and often ancillary, experiments with the creation of new types of monetary IOUs. This observation takes us back into the realm of law and institutions, and the question of whether customers—in search of good payments—may be exposing themselves to the risk of bad money. As we have seen, these risks stem first and foremost from the potential application of general corporate bankruptcy law and its destructive impact on money's moneyness. As explored in the next chapter, not all of these new monetary experiments effectively insulate customers from these important risks. This raises a second question—examined in greater detail in chapter 6—about whether existing regulatory frameworks serve to make these monetary IOUs any more credible. If they do not, the burden inevitably falls on policymakers to design frameworks that strike a more effective balance between the inherent opportunities and dangers of Gresham's new law.

5

Money in the Shadow of Bankruptcy

WHERE IS OUR MONEY?

—MT GOX CUSTOMER

On a cool and overcast morning in February 2014, Mt Gox, then the world's largest cryptocurrency exchange, filed for bankruptcy protection in Tokyo, Japan.[1] While the filing attracted only modest coverage in the financial press, it was seismic news within the burgeoning BTC community, where at the time Mt Gox was responsible for the lion's share of global trading volumes.[2] Rumors that the exchange had been hacked had been circulating for months, and it now appeared that as much as $460 million worth of BTC belonging to both the exchange and its customers had been stolen.[3] As of the bankruptcy filing, Mt Gox reported Japanese assets of ¥6.5 billion ($65 million) against debts of over ¥3.8 billion ($38 million), payable to its 127,000 customers and other creditors. There was also the small matter of roughly 850,000

---

1. Application of MtGox Co., Ltd. for the Commencement of a Civil Rehabilitation Procedure, filed in Tokyo District Court (February 28, 2014), https://www.mtgox.com/img/pdf/20140228 -announcement_eng.pdf. (Mt Gox would subsequently also file for bankruptcy protection in the US.)

2. Robert McMillan & Cade Metz, "The Rise and Fall of the World's Largest Bitcoin Exchange," *Wired* (November 6, 2013).

3. Robert McMillan, "The Inside Story of Mt. Gox, Bitcoin's $460 Million Disaster," *Wired* (March 3, 2014).

missing bitcoins. In the midst of the chaos and uncertainty leading up to the bankruptcy—which eventually forced Mt Gox to impose a freeze on any withdrawals—one of these customers flew from London to Tokyo, where he planted himself outside the exchange's headquarters with a sign that read simply, "MT GOX WHERE IS OUR MONEY?"[4]

This story highlights two important and inescapable facts. The first is that people often have vague, distorted, and sometimes downright unhelpful notions about what constitutes "money." There are a variety of possible reasons why people entertain, and often cling to, these notions. As a starting point, people may perceive themselves as too busy, lacking the necessary expertise, or simply uninterested in understanding the nature and sources of money. People can also fall prey to deceptive marketing practices—especially where they are told that they can generate a "risk-free" return on their hard-earned savings. Along the same vein, they may infer from the use of language like crypto*currency,* bit*coin,* or *Cash* App that a particular asset possesses the qualities of money—that it embodies both a reliable store of nominal value and a convenient means of payment. And, last but not least, they may value the convenience of making fast, cheap, or convenient payments *today,* but without fully considering the longer-term trade-offs that may affect their ability to access and use their money *tomorrow and beyond.* Ultimately, what unites all of these potential reasons is the reality that people often fail to ask important questions about what money is, where it comes from, and whether a given monetary IOU can really be trusted as good money.

The second inescapable fact is that the application of conventional corporate bankruptcy law has a marked tendency to confound these unhelpful notions: making people pay, often dearly, for their failure to critically examine the nature and sources of the promises they call "money." For as we have already seen, while virtually anyone can make these promises, the challenge is making sure they remain credible in the shadow of bankruptcy. Unfortunately, it is precisely at this point that the people to whom these promises have been made are probably not going to like the answers to the questions they never asked. For the customers of Mt Gox, these answers demonstrate beyond a shadow of a doubt that the exchange's promises were not actually money—at least not when it really counted. As a matter of fact, almost a full decade after Mt Gox filed for bankruptcy, customers were still

4. Ben McLannahan, "Bitcoin Exchange Mt Gox Files for Bankruptcy Protection," *Financial Times* (February 28, 2014).

waiting for the conclusion of the bankruptcy process, at which point they stand in line to receive only a small fraction—perhaps around one-fifth—of their original investments.[5]

It is perhaps tempting to frame Mt Gox as an isolated example—a cautionary tale about the dangers of fraud and cyber theft in cryptoland. For many, this temptation has only grown stronger in the wake of a string of high-profile crypto bankruptcies in the summer and fall of 2022. This "crypto winter" saw the failure of leading crypto lending platforms, like Celsius and BlockFi, along with the bankruptcies of several cryptocurrency exchanges, including Voyager Digital and, most significantly, FTX. At the time of its collapse, FTX was the third-largest cryptocurrency exchange in the world by trading volume, serving millions of customers trading BTC, ETH, and other digital assets.[6] In its initial bankruptcy filings, FTX disclosed that it owed somewhere between $10 billion and $50 billion to its more than one million creditors, including customers holding fiat currency and stablecoin balances via the exchange.[7] While the actual amount of FTX's outstanding liabilities—along with any net shortfall—remains unclear, the downfall of FTX and other crypto intermediaries has driven home the harsh reality that bankruptcy is the ultimate promise-breaker and, therefore, anathema to any aspiring monetary IOUs.

Yet there is nothing about these crypto intermediaries that makes them inherently unique, or any more or less vulnerable to the destructive impact of corporate bankruptcy law than other components of the shadow monetary system. Indeed, while the volatility of BTC and other digital assets has exposed the fact that many of the emperors of crypto had no clothes, the basic legal structure and regulation of these intermediaries is often broadly similar, if not identical, to seemingly less risky financial institutions, like PayPal, Circle, or Wise. In the event any of these institutions and platforms were to fail—whether as a result of mismanagement, operational risks, fraud, or significant losses on their ballooning investment portfolios—their customers would likely experience more or less the same fate as those of Mt Gox and,

5. Details of the Mt Gox plan of rehabilitation are available at https://www.mtgox.com/.

6. In its bankruptcy filing, FTX disclosed that its US trading arm served approximately one million customers and that its global (non-US) arm served "millions" more; *FTX Trading Ltd., et al.*, Case No. 22-11-068, U.S. Bankruptcy Court for the District of Delaware, Affidavit of John Ray III (filed November 17, 2022).

7. See Alameda Research LLC, Voluntary Petition for Non-individuals Filing for Bankruptcy, Case 22–11066 (filed November 11, 2022) (indicating FTX's liabilities); *FTX Trading Ltd., et al.*, Case No. 22-11-068, U.S. Bankruptcy Court for the District of Delaware, Motion of Debtors for Entry of an Order Modifying Certain Creditor List Requirements 6 (filed November 14, 2022).

potentially, FTX. This makes these failures valuable case studies for illuminating the dangers of Gresham's new law. For these purposes, the question is not whether or how they might fail, but what impact their failure would have on the credibility of their monetary IOUs.

This chapter explores this question in greater depth. It begins by describing in more detail why the monetary IOUs issued by these institutions and platforms are so vulnerable to the core substantive and procedural requirements imposed by corporate bankruptcy law. Ironically, this vulnerability takes us back to the early English case law that, as we have already seen, was so pivotal to the emergence of fractional reserve banking. It then chronicles the growing number of real-world case studies that vividly illustrate this vulnerability and the destructive impact of bankruptcy law on the credibility of their monetary IOUs. Last, this chapter explains why people and businesses might still want to hold the monetary IOUs of these vulnerable institutions and platforms: effectively discounting, if not altogether disregarding, the risks that bankruptcy poses to their money. This chapter sets the stage for the next, where we examine how these institutions and platforms, and the regulators responsible for overseeing them, have attempted to reduce this vulnerability and, ultimately, whether these efforts have successfully protected customers from the risks of bad money.

The Contract Killer

In virtually every country on the planet, corporate bankruptcy law dictates what happens in the event that a corporation or other business enterprise is unable to pay its outstanding debts.[8] Yet rather than dictating a specific result, bankruptcy law is generally designed to coordinate the *process* of restructuring the bankrupt firm's liabilities, ultimately with the goal of returning the firm to solvency and giving its (new) owners the chance to rebuild the struggling business. Where this is not possible, bankruptcy law also typically coordinates the process of winding the firm down and liquidating its remaining assets for the benefit of its creditors. While the mechanics of these bankruptcy processes and their objectives vary from country to

---

8. For a basic overview and comparison of corporate bankruptcy law across jurisdictions, see Philip Wood, *Principles of International Insolvency* (2007). For a conceptual framework identifying and describing the core features of corporate bankruptcy law across jurisdictions, see Horst Eidenmuller, "Comparative Corporate Insolvency Law," European Corporate Governance Institute Law Working Paper No. 319-206 (July 2017).

country, the legal frameworks in most jurisdictions contemplate several core procedural and substantive requirements.

When a firm files for bankruptcy, this typically triggers two procedural events by operation of law. The first event is the creation of an entirely new legal entity, often referred to as the bankruptcy estate.[9] This estate generally comprises all the legal and equitable interests of the bankrupt firm in any property at the moment of the bankruptcy filing, along with any interest in property subsequently received by the firm or otherwise recovered by a court-appointed bankruptcy trustee.[10] The second event is the imposition of an automatic stay that prevents the bankrupt firm's creditors from immediately seeking to seize this property in connection with the enforcement of their outstanding debts.[11] Typically, the automatic stay applies to almost all the firm's creditors, and to all the bankruptcy estate's property, wherever in the world this property is located.[12]

The rationale for the automatic stay is often framed as solving a potentially acute coordination problem. Specifically, by preventing individual creditors from immediately rushing in to seize the assets of the bankruptcy estate, the stay provides the management of the bankrupt firm, or the bankruptcy trustee, with breathing space to explore the possibility of negotiating a sustainable restructuring.[13] In effect, the hope is that the bankruptcy process can be used to maximize the value of the firm going forward and avoid potentially destructive competition among creditors that might otherwise result in unnecessary liquidation. Reflecting this rationale, the automatic stay generally remains in place until the very end of the bankruptcy process.[14]

Yet in bankruptcy law, as in life, there is never a free lunch. While the automatic stay may in many cases help maximize the value of the bankrupt firm, extracting this value almost inevitably comes at the expense of time. Creditors must typically wait until the conclusion of the bankruptcy

9. For the relevant US law, see 11 U.S.C. § 541(a).

10. See, e.g., 11 U.S.C. § 541(a)(1); see *Lehman Bros., Holding Inc.*, 422 B.R. 407, 418 (U.S. Bankruptcy Court, S.D.N.Y., 2010).

11. See, e.g., 11 U.S.C. § 362(a).

12. In many jurisdictions, there are several classes of creditors not subject to the automatic stay. Notably, this "superpriority" typically applies to sophisticated financial creditors that enter into securities transactions, derivatives or repo agreements, or other specified contracts with the bankrupt firm.

13. See Thomas Jackson, *The Logic and Limits of Bankruptcy Law* (1986); Jackson & Douglas Baird, "Corporate Reorganizations and the Treatment of Diverse Ownership Interests," 51 University of Chicago Law Review 97 (1984).

14. While a court can theoretically lift the stay for cause, this still requires the creditors to go to court to seek this specific relief; see, e.g., 11 U.S.C. § 362(d).

process before getting paid back—a process that can take several years. As of 2022, the World Bank estimated that the average length of corporate bankruptcy proceedings in countries like the United States, the United Kingdom, Canada, and Singapore was approximately one year. This average jumps to almost two years in countries like Sweden and China, three years in Switzerland and the Bahamas, and over four years in Kenya and Brazil.[15] What's more, these figures are only estimates, with larger and more complex bankruptcies often taking considerably longer to complete. The US bankruptcy of Lehman Brothers, for example, took over fourteen years from the first filing in September 2008 until the final proceeds of the liquidation were paid out to creditors in the fall of 2022.[16] As of writing, the Japanese bankruptcy of Mt Gox is still ongoing over ten years after the embattled exchange announced it was closing its doors.

Crucially, the automatic stay only applies to the property of the bankruptcy estate. As a consequence, if any property in the possession of a firm at the time of its bankruptcy actually belongs to someone else, the automatic stay would not technically prevent the owner of this property from immediately seizing it. Thus, for example, if you asked your accountant if you could keep a cache of diamonds in her office safe, and the accounting firm filed for bankruptcy while the diamonds were in its possession, you would be entitled to take them back notwithstanding any debts the firm owed to its creditors. Yet, even in these types of cases, because contraventions of the automatic stay can attract significant sanctions from the bankruptcy court, the owners of this property typically seek the court's permission before attempting to assert their legal rights. Accordingly, even where property does not belong to the bankruptcy estate, there can still be significant procedural delays before the property is returned to its rightful owners.

In addition to procedural requirements like the automatic stay, corporate bankruptcy law also typically includes important substantive requirements governing the claims of different creditors over the property of the bankruptcy estate. The first set of requirements lays down the relative priority of different classes of creditors. Metaphorically speaking, if the property of the estate is a jug of water, these priority rules determine who gets to drink first and how much. In general, secured creditors have first priority

15. World Bank, "Business Enabling Environment: Alternative Existing Indicators for the Year 2020" (updated to September 30, 2021), https://www.worldbank.org/en/programs/business-enabling-environment/alternative-existing-indicators#3.

16. See Jonathan Stempel, "After 14 Years, Lehman Brothers' Brokerage Ends Liquidation," Reuters (September 28, 2022).

up to the entire value of their secured claims. This is followed by enumer-
ated classes of unsecured creditors that are given a statutory preference;
for example, the bankruptcy trustee, tax authorities, trade creditors, and
employees.[17] Standing last in line are then the general unsecured creditors
of the bankrupt firm.

Within each class of creditors, bankruptcy law typically envisions a second substantive rule, often known as the equal treatment or *pari passu* rule.[18]
The pari passu rule dictates that creditors of a given class share in any distribution of the bankruptcy estate's property on a pro rata or proportionate
basis. Thus, if a given creditor had a claim equal to 10 percent of the total
claims owed to the creditors of that class, that creditor would be entitled to
10 percent of whatever sum of money that class was ultimately entitled
to receive from the bankruptcy estate. The pari passu rule has especially
important implications for general unsecured creditors, who are therefore
forced to compete with each other for whatever scraps of the estate remain
after other, more senior, creditors have been made whole. Depending on
the amount and structure of the firm's debts, this could mean that there is
little or nothing left in the jug.

Taken together, the application of the automatic stay, priority rules, and
the pari passu rule are particularly bad news for one peculiar species of debt
contracts: monetary IOUs. As we have seen, these IOUs are designed to
facilitate their immediate transfer, at full nominal value, to complete strangers, at any time. Put differently, these contracts are designed to be highly,
if not universally, liquid. Yet upon the bankruptcy of firms that issue these
IOUs, the immediate application of the automatic stay effectively prohibits
the creditors that hold these claims from enforcing their legal rights to withdraw or otherwise transfer them—a prohibition that may remain in place
for months, years, or even decades. In this way, the strict and automatic
application of the stay catalyzes an elemental change in the nature of these
IOUs, transforming them from extremely liquid assets into what are essentially frozen and often fundamentally immovable claims for the duration of
the bankruptcy process.[19]

---

17. See, e.g., 11 U.S.C. § 507.

18. See, e.g., 11 U.S.C. § 726(b).

19. While the holder of a monetary IOU may be able to sell these claims to a third party,
this almost invariably requires the holder to accept a discount to their nominal (face) value. Sale
or no sale, the effect is to reduce the liquidity of these claims, thereby eroding their value as a
source of money.

Compounding matters, bankruptcy law can also erode the ostensibly fixed nominal value of these monetary IOUs. Where the holders of monetary IOUs are deemed to be general unsecured creditors, priority rules mean that their interests are subordinated to the claims of the bankrupt firm's secured creditors, those that enjoy a statutory preference, and any counterparties not subject to the automatic stay. The application of the pari passu rule also means these creditors will be forced to share equally in whatever pool of assets remains at the conclusion of the bankruptcy process. In many cases, these creditors will include not only the holders of monetary IOUs but also a wide variety of other parties that were owed money by the bankrupt firm. This raises the distinct prospect that the holders of these IOUs may get back only pennies on the dollar, and perhaps even nothing at all. Viewed in this stark and unflattering light, the application of these core bankruptcy rules destroys the very essence of the bargain at the heart of these contracts. Make no mistake: when it comes to monetary IOUs, bankruptcy law is a cold-blooded contract killer.

The Untouchables

Nevertheless, there are some particularly hardy varieties of monetary IOUs that even bankruptcy law cannot kill. In many jurisdictions, corporate bankruptcy law includes a series of exemptions—often referred to as carveouts or "safe harbors"—from the application of the automatic stay for certain types of executory debt contracts. Where a creditor of a bankrupt firm is owed money pursuant to one of these contracts, they are generally entitled to seize and liquidate property in satisfaction of this debt almost immediately after the debtor firm files for bankruptcy. Indeed, in many cases, they can demand that struggling firms post property as collateral against its debts right up to the eve of bankruptcy. The practical effect of these safe harbors is to give the counterparties to these contracts superpriority over the bankrupt firm's other creditors: enabling them to avoid the uncertainty, cost, and delay associated with the bankruptcy process and eliminating the need for them to participate in the potentially destructive competition for the firm's remaining property.[20]

---

20. For a detailed discussion of the potential impact of these superpriorities, see Mark Roe, "The Derivatives Market's Payment Priorities as Financial Crisis Accelerator," 63 Stanford Law Review 539 (2011), and Ed Morrison & Franklin Edwards, "Derivatives and the Bankruptcy Code: Why the Special Treatment?," 22 Yale Journal on Regulation 101 (2005).

One of the primary rationales for the creation of these bankruptcy safe harbors is that the strict application of the automatic stay can undermine the smooth and orderly functioning of systemically important financial markets. This includes wholesale money markets like the $4.5 trillion market for US-dollar-denominated repurchase or "repo" contracts.[21] Repo markets have long been used by banks and other financial institutions as a critical source of short-term financing—the modern-day version of Bagehot's Lombard Street. These once obscure markets catapulted to fame in the thick of the global financial crisis, when the "run on repo"[22] became one of the sparks that ignited the fire, ultimately illuminating the size, fragility, and complex inner workings of the so-called shadow banking system.[23]

Legally speaking, repo contracts typically involve the sale and subsequent repurchase of a specified basket of collateral assets, often including government debt, corporate bonds, or other fixed-income securities. Yet, economically speaking, these contracts are perhaps best understood as short-term collateralized loans, with the borrower essentially exchanging the collateral basket for cold hard cash. In the United States, around 50 percent of repo loans are currently extended on either an "open" or "overnight" basis,[24] meaning that the lender can decide to immediately terminate the contract, or simply not roll it over, on any given day. Together with the liquidity and credit quality of the posted collateral, the ability of repo lenders to demand their money back on such short notice is an important part of what makes repo markets vulnerable to destabilizing runs. Importantly, it is also what gives these contracts the basic look and feel of monetary IOUs—the wholesale equivalent of retail bank deposits.

The bankruptcy safe harbors for repo contracts highlight an important yet often neglected difference between conventional money markets and the new monetary experiments described in chapter 4. Whereas conventional money markets are largely the domain of banks, broker-dealers, hedge funds, and other sophisticated financial institutions that can avail themselves of the protections afforded by the repo and other bankruptcy safe harbors,

21. US Office of Financial Research (OFR), OFR Short-Term Funding Monitor, "Repo Transaction Volumes by Venue" (January 2023), https://www.financialresearch.gov/short-term -funding-monitor/.

22. See Gary Gorton & Andrew Metrick, "Securitized Banking and the Run on Repo," National Bureau of Economic Research Working Paper 15223 (August 2009).

23. See Zoltan Pozsar, Tobias Adrian, Adam Ashcraft, & Hayley Boesky, "Shadow Banking," 19 Federal Reserve Bank of New York Economic Policy Review 1 (2013).

24. See OFR, OFR Short-Term Funding Monitor, "Tenor" (January 2023), https://www .financialresearch.gov/short-term-funding-monitor/market-digests/tenor/chart-27/.

these new monetary experiments cater to the needs of less sophisticated consumers and businesses that—often unbeknownst to them—stand fully exposed to the destructive force of bankruptcy law. Compounding matters, where these two very different types of creditors find themselves owed money by the same bankrupt firm, the safe harbors would likely operate to ensure that the institutional holders of conventional money market instruments would get paid back almost immediately and in full. By definition, this would leave less property in the bankruptcy estate for eventual distribution to the firm's other creditors, including the retail holders of any monetary IOUs not protected by a safe harbor.

By tilting the legal scales decidedly in favor of more sophisticated institutional creditors, the repo and other bankruptcy safe harbors effectively flip the elemental logic of customer protection on its head.[25] Specifically, the safe harbors shield some of the most financially sophisticated creditors in the world from the full force and impact of bankruptcy law while simultaneously leaving less sophisticated creditors to the law of the bankruptcy jungle: caveat emptor. In the process, the safe harbors drive a wedge between different types of monetary IOUs—giving those that benefit from them a far greater degree of moneyness than those that do not. For the holders of these untouchable monetary IOUs, the shadow of bankruptcy may seem like little more than welcome protection from the hot summer sun. Yet for basically everyone else, this shadow represents a looming existential threat, forcing them to find other avenues for protecting the liquidity and value of their money. Not by chance, these avenues take us back to the very beginning of our story and the venerable English case law that paved the way for the emergence of modern banking, money, and payments.

Foley v. Hill Revisited

What becomes clear from this broad overview of the basic mechanics of corporate bankruptcy law is that the fate of a monetary IOU ultimately hinges on the nature of the legal claim it creates against a bankrupt firm. Where this claim is characterized as debt, the holders of any monetary IOUs that do not enjoy a safe harbor are lumped in with the firm's other creditors—at which point they become subject to the harsh strictures of the automatic

---

25. This logic is premised on the assumption that less sophisticated consumers should receive more legal protection; see John Armour, Dan Awrey, Paul Davies, Luca Enriques, Jeff Gordon, Colin Mayer, & Jennifer Payne, *Principles of Financial Regulation*, chapter 10 (2016).

stay, priority rules, and the pari passu rule. Conversely, where this claim is characterized as a property interest, or otherwise enjoys equivalent legal protections that carve it out from the bankruptcy estate, these holders may, at least eventually, be entitled to the return of their money. Indeed, even in cases where there is not enough money to guarantee full recovery, the fact that the holders of these monetary IOUs do not have to compete over the scraps means they receive more, and faster, than if they had been general unsecured creditors.

The process of determining the legal nature of these claims is typically an extremely fact-driven exercise.[26] In theory, there are several different avenues for the holders of these claims to argue that their monetary IOUs represent a property or other interest separate and apart from the assets of the bankruptcy estate. In many cases, the first and most straightforward avenue will be to demonstrate the existence of an *express trust* acknowledging that the issuer of the monetary IOU is holding property as trustee on their behalf. Where an express trust is found to exist, the holders of these IOUs will then enjoy the rights of beneficial ownership in any deposited property, and the property in question will not be available for distribution to the bankrupt firm's creditors. Importantly, however, the finding of an express trust is generally contingent on the existence of a written document—e.g., contractual terms and conditions—that evidences a clear intention to create a trust for the benefit of an identifiable class of beneficiaries.[27] And even when these beneficiaries include the holders of a firm's monetary IOUs, they will still need to apply to the bankruptcy court for an order acknowledging the existence of the trust and authorizing the transfer of the property to the beneficiaries.

A second potential avenue of legal recourse involves the holders of a bankrupt firm's monetary IOUs arguing that their claims are protected by what is known as a *constructive trust*—an implied trust created by a court to protect against the unjust enrichment of a party that holds legal title to a particular asset. Whereas the existence of an express trust depends on the ex ante intentions of the contracting parties, the existence of a constructive trust thus depends on ex post judicial intervention. As famously explained by Justice Benjamin Cardozo, "A constructive trust is the formula through which the conscience of equity finds expression. When property has been

---

26. For a detailed synthesis of these avenues in the context of cryptocurrency exchanges, see Adam Levitin, "Not Your Keys, Not Your Coins: Unpriced Credit Risk in Cryptocurrency," 101 Texas Law Review 877, 25–52 (2023).

27. As described in the next chapter, express trusts can also be created by statute or regulation.

acquired in such circumstances that the holders of the legal title may not in good conscience retain the beneficial interest, equity converts him into a trustee."[28]

Yet predicting if and when courts will exercise their equitable jurisdiction to create a constructive trust is notoriously difficult. Different jurisdictions also take radically different approaches to recognizing the existence of constructive trusts. In the United States, for example, some states require a court order creating the trust prior to the initiation of bankruptcy proceedings, while others do not recognize them at all.[29] Further complicating matters, constructive trusts are often viewed with particular skepticism in the context of corporate bankruptcy proceedings, where carving out property from the bankruptcy estate can have potentially enormous distributional implications for the firm's creditors. And, of course, the creation of any constructive trust still requires the potential beneficiaries to incur the time and expense of going to court to establish and enforce their legal rights.

A third, and somewhat related, avenue is bailment. In a nutshell, a *bailment* relationship involves the delivery of property from one person to another for a specific purpose, pursuant to a contract that envisions that the property will be returned when that purpose has been achieved or when the owner retakes possession. Like express and constructive trusts, bailment thus draws a sharp distinction between the party in possession of property and its ultimate owner. Returning to our diamond example, the accountant holding your cache in the office safe would potentially be acting as your bailee, provided that she agreed to do so and that you—the bailor—do not have access to the office or know the combination to the safe.

Historically, the concept of bailment has generally only applied to physical property, like diamonds, wheat, and other commodities. Nevertheless, in theory, there is no compelling reason why it could not be extended to intangible assets like financial instruments held on the books of an intermediary.[30] Yet, once again, the existence of a bailment relationship inevitably hinges on the facts of a given case, including the detailed terms of the contract between the putative bailor and bailee. Where the contract clearly envisions that one party will deliver and completely relinquish control of property to another party, and where the receiving party agrees to return the exact same property, a court may be willing to entertain the existence of a

28. *Beatty v. Guggenheim Exploration Co.*, 225 N.Y. 380, 386 (1919).

29. For a discussion, see Levitin, "Not Your Keys, Not Your Coins," 32–33.

30. For a discussion, see Danielle D'Onfro, "The New Bailments," 97 Washington Law Review 97 (2022).

bailment relationship. However, where the delivering party retains a degree of control, or where the contract simply envisions the return of equivalent property, or property of equal value, the relationship will be characterized as debt, and ownership of the property itself will reside in the bankruptcy estate.[31]

Notably, all three of these legal avenues—and bailment in particular—share important parallels, and in many respects a common jurisprudential lineage, with the early English case law on bank deposit taking that culminated in the House of Lords decision in *Foley v. Hill*. As we saw in chapter 1, the decision in *Foley*, like many English cases before it, drew a distinction between the common law remedies of detinue and debt. Whereas detinue recognized the property rights of the depositor and required the party holding it to return that exact same property, debt merely required them to return an equivalent sum of money. Ultimately, it was the fact that English courts held that the legal obligations of the goldsmiths to their depositors were properly characterized as *loans*—and hence *debt* contracts—that gave these fledgling bankers full legal title to deposited property, thereby supporting the emergence of fractional reserve banking. The fact that depositors are unsecured creditors is also precisely why, in the absence of the financial safety net, they are so exposed to the risk of bankruptcy. In this critical and yet often underappreciated respect, the fragility of banks, their vulnerability to destabilizing runs, and the rationale for the financial safety net can all be traced back to the decision to view their monetary IOUs as a species of unsecured debt.

These parallels become even more evident once we introduce what was historically an important exception to the general rule that bank depositors are simply unsecured creditors. This exception, known as the "bagging rule," dictated that money deposited with a protobank in a sealed bag, locked chest, or other vessel bearing the mark of the depositor would remain the depositor's property. As both a legal and practical matter, delivering money in a bag, signed and sealed by the depositor, served two important purposes. First, despite the bank having physical possession of the deposited money, the seal effectively prevented it from lending the money to other customers. Second, in the event of a subsequent dispute, the fact that the contents of the bag—otherwise indistinguishable gold and silver coins—were secured and clearly marked enabled a court to easily verify that the money belonged to a specific depositor. In effect, the practice of sealing

---

31. See *Powder Co. v. Burkhardt*, 97 U.S. 110 (1878); *Strum v. Boker et al.*, 150 U.S. 312 (1893).

the coins in a bag came to be understood as a signal to the court that the bank had agreed to act in a capacity equivalent to that of a bailee, thus carving out the depositor's property from the property of the bank itself.[32]

The nature, availability, and application of these and other equivalent legal remedies vary across jurisdictions. Nevertheless, these remedies all share two things in common. First, where they are available, these remedies draw a hard-and-fast distinction between the property of the bankrupt firm and that of its customers—providing the latter with relief from the strict application of bankruptcy law. Second, they all force these customers to go to court to affirmatively prove and enforce their legal rights, introducing potentially significant legal uncertainty, monetary costs, and temporal delays into the process of getting their money back. Importantly, the uncertainty, cost, and delay associated with this process is likely to be even greater where there are allegations of fraud, where the bankrupt firm has commingled customer property with its own or that of other customers, where the firm has used or disposed of customer property for its own purposes, or where it has failed to keep accurate books and records. Especially in these more complex cases, even if customers can successfully establish their legal rights to property outside the bankruptcy estate, there is still no guarantee that the bankrupt firm will have enough money left to make them whole.

For the vast majority of retail bank depositors, the financial safety net effectively solves all of these problems. While their deposits are still characterized as debt, deposit insurance schemes and bank resolution frameworks effectively combine to ensure that they will have continuous access to their money—thereby eliminating the uncertainty, cost, and delays otherwise associated with the bankruptcy process. But for the growing number of people and businesses that hold monetary IOUs issued by financial institutions and platforms other than banks, which by definition are not protected by this safety net, these problems are exactly what awaits them in the event of bankruptcy. Viewed in this light, *Foley v. Hill*, the bagging rule, bailment, and trust law all provide us with a window to a long forgotten world, before the creation of the financial safety net, when depositors and their money were easily parted. This begs an important question: Is the future of money on a collision course with its past?

---

32. For a comprehensive overview of the rationale for, and jurisprudence developing, the bagging rule, see David Fox, "*Banks v. Whetson* (1596)," in Douglas, Hickey, & Waring (eds.), *Landmark Cases in Property Law* (2015).

Back to the Future

For better or worse, we no longer need to exhume obscure and, in many ways, antiquated English case law to answer this question. Like so many crises before it, the crypto winter that began in the spring of 2022 exposed the shaky legal foundations on which many of the new financial intermediaries that have emerged to support digital asset markets currently rest. The first signs of trouble appeared in May, when an algorithmic stablecoin, known as TerraUSD, lost its peg, wiping out over $18 billion in market capitalization in a matter of days. This was immediately followed by the collapse of TerraUSD's sister coin, LUNA, destroying another $11 billion.[33] These widely unexpected and high-profile failures spooked the crypto market, with the price of one BTC falling from almost $40,000 to less than $20,000 in a little over a month.[34] This precipitous price decline had a predictable impact on leveraged crypto investors like Three Arrows Capital, which defaulted on a $660 million loan to crypto lending platform Voyager Digital before being unable to meet a margin call from another crypto lender, BlockFi.[35] The growing market turmoil put the balance sheets of these crypto lenders under severe strain. In July, Voyager filed for bankruptcy protection,[36] followed a week later by the bankruptcy of another major crypto lender, Celsius Network.[37]

The storm would continue to rage on into the fall and winter of 2022. In November, cryptocurrency exchange FTX, which had agreed to buy Voyager's assets out of bankruptcy, announced that it was itself filing for bankruptcy protection amid widespread allegations of fraud, mismanagement,

33. See Krisztian Sandor & Ekin Genç, "The Fall of Terra: A Timeline of the Meteoric Rise and Crash of UST and LUNA," *CoinDesk* (December 22, 2022), https://www.coindesk.com/learn /the-fall-of-terra-a-timeline-of-the-meteoric-rise-and-crash-of-ust-and-luna/.

34. See Coinmarketcap.com, BTC price history, https://coinmarketcap.com/currencies /bitcoin/(reporting a BTC price of $39,695 on May 5, 2022, and $19,010 on June 18, 2022).

35. See Kadhim Shubber & Joshua Oliver, "Crypto Hedge Fund Three Arrows Fails to Meet Lender Margin Calls," *Financial Times* (June 16, 2022), https://www.ft.com/content/126d8b02 -f06a-4fd9-a57b-9f4ceab3de71.

36. See Brian Newar, "Voyager Digital Files for Chapter 11 Bankruptcy, Proposes Recovery Plan," *Cointelegraph* (July 6, 2022), https://cointelegraph.com/news/voyager-digital-files-for -chapter-11-bankruptcy-proposes-recovery-plan.

37. See Olga Kharif & Joanna Ossinger, "Crypto Lender Celsius Files for Bankruptcy after Cash Crunch," *Bloomberg* (July 13, 2022), https://www.bloomberg.com/news/articles/2022-07 -14/crypto-lender-celsius-files-for-bankruptcy-in-cash-crunch?leadSource=uverify%20wall.

and bad portfolio investments.[38] The fallout would quickly engulf BlockFi, which had lent over $1 billion to FTX.[39] And, as of January 2023, the latest major domino to fall was Genesis Global, a major crypto brokerage firm that primarily served institutional investors.[40] While many are still in their early days, these and other crypto bankruptcies will inevitably test the credibility of the monetary IOUs issued by these once dazzling, but now rapidly imploding, stars of the crypto universe.

Among these ongoing bankruptcy proceedings, the New York case in *Celsius Network* was the first to directly address the legal treatment of monetary IOUs. Celsius was an archetypal crypto lending platform. The platform gave its customers the option to deposit, lend, and borrow against BTC, ETH, and other digital assets in two different ways. The first involved opening what Celsius described as a "Custody" account. The second was marketed as an "Earn" account. As this marketing language suggests, the key difference between the Custody and Earn accounts was that the latter entitled customers to earn "rewards" on their deposits, typically in the form of interest payments denominated in the deposited assets. As of January 2022, Celsius was promising to pay its Earn customers an annualized interest rate of up to 18 percent on their deposits at a time when traditional savings accounts typically offered less than 1 percent.[41] Celsius then lent out the crypto deposited in its customers' Earn accounts, theoretically using the interest on these loans to pay out the promised rewards. In reality, Celsius turned out to be little more than a complex Ponzi scheme.[42]

In January 2023, the court in *Celsius* was asked to determine who owned the digital assets held in the platform's 600,000 Earn accounts immediately

38. *FTX Trading Ltd.*; David Yaffe-Bellany, "FTX Assets Still Missing as Firm Begins Bankruptcy Process," *New York Times* (November 22, 2022), https://www.nytimes.com/2022/11/22/business/ftx-bankruptcy-sam-bankman-fried.html.

39. See Lauren Hirsch, David Yaffe-Bellany, & Ephrat Livni, "BlockFi Files for Bankruptcy as FTX Fallout Spreads," *New York Times* (November 28, 2022), https://www.nytimes.com/2022/11/28/business/blockfi-bankruptcy-cryptocurrency-ftx.html.

40. See Stephen Alpher & Danny Nelson, "Genesis' Crypto Lending Businesses File for Bankruptcy Protection," *CoinDesk* (January 20, 2023), https://www.coindesk.com/business/2023/01/20/genesis-global-files-for-bankruptcy-protection/.

41. See Zeke Faux & Joe Light, "Celsius's 18% Yields on Crypto Are Tempting—and Drawing Scrutiny," *Bloomberg* (January 27, 2022), https://www.bloomberg.com/news/articles/2022-01-27/celsius-s-18-yields-on-crypto-are-tempting-and-drawing-scrutiny?leadSource=uverify%20wall.

42. See Bryce Elder, "Scenes from a Celsius Bankruptcy Report," FTAlphaville blog (January 30, 2023), https://www.ft.com/content/6e74511e-0b94-44d6-beeb-df52bec1476c; *Celsius Network LLC, et al.*, U.S. Bankruptcy Court, S.D.N.Y., Case No 22–10964, Final Report of Shoba Pillay, Examiner (January 30, 2023).

before the firm filed for bankruptcy.[43] At the moment of filing, these assets were collectively worth approximately $4.2 billion, including $23 million worth of stablecoins. The legal arguments followed a familiar pattern in these types of cases. Earn customers argued that the assets were their rightful property and should be returned to them as soon as possible. The bankruptcy trustee and other creditors argued that they were properly a part of the bankruptcy estate and therefore available to pay for the firm's ongoing operating expenses and, as necessary, eventually distributed to its creditors in accordance with the priority and pari passu rules. At the crux of these competing arguments were the contractual terms and conditions attached to Earn accounts, which include the following language:

> In consideration for the Rewards payable to you on the Eligible Digital Assets using the Earn Service . . . you grant Celsius . . . all right and title to such Eligible Digital Assets, including ownership rights, and the right, without further notice to you, to hold such Digital Assets in Celsius' [*sic*] own Virtual Wallet or elsewhere, and to pledge, re-pledge, hypothecate, rehypothecate, sell, lend, or otherwise transfer or use any amount of such Digital Assets, separately or together with other property, with all attendant rights of ownership.[44]

The terms and conditions then go on to state:

> In the event that Celsius becomes bankrupt . . . and Eligible Digital Assets used in the Earn Service or as collateral under the Borrow Service [a lending product that enables customers to pledge digital assets as security] may not be recoverable, and you may not have any legal remedies or rights in connection with Celsius' [*sic*] obligations to you other than your rights as a creditor.[45]

On a plain reading, the terms and conditions are thus clear and unambiguous: the digital assets were the property of the bankruptcy estate, relegating Earn customers to the status of unsecured creditors in a failed Ponzi scheme.

So what exactly was the legal basis of the customers' argument for why, contrary to the terms and conditions, they should be viewed as the rightful owners of these assets? Among the litany of arguments advanced by counsel for the customers, two in particular stand out. The first argument was that

43. *Celsius Network LLC, et al.*, U.S. Bankruptcy Court, S.D.N.Y., Case No. 22-10964, Memorandum Opinion and Order Regarding Ownership of Earn Account Assets (January 24, 2023).

44. *Celsius Network LLC, et al.*, Memorandum Opinion and Order, 10.

45. *Celsius Network*, 11.

most Earn customers had probably never read the terms and conditions. While empathizing with the frustrations of these customers, the court quickly dismissed this argument—observing that to hold otherwise would destroy the "certainty and predictability required for modern commerce in the digital era."[46] The second argument was that the ubiquitous use of the word *loan* elsewhere in the terms and conditions was inconsistent with the idea that ownership of the assets was transferred to Celsius at the moment the customer deposited them. As summarized by the court, the essence of this argument was that, from a layperson's perspective, the use of the term *loan* somehow created the expectation that the customer would retain ownership over the assets, but also temporarily permit Celsius to use them in its own business.

Immediately, this second argument should raise the eyebrows of anyone who has ever encountered the House of Lords decision in *Foley v. Hill*. As we have seen, the entire basis for fractional reserve banking is that deposits are loans, with the property rights in deposited assets being transferred from the depositor to the bank itself. As if to drive this point home, the court in *Celsius* quoted at length from a New York precedent adopting the logic in *Foley*: "Under New York law, a bank and its depositor stand in a debtor-creditor relationship that is contractual in nature. The bank owns the deposit, the depositor has a claim to payment against the bank, and the bank has a corresponding obligation to pay its depositor."[47] Describing this position as "black letter law," the court therefore dismissed the argument that Earn customers should expect to be treated as anything other than general unsecured creditors.[48]

The decision in *Celsius Network* provides us with something a temperature check for the treatment of monetary IOUs in bankruptcy. Three things stand out. First, this was a relatively straightforward case involving crystal clear terms and conditions and, at least at the time, no documented evidence of fraud, commingling of customer funds, or other conduct that might have complicated the case, even if it might have also perhaps tipped the scales of equity in the favor of Earn customers.[49]

---

46. *Celsius Network*, 33.

47. *Masterwear Corp.*, 229 B.R. 301, 310 (U.S. Bankruptcy Court, S.D.N.Y. (1999).

48. *Celsius Network LLC, et al.*, Memorandum Opinion and Order, 40.

49. While the Earn customers and several intervenors did allege fraud and commingling had taken place, they did not submit any evidence in support of these allegations as part of their request for the return of Earn assets. In the end, the finding that the assets were not the customers' property also rendered the allegation of commingling moot.

Second, notwithstanding the relative simplicity of the case, the court's opinion came down almost six months after the initial bankruptcy filing. Customers would have experienced the costs of this delay not only in terms of lost time but also lost money. While the total amount spent on legal fees is not publicly available, the opinion lists forty-one different lawyers from no less than eleven law firms, the US Office of the Trustee, and the states of Washington, Vermont, and Texas. Not only would Earn customers likely have to shoulder some of the resulting legal fees, but Celsius itself would have incurred fees in opposing the customers' request for the return of the deposited assets. Importantly, these fees are generally paid out of the bankruptcy estate. They also enjoy a statutory preference, with the result that Celsius's lawyers get paid first, out of assets that might otherwise have been distributed to the firm's unsecured creditors. Put bluntly, not only did Earn customers lose on the merits, they also probably guaranteed themselves a lower payout at the conclusion of the bankruptcy process.

Third, and perhaps most critically, the decision in *Celsius Network* treated all Earn customers as a single class of claimants, regardless of the nature of the assets they had originally deposited into their accounts. While this may seem like a trivial observation, the practical effect was to give Earn customers who had deposited roughly $23 million in relatively safe stablecoins the exact same legal rights and protections as customers holding over $4 billion in far more speculative, volatile, and potentially worthless digital assets. Yet this is exactly the result that would have always been dictated by bankruptcy law: once it has been established that someone is a general unsecured creditor, priority rules push them to the back of the line, where the pari passu rule then forces them to compete with other unsecured creditors over the last remnants of the bankruptcy estate. In this bleak postbankruptcy world, it simply doesn't matter whether these creditors thought they were holding a monetary IOU or a lottery ticket. In the eyes of bankruptcy law, they are one and the same.

The question naturally turns to the broader implications of bankruptcy law's treatment of monetary IOUs as reflected in the *Celsius* case. In terms of the growing number of ongoing bankruptcy proceedings involving crypto intermediaries, the *Celsius* decision is almost certainly a harbinger of very bad things to come. The use of "custody" and "earn" accounts is a common feature across many of the most popular cryptocurrency exchanges and lending platforms, with the former typically contemplating that customers retain ownership of deposited assets and the latter transferring ownership to the exchange or platform. This includes bankrupt intermediaries BlockFi and FTX, where the bankruptcy court in both cases will almost inevitably have to grapple with the same issues as the court in *Celsius*.

As we explore in chapter 6, the structure of the Celsius terms and conditions also reflects something of an emerging standard within the crypto industry—albeit one with a high degree of variance around the mean. Yet, as we will see, there are still a great many exchanges and lending platforms that do not provide sufficient clarity around the ownership of deposited assets or the legal rights of customers in the event of bankruptcy. Should these intermediaries ever file for bankruptcy, this lack of clarity will likely translate into even greater legal uncertainty, higher costs, and longer delays before customers recover any of their money.

Lastly, while it may be tempting to confine this discussion to crypto, the reality is that any firm that issues monetary IOUs outside the financial safety net is exposing its customers to these exact same risks. The terms and conditions for popular P2P payment platforms, like PayPal, Venmo, and Wise, clearly disclose that customers holding balances in their accounts will be treated as unsecured creditors in the event of bankruptcy. Even in the absence of this disclosure, the basic structure and mechanics of corporate bankruptcy law more or less dictate this result. And while the bankruptcy of these platforms may seem like a remote possibility, this is still an enormous risk to take with our money. Indeed, the question is probably not *if* one of these platforms will eventually fail but *when*. That being the case, it is important to try to better understand why a large and growing number of people and businesses appear willing, and often eager, to hold money in the shadow of bankruptcy.

What We Do in the Shadows

There are several reasons why people might be attracted to the shadow monetary system notwithstanding the risks that bankruptcy poses to the liquidity and value of their monetary IOUs. In theory, the first and most obvious reason is that bad money often comes bundled together with good payments: offering people cheaper, faster, more convenient, more secure, and more accessible ways to send and receive money. Yet in practice, it is often far from clear whether this technological superiority in the realm of payments necessarily translates into net gains for consumers once the risks of bankruptcy are taken into account. Where these net benefits remain unclear, we must inevitably go in search of other, more compelling, explanations.

One potential explanation is that these risks never even enter our con-
sciousness. Indeed, while the benefits of PayPal, Venmo, M-PESA, and Alipay
are intuitively easy for customers to grasp, understanding the attendant risks
demands a threshold investment of time, expertise and, yes, even money
itself. Having purchased and read this book, you have made an investment
in understanding the nature and sources of money, the important role of the
financial safety net, and the risks that bankruptcy poses to the credibility
of monetary IOUs. This information is not naturally endowed; it must be
learned. Yet, understandably, the vast majority of people are too busy, lack
what they believe is the requisite background or expertise, or are simply
not interested in learning about the problem of bad money. Indeed, they
may have never even been exposed to the idea that money was something
they actually needed to learn about. Whatever the reason, these people are
unaware of the existence of these risks and, therefore, prone to viewing the
emergence of the shadow monetary system as a pure, unalloyed good.

Even when people are not completely unaware, their understanding of the nature, sources, and credibility of money is often anchored in
their previous experiences. For many of us, those experiences have until
very recently revolved almost entirely around conventional deposit-taking
banks. Yet these experiences can distort our understanding of how money
works—and sometimes doesn't—once we remove something as critical,
and often undervalued, as the financial safety net. Once again, the products and services provided by crypto intermediaries offer an illuminating
example. Many have observed that the combination of "custody" and "earn"
accounts offered by major cryptocurrency exchanges and lending platforms
bears something of a superficial similarity to the historical distinction
between bank checking and savings accounts. In theory, this similarity can
be seen as inviting the expectation that, like most conventional checking and
savings accounts, transferring money from one account to the other does not
fundamentally change the customer's legal rights. And in practice, there is at
least some anecdotal evidence to suggest that this is exactly what customers
expect. As one unfortunate customer of the failed crypto lending platform
Genesis told the *Financial Times* after transferring crypto from his custody
account to his earn account, "I thought I was just parking the money in a
high-yield savings account and I can get it out at any time."[50] Ultimately, of

---

50. Nikou Asgari, "'Nightmare': Collapse of Leading Crypto Lender Traps Investors,"
Financial Times (January 20, 2023), https://www.ft.com/content/64648e10-cc09-4304-a274
-87b66d37d3bc.

course, any functional similarity was entirely irrelevant once the platform filed for bankruptcy. While a high-yield savings account would have likely been protected by deposit insurance and other elements of the financial safety net, the terms and conditions of the customer's earn account almost inevitably leave them exposed to the uncertainty, delay, and potential loss that comes with being a general unsecured creditor.

This example highlights a critical point. Our previous experiences may serve us well where there is little or no change in the nature or sources of money over time. The real challenge to our ignorance is dynamism. Indeed, it is only where our previous experiences have created expectations that risk being confounded by the emergence of new types of monetary IOUs that things like the impact of bankruptcy law come front and center. It is also at precisely this point that we encounter a fundamental distinction between Gresham's old and new laws. Gresham's old law was premised on the idea that people paid close attention to differences in the quality of money. These differences then dictated decisions about which money to hoard or export and which to use as a means of payment. Gresham's *new* law stands this premise on its head. Rather than actively attempting to profit from differences in the quality of money, the reality is that we have become almost completely indifferent to them. As we have seen, this indifference is a function of the financial safety net, the elimination of bankruptcy as a threat to the credibility of monetary IOUs, and the resulting dominance of bank deposits as a source of money in the modern economy. Yet while this indifference is arguably rational in a world where the nature and sources of money are relatively static and homogeneous, it presents complex challenges in one shaped by rapid monetary change and increasing heterogeneity.

A second potential explanation—one that builds on the anchoring effects of our previous experiences—is based on language. PayPal, Wise, and other P2P payment platforms routinely advertise that they give customers the ability to send and receive "money" and not, for example, "magic internet tokens." The clear implication is that the monetary IOUs issued by these platforms are close functional substitutes for the money their customers are most familiar with: conventional bank deposits. If anything, the use of this language is even more pronounced within the crypto ecosystem, where labels like "stablecoin" and "cryptocurrency" serve to cloak the entire industry in a vague, and often very inaccurate, sense of moneyness. Embarrassingly, even the law has sometimes sought to compete in these linguistic gymnastics. After El Salvador adopted BTC as legal tender in 2021, the cryptocurrency automatically became "money" in most of the United States pursuant to state commercial law.[51] Yet the narrow use of the term *money* under these state laws—essentially limited to the perfection of security interests—was completely unrelated to its actual use as a store of nominal value or a means of payment. Nor did it mean that BTC was subject to US regulation.

Ultimately, where people lack a baseline level of understanding, or base decisions on their previous experiences, the pervasive use of this language can influence their understanding of what qualifies as money, where they hold it, and how they use it to make payments. Where these understandings, practices, and patterns become entrenched and widespread, this can then further reinforce the use of this language. In this way, language and experience can shape consumer expectations about how money works in both good times and bad. The problem, of course, is that while different types of monetary IOUs may appear to be close functional substitutes when the party is in full swing, the shadow of bankruptcy means that they often behave very differently when the music stops.

Beyond a basic lack of understanding, or an overreliance on their own previous experience, people's decisions may also be influenced by a variety of other behavioral biases. Two potentially important biases at the intersection of money and bankruptcy are hyperbolic discounting and salience. *Hyperbolic discounting* reflects the tendency of people to value the costs and benefits of a given decision that will materialize in the short run disproportionately higher than those that will materialize over the long run.[52] *Salience*, meanwhile, reflects the parallel tendency to base decisions on the most prominent, easy-to-understand, or immediately available information, while simultaneously disregarding more complex, less certain, or less tangible information.[53] Taken together, these biases can drive people to make bad decisions by focusing myopically on easily quantifiable, short-term benefits—like faster, cheaper, and more convenient payments—at the expense of harder-to-quantify,

---

51. See Brian McCall, "How El Salvador Has Changed U.S. Law by a Bit: The Consequences for the UCC of Bitcoin Becoming Legal Tender," 74:3 Oklahoma Law Review 313 (2022).

52. In more formal terms, hyperbolic discounting is characterized by a relatively high subjective discount rate over short time horizons, combined with a relatively low discount rate over long time horizons. This discount rate structure creates an intertemporal conflict between our preferences (i.e., between what we want today and what we will want tomorrow); see David Laibson, "Golden Eggs and Hyperbolic Discounting," 112:2 Quarterly Journal of Economics 443, 445 (1997).

53. The notion of salience can be traced back to Daniel Kahneman and Amos Tversky's groundbreaking work on availability bias: "Availability: A Heuristic for Judging Frequency and Probability," 5 Cognitive Psychology 207 (1973).

longer-term costs—like the risk that bankruptcy may one day destroy the function and value of their hard-earned money.

Yet the problem goes deeper than a simple lack of understanding, the seemingly benign use of imprecise language, or potential behavioral biases. The *real* problem, and hence the far more troubling explanation, is that the combination of these factors can be exploited by unscrupulous financial institutions and platforms looking to make a buck by making bad money. This exploitation can take a variety of forms. As described in greater depth in the next chapter, these institutions and platforms are often in a position to select the regulatory frameworks that impose the fewest constraints on how they are permitted to hold and use customer funds, maximizing their own revenue streams at the expense of consumer protection. Thereafter, they can design and market products that foreground potential benefits—like Celsius's astounding 18 percent annual return on its Earn account—while burying disclosure of the associated risks in the fine print that, as the lawyers for Celsius's customers took great pains to point out, hardly anyone ever reads.

Finally, and most importantly, these institutions and platforms can deliberately give customers the false impression that their monetary IOUs are protected by the conventional financial safety net. In March 2002, on the eve of its original IPO, PayPal disclosed that it planned to obtain "pass-through" deposit insurance from the FDIC "for our customers."[54] Yet nowhere in their disclosure did PayPal make it clear that pass-through deposit insurance only indirectly protects customers against the failure of the bank in which their funds are deposited, and not against the bankruptcy of the platform itself. Twenty years later, both FTX and Genesis would take a page out of this same playbook before eventually being reprimanded by the FDIC for misleading their customers.[55] The subject matter of these omissions and misstatements is extremely telling. These firms were not misleading customers about the quality of their payment services. Rather, they were attempting to enhance the perceived credibility of their monetary IOUs by invoking

54. See PayPal, Inc. Securities & Exchange Commission Form 10-K, 9, 23–24 (March 1, 2002), https://www.sec.gov/Archives/edgar/data/1103415/000091205702009834/a2073071z10-k405.htm.

55. See Nikhilesh De, "FDIC Orders Crypto Exchange FTX US, 4 Others to Cease 'Misleading' Claims," *CoinDesk* (August 19, 2022), https://www.coindesk.com/policy/2022/08/19/fdic-orders-ftx-us-4-other-companies-to-cease-and-desist-misleading-consumers/; Emily Peck & Matt Phillips, "As Crypto Crated, Gemini Talked to Customers about FDIC Insurance," *Axios* (January 30, 2023), https://www.axios.com/2023/01/30/as-crypto-cratered-gemini-talked-to-customers-about-fdic-insurance.

Adoption of Online Payment Accounts by U.S. Consumers (percentage of total)

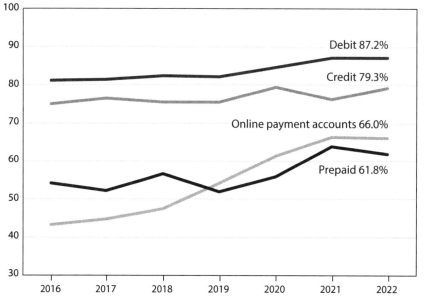

FIGURE 5.1. Adoption of Online Payment Accounts by US Consumers. *Source*: Federal Reserve Bank of Atlanta (2022).

one of the fundamental shibboleths—FDIC deposit insurance—that people have long used as a symbol of good money.

Obviously, it is difficult to completely disentangle these and other potential explanations for why people are increasingly comfortable entrusting their money to financial institutions and platforms that reside outside the perimeter of the financial safety net, where the law of the bankruptcy jungle still prevails. Yet as we saw in chapter 4, people are relying more than ever on firms like PayPal, Alipay, and M-PESA to hold and move their money. This is true even in jurisdictions like the United States, which has often lagged far behind other countries in the adoption of new payments technology. Taken from the Atlanta Fed's 2021 Survey and Diary of Consumer Payment Choice, figure 5.1 reveals the growing popularity of these nonbank payment platforms.[56] Strikingly, this data shows a healthy 57 percent

56. Federal Reserve Bank of Atlanta, 2021 Survey and Diary of Consumer Payment Choice, 7 (October 13, 2022), https://www.atlantafed.org/banking-and-payments/consumer-payments /survey-and-diary-of-consumer-payment-choice.

increase in the number of US consumers using online payment accounts, like PayPal and Venmo, between 2016 and 2021.

Especially when compared to the relatively stagnant use of conventional credit and debit cards, the sharp rise in the use of nonbank payment platforms suggests these new institutions and platforms are making significant strides in the competition for our (virtual) wallets. They are doing so by capitalizing on their technological superiority to offer cheaper, faster, more convenient, more secure, and more accessible payments. Yet they are also doing so in the constant shadow of bankruptcy, thereby exposing their customers to potentially catastrophic risks. Make no mistake: what we are witnessing is Gresham's new law in action.

Brass Tacks

Quite understandably, nobody wants to think about bankruptcy law when they are buying concert tickets online, splitting a restaurant check, or sending money to their kids in college. For decades, the unique privileges and protections of the financial safety net effectively meant that we didn't have to: that we could go about our daily lives safe in the knowledge (or ignorance) that insured bank deposits were fundamentally good money. But ongoing changes in the way we make payments mean that we increasingly find ourselves under bankruptcy's shadow. The question then becomes whether the new institutions and platforms that we use to make cheaper, faster, safer, and more convenient payments have taken full advantage of the available strategies for insulating us from the destructive impact of bankruptcy on the credibility of their monetary IOUs. We also need to question whether the regulatory frameworks currently governing these institutions and platforms adequately protect us from any residual risks. These questions are explored in the next chapter. Ultimately, if the answer is no, we need to understand that we are choosing good payments over good money—putting us on a collision course with Gresham's new law.

6

The Old Law of New Money

The higher your fence, the more likely people are just going to dig under it.

—UNKNOWN

One might reasonably ask whether the shadow of bankruptcy really looms all that large over the financial institutions and platforms that populate the shadow monetary system. Put differently: is the problem of bad money ultimately just a theoretical one? Intuitively, the answer to this question depends in large measure on the balance sheets of these institutions and platforms, including what they actually do with the money their customers have entrusted to them. If these institutions and platforms can credibly commit to hold relatively safe and highly liquid assets, and can otherwise insulate their customers from the risks of bankruptcy, then the answer may very well be yes. But if they invest in more risky and illiquid assets, or relegate their customers to the status of general unsecured creditors, then the problem of bad money will remain an ever-present threat—like a hidden weakness in their institutional DNA, waiting to reveal itself in times of stress and critically undermining the financial health of their unsuspecting customers.

The case of MoneyGram offers an instructive and cautionary tale. Like PayPal, Venmo, and Wise, MoneyGram is a P2P payment platform that gives customers the ability to send and receive money over the internet. On the surface, this looks like a relatively safe—perhaps even boring—business, with MoneyGram simply acting as a conduit between its nearly 150 million customers all over the world. Yet looks can sometimes be deceiving. In the years leading up to the global financial crisis, MoneyGram invested hundreds of millions of dollars in risky and illiquid mortgage-backed securities—the very same securities that would soon bring the entire financial system to its knees. As the market value of these securities plummeted between the summer of 2007 and the spring of 2008, MoneyGram experienced a severe liquidity crisis and was ultimately forced to announce that it would take a loss of over $260 million on these investments.[1] This liquidity squeeze had a predictable effect on the firm's share price, which fell from a peak of over $240 in July 2007 to just under $16 in March 2008.[2] On the verge of bankruptcy, MoneyGram was eventually bailed out by a consortium, led by Thomas H. Lee Partners and Goldman Sachs, that collectively injected over $1.5 billion in new equity and debt.[3] Had it not received this sizable and timely recapitalization, MoneyGram may have been forced into bankruptcy, exposing its customers to significant payment delays and hundreds of millions of dollars in potential losses.

Up to this point, our analysis has revolved around the legal rights and obligations attached to a firm's *liabilities* and whether we should view them as credible monetary IOUs. Yet, as the MoneyGram case clearly demonstrates, understanding the structure and composition of a firm's *assets* is equally important for determining whether these IOUs should be understood as good or bad money. This observation should not come as a surprise. After all, the fragility of conventional deposit-taking banks is not simply a function of the fact that they issue short-term and highly liquid deposits, but that they combine these deposits with investments in longer-term, risky, and illiquid loans and other assets. The question thus becomes whether the balance sheets of the financial institutions and platforms that populate the shadow monetary system exhibit this same type of fragility and what, if anything, they do to manage the resulting risks.

In theory, this fragility can be managed in one of two ways. The first involves the creative use of contractual, institutional, and other commitment mechanisms by the institutions and platforms themselves. These

1. See MoneyGram International, Inc., Form 10-K, 9 (March 25, 2008), http://ir.moneygram .com/static-files/5090f7d4-214b-484d-92bf-becc053403da.

2. Closing stock prices of $240.80 on July 2, 2007, versus $15.92 on March 24, 2008; from Yahoo Finance.

3. See Thomas H. Lee Partners, news release, "MoneyGram Completes Comprehensive Recapitalization with Investor Group Led by Thomas H. Lee Partners, L.P. and Goldman Sachs" (March 25, 2008), http://www.thl.com/newsroom/press-release?year=2008&id=1442.

private law strategies include contractual portfolio constraints, the use of trusts, bailment, and other property law tools, and structural separation. Whereas portfolio constraints serve to reduce the probability of bankruptcy, trusts, property law, and structural separation all serve to ringfence customer funds from a firm's other assets, thereby eliminating the unwelcome prospect of having to compete with unsecured creditors in the event of bankruptcy. While these mechanisms are not a complete prophylactic, their judicious use can both protect customers from potentially significant losses and, when bankruptcy strikes, speed up the time frame for getting their money back.

Where these private law mechanisms are underutilized or otherwise incomplete, the second way that we can manage the risks of fragility is through *public regulation*. Among other potential benefits, regulation can make it mandatory for financial institutions and platforms to use mechanisms like portfolio constraints, trusts, and structural separation to protect customer funds from the risks of bankruptcy. Regulation can also be used to create bespoke resolution frameworks as a substitute for conventional corporate bankruptcy law, ultimately with the objective of increasing the speed and certainty of the resolution process. In these and other ways, regulation can both reduce the degree of monetary heterogeneity and enhance the credibility of the monetary IOUs issued by these institutions and platforms. Viewed from this perspective, rather than simply representing the imposition of an unwelcome burden, well-designed regulation can actually give these new players the opportunity to compete with banks on a more level playing field.

This chapter explores the current state of play in greater depth, examining the use of both private law mechanisms and existing regulatory frameworks to address the risks of bad money. There are three key takeaways. The first is that the use of private law mechanisms currently appears to be very limited within the shadow monetary system. Second, while this theoretically opens the door for public regulation, many of the existing regulatory frameworks—especially in the United States—are antiquated and inadequate rule books that are simply not fit for purpose in the digital age. These rule books have created bountiful opportunities for regulatory arbitrage, allowing a variety of new financial institutions and platforms to dig tunnels around, under, and even into the conventional financial safety net. Third, the United States and many other countries have a great deal to learn from those jurisdictions where new regulatory frameworks have grown up alongside the emergence, evolution, and spectacular growth of the shadow monetary system. These lessons relate not only to the all-important question of how to legally engineer good money, but also how to ensure the type of coordinated investments in network infrastructure necessary to deliver better payments.

Digital Free Banking

The original idea behind free banking was that firms meeting certain conditions—including the requirement to post collateral against the issuance of monetary IOUs—should be free to issue paper currency without first receiving a special legal charter from the state. As we saw in chapter 1, it is debatable whether the relatively brief experiments with free banking in the United States were always "free" in this technical sense, and there is a lively if somewhat niche debate about whether other experiments in countries like Switzerland, Canada, and Scotland remained true to this original idea, how successful they were, and the reasons for their eventual demise.[4] Yet, in theory, one can still imagine a world in which financial institutions and platforms engineer monetary IOUs that rely solely on private legal and institutional strategies to support their nominal value and use as a means of payment: a new *digital* free banking.

The first and arguably most elemental private law strategy for enhancing the credibility of monetary IOUs involves the use of contractual portfolio restrictions. In a nutshell, portfolio restrictions dictate the types of financial assets in which institutions and platforms can invest: typically limiting them to cash, cash equivalents, and other high-quality liquid assets (HQLA) like short-term government debt, repurchase agreements, and other money market instruments. Portfolio restrictions reside at the heart of long-standing proposals for so-called narrow banking.[5] These proposals seek to sever the institutional link between the issuance of monetary IOUs and the ability to invest in longer-term, risky, and illiquid commercial loans, equity and debt securities, and other speculative assets. In effect, by enshrining the contractual commitment to limit their investments to HQLA, portfolio restrictions are designed to reduce the risk of bankruptcy, along with the associated uncertainty, delay, and potential costs for the holders of a firm's monetary IOUs. Nevertheless, while portfolio restrictions can reduce the *probability* of financial distress, they ultimately do very little to protect customer

---

4. For a flavor of these debates, see Lawrence White, *Free Banking in Britain: Theory, Experience and Debate 1800–1845* (2nd ed., 1995); White (ed.), *Free Banking, Volumes 1–3* (1993); and Kevin Dowd (ed.), *The Experience of Free Banking* (1992).

5. The intellectual roots of narrow banking, along with the similarities and differences between it and the blueprint advanced in this book, are explored in chapter 7.

funds once an institution or platform actually enters the bankruptcy process. Indeed, when used on their own, these restrictions do absolutely nothing to ringfence customer funds from the other assets of the bankruptcy estate, thus potentially forcing the holders of a firm's monetary IOUs to compete with its other unsecured creditors.

A second, and highly complementary, private law strategy involves the use of trusts, bailment, and other equivalent property law mechanisms. These mechanisms share a common feature in that they enable contracting parties to draw a clear distinction between the party *in possession or control* of an asset and its ultimate *beneficial owner*. Importantly, where a firm uses these mechanisms to earmark customer assets, bankruptcy courts typically recognize the resulting separation: thus carving these assets out from the bankruptcy estate and thereby ensuring that customers do not have to compete with the firm's general unsecured creditors.

This ringfencing of customer funds from a firm's other assets can play an important role in supporting the value of its monetary IOUs. Yet, just like portfolio restrictions, these property law mechanisms have their limits. As a preliminary matter, a customer seeking the protections afforded by these mechanisms is required to go to court to establish their existence. Even where customers can easily meet this evidentiary burden—e.g., by producing a contract, trust deed, or other documentary evidence—they may still face significant procedural delays while the bankruptcy court, trustee, or administrator verifies the existence and validity of these mechanisms, together with the identities and entitlements of all the protected beneficiaries. In many cases, the relevant legal costs may also be recoverable directly out of the ringfenced assets. Accordingly, while trusts, bailment, and other property law mechanisms can often effectively insulate customer funds from the law of the bankruptcy jungle, they do not completely eliminate the potential delays and other costs associated with the bankruptcy process itself.

This takes us to a third, and more institutionally oriented, strategy for enhancing the credibility of monetary IOUs: structural separation. While structural separation can take many different forms, the essence of this strategy involves a parent firm creating a wholly owned subsidiary for the limited purpose of issuing monetary IOUs and holding the corresponding collateral assets. Where the two firms are recognized as having separate legal personality, the bankruptcy of the parent will therefore not automatically trigger the bankruptcy of its subsidiary. The subsidiary can then further reduce the probability of its own bankruptcy by adopting tight portfolio restrictions, along with a prohibition against conducting non-payment-related activities or lending to its corporate parent or affiliates. The subsidiary can also hold all of its assets in trust for the benefit of customers, adding an additional layer of protection between the assets and operations of the parent and the holders of the subsidiary's monetary IOUs. For its part, the parent can also reduce the risk of the subsidiary's bankruptcy by injecting a sufficient cushion of equity capital to absorb any volatility in the value of the ringfenced customer assets. In this way, structural separation—especially when used alongside these other strategies—can serve as a legal and economic firewall between the business risks and potential bankruptcy of the parent firm and the credibility of its subsidiary's monetary IOUs.

The problem as it stands today is not that these strategies can't work—it's that they are nowhere close to being widely used. A 2019 survey commissioned by the Swift Institute revealed that, across almost every segment of the shadow monetary system, these strategies were employed very sparingly (see figure 6.1).[6] The survey was based on a deep dive into the contractual terms and conditions and other legal documentation for just over one hundred P2P payment platforms, mobile money platforms, and cryptocurrency exchanges. Strikingly, it found that less than 10 percent of these institutions and platforms used contractual portfolio restrictions and less than 7 percent employed any form of structural separation. And while close to 40 percent of surveyed firms used trusts or other equivalent legal mechanisms, fully half of these firms came from one segment: mobile money. Mobile money platforms were also the only firms targeted by the survey that used structural separation to protect customer funds. If this survey is representative, then the dawn of digital free banking has come in a blaze of red: an ominous warning of a gathering storm.

The potential explanations for why financial institutions and platforms have been hesitant to adopt these strategies are not particularly hard to fathom. Firms like PayPal, Alipay, Tether, and Circle sit on tens of billions of dollars in customer funds. Investing these funds in risky financial assets can be a relatively easy way for them to generate additional revenue, effectively subsidizing their core payments businesses. Similarly, cryptocurrency exchanges make money not by simply holding digital assets on behalf of their customers but by using them in their trading, lending, and borrowing activities. Viewed in this light, the adoption of contractual portfolio

---

6. Dan Awrey & Kristin van Zwieten, "Mapping the Shadow Payment System," Swift Institute Research Paper No. 2019-001 (November 2019).

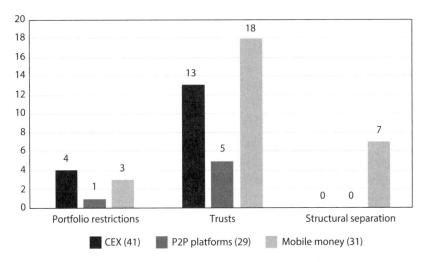

FIGURE 6.1. The Use of Private Legal and Institutional Strategies within the Shadow Monetary System. *Source*: Awrey & van Zwieten (2019).

restrictions, or placing assets in trust for customers, can have a real impact on their bottom line. Moreover, where customers do not fully understand, or otherwise undervalue, the important role these strategies can play in protecting them, there is little reason for these firms to *voluntarily* commit to using them—even if doing so would ultimately transform their monetary IOUs into good money.

This is not to say that there has not been some modest progress. Conventional P2P payment platforms, like PayPal, have long disclosed the risks that bankruptcy would pose for their customers. In May 2022, the largest cryptocurrency exchange in the United States, Coinbase, made headlines when it too publicly disclosed that its customers were at risk of being treated as unsecured creditors in the event of the exchange's bankruptcy.[7] Shortly thereafter, Coinbase updated its terms and conditions to "clarify" that customers retained property rights in deposited crypto that, it believed, would prevent them from being included as part of the firm's bankruptcy estate.[8]

7. See Jeremy Hill, "Coinbase Lets Users Know What a Bankruptcy Could Mean for Their Crypto," *Bloomberg* (May 11, 2022), https://www.bloomberg.com/news/articles/2022-05-11/coinbase-gives-256-billion-reminder-about-agonies-of-bankruptcy#xj4y7vzkg.

8. See Paul Grewal, Coinbase General Counsel, "Setting the Record Straight: Your Funds Are Safe at Coinbase—and Always Will Be," Coinbase blog post (June 1, 2022), https://www.coinbase.com/blog/setting-the-record-straight-your-funds-are-safe-at-coinbase-and-always-will-be The post states the view that Coinbase customer assets are protected by Article 8 of the Uniform

There are also some early signs that other cryptocurrency exchanges may be following suit—although, as we have already seen in connection with the Celsius bankruptcy, these protections do not necessarily extend to their staking or yield farming products. Looking ahead, the ongoing fallout from the Celsius, FTX, BlockFi, and Genesis bankruptcies may also spur more industry players to rethink their current approaches to the legal and institutional protection of customer assets. Yet this is still only one relatively small and exotic corner of the shadow monetary system. And with the exception of mobile money platforms—explored in greater detail below—customers are often afforded limited protections beyond disclosure. Until this changes, and absent government intervention, the fiat currency balances, stablecoins, and other monetary IOUs issued by, or otherwise held with, these institutions and platforms will remain deep in the shadow of bankruptcy.

Old Fences, New Neighbors

Ultimately, of course, one of the reasons why the financial institutions and platforms that populate the shadow monetary system might not have voluntarily adopted strategies like portfolio restrictions, trusts, or structural separation is because they were already required to do so under applicable regulatory frameworks. Indeed, almost all P2P payment platforms, centralized cryptocurrency exchanges, and mobile money platforms are subject to some type of prudential regulation. The question then becomes whether this regulation makes any better use of these strategies, or otherwise reflects the existential risks that the bankruptcy of these institutions and platforms would pose to their monetary IOUs.

The answer to this question demands that we take a short journey back in time. Long before the invention of the internet, there was another breakthrough in long-distance telecommunications that promised to revolutionize finance: the telegraph. In the United States, firms like Western Union, American Telegraph Company, and United States Telegraph Company were quick to capitalize on this new technology: offering their customers the ability to transfer money rapidly across long distances using the country's expanding network of telegraph lines. Customers would deliver money to a branch office in one location, which would then telegraph a coded message

---

Commercial Code, which gives customers a pro rata interest in the commingled customer assets held by Coinbase. If true, this would provide a measure of protection for customers by eliminating the threat of competition with unsecured creditors *other than other customers*. Nevertheless, it does not guarantee that the ringfenced assets would be sufficient to fully compensate these customers.

to a branch at another location instructing it to deliver payment to the designated recipient. While the underlying technology would eventually shift from the telegraph to the telex, and ultimately to the internet, these money transmitters remain an important part of the domestic and international payment system.

In the United States, responsibility for the prudential regulation of money transmitters falls to each of the fifty states. These state regulatory frameworks typically employ three principal strategies to ensure the safety and soundness of money transmitters. Sometimes referred to as the "three-legged stool," these strategies include permissible investment restrictions, minimum net worth requirements, and surety bond and other security requirements.[9] Together, these strategies are explicitly designed to "preserve public confidence in the financial services sector" and "protect customers from harm, including all forms of loss."[10] At least in theory, one might therefore assume that these state regulatory frameworks provide customers with a relatively high level of protection against the risks of bankruptcy.

The reality is significantly more complicated. Let's start with permissible investment restrictions. At their core, these restrictions are simply a species of portfolio constraint, dictating the type of investments that money transmitters can and cannot make with customer funds. While there is an enormous degree of heterogeneity across states, arguably the most remarkable feature of these "restrictions" is the discretion they give money transmitters to invest in a wide range of risky financial instruments.[11] To take just one example, over 60 percent of states currently permit money transmitters to invest customer funds in the shares of publicly traded corporations.[12] While some states impose caps or concentration limits on these equity investments, almost half do not.[13] Even more remarkably, there are currently twelve states that do not impose any restrictions whatsoever on the assets in which money

9. See Conference of State Banking Supervisors (CSBS), "MSB Model Law—Executive Summary," 5 (September 2019), https://www.csbs.org/sites/default/files/2019-10/Executive%20Summary%20-%20Draft%20Model%20Law%20%28Sept%202019%29.pdf.

10. CSBS, "MSB Model Law," 2. See also Uniform Law Commission, *Uniform Money Services Act,* 35, 38, 60–61,63–64 (2004), commentary to section 204 (surety bond requirements), section 207 (net worth requirements), and sections 701 and 702 (permissible investment restrictions), https://www.uniformlaws.org/viewdocument/final-act-8?CommunityKey=cf8b649a-114c-4bc9 -8937-c4ee17148a1b&tab=librarydocuments.

11. All data on state-level money transmitter laws is from Dan Awrey, "Bad Money," 106:1 Cornell Law Review 1 (2020).

12. Awrey, "Bad Money," appendix A.

13. Awrey, appendix A. In a nutshell, a cap sets the maximum percentage of a money transmitter's portfolio that can be invested in any given class of financial instrument; a concentration

transmitters may invest. This stands in stark contrast to the small handful of states that limit a money transmitter's investments to HQLA. And, of course, these restrictions only apply to customer funds—leaving money transmitters free to take whatever risks they want using their other sources of investment capital.

The permissible investment restrictions in the majority of states also contain a potentially devastating loophole. Specifically, of the thirty-eight states that currently impose permissible investment restrictions, twenty-eight of them permit money transmitters to invest customer funds in "accounts receivable"—including the accounts receivable payable by a money transmitter's own affiliates, delegates, or authorized agents.[14] Distilled to their essence, accounts receivable represent money that is owed to a firm by a third party. Economically speaking, an "investment" in accounts receivable is thus more accurately characterized as a loan. In other words, the permissible investment restrictions in more than half of all US states currently permit money transmitters to use customer funds for the purpose of extending loans to other legal entities within their own corporate groups. Where these entities are not themselves money transmitters, or not otherwise subject to prudential regulation, the practical effect is to remove any restrictions on how they can invest the funds borrowed from their money transmitter affiliates. Where these entities then use the proceeds of these loans to make risky or illiquid investments, or where the loans are not repayable on demand, this inevitably leaves money transmitters vulnerable to the risk that their affiliates might one day be unable to pay their debts. Like other risky investments, the unconstrained freedom to make these intragroup loans thereby increases the probability of a money transmitter's bankruptcy, and with it the prospect that its customers will be forced to bear at least some of the consequent losses.

The second leg of the stool consists of minimum net worth requirements. Like bank capital requirements, net worth requirements are designed to ensure that a money transmitter holds sufficient retained earnings and equity capital to absorb a threshold level of losses without triggering the firm's bankruptcy. By reducing the probability of bankruptcy, these requirements serve to provide a money transmitter's customers with a degree of protection against the destructive impact of mechanisms like the automatic stay,

---

limit sets the maximum percentage that can be invested in any single issuer and/or instrument within each class.

14. Awrey, appendix A.

priority rules, and the pari passu rule on the value of their monetary IOUs. Yet, just like permissible investment restrictions, these requirements exhibit an incredible degree of heterogeneity across states: ranging from zero in six states to up to $3 million in Washington and Oklahoma. Similarly, while some states only impose minimum net worth requirements, others combine minimum requirements with a hard cap on the amount of equity and retained earnings that money transmitters must hold. Reflecting their origins in regulating telegraphic wire transfer services like Western Union, many states also still calibrate these requirements on the basis of the number of physical locations—i.e., branch offices—that a money transmitter operates within a given state.

Ultimately, these net worth requirements contemplate an incredibly thin layer of protection against the threat of bankruptcy. This should hardly come as a surprise given that these requirements do not generally reflect the size of a money transmitter's balance sheet or the risk profile of its assets. It is also important to note that these requirements are not cumulative; with the implication that a single money transmitter operating across all fifty states can theoretically satisfy its net worth requirements in each state by simply complying with the laws in the state with the highest requirements. Take PayPal, for example. As a preliminary matter, PayPal obviously does not have any physical branches. Hence, any state that uses the number of branch offices to calculate net worth requirements is almost certainly bound to set its minimum net worth requirement far too low. More importantly, PayPal can comply with its net worth requirements in all states by holding the $3 million in retained earnings and equity required in both Washington and Oklahoma. Given that PayPal reported total assets of just over $78 billion at the end of 2022,[15] this translates into an effective minimum net worth requirement of just under 0.004 percent.[16] To put this figure into perspective, as of June 30, 2022, the average CET1 capital level for US bank holding companies was between 11 and 12 percent of risk-weighted assets.[17] While one might reasonably object to this comparison on the grounds that banks take more risks, given the demonstrated laxity of permissible investment restrictions it would seem unwise to simply take this for granted.

15. See PayPal, Inc., 2022 Annual Report (April 13, 2023), https://investor.pypl.com /financials/annual-reports/default.aspx.

16. Calculated as $3,000,000/$78,717,000,000 = 0.0000381112.

17. See Federal Reserve Board of Governors, *Financial Stability Report*, 32 (November 2022), https://www.federalreserve.gov/publications/files/financial-stability-report-20221104.pdf.

The third and final leg of the stool includes surety bond, letter of credit, bank deposit, insurance, or other security requirements. These requirements are designed to ensure that a money transmitter puts aside, or otherwise makes available, a minimum amount of money or other HQLA for distribution to its customers in the event of the firm's bankruptcy.[18] Like permissible investment restrictions, these security requirements vary significantly from state to state. Whereas several states—including Georgia, Hawaii, Idaho, Nevada, and Washington—have minimum security requirements as low as $10,000, Michigan and Kentucky require a minimum of $500,000 and Pennsylvania requires a cool $1 million. In many cases, these minimums are then augmented by supplemental amounts, typically calibrated on the basis of the volume of payments processed by a money transmitter, the number of physical locations it operates within the relevant state, or any deterioration in its financial condition. Many states also impose a cap on these requirements, ranging from to $125,000 in Alaska to $7 million in California.

Unlike minimum net worth requirements, these security requirements are typically cumulative. As a result, money transmitters are required to satisfy the minimum security requirement, plus any supplemental amounts, in each state. For this reason, these requirements often provide customers with a marginally higher level of protection than net worth requirements. Returning to our PayPal example, and assuming that it was subject to the maximum security requirement in each state, it would be required to set aside or otherwise make available somewhere in excess of $42 million in security against its monetary IOUs to US customers. This figure excludes any supplemental amounts that PayPal would be required to post in the event of any deterioration in its financial position. While this is undoubtedly a significant sum, it obviously pales in comparison to the tens of billions of dollars currently sitting in PayPal's customer accounts. Moreover, these security requirements provide customers in different states with very different levels of protection against a money transmitter's bankruptcy. Perhaps most importantly, insofar as these requirements are expressed as fixed amounts, or are based on the number of physical locations or the volume of payment flows, they may not reflect the aggregate size of the positive account balances held by customers within each state. This can result in state-by-state

---

18. Whereas surety bond and bank account requirements envision that money transmitters will put aside liquid assets, letters of credit envision that they will arrange (and pay for) a guarantee from a bank pursuant to which the bank agrees to pay the specified amount to customers in the event of the firm's bankruptcy.

mismatches between the amount of available security and the number and value of potential customer claims against a bankrupt money transmitter.

In theory, one relatively straightforward way of addressing the manifest shortcomings of both minimum net worth and security requirements is by ringfencing customer funds from a money transmitter's other assets. This can be achieved using a variety of now familiar legal strategies, including trusts and structural separation. For example, regulators might require money transmitters to place customer funds in trust for the benefit of their customers— thereby preventing the distribution of these assets to the firm's other creditors in the context of any future bankruptcy proceeding. Money transmitters could also be required to place customer funds in a dedicated bankruptcy-remote subsidiary that could then continue to honor its financial obligations in the event of the parent firm's bankruptcy. Yet, despite the existence and potential usefulness of these ringfencing strategies, only thirty states currently require money transmitters to place customer funds in trust and no states require structural subordination.[19] Even in these states, there remains the thorny question of whether, when the monetary rubber eventually hits the bankruptcy road, the presiding court will deem the trust to be validly constituted.

This survey of state money transmitter laws suggests that the three-legged stool is very wobbly indeed. Money transmitters have wide latitude to invest customer funds in risky and potentially illiquid assets. These risks are amplified by the fact that large money transmitters are required to hold a razor thin layer of equity capital, heightening the risk of bankruptcy and, thereafter, exposing customers to potentially significant volatility in the value of these assets. And to top it all off, there is no universal requirement for these assets to be ringfenced from a money transmitter's other assets or activities, thereby almost guaranteeing that customers will be forced to compete with the firm's other creditors in the event of bankruptcy.

Admittedly, none of this would matter very much if we were still talking about regulating telegraphic wire transfer services like Western Union. These old-school money transmitters only held customer funds for a very brief period of time—typically only as long as it took for the intended recipient to get to the nearest branch. The fleeting nature of these holdings meant that money transmitters were not in a position to invest customer funds in risky and illiquid assets, and that customers were only briefly exposed to the risk that a firm might be forced into bankruptcy. But times have most certainly changed. Today, the list of financial institutions and platforms

---

19. Awrey, "Bad Money," appendix A.

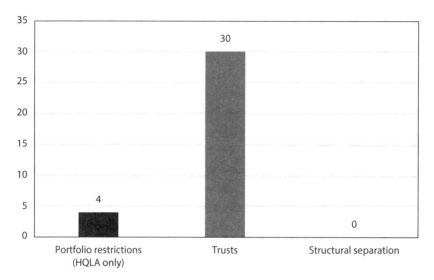

FIGURE 6.2. The Use of Legal and Institutional Strategies in US State MSB Regulation. *Source*: Awrey (2020).

licensed and regulated in the United States as money transmitters is a veritable *Who's Who* of the shadow monetary system. The list includes popular P2P payment platforms like PayPal, MoneyGram, and Wise. It includes many of the recently fallen stars of the crypto universe like FTX, Celsius, BlockFi, Genesis, and Voyager Digital. And, until very recently, it also included Circle—the issuer of the popular USDC stablecoin. Importantly, unlike their predecessors, these new-school money transmitters have used customer funds to accumulate vast pools of longer-term investment capital—transforming themselves from mere conduits into true financial intermediaries. Yet, despite this transformation, these institutions and platforms have been and remain, as of writing, regulated by antiquated and inadequate regulatory frameworks left over from the age of the telegraph.

New Fences, Noisy Neighbors

This is not to say that the United States is completely and irretrievably stuck in the past. To the contrary, the perceived promise and perils of crypto have spurred policymakers in several states to either update their existing regulatory frameworks governing money transmitters or create entirely new frameworks for cryptocurrency exchanges, crypto lenders, and stablecoin issuers. The former approach is exemplified by the efforts of the Conference of State Bank Supervisors, which released its "modernized" Model Money Transmission Act in January 2022, in part to incorporate digital assets.[20] The latter approach has been championed by the New York State Department of Financial Services (NYDFS), which launched its groundbreaking "Bitlicense" in June 2015.[21] The Bitlicense framework applies to all "virtual currency business activity" that has a nexus with the state of New York or one of its residents. The activities captured by this definition include receiving virtual currency for transmission; transmitting virtual currency; storing, holding, or maintaining custody or control of virtual currency on behalf of customers; buying and selling virtual currency as a business on behalf of customers; or controlling, administering, or issuing a virtual currency.[22] This extremely broad definition reflects both the nebulous and rapidly evolving structure of the crypto ecosystem and the desire on the part of the NYDFS to capture the widest possible range of crypto-related activities.

The Bitlicense framework requires any firm conducting virtual currency business activity to obtain a license from the NYDFS.[23] Thereafter, the framework subjects licensed firms to basic prudential regulation and supervision, including capital, examination, reporting, recordkeeping, and cybersecurity requirements.[24] The framework also requires licensed firms to fully disclose all material risks, including the fact that virtual currencies are not legal tender, that customers are not protected by the FDIC or other deposit insurance schemes, and that mechanisms designed to protect customer assets may not be sufficient to completely cover all potential losses.[25]

Importantly, the Bitlicense framework also incorporates a number of strategies designed to protect customer assets in the event of a licensee's bankruptcy. As a starting point, licensees are required to maintain a US dollar surety bond or trust account for the benefit of their customers in a form and amount acceptable to the NYDFS. Where a licensee elects to use

---

20. CSBS, Model Money Transmission Modernization Act (January 6, 2022). As of writing, only two states—West Virginia and South Dakota—have introduced legislation that, if enacted, would adopt the CSBS's proposed new model.

21. See New York Regulations, 23 CRR-NY § 200 et seq.

22. 23 CRR-NY § 200.2.

23. 23 CRR-NY § 200.3. The framework contemplates exemptions for banks chartered in New York that have been authorized to engage in virtual currency business activity and for merchants and customers who use virtual currency solely for the purchase or sale of goods or services or for investment purposes.

24. 23 CRR-NY § 200.8 (capital requirements), § 200.12 (recordkeeping requirements), § 200.13 (examination requirements), § 200.14 (reporting requirements), and § 200.16 (cybersecurity requirements).

25. 23 CRR-NY § 200.19(a).

a trust account, this account must be maintained with a qualified custodian.[26] Eligible custodians include New York limited purpose trust companies, like Paxos Trust, Coinbase Custody Trust, and Fidelity Digital Asset Services, which have been licensed by the NYDFS to engage in virtual currency business activities.[27] Licensees that store, hold, or maintain custody or control of virtual currency on behalf of a customer are then subject to portfolio restrictions that require them to hold the same type and amount of virtual currency as that owed, or otherwise obligated, to that customer.[28] Thus, if a customer holds 100 BTC with a licensee, the licensee must also hold 100 BTC, effectively mirroring its customer's position. Licensees are also prohibited from selling, transferring, assigning, lending, hypothecating, pledging, or otherwise using or encumbering customer assets, except in connection with the sale, transfer, or assignment of these assets at the customer's direction.[29]

In the eyes of many observers, New York's Bitlicense framework is the current gold standard of crypto regulation—at least in the United States.[30] Nevertheless, when evaluated against the all-important benchmark of whether licensees issue fundamentally credible monetary IOUs, the framework arguably suffers from a number of serious, and potentially fatal, flaws. The capital requirements, surety bonds, and other key prudential requirements are generally left to the discretion of the NYDFS on a case-by-case basis, raising the unsettling prospect of significant legal heterogeneity in the rules applied to different licensees. These firm-specific requirements are also not publicly disclosed, leaving both customers and intrepid researchers to speculate about their precise substance, scope, and likely effectiveness. Similarly, while the framework contemplates tight portfolio restrictions in connection with a customer's *crypto* assets, there is no mention whatsoever of any constraints on how a licensee can invest *fiat currency* balances. And

26. 23 CRR-NY § 200.9(a).

27. For an overview of New York limited purpose trust companies and their regulation, see NYDFS, "Organization of a Trust Company for the Limited Purpose of Exercising Fiduciary Powers," https://www.dfs.ny.gov/apps_and_licensing/banks_and_trusts/procedure_certificate_merit_trust_comp.

28. 23 CRR-NY § 2009(b). In response to the 2022 crypto winter, the NYDFS also issued guidance to Bitlicense holders and limited purpose trust companies regarding the custody of virtual assets: NYDFS, Industry Letter, "Guidance on Custodial Structures for Consumer Protection in the Event of Insolvency" (January 23, 2023).

29. 23 CRR-NY § 2009(c).

30. See, e.g., NYDFS, "Superintendent Linda A. Lacewell Announces PayPal to be the First Approved Entity for DFS Conditional BitLicense," press release (October 21, 2020) (quoting Charles Cascarilla, then CEO of Paxos, as referring to New York as "the gold standard of cryptocurrency regulation").

most importantly, both Bitlicense holders themselves and the limited purpose trust companies they use as custodians are still subject to general corporate bankruptcy law, opening the door to potentially significant delays in
connection with the recovery of customer assets.[31] Where licensees elect to
maintain a surety bond instead of placing customer assets in trust, or where
losses on any investments using fiat currency balances exceed the nominal
value of the licensee's monetary IOUs, there is also the risk that customers
may not get all of their money back at the conclusion of the bankruptcy
process. Collectively, this unique combination of binding legal constraints
and critical flaws may help explain why—despite an explosion in the number
of cryptocurrency exchanges, crypto lending platforms, and stablecoins in
recent years—only twenty-four firms registered under the new framework
between June 2015 and March 2023.[32]

Outside the United States, several other jurisdictions have also begun to
experiment with regulatory frameworks that specifically target digital assets
and intermediaries. Japan was a notable early mover. Following the bankruptcy of Mt Gox in February 2014, the Japanese government introduced
a series of regulatory reforms designed to improve oversight of cryptocurrency exchanges and better protect customer assets. In 2016, Japan amended
its Payment Services Act to create a mandatory licensing framework for all
cryptocurrency exchanges, imposing disclosure, minimum capital, operational risk, and other prudential requirements.[33] Crucially, the framework
also mandated the strict segregation of customer assets, legally and opera-
tionally ringfencing them from the assets and activities of the exchanges
themselves.[34] This framework was subsequently strengthened in 2019 and,
in 2022, expanded to encompass banks, trust companies, and other intermediaries engaged in the issuance of stablecoins.[35]

---

31. By construction, BitLicense holders do not include New York chartered banks; see the
exemption under 23 CRR-NY § 200.3. New York banking law also expressly excludes limited
purpose trust companies from the definition of a bank; see N.Y. Laws, Chapter 2, Article 1, § 2.

32. See NYDFS, "Virtual Currency Businesses" (listing all Bitlicense holders and limited
purpose trust companies licensed to engage in virtual currency business activities), https://www
.dfs.ny.gov/virtual_currency_businesses.

33. Act No. 62 of 2016, Act to Amend Parts of the Bank Act and Other Acts in Order to
Correspond with Changes in the Environment Made by Information and Communications Technologies, KANPO, Extra No. 123 (June 3, 2016), Article 63–2 et seq.

34. Act No. 62 of 2016.

35. See Taiga Uranaka & Yuki Hagiwara, "Japan Passes Stablecoin Bill That Enshrines Investor
Protection," *Bloomberg* (June 2, 2022), https://www.bloomberg.com/news/articles/2022-06-03
/japan-passes-stablecoin-bill-that-enshrines-investor-protection#xj4y7vzkg.

The benefits of Japan's new regulatory framework became readily apparent following the bankruptcy of FTX in November 2022. Reflecting the strict segregation of customer assets, customers of FTX Japan were paid back in full within three months of the initial bankruptcy filing.[36] This stands in stark contrast to the customers of FTX's US subsidiary—a state-licensed money transmitter—who now find themselves in the midst of a complex and expensive bankruptcy process that, by all accounts, is likely to drag on for several years. Given the lack of effective internal controls, the dense and opaque thicket of intragroup exposures, and the pervasive use of customer assets in connection with FTX's own investment activities, it is also highly likely that these customers will ultimately get back little of their money at the conclusion of this process.

For many, these new regulatory frameworks offer a glimpse into the future—a potential blueprint for regulating digital assets and intermediaries. Yet they also offer important lessons about how *not* to regulate money and payments. First and foremost, neither the New York Bitlicense nor the ongoing Japanese reforms completely remove customer assets from the shadow of bankruptcy. While the fact that the customers of FTX Japan only had to wait three months for the return of speculative digital assets like BTC and ETH is an exceptional result when compared with the plight of general unsecured creditors, it comes nowhere close to the next-business-day time frame targeted by the FDIC and many other deposit insurance schemes. This is no small point. Indeed, we might expect the same three months to feel like an eternity where the assets in question were monetary IOUs used by customers every day to pay their rent, buy groceries, and keep the lights on. Ultimately, the functional requirements of monetary IOUs are just different from other financial assets, and the regulatory frameworks that govern them must take these differences into account.

Second, these new regulatory frameworks specifically target financial institutions and platforms within the emerging crypto ecosystem. This raises important and awkward questions about why policymakers would want to legally privilege one type of technology over another—especially where this technology has yet to prove its worth in the realm of money and payments. Given the inevitability of future technological advancements, it also raises the prospect that these new frameworks will eventually meet

---

36. See Megumi Fujikawa, "Some FTX Customers Can Withdraw Their Money—in Japan, at Least," *Wall Street Journal* (February 21, 2023), https://www.wsj.com/articles/some-ftx -customers-get-their-money-backin-japan-at-least-3e0f2d15.

the same fate as the now antiquated state money transmitter laws. While it's imperative that policymakers respond to developments at the edge of today's technological frontier, the real and far more important challenge is designing regulatory frameworks that can both capture and adapt to future rounds of technological and institutional innovation.

Finally, these new regulatory frameworks understandably focus on the prudential regulation of crypto intermediaries, along with the parallel objective of protecting customer assets. These are obviously laudable objectives, and the resulting regulation can, at least in theory, play an important role in ensuring that these intermediaries issue *good money*. Conversely, these new frameworks often all but ignore how regulation targeting issues like network governance, access, and interoperability can play a critical role in promoting *good payments*. Intuitively, the failure to simultaneously pursue both sets of objectives will inevitably impose a ceiling on the potential benefits stemming from the creation of these frameworks, effectively forcing new monetary trains to ride on the same old payment rails.

Les Clôtures Européennes

Another group of countries that has made early and significant strides in the regulation on the shadow monetary system are the twenty-seven member states of the European Union. On the surface, the EU shares a number of important parallels with the United States, including a large and powerful incumbent banking system, a thriving fintech ecosystem focused on harnessing new technology to improve money and payments, and a federal political system that can introduce significant coordination costs, lead to messy jurisdictional turf wars, and create opportunities for destabilizing regulatory arbitrage. Yet, unlike the United States, the EU has actually been able to design and implement a relatively harmonized regulatory framework governing large swaths of the shadow monetary system.

The bedrock of this pan-European regulatory framework are two directives: the Payment Services Directive (PSD2) and E-Money Directive (EMD2).[37] Together, these directives apply to an exhaustive list of "payment institutions," including P2P payment platforms, electronic money remittance services, credit card companies, and other institutions and platforms

---

37. Directive 2015/2366 of the European Parliament and Council on Payment Services (November 25, 2015) (PSD2) and Directive 2009/110/EC of the European Parliament and Council on the Taking Up, Pursuit, and Prudential Supervision of the Business of Electronic Money Institutions (September 16, 2009) (EMD2).

that issue "electronically stored monetary value in the form of claims on the issuer"—in short, monetary IOUs.[38] Payment institutions covered by PSD2 and EMD2 are required to obtain authorization from the competent regulatory authority in a member state before undertaking payment services. Once authorized, they are then required to comply with detailed rules governing minimum capital, financial reporting, recordkeeping, outsourcing, and other matters.[39]

The most important of these rules for our purposes are those dealing with the investment and safeguarding of customer funds. The directives give authorized payment institutions two realistic options.[40] The first is to deposit customer funds in a conventional bank account. The second is to invest them in "secure, liquid low-risk assets" more or less equivalent to HQLA. In at least some member states, this second option is then augmented by implementing regulations that prohibit payment institutions from pledging, rehypothecating, or otherwise using customer assets, and require them to hold these assets via a qualified third-party custodian. Under both options, payment institutions are prohibited from "commingling" customer funds with the funds of the payment institution itself. Payment institutions are also required to insulate customer funds against potential claims from their other creditors in the event of bankruptcy, although the precise strategies for achieving this are left up to each member state. On their face, PSD2 and EMD2 are thus far more sensitive to the risks that bankruptcy poses to the customers of these institutions than US state money transmitter laws.

By the standards of many modern regulatory frameworks, PSD2 and EMD2 are now both fairly long in the tooth. The first iteration of the PSD was finalized in 2007, with the first EMD following two years later.[41] And while both directives have been subsequently updated to reflect new market developments, neither was designed to explicitly address the unique policy

---

38. See PSD2, Annex 1; EMD2, Articles 2.1 and 2.

39. These rules are set out in both the directives themselves and the implemented regulations adopted in each member state.

40. See PSD2, Article 10(1)(a). PSD2 also contemplates the possibility that authorized payment institutions may take out an insurance policy or guarantee in the amount of its outstanding obligations to customers payable in the event of the institution's bankruptcy; see Article 10(1)(b). As of writing, however, there is little evidence of market demand for insurance policies. This should not be all that surprising given that, while the other two options both yield interest income, insurance policies would inevitably require payment institutions to make periodic premium payments.

41. Directive 2007/64/EC of the European Parliament and Council on Payment Services in the Internal Market (November 13, 2007) and Directive 2009/110/EC (September 16, 2009).

challenges arising from the emergence and rapid growth of the crypto ecosystem. To address this gap, the European Commission has recently adopted a new Markets in Crypto Assets (MiCA) Regulation.[42] Most of MiCA is dedicated to creating a regulatory framework for the classification, issuance, and trading of digital assets, like BTC, ETH, and XRP. However, MiCA also imposes significant new obligations on crypto intermediaries, including authorization requirements, minimum capital requirements and, importantly, relatively strict rules governing the ownership and safekeeping of the crypto assets and fiat currency balances held on behalf of their customers. Simultaneously, MiCA requires the authorization of stablecoin issuers and subjects them to ongoing disclosure, reporting, capital, and liquidity requirements, and enshrines the right of customers to redeem their stablecoin holdings for free and at any time. Stablecoin issuers are also required to hold customer assets with third-party custodians and, uniquely, the market value of the assets held in custody must actually *exceed* the aggregate nominal value of the issuer's outstanding monetary IOUs. MiCA also envisions enhanced prudential regulation and supervision of any "systemically significant" stablecoins.

There is a great deal to applaud about the EU's evolving approach to the regulation of money and payments. The portfolio restrictions under PSD2 and EMD2 are far more homogeneous and strict than those in the United States, with the overcollateralization contemplated by MiCA offering stablecoin holders an additional layer of protection against any volatility in the market value of portfolio assets. The directives are also far more explicitly conscious of the need to protect customer assets in the event of bankruptcy, even while the precise strategies for achieving this objective vary from framework to framework and from member state to member state. In particular, where financial institutions and platforms are required to ringfence customer assets by placing them in trust and holding them through a bank or qualified custodian, this all but eliminates the prospect that customers would be forced to watch as the application of the automatic stay, priority rules, and pari passu rule slowly and inexorably chip away at the nominal value of their monetary IOUs.

Yet the EU's approach is still far from perfect. The fact that the institutions and platforms subject to PSD2, EMD2, and MiCA can engage in a wide range

---

42. Final Proposal for a Regulation on Markets in Cryptoassets 2020/0265 (COD)/ COM(2020) 593 (adopted April 20, 2023). Technically, MiCA does not apply to PSD2 payment instruments but does apply to e-money under EMD2.

of financial services *other than money and payments* inevitably increases the probability of financial distress and, ultimately, bankruptcy. Where these platforms and institutions are not exempt from general corporate bankruptcy law, the domestic implementing regulations and bankruptcy procedures in each member state can still introduce significant delays in the process of returning customer funds.[43] In this respect, it is notable that neither PSD2 nor EMD2 provide a time frame within which the customers of failed institutions and platforms should expect to get their money back. And even outside bankruptcy, MiCA contemplates the imposition of liquidity fees and the temporary suspension of withdrawals during periods of institutional distress that, while designed to prevent destabilizing runs, would deprive customers of immediate access to their money.

More broadly, the EU approach also reflects the same fundamental shortsightedness as many of its peers in other jurisdictions. While PSD2, EMD2, and MiCA all make significant progress toward addressing the inherent dangers of bad money, they collectively do almost nothing to promote the type of experimentation, competition, and innovation that might one day yield better payments. They do not create a harmonized framework for expanding access to basic financial market infrastructure beyond conventional deposit-taking banks. Indeed, quite to the contrary, they envision that new institutions and platforms will continue to use banks as both the custodians of customer assets and the gatekeepers of the conventional payment system. Nor have these new regulatory frameworks been accompanied by new governance frameworks or public investment designed to promote the type of open access or technological interoperability that would serve to level the competitive playing field. In the absence of these types of more farsighted and ambitious policy initiatives, the longer-term benefits of these regulatory frameworks, and of the new institutions and platforms they were created to support, may ultimately be very limited.

Trusting M-PESA

A continent away, Kenya faced a distinctly different challenge. Safaricom, the creator and administrator of M-PESA, had already figured out how to use its existing telecommunications infrastructure as a springboard for

---

43. There is also the risk that regulatory authorities in member states may fail to successfully implement and monitor compliance with the rules designed to ringfence customer assets; see, e.g., *In the matter of Lehman Brothers International (Europe) (In Administration) and in the matter of the Insolvency Act 1986* [2012] UKSC 6.

leapfrogging the conventional banking system to deliver better payments. The challenge was how to protect customer funds from the risks associated with the wider commercial enterprise, thereby promoting public trust in M-PESA as good money. Intuitively, we might have expected this challenge to be particularly daunting in a country where a large segment of the population had historically not been customers of banks or other financial institutions and where, accordingly, Safaricom could not simply tap into an existing wellspring of public trust in the financial system.

The solution that Safaricom hit upon combined several of the private legal and institutional strategies that we have explored in this chapter. The first strategy was structural separation: with Safaricom creating a dedicated bankruptcy remote subsidiary, M-PESA Holding Co. Limited, specifically for the purpose of establishing and maintaining the accounts through which customers hold and transfer M-PESA balances.[44] Second, the funds received from customers in connection M-PESA balances are automatically held in an express trust established for their sole benefit, with M-PESA Holding Co. itself serving as the trustee.[45] Lastly, pursuant to the terms of the trust deed, these customer trust funds are subject to tight portfolio restrictions, with the trustee only permitted to invest them in commercial bank accounts and short-term debt securities issued by the Kenyan government.[46] Any trust funds deposited with commercial banks are also covered by pass-through deposit insurance provided by the Kenya Deposit Insurance Corporation (KDIC), thereby protecting M-PESA customers against the risk of bank failure.[47]

Of course, it is extremely unlikely that Safaricom would ever enter bankruptcy. But that's not really the point. Low-probability, high-impact events—like widespread disruption to basic financial market infrastructure—can be extremely damaging to both economic activity and public trust in core social institutions. Against this backdrop, the combination of structural separation, trusteeship, and tight portfolio restrictions gives M-PESA customers a very high level of protection against these types of disruptive events. Structural

44. Declaration of Trust in Favour of All M-PESA Account Holders of Safaricom Limited, February 27, 2007, amended and restated June 19, 2008, https://www.safaricom.co.ke/images/deed_of_amendment_to_declaration_of_trust_-_mpesa_account_holders.pdf.

45. M-PESA Trust Deed, Article 1.

46. M-PESA Trust Deed, Article 6(1).

47. For a description of how this pass-through deposit insurance framework operates, see Ryan Defina, Bert Van Roosebeke, & Paul Manga, "E-Money and Deposit Insurance in Kenya," International Association of Deposit Insurers, Fintech Brief No. 6 (December 2021).

separation ensures that M-PESA Holding Co. would not automatically be ensnared in a Safaricom bankruptcy. If M-PESA Holding did enter bankruptcy, holding funds in trust would then ensure that these assets were not available for distribution to any of the firm's other creditors.[48] It would also likely translate into faster payouts for customers, reducing potential inconvenience and ensuring that they could continue to pay for the necessities of life. And, behind the scenes, narrow and binding restrictions on the types of assets in which trust funds can be invested dramatically reduce the indirect exposure of customers to market, credit, and liquidity risks. In fact, given the narrow range of eligible assets—KDIC-insured bank deposits and Kenyan sovereign debt—these portfolio restrictions effectively create a de facto public backstop for M-PESA's monetary IOUs. Accordingly, while much has been made about how M-PESA has transformed the payment system in Kenya and many other emerging markets, Safaricom and Kenyan regulators also deserve credit for how they have adeptly used these legal, institutional, and regulatory strategies to successfully engineer good money.[49]

Shadow Money, with Chinese Characteristics

Like Safaricom, the challenge for Alipay and WeChat Pay was never how to leapfrog China's archaic incumbent banking system. All these new platforms needed to do was harness existing technology, like the internet and smartphones, to provide customers with a safe, fast, and convenient way to make electronic payments. And Chinese customers clearly liked what they saw: with the total dollar volume of payments processed by Alipay and WeChat Pay growing from well under $1 trillion in 2013 to almost $35 trillion in 2019.[50] Yet as these twin tech behemoths grew in size and economic importance, they also increasingly found themselves in the political

48. On this point, two additional things that M-PESA Holding, or its regulator, could theoretically do to further enhance the credibility of its monetary commitments would be to impose activity restrictions and a prohibition against incurring debts other than those to M-PESA customers and other system participants in the normal course of its payment activities.

49. Indeed, this model has subsequently been replicated by mobile money operators in several other jurisdictions; see Jonathan Greenacre & Ross Buckley, "Using Trusts to Protect Mobile Money Customers," Singapore Journal of Legal Studies 59 (2014).

50. See Tim Massad, "Facebook's Libra 2.0: Why You Might Like It Even If You Can't Trust Facebook," Brookings Institution Studies in Economics, 42–43 (December 2021) (citing Chinese-language sources on the dollar volume of payments and comparative payment volumes for Alipay and WeChat Pay for 2013, 2016, and 2019).

crosshairs, especially after Xi Jinping's rise to power in 2013.[51] Having once been celebrated as national champions and important catalysts of China's technological and financial revolution, and having greatly benefited from both political connections and regulatory forbearance during the first phase of their meteoric rise, Alipay and WeChat Pay were about to get an abrupt wake-up call.

The shift in China's regulatory approach to Alipay, WeChat Pay, and other P2P payment platforms involved several incremental, if progressively bolder, steps. This shift began modestly enough in 2010, when the PBOC introduced a new regulatory framework designed to promote the safety and soundness of P2P payment platforms and establish a baseline level of consumer protection.[52] Over time, this framework evolved to include customer disclosure requirements, conflict of interest rules, and the imposition of a minimum capital requirement equal to 10 percent of a platform's average daily customer balances. Platforms were also required to establish a reserve fund and compensation scheme to cover any customer losses.

Yet as time passed, the PBOC's approach took a decidedly more interventionist turn. In January 2017, the PBOC announced that it would require payment platforms to deposit 20 percent of customer funds in a non-interest-bearing custodial account held at a commercial bank.[53] The 20 percent minimum was increased to 50 percent in June 2018, and then to 100 percent effective January 1, 2019.[54] The custody requirement has also evolved over time, with P2P payment platforms now required to deposit customer funds directly into a dedicated reserve account with the PBOC itself.[55] By the time

51. For a detailed description of the shift in the political climate facing Alipay and WeChat Pay, see Martin Chorzempa, *The Cashless Revolution: China's Reinvention of Money and the End of America's Domination of Finance and Technology* (2022).

52. PBOC, Administrative Measures for the Payment Services Provided by Non-financial Institutions (June 14, 2010, effective September 1, 2010), CLI.4.134238 (EN), and Administrative Measures for the Online Payment Business of Non-banking Payment Institutions (December 28, 2015, effective July 1, 2016), CLI.4.261833 (EN); China Banking Regulatory Commission, Administrative Measures for the Capital of Commercial Banks (for Trial Implementation) (June 7, 2012, effective January 1, 2013), CLI.4.176745 (EN).

53. PBOC, Notice of the General Office of the People's Bank of China on Matters Concerning Implementing the Centralized Deposit of the Funds of Pending Payments of Clients of Payment Institutions (January 13, 2017), art. 3, CLI.4.288811 (EN). See also Gabriel Wildau & Yizhen Jai, "Central Bank Takes Steps to Ensure Ant Financial and Tencent Do Not Grow Too Powerful," *Financial Times* (January 1, 2019).

54. PBOC, Notice of the General Office of the People's Bank of China on Matters Concerning Complete Centralized Deposit of the Funds of Pending Payments of Clients of Payment Institutions (June 29, 2018), art. 1, CLI.4.316748 (EN).

55. PBOC, Notice Concerning Complete Centralized Deposit (June 29, 2018).

these requirements were fully implemented, it was estimated that Alipay and WeChat Pay had collectively amassed over $143 billion in customer funds, with the requirement to deposit these funds in a non-interest-bearing reserve account translating into as much as $1 billion per year in lost interest income.[56] While the PBOC subsequently reversed its decision not to pay interest on these reserve balances, the practical effect of these requirements was to eliminate the once unfettered discretion that Alipay and WeChat Pay enjoyed over the enormous float of customer funds generated by their vast financial and commercial empires.

Quite clearly, the PBOC's approach is a reflection of China's unique political environment, where this level of state control over strategically important infrastructure and industries is not unusual. Yet this approach also reflects a very specific, and in many ways compelling, vision for how public policy can be used to promote both good money and good payments. As a starting point, by requiring P2P payment platforms to deposit all customer funds in a ringfenced central bank reserve account, the PBOC is effectively eliminating their exposure to a platform's bankruptcy. Even better, the PBOC is replacing this exposure with one to an entity—the PBOC itself— that is not subject to the harsh strictures of corporate bankruptcy law. As a consequence, the PBOC's custody rules essentially create a public backstop, protecting customers from the risks of illiquidity and potential losses that might otherwise arise from the failure of Alipay, WeChat Pay, or other P2P payment platforms.

The PBOC's custody rules can also be viewed as one of the critical linch-pins of China's plan to revitalize its once moribund bank-based payment system. In addition to bringing P2P payment platforms within the perim-eter of financial regulation and requiring them to deposit customer funds in central bank reserve accounts, the PBOC has also taken steps to centralize and expand access to its basic financial market infrastructure.[57] The most important of these steps took place in 2017, when the PBOC created a single national clearinghouse—NetsUnion Clearing Corporation—and gave it sole responsibility for clearing and settling payments between banks, P2P pay-ment platforms, and other system participants.[58]

---

56. See Wildau & Yizhen, "Central Bank Takes Steps."

57. See Massad, "Facebook's Libra 2.0," 48.

58. For a more detailed description of NetsUnion, see "NetsUnion Clearing Corporation," *China Banking News* (July 23, 2018), https://www.chinabankingnews.com/wiki/netsunion-clearing-corporation/.

The practical effect of these steps has been to greatly enhance the interoperability of the Chinese payment system, allowing people and businesses to transfer money more seamlessly between P2P payment platforms, banks, and their billions of customers. And while the resulting centralization of China's payment infrastructure might be viewed as robbing Alipay and WeChat Pay of two of their most important comparative advantages—convenience and ubiquity—the fact that they now operate on the same clearing and settlement rails as conventional deposit-taking banks and, perhaps more importantly, *as each other* arguably gives them more powerful incentives to stay one step ahead of the technological curve. Should these incentives ultimately translate into ongoing improvements to their consumer-facing payment applications, along with the quality of their broader universe of products and services, then Chinese consumers will benefit from not only better money but also better payments and perhaps even a more dynamic economy.

Making Payment Networks Work

As the recent experiences of both Kenya and China demonstrate, it's not enough to simply create new regulatory frameworks designed to bolster the credibility of monetary IOUs issued by institutions and platforms outside the conventional banking system. While prudential regulation can help engineer good money, it does not eliminate the legal and technological barriers that have long prevented these new institutions and platforms from gaining full and unfettered access to incumbent payment networks. Nor does this regulation guarantee that incumbents and new entrants will come together to develop common technical standards or coordinate investments in the next generation of payment networks. All of this points in the direction of a potentially valuable—and perhaps even essential—role for regulators in promoting policy objectives such as open access and interoperability. In short, both logic and experience suggest that regulators may sometimes need to play a more proactive, muscular role in the ongoing *governance* of financial market infrastructure.

To date, it is this governance role that has been largely absent from recent regulatory initiatives like the New York BitLicense and the EU's MiCA. Yet there are other jurisdictions that have taken this role more seriously—often with impressive results. Take Brazil, for example. Less than five years ago, Brazil was home to one of the world's slowest and most expensive electronic payment systems. Predictably, the high cost of making electronic payments drove extremely high rates of cash usage and stubbornly high levels of financial exclusion.[59] To address these persistent challenges and advance its legal mandate to promote "financial citizenship," the Brazilian Central Bank introduced a new real-time payment network, known as Pix, in November 2020. Today, Pix's retail customers can send and receive money for free using a mobile phone app, without the need to open a bank account or share sensitive personal information with payors.

Importantly, not only did the Brazilian Central Bank take the lead in developing Pix, it also made a series of forward-looking decisions about network access and governance. These decisions included building an open API and then requiring all incumbent banks to invest in the technological upgrades necessary to connect to the new system. They also included opening up access to the Pix system to institutions and platforms outside the conventional banking system, thus taking advantage of their technologically superior products and services to drive network adoption, expansion, and innovation. The results have been staggering. Less than three years after its introduction, Pix is now used by approximately 80 percent of Brazil's adult population, more than thirteen million private firms, and even the Brazilian government.[60] The rapid adoption of Pix has also been accompanied by a dramatic decrease in Brazil's unbanked population. Indeed, even incumbent banks have reaped the benefits, generating significantly higher fees from the almost fivefold increase in the volume and size of electronic payments.

India offers yet another compelling example. In 2016, a joint venture between the Reserve Bank of India—the country's central bank—and the Indian Bankers Association announced the launch of the Unified Payments Interface (UPI). Like Pix, UPI is an open API built on top of the central bank's existing real-time settlement system. Unlike Pix, UPI was developed in cooperation with incumbent banks. Users must also have a bank account to send and receive payments via UPI. The introduction of UPI has supported a wave of technological innovation that today enables over three hundred million customers and fifty million small businesses—everyone from taxi drivers, to roadside barbers, to textile workers—to send and

59. "Digital Payments Have Gone Viral in Brazil," *The Economist* (May 14, 2022); see also Angelo Duarte, Jon Frost, Leonardo Gambacorta, Priscilla Koo Wilkens, & Hyun Song Shin, "Central Banks, the Monetary System, and Public Payment Infrastructures: Lessons from Brazil's Pix," Bank for International Settlements Bulletin No. 52 (March 23, 2022).

60. IMF, "Pix: Brazil's Successful Instant Payment System," IMF Western Hemisphere Department (July 31, 2023), https://www.elibrary.imf.org/view/journals/002/2023/289/article -A004-en.xml.

receive payments via their mobile phones at a tiny fraction of the cost of electronic payments in many other jurisdictions.[61] In the process, UPI has quickly put India at the forefront of digital innovation and financial inclusion.

These and other examples are a reminder that promoting experimentation, competition, and innovation is often not simply a matter of adopting market-supporting laws and institutions. This is especially true when it comes to the development, maintenance, and upgrades to financial market infrastructure—where economies of scale, network effects, and powerful incumbents often erect barriers to the adoption of new technology. In these cases, policymakers will sometimes need to get their hands dirty and directly involve themselves in important decisions about network access, investment, and stability—not just *supporting* markets but actively *shaping* them in pursuit of important social objectives, like fast, cheap, and inclusive payments.

The Reckoning

We can now start to put all the pieces together. The financial safety net, bank regulation and supervision, and restrictions on access to basic financial market infrastructure have entrenched banks at the apex of our systems of money and payments. Yet the comparative disadvantage of banks in the development and application of new payments technology, combined with the weakened incentives of incumbency, have opened the door to the emergence and rapid growth of the shadow monetary system and a new breed of financial institutions and platforms. However, while these new institutions and platforms are fast revolutionizing the way we make payments, many struggle to compete with banks in the legal and institutional engineering of good money. This disadvantage is compounded by regulatory frameworks that too often fail to protect customers from the risks of bankruptcy, violate basic principles of technological neutrality, or are simply not designed for the digital age.

Viewed together, these pieces reflect the core predictions of Gresham's new law. In a great many cases, the development and application of the new technology being used to deliver good payments is moving faster than the evolution of the laws and institutions that deliver good money. Where people and businesses value good payments today and discount the risks of bankruptcy tomorrow, the resulting shift of assets and activity into the

---

61. Mujib Mashal & Hari Kumar, "Where Digital Payments, Even for a 1-Cent Chai, Are Colossal in Scale," *New York Times* (March 1, 2023).

shadow monetary system increases the risk that bad money will drive out good. This hydraulic process makes it more likely that this system will one day come crashing down. If and when it does, the carnage will pose significant risks for customers, for the safety and soundness of banks and other financial institutions, and perhaps even for the stability of our monetary and financial systems. Yet the dynamics of Gresham's new law are far from universal. Nor are the resulting risks somehow unavoidable. While some of the case studies explored in this book demonstrate these potentially destructive dynamics, others offer important lessons about how we might arrest them: thereby harnessing the benefits of new payments technology while also enhancing the stability of our monetary systems. Drawing on these lessons, the final chapter lays out a blueprint for legal and institutional reform for countries—like the United States—that have fallen behind the technological and regulatory curve.

7

A Blueprint for Reform

> The basic dilemma is this: Our monetary and banking institutions
> have evolved in a way that entangles competition among financial
> intermediary firms with the provision of transactions media. The
> entanglement is the source of risks of default and breakdown.
> Protection against those risks has brought the government
> interventions now seen to have inefficient by-products: bureaucratic
> surveillance, deposit insurance, lender-of-last-resort guarantees
> by central banks. There is no possible complete resolution of this
> dilemma, but we may hope to limit its scope.[1]
>
> —JAMES TOBIN

This book has explored a long-standing and fundamental tension embedded
deep within the structure of our financial system. This tension is a product
of the fact that we rely on banks to perform three critical and, at least as
presently constituted, intertwined functions. The first is the provision of
loans and other types of financing to people, businesses, and governments,
thereby necessitating that banks hold risky and often illiquid longer-term
assets. The second is *money creation*, with short-term and highly liquid
bank deposits representing by far and away the largest source of money
in the modern economy. The third is *payments*, where banks serve as both
the gatekeepers and custodians of the vast and sprawling network of financial

1. James Tobin, "Financial Innovation and Deregulation in Perspective," 3 Bank of Japan
Monetary & Economic Studies 19, 20–21 (1985).

plumbing that moves money across time and space in satisfaction of our financial obligations. As economist Matthew Klein recently put it, this essentially makes banks "speculative investment funds grafted on top of critical infrastructure."[2]

The institutional bundling of financing, money, and payments has made banks a uniquely important part of our financial system and economy. But it is also what makes them inherently fragile. To address this fragility, and contain the systemic impact of both idiosyncratic bank failures and wider banking panics, policymakers have erected a strong financial safety net that includes lender-of-last-resort facilities, deposit insurance schemes, and bank resolution frameworks. To limit reliance on this safety net, they have also created comprehensive and costly frameworks of prudential regulation and supervision. Collectively, these policy decisions have greatly reduced the fragility of banks: transforming otherwise risky deposits into good money and promoting their widespread use as a means of payment. Yet, as we have seen, these same regulatory frameworks can also erect significant barriers to entry, undercut competition, impede the development and adoption of new technology, spur destabilizing regulatory arbitrage, and exacerbate the too-big-to-fail problem.

As the quote from Nobel laureate James Tobin at the beginning of this chapter illustrates, this book is not the first attempt to expose this tension or advance a potential blueprint for reform. Like any book on money, it stands on the shoulders of giants—both in terms of its understanding of the fundamental problem and the range, desirability, and limits of possible solutions. Yet these giants could never have predicted the sweeping technological changes that have revolutionized banking, money, and payments over the past two decades. These changes are the drivers behind Gresham's new law. They are also the motivation for reimagining what a more stable, competitive, convenient, and accessible system of money and payments might look like—and for laying out a blueprint for how we might achieve it.

This blueprint is built on three pillars. The first is a *dedicated payments charter*. This charter would be available to financial institutions, platforms, and technology firms that issue monetary IOUs in connection with their core payments business. Access to the charter would come with several important strings. First, these firms would be required to incorporate a separate ring-fenced subsidiary—a payments entity—that would obtain the charter and

    2. Klein, "Thoughts on Bank Bailouts," *The Overshoot* (March 13, 2023), https://theovershoot .co/p/thoughts-on-the-bank-bailouts.

serve as the sole vehicle through which the firm issues monetary IOUs and processes payments. Second, the charter would prohibit any payments entity from engaging in financial intermediation. This "no intermediation" rule would prevent charterholders from using customer funds to make risky investments. Thus, for every dollar, pound, euro, or tether that a payments entity accepts on behalf of its customers, an equal amount—denominated in the same currency—would automatically be set aside for their benefit. To ensure that these customers are always at the top of the creditor pecking order, a payments entity would also be prohibited from entering into any other lending or borrowing arrangements, including with its parent or other affiliates. Compliance with these requirements would then be subject to ongoing prudential supervision tailored to reflect the narrow business model of payments entities.

The second pillar is an *open access rule* that gives these payments entities a legal right to directly connect to basic financial market infrastructure. First and foremost, this rule would give charterholders automatic access to central bank reserve accounts, along with a corresponding requirement that payments entities deposit all customer funds directly into these accounts. Access to central bank reserve accounts would then be the first step toward ensuring access to clearinghouses, financial communication networks, and other electronic payment infrastructure. The owners and operators of this infrastructure would then be subject to an interoperability rule imposing an affirmative obligation on them to take all reasonable measures to eliminate any technological and operational barriers that, as a practical matter, might prevent payments entities from connecting to their networks. This interoperability rule would include a mechanism for allocating the initial and ongoing costs of any resulting system upgrades among these owners and operators, incumbent network participants, and potential new entrants.

The third pillar of this blueprint is a *new governance structure* for the payment system. At present, decisions about payment system access, interoperability, and whether to invest in the development and adoption of new technology are often the product of opaque, informal, and sometimes uncoordinated processes involving only a handful of public and private sector stakeholders. These stakeholders include central banks, the owners and operators of incumbent financial market infrastructure and, of course, banks. As a governance matter, these processes can make it difficult to observe what decisions are being made about payment system design, why, and by whom. There is also the risk that aspiring new entrants may not get a seat at the table. For these reasons, we might expect these processes to

FIGURE 7.1. A Blueprint for Good Money and Good Payments

Good money	Good payments
• A payments charter • A "no intermediation" rule • Structural separation • Borrowing, lending, and activity restrictions • A simplified resolution framework	• An open access rule for central bank reserve accounts • An interoperability rule for financial market infrastructure • A new payments governance framework

entrench the technological status quo and protect incumbents from vigorous competition. We might also expect these processes to yield decisions that are not always in the best interests of customers or consistent with the pursuit of broader public policy objectives. This final pillar would see these processes replaced with a more formal, transparent, and representative governance structure designed to harness the comparative advantages of different stakeholders, better coordinate decisions about payment system design, and ultimately ensure that these decisions are made in the public interest.

Together, these three pillars hold out enormous potential benefits for consumer protection, for competition and innovation, and for the stability of the financial system. The new payments charter would create a parallel system of money and payments—one that eliminates the fragility associated with fractional reserve banking, effectively ringfences customers' funds from the risks of bankruptcy, and prevents the transmission of cross-sector risks between banks and payments entities. The open access and interoperability rules would then ensure that these payments entities compete with banks on a more level playing field, while the governance structure would provide a platform for coordinating future infrastructure improvements, and for ensuring that these improvements benefit everyone—not just incumbent players.

Like all architects, policymakers will inevitably be forced to confront a wide range of practical challenges and objections when attempting to turn this blueprint into reality. These challenges include how to eliminate, or at the very least limit, opportunities for destabilizing regulatory arbitrage. The objections, meanwhile, include questions around what space the new payments charter leaves for firms to profit from their investments in new technology and what impact greater competition in payments might have on both financial intermediation and the stability of the conventional banking system. These challenges and objections are extremely important and should not simply be dismissed out of hand. Yet, upon closer inspection, they are also not insurmountable. Nor when compared with the fragility and competitive distortions created by the current bundled system do they seem like a high price to pay for good money and better payments.

The Payments Charter

The grant of charters to conventional deposit-taking banks is often framed as creating a *franchise* relationship. As explained by professors Robert Hockett and Saule Omarova, this framing envisions that "the sovereign public, as franchisor, effectively licenses private financial institutions, as franchisees, to dispense a vital and indefinitely extensible public resource: the sovereign's full faith and credit."[3] Put differently, just like McDonald's gives its franchisees the right to use the Golden Arches to sell cheeseburgers, the government gives banks the right to use the unique privileges and protections of the financial safety net to sell their monetary IOUs as good money. In return, franchisee banks agree to submit themselves to prudential regulation and supervision by the franchisor, theoretically designed to ensure that banks do not abuse this franchise relationship.

Borrowing this framing, the payments charter effectively envisions the creation of a second franchise—one designed to produce a competing product but in a different package and, ultimately, demanding far less from the government as franchisor. The key differences between these two franchises stem from the ability of the franchisee to engage in financial intermediation. As we saw in chapter 1, fractional reserve banking gives banks the ability to create money, with the extension of new loans mechanically resulting in the creation of new deposits. Subject to applicable regulation, banks are also typically permitted to make investments in equity and debt securities, real estate, commodities, and other financial assets. In stark contrast, the payments charter would completely prohibit charterholders from creating new money or using customer funds to make risky investments. No loans, no stocks, no bonds, no mortgage-backed securities—no credit, liquidity, or maturity transformation whatsoever. This strict and all-encompassing prohibition is the essence of the no intermediation rule.

---

3. Hockett & Omarova, "The Finance Franchise," 102 Cornell Law Review 1143, 1147 (2017). See also Morgan Ricks, *The Money Problem: Rethinking Financial Regulation* (2016) (describing bank charters as creating a public-private partnership).

By itself, the no intermediation rule is not a new idea. The basic prescription bears a strong resemblance to Irving's Fisher's 100% money, the Chicago plan, and other so-called narrow banking proposals. These proposals are part of a long and distinguished line of academic literature pioneered by economists including Fisher, Henry Simons, Milton Friedman, James Tobin, and Robert Litan that was motivated by the desire—as Litan colorfully described it—to "break the Gordian knot between deposit taking and commercial lending."[4] These narrow banking proposals saw renewed interest in the wake of the global financial crisis,[5] and then again after the failure and controversial bailout of Silicon Valley Bank in March 2023.[6]

Yet *this* version of the no intermediation rule would differ from its predecessors in two important respects. First, whereas narrow banking proposals almost universally envision dismantling the conventional banking system, the new payments charter would represent a second, parallel, and completely separate regulatory track alongside existing bank charters. This is no small difference: whereas the payments charter would be in part designed to promote greater diversity, competition, and innovation, most narrow banking proposals risk creating an institutional and regulatory monoculture in money and payments. Second, and more importantly, previous narrow banking proposals have all been motivated by the perceived perils of fractional reserve banking and its potential impact on both financial and monetary stability. The payments charter, on the other hand, is simply the first pillar in a more comprehensive and ambitious blueprint designed to strike a better balance between the often competing objectives of promoting more vibrant competition and innovation, protecting consumers, and preventing monetary and financial instability. Viewed through this wider lens, the motivation for the no intermediation rule is ultimately Gresham's new law and the corresponding need for laws and institutions that better reflect both the opportunities and risks stemming from rapid technological change.

The no intermediation rule raises an important threshold question about the nature of the assets that payments entities should be permitted to hold.

---

4. Litan, *What Should Banks Do?*, 145 (1987). See also, e.g., Fisher, *100% Money* (1936); Simons, "A Positive Program for Laissez Faire: Some Proposals for a Liberal Economic Policy," in Gideonse (ed.), *Public Policy Pamphlet No. 15* (1934); Friedman, *A Program for Monetary Stability* (1963); Tobin, "Financial Innovation and Deregulation."

5. See, e.g., Adam Levitin, "Safe Banking: Finance and Democracy," 83 University of Chicago Law Review 357 (2016); John Kay, *Narrow Banking: The Reform of Banking Regulation* (2009).

6. See, e.g., Mihir Desai & Sumit Rajpal, "How 'Payment Banks' Could Prevent the Next Bank Collapse," Harvard Business Review (March 17, 2023), https://hbr.org/2023/03/how-payment-banks-could-prevent-the-next-bank-collapse.

In theory, there are two basic options. The first is to permit payments entities to invest customer funds in government debt securities and other HQLA. Yet even these ostensibly safe government securities are sometimes prone to bouts of market illiquidity. Put bluntly, the assets that qualify as HQLA are not always high quality or liquid. In the United States, there are also growing concerns that the increasingly complex, fragmented, and fragile structure of US treasury markets might contribute to future market instability and potential breakdown.[7] Further complicating matters, the mechanics of bond market pricing mean that the market value of these securities inevitably declines during periods of rising interest rates.[8] Since all the liabilities of payments entities would be monetary IOUs with a fixed nominal value, marking these securities to market during these periods could lead to states of the world where their outstanding liabilities exceeded the market value of their collateral assets. Conversely, holding these assets at their acquisition cost would obscure their true liquidity position, forcing payments entities to take real, crystallized losses when selling them for the purposes of honoring customer redemption requests. To address these market risks, payments entities would need to be subject to additional rules envisioning either the overcollateralization of monetary IOUs or the imposition of minimum equity capital requirements. The need for these rules reflects an unavoidable trade-off: once policymakers permit even a tiny amount of financial intermediation, prudence demands additional layers of regulation, which in turn cuts against the benefits of the payments charter.

The second and more straightforward option would be to hold customer funds directly in the payment system's ultimate settlement asset: central bank reserve balances. Importantly, this option would pose none of the challenges stemming from potential market illiquidity, instability, or mark-to-market losses encountered in connection with investments in government debt securities or other HQLA. As a consequence, it would not demand any additional regulation designed to insulate customers from the resulting market, liquidity, and other risks. As explored in greater detail below, this

7. See, e.g., US Department of the Treasury, Interagency Working Group for Treasury Market Surveillance, "Enhancing the Resilience of the U.S. Treasury Market: 2022 Staff Progress Report" (November 10, 2022), https://home.treasury.gov/system/files/136/2022-IAWG-Treasury-Report .pdf. See also Yesha Yadav, "The Failed Regulation of U.S. Treasury Markets," 121 Columbia Law Review 1173 (2021).

8. Bonds and other debt securities typically envision coupon payments at a fixed rate of interest reflecting their intrinsic credit and other risks. Where interest rates rise, the fixed coupon payments attached to these securities mean that the only way this change can be reflected is through a decline in their market price.

option might involve some incremental trade-offs. Nevertheless, requiring payments entities to hold all customer funds in central bank reserve balances would represent the purest embodiment of the no intermediation rule.

Beyond the no intermediation rule itself, the new payments charter would obviously demand the creation of a new regulatory and supervisory framework. The entry point for this framework would be a chartering requirement. Any financial institution, platform, technology firm, or other enterprise that sought to issue monetary IOUs as part of its business would have two basic options.[9] The first would be to apply for and obtain a conventional bank charter. The second would be to incorporate a new subsidiary and charter it as a payments entity. Once chartered, the payments entity would be permitted to accept funds from customers in exchange for the issuance of monetary IOUs. The funds received by the payments entity would then be subject to the no intermediation rule, and the monetary IOUs the payments entity issued would be the only debts it was permitted to incur. Most importantly, the payments entity would be strictly prohibited from lending money to, or borrowing money from, its parent firm or other affiliates. This prohibition against other indebtedness would be designed to prevent the type of dense counterparty exposures that, as recently revealed by the crypto winter, so often sow the seeds of financial contagion. While the new framework would place no additional restrictions on the activities or financing of the parent firm, the payments entity itself would also be prohibited from undertaking any business other than payments.[10] This combination of structural separation, portfolio restrictions, and activity constraints would serve to completely ringfence the business and balance sheet of the payments entity from those of its parent and wider corporate group.

Compliance with this new regulatory framework would obviously require ongoing supervision by a regulatory authority—most likely an existing bank regulator, like the Federal Reserve or the OCC. Yet, given the incredibly simple balance sheets of payments entities, the complete absence of financial intermediation, and their narrow range of permitted activities, this supervision would not need to be nearly as intensive or costly as the prudential

9. In practice, this would also demand the articulation of a tractable legal definition of what constitutes a "monetary IOU." A useful starting point for this definition is arguably the existing definitions of "payment instrument," "money," and "monetary value," as defined under US state money transmission laws; for further details, see Dan Awrey, "Bad Money," 106:1 Cornell Law Review 1 (2020), appendix A.

10. Of course, if a bank or other financial institution that incorporated and chartered a payments entity was subject to such activity restrictions, these restrictions would continue to apply.

supervision of conventional deposit-taking banks. Indeed, rather than focusing on complex variables like capital adequacy, asset quality, earnings, and liquidity management, supervisors could instead focus on simply verifying ongoing compliance with the core ringfencing rules. They would also need to ensure that payments entities keep accurate and up-to-date customer records and that they have in place adequate policies and procedures governing compliance with anti-money-laundering rules, fraud detection, and operational resilience.[11] By tailoring this supervisory framework to reflect the narrow business model of payments entities, the payments charter would create valuable optionality: giving technology firms developing products and services at the frontier of money and payments a more viable alternative to obtaining a conventional bank charter.

Together, these new regulatory and supervisory frameworks would greatly reduce the risk that a payments entity would be forced into bankruptcy. Indeed, given the strict portfolio and borrowing restrictions imposed on payments entities, the most likely reason for their bankruptcy would henceforth be an operational risk failure, such as management fraud or a successful cyberattack. Still, in order to completely remove payments entities from the shadow of bankruptcy, policymakers would need to take two additional steps. The first step would be to explicitly exempt these entities from conventional corporate bankruptcy law. In countries like the United States, this would put them on the same legal footing as federal and state-chartered banks. The second, and corresponding, step would then be to create a special resolution framework as a replacement for the bankruptcy process. Once again, given the narrow business model of payments entities, this framework would be far more streamlined than those designed to coordinate the restructuring, sale, or wind-down of failing banks. In most cases, the key priorities in the resolution process would simply be confirming the identity of customers, determining how much they are owed, and soliciting instructions for where to send their money. Given this relatively straightforward process, it seems reasonable to expect that it could be completed within a relatively short span of time—ideally matching the next-business-day standard targeted by the FDIC and many other conventional deposit guarantee schemes.

Outside the United States, policy experiments involving stand-alone payments charters are already well under way. In Europe, we have already

---

11. Any residual operational risks impacting customers could be mitigated by requiring the parent firm of any payments entity to obtain an insurance policy against these risks. Ideally, this policy should be for the express benefit of customers.

seen how PSD2 and EMD2 provide a bespoke regulatory pathway for P2P payment platforms. In China and India, legal frameworks for the authorization and regulation of nonbank payment service providers are now well established.[12] In Canada, the Bank of Canada has recently rolled out a new licensing framework for retail payments activities.[13] And in the UK, the Bank of England is in the process of developing a new regulatory framework for stablecoin issuers. These and other frameworks are far from perfect; indeed, almost all of them would benefit from additional measures designed to insulate customer funds from the risk of bankruptcy and ensure the rapid and orderly resolution of chartered firms. In some jurisdictions, there are also lingering questions around the effectiveness of current supervisory frameworks and the level of industry compliance with existing rules.[14] Yet all of these policy experiments are still light-years ahead of the United States, where antiquated and inadequate state money transmitter laws and technology-specific charters like the New York Bitlicense remain the only viable alternatives to conventional bank charters. Accordingly, while the United States is often and rightly viewed as a global leader in financial services, the reality—at least when it comes to money and payments—is that it now finds itself falling farther and farther behind the technological and regulatory curve. A new federal payments charter would be an important first step toward closing this gap.

Open Access and Interoperability Rules

The regulatory, supervisory, and resolution frameworks that would accompany the new payments charter are all designed for a singular purpose: promoting good money. Yet, implemented on their own, these new frameworks would only be a necessary but insufficient condition for fostering the type of dynamic experimentation, competition, and innovation needed to promote good payments. Indeed, so long as incumbent banks enjoy privileged access to central bank reserve accounts and other financial market infrastructure,

12. See PBOC, Administrative Measures for the Payment Services Provided by Non-financial Institutions, (June 14, 2010, effective September 1, 2010), CLI.4.134238 (EN); PBOC, Administrative Measures for the Online Payment Business of Non-Banking Payment Institutions (December 28, 2015, effective July 1, 2016), CLI.4.261833 (EN); Indian Payment and Settlement Systems Act (2007) and associated regulations.

13. See Retail Payment Activities Act, S.C. 2021, c. 23, s. 177; "Retail Payment Activities Regulations," Part I, 157:6 Canada Gazette (February 11, 2023).

14. See, e.g., Laura Noonan, "UK Regulator Attacks 'Unacceptable' Risk Posed by Payments Groups," *Financial Times* (March 16, 2023), https://www.ft.com/content/1fa1139c-faf7-4ce8-b0b9-f32f0d07da44.

there is little reason to believe that they will not continue to remain unchallenged at the apex of our systems of money and payments. Beyond the payments charter itself, policymakers must therefore ensure that institutions and platforms holding a payments charter enjoy legal and operational access to this infrastructure, and that they play a role in key decisions about the technological design of payment networks.

Logically, the first step toward achieving these objectives is ensuring that payments entities have direct access to central bank reserve accounts. In many jurisdictions, expanding access to these accounts would involve a relatively straightforward and modest change to existing central bank policy, with the regulatory framework governing payments entities also serving as a condition of eligibility for opening an account. Yet, in the United States, granting payments entities access to Federal Reserve master accounts would also require an act of Congress amending Section 13(1) of the Federal Reserve Act. At the very least, this amendment should explicitly acknowledge that payments entities are legally eligible to open master accounts. However, given the Fed's historical antipathy toward granting master account applications by novel banks, like Custodia and TNB, there is also a compelling argument for going beyond mere eligibility and including a presumption that an application *will* be granted unless doing so would pose a clear risk to the stability or integrity of the US financial system. This presumption could then be combined with a process whereby the Fed would be entitled to deny the application within a set time frame, on the basis of specific evidence and upon publicly disclosing its reasons for doing so.

The narrow business model of payments entities means that granting them access to reserve accounts would pose little or no credit risk to central banks. Given the potential benefits in terms of greater competition and innovation, it should therefore come as no surprise that other jurisdictions have already started to experiment with expanding access. As we have already seen, access to PBOC reserve accounts has been one of the linchpins of China's approach toward the regulation of P2P payment platforms like WeChat Pay and Alipay since 2018. In 2019, the Bank of England published a formal process and eligibility criteria for nonbank payment service providers seeking direct access to the Bank's settlement accounts.[15] Less than a year later, Singapore announced that nonbank payment service providers

15. Bank of England, "Access to UK Payment Schemes for Non-bank Payment Service Providers" (December 2019), https://www.bankofengland.co.uk/-/media/boe/files/markets/other-market-operations/accessfornonbankpaymentserviceproviders.pdf.

would be allowed to directly connect to both its Fast and Secure Transfers (FAST) and PayNow real-time payment systems.[16] And in the years since, Canada, Australia, India, and a host of other countries have all signaled their intention to follow suit, thereby breaking the stranglehold that banks have historically enjoyed over access to basic central bank settlement architecture.[17] By all accounts, the train is leaving the station—and often on new rails. The only question is whether the United States will be on board.

Beyond expanding access to central bank reserve accounts, plugging chartered payments entities directly into existing payment networks would require legal and operational interoperability with clearinghouses and other financial market infrastructure. Broadly speaking, this interoperability has two components: clearing and settlement. *Clearing interoperability* requires network participants to develop and adopt technologically compatible systems for communicating, verifying, and reconciling electronic payment instructions. Clearing interoperability thus encompasses a wide variety of network features: ranging from relatively mundane decisions about the formatting of payment messages, to highly technical issues around the design of APIs, and more fundamental design questions like whether to adopt a centralized hub-and-spoke or decentralized peer-to-peer payment network.[18] *Settlement interoperability* then requires network participants to identify a common asset or assets, the delivery of which will satisfy their obligations pursuant to the payment instructions. If clearing interoperability is about making sure all the different pipes fit snugly together to form a coherent system of financial plumbing, settlement interoperability dictates the nature and quality of the liquid that flows through the pipes.

Access to central bank reserve accounts would effectively solve the challenge of settlement interoperability, with both chartered payments

---

16. Monetary Authority of Singapore, "Non-bank Financial Institutions to Have Access to Fast and PayNow" (November 30, 2020), https://www.mas.gov.sg/news/media-releases/2020/non-bank-financial-institutions-to-have-access-to-fast-and-paynow.

17. See, e.g., Bank of Canada, "Access to Bank of Canada Settlement Accounts for the Real-Time Rail" (October 2022), https://www.bankofcanada.ca/wp-content/uploads/2022/09/Access-to-Bank-of-Canada-Settlement-Accounts-for-the-Real-Time-Rail.pdf; "Australia's Wholesale CBDC Trial Allowed Access to Non-banks," *Ledger Insights* (December 8, 2021), https://www.ledgerinsights.com/australias-wholesale-cbdc-trials-allowed-access-to-non-banks/; "RBI to Give Some Non-banks Access to Payment Systems," *Central Banking* (April 15, 2021), https://www.centralbanking.com/central-banks/financial-stability/fmi/7822686/rbi-to-give-some-non-banks-access-to-payments-systems.

18. For a flavor of the types of technical challenges that payment networks must address in order to ensure clearing interoperability, see International Standards Organization, "Universal Financial Industry Message Scheme," https://www.iso20022.org/about-iso-20022.

entities and incumbent banks settling payments in reserve balances. The real challenge is clearing interoperability. In a world of rapid technological change, promoting clearing interoperability would force policymakers to successfully navigate a series of thorny trade-offs. As we saw in chapter 3, seemingly inconsequential technical decisions about network design can be used to erect artificial barriers to interoperability, thereby shielding incumbents from competition and preventing new and possibly better technologies from emerging and taking hold in the marketplace. In much the same way that Tesla can design charging stations that prevent other electric vehicle brands from connecting to its network infrastructure, incumbent payment networks can thus design clearing systems and processes in ways that render them more or less incompatible with the technology used by aspiring new entrants.

The prospect that decisions about network design would be made solely by incumbent players, acting in their narrow self-interest, provides a strong rationale for the imposition of some kind of interoperability rule. This rule would represent an affirmative obligation on the part of clearinghouses and other financial market infrastructure providers to take whatever steps were reasonably necessary to ensure that chartered payments entities did not encounter any significant legal, technological, or operational barriers when attempting to connect to a payment network.[19] In effect, this rule would encourage incumbent networks to coordinate with aspiring new entrants to identify and minimize any potential barriers, thereby lowering the costs of establishing and maintaining a network connection.

The design and implementation of this interoperability rule would demand that policymakers thread a difficult needle. On the one hand, the effectiveness of this rule in deterring anticompetitive conduct and practices would be bolstered by a strong and unequivocal commitment to interoperability, coupled with strict and vigorous enforcement. On the other hand, forcing incumbent networks to ensure interoperability with each successive wave of technological change—no matter how fluid or unproven—would be unrealistic and almost certainly inefficient. This points to the desirability of retaining some degree of flexibility in the rule's application, reserved for those cases where strict enforcement is unlikely to yield meaningful public benefits.

---

19. For an example of this type of clearing interoperability rule in other contexts, see § 17A of the U.S. Securities Exchange Act, governing securities clearing, as described in Dan Awrey & Joshua Macey, "Open Access, Interoperability, and DTCC's Unexpected Path to Monopoly," 132 Yale Law Journal 96 (2022).

Further complicating matters, even where interoperability is likely to yield significant benefits, there is still the question of how to allocate the initial and ongoing costs associated with the necessary technological and operational upgrades. Once again, trade-offs abound. Allocating all, or even the lion's share of these costs to prospective new entrants would increase the already high barriers to market entry.[20] Where incumbent networks were then responsible for designing and implementing the necessary upgrades, there is also the possibility that they will possess both a lack of expertise in the relevant technology and poor incentives to cost-effectively integrate it with their existing clearing systems. Conversely, allocating the costs entirely to incumbent players could lead to chronic overinvestment, with aspiring new entrants effectively forcing incumbent networks to take significant risks on new and still unproven technology.

On the flip side, there is also the question of how to divide up the cost savings where interoperability lays the groundwork for network upgrades that generate significant efficiency gains. In theory, there is a compelling argument for allocating a disproportionate share of these gains to the new entrants that develop and champion a particular technology, thereby spurring incumbent players to invest in the relevant network improvements. Yet in practice, this would also seem to create a marginal disincentive for incumbents to invest in greater interoperability in the first place. Over time, it could also generate new competitive distortions as these cost advantages transform new entrants into powerful and entrenched incumbents. And, more generally, measuring the different financial, human, technological, and other contributions of various players toward these network improvements would often be highly case-specific, extremely difficult, and fundamentally contestable. Like the application of the interoperability rule itself, these complex trade-offs suggest that policymakers should eschew prescriptive ex ante rules governing the allocation of these costs and benefits in favor of a more flexible and contextualized approach.

These trade-offs lay bare a fundamental challenge in the governance of financial market infrastructure. The goal of interoperability is to level the legal, technological, and operational playing field—to balance the competing objectives of promoting long-term investment in network infrastructure and ensuring that these investments do not entrench market power, undercut

---

20. Awrey & Macey, "Open Access, Interoperability, and DTCC" (describing how the SEC's interoperability rule inadvertently imposed higher connection costs on newer, smaller entrants, thereby impeding competition and ultimately contributing to the DTCC's current monopoly).

vigorous competition, or stifle innovation. Put differently, the goal is to encourage incumbent networks to extract efficiency benefits at the edge of today's technological frontier, while simultaneously carving out space for new entrants to push that frontier tomorrow and beyond. Striking this balance is no easy task. Nor is it one that a well-designed payments charter, expanded reserve account access, and a flexible interoperability rule are likely to achieve on their own. This suggests the need for a third and final pillar of the blueprint: a new governance structure for the payment system itself.

A New Governance Framework

Any joint enterprise demands that stakeholders strike a delicate balance between competition and coordination. Competition spurs investment and innovation and prevents the concentration and entrenchment of market power. Yet too much competition can lead to overinvestment and deadweight losses. This is especially true in infrastructure industries like payments, where economies of scale, network effects, and path dependence can drive the market toward concentration—leaving a trail of promising but ultimately failed experiments in their wake. Indeed, even healthy levels of competition, investment, and innovation will often need to be intentionally channeled toward their most productive and socially useful ends. In both cases, the common denominator is the need for constructive coordination as a complement to the process of creative destruction.

At present, the dynamics of competition and coordination tend to play out in relatively obscure corners of our financial and political systems. Perhaps nowhere is this more true than in the United States. While specific examples abound, the policy decisions surrounding the ongoing shift to real-time payments provide an illustrative case in point. In 2017, to little fanfare outside the payments industry, a consortium of the largest US banks introduced the country's first real-time payments system, known as RTP.[21] The RTP platform is essentially a clearing system built directly on top of the Federal Reserve's existing settlement architecture. RTP maintains a master account with the Fed, with each participating bank maintaining a subaccount for the purpose of settling payments with other network participants.

---

21. See The Clearing House, "First New Core Payments System in the US in More Than 40 Years Initiates First Live Payments," press release (November 14, 2017), https://www.theclearinghouse.org/payment-systems/articles/2017/11/20171114-rtp-first-new-core-payments-system.

The RTP platform then enables participants to send and receive payment instructions in real time, with the corresponding debits and credits taking place instantaneously on the balance sheet of the Federal Reserve—all within RTP's own master account.

Two years later, the Federal Reserve announced its intention to develop and roll out its own real-time payment system, christened FedNow.[22] In many respects, the announcement was the culmination of several years' work, largely under the auspices of a Fed-sponsored group called the Faster Payments Task Force. Established in May 2015, the task force was created to "identify and evaluate alternative approaches for implementing safe, ubiquitous, faster payments capabilities in the United States."[23] The task force's participants were drawn from a wide range of stakeholders, including government, large commercial banks, small and medium-sized banks, nonbank financial institutions, business payment users, and consumer advocacy groups. Under the stewardship of its steering committee, the task force identified the most desirable attributes of a faster payment system, solicited evidence regarding the current state of technological capabilities, identified alternative paths forward, and leveraged both its own expertise and that of independent experts to evaluate the likely effectiveness of each path in achieving the desired attributes. The task force then developed a series of detailed recommendations focusing on the governance, regulation, infrastructure development, sustainability, and evolution of any new real-time payment system. The task force's final report—optimistically entitled "A Call to Action"—was published in July 2017.[24] It would be the last document the Task Force ever published. Five months after the report was issued, twenty-five of the country's largest banks would announce their intention to unilaterally move forward with the introduction of RTP. And almost exactly six years later, the Fed would finally launch the much-delayed FedNow.

---

22. Federal Reserve, Notice and Request for Comment, *Federal Reserve Actions to Support Interbank Settlements of Faster Payments*, Docket No. OP-1670, 84 Fed. Reg. 39297 (August 9, 2019). Ten months earlier, the Fed had solicited comment on potential actions it might take to promote ubiquitous, safe, and efficient faster payments: Federal Reserve, Request for Comments, *Potential Federal Reserve Actions to Support Interbank Settlement of Faster Payments*, Docket No. OP-1625, 83 Fed. Reg. 57351 (November 15, 2018).

23. Faster Payments Task Force Charter (May 2015), https://fasterpaymentstaskforce.org /meet-the-task-force/mission-and-objectives/.

24. Faster Payments Task Force, "The U.S. Path to Faster Payments: Final Report Part 2: A Call to Action" (July 2017), https://fasterpaymentstaskforce.org/wp-content/uploads/faster -payments-task-force-final-report-part-two.pdf.

This example is notable for several reasons. First, despite the work of the Faster Payments Task Force, major banks, and the Federal Reserve, the United States was still nowhere near the vanguard of jurisdictions pushing toward real-time payments. Second, notwithstanding the valiant efforts of the task force, a small, powerful, and homogeneous subset of its stakeholders ultimately decided to move ahead with real-time payments on their own. And while the service they created—RTP—is currently state of the art, decisions about its design, future upgrades, and network access are controlled entirely by The Clearing House, an industry trade association owned by the world's largest banks.[25] Compounding matters, because RTP transactions all flow through Fed master accounts, only banks enjoy direct access to these new real-time payment rails. Last, the task force's final report included a series of forward-looking recommendations about how to promote greater interoperability, improve cross-border payments, and ensure "broader access to Federal Reserve settlement services" in order to "level the playing field and enhance competition."[26] Yet, rather than take up this baton, the Federal Reserve decided instead to develop its own real-time payment system—a system that, if it ever truly gets off the ground, will reflect few if any of these recommendations. Equally important, it's not entirely clear whether FedNow can successfully compete with either the increasingly popular RTP or more established players like ACH.

These hugely impactful decisions—to let RTP use the Fed's settlement architecture, to push forward with FedNow despite the launch of RTP, and to deprioritize important policy objectives like open access and interoperability—were made largely out of the public eye. Beyond the normal notice and comment procedure in connection with the creation of FedNow, we do not really know what process the Fed followed, which stakeholders it consulted, or how it arrived at these decisions. This is not to say that these decisions were not ultimately made in the public interest. But the opaque, informal, and seemingly ad hoc governance structure used to make them means that we are essentially left to trust that this was indeed the case. And all the while, American businesses and consumers are saddled with slower, less convenient, and more expensive payments than their peers in almost every other highly developed country. Putting all of this together, the evidence suggests that the current US governance model—and

---

25. For a complete list of The Clearing House's owners, see "Owner Banks," https://www.theclearinghouse.org/About/Owner-Banks.

26. Faster Payments Task Force, "Call to Action," 31.

in many ways the lack thereof—has delivered neither effective coordination nor healthy and vibrant competition.

Ironically, the very first recommendation of the Faster Payments Task Force was to establish a more formal, transparent, and permanent governance framework for the US payment system.[27] While the task force originally envisioned a voluntary, industry-led initiative, the subsequent disjointed and increasingly divergent trajectories of RTP and FedNow highlight the need for greater coordination between incumbent banks, aspiring new entrants, and public policymakers. This new governance framework would have several core institutional features. As a starting point, the framework should fall under the oversight of a single public sector body. This body could be a stand-alone payments regulator or "council" of existing financial, competition, and consumer protection regulators modeled on the FSOC. It could also be folded into a broader "digital authority," with responsibility for protecting consumers and promoting competition across all digital platform markets.[28] The only thing it should not be is an appendage of existing prudential regulators, where jurisdictional turf wars and regulatory capture would almost inevitably undercut its efficacy and independence. This body would then be given a statutory mandate to promote specific objectives like competition, consumer protection, and financial inclusion. It would also be subject to administrative procedures designed to hold it accountable for advancing these objectives.

This new body would perform two principal roles. The first would be to monitor and enforce compliance with the open access and interoperability rules. The second would be to coordinate long-term planning and investment in the technological infrastructure supporting the US payment system. Whereas the first role would demand that Congress vest the new body with specific regulatory, supervisory, and enforcement powers, the second would rely on the background threat of enforcement to bring stakeholders to the table for the purposes of coordinating private and public sector investments in cheaper, faster, safer, more convenient, and more interoperable payments infrastructure. Like the Faster Payments Task Force, this body would be required to solicit the views of a diverse range of industry, public sector, and community stakeholders. This representation could even be hardwired into the body's own governance structure through, for example, the creation

27. Faster Payments Task Force, 30, 35–37.
28. See, e.g., Stigler Center for the Study of the Economy and the State, "Stigler Committee on Digital Platforms Final Report," 83–85 (2019), https://www.chicagobooth.edu/-/media/research/stigler/pdfs/digital-platforms---committee-report---stigler-center.pdf.

of standing advisory committees. These views would be incorporated into an ongoing process—overseen by the new body—for establishing investment priorities, identifying and evaluating different options for advancing them, and generating stakeholder consensus around the most desirable path forward. Yet, unlike the task force, the new body would be responsible for translating this consensus into action—and for justifying these actions, and any inaction, to both lawmakers and the public. While the details of this new governance framework would obviously need to be fleshed out, the ultimate goal would be to foster both greater competition and coordination and, crucially, to harness them in pursuit of the public interest.

Without a doubt, designing, implementing, and establishing the credibility of this new governance framework would be the most difficult pillar of this blueprint to successfully execute. Indeed, it might not even be possible in the current political climate, where distrust among stakeholders is high. And, as always, the devil is in the details. For example, recent reforms to the governance framework in Canada designed to spur the modernization of the country's outdated payment infrastructure have been slow to yield meaningful results, in part because they further entrenched the power of incumbent banks.[29] Yet, as we have seen, several other countries—most notably India and Brazil—have recently been able to overcome resistance from incumbent players to introduce significant technological upgrades to their domestic payment systems.[30] Ultimately, the fact that something is hard is not a compelling reason not to do it. The only question is whether the juice is worth the squeeze.

Move Fast, but Don't Break Things

The benefits of this blueprint all stem from the observation that money and payments pose two very different sets of policy challenges. The challenge at the heart of creating good money is whether the law and institutions can be used to engineer monetary IOUs with a stable nominal value. The challenge for good payments is whether technology can be used to ensure that

29. See Jon Victor, "How the Push to Modernize Canada's Payment Systems Went Off the Rails," *The Logic* (March 17, 2022), https://thelogic.co/news/the-big-read/how-the-push-to-modernize-canadas-payment-systems-went-off-the-rails/.

30. See, e.g., Mujib Mashal & Hari Kumar, "Where Digital Payments, Even for a 10-Cent Chai, Are Colossal in Scale," *New York Times* (March 1, 2023); Angelo Duarte, Jon Frost, Leonardo Gambacorta, Priscilla Koo Wilkens, & Hyun Song Shin, "Central Banks, the Monetary System, and Public Payment Infrastructures: Lessons from Brazil's Pix," Bank for International Settlements Bulletin No. 52 (March 23, 2022).

these monetary IOUs are transferred in a fast, safe, convenient, and accessible way—thereby promoting their widespread use as a means of payment. It is only once we understand these challenges as fundamentally distinct that the potential benefits of this blueprint come squarely into view.

FOR CUSTOMER PROTECTION

Any attempt to inventory these potential benefits must necessarily begin with those that will flow to the people and businesses that have historically taken good money for granted. As chronicled in chapter 4, for well over a decade, these everyday customers have been channeling more and more of their money into and through the shadow monetary system: exposing themselves to the risks of bankruptcy and the prospect of lengthy repayment delays and potentially devastating losses. Together, the core features of the payments charter—the no intermediation rule, structural separation, and borrowing, lending, and activity restrictions—would all but eliminate these risks. By removing intermediation and credit risk from the equation, they would also greatly dampen the incentives that might otherwise drive customers to engage in destabilizing runs. And even where the businesses that held a payments charter ultimately floundered and failed, the proposed resolution framework would ensure that customers were repaid rapidly and in full.

Of course, one might counter that these same people and businesses could always deposit their money in an insured bank account. And this is often true—at least up to the limits imposed by the relevant deposit insurance scheme. Yet if we can take anything away from Gresham's new law, it's that this too often creates a trade-off between good money and good payments. So long as customers value good payments over good money during periods of financial stability, they will continue to behave in ways that expose them to the risks of destabilizing runs and bankruptcy when this stability evaporates. Once again, the payments charter would eliminate these risks, thereby promoting a return to the world in which customers could trust that their money would always be there for them—no questions asked.

FOR COMPETITION AND INNOVATION

Customers would also benefit from the cheaper, more convenient, and more accessible payment options generated by a more diverse, competitive, and innovative financial ecosystem. The blueprint would help spur competition and innovation in three principal ways. First, the payments charter would render the monetary IOUs of payments entities true functional substitutes for insured bank deposits, thereby eliminating the distinction between good and bad money. Second, by ensuring that payments entities enjoy direct access to central bank reserve accounts, clearinghouses, and other basic financial market infrastructure, the open access and interoperability rules would level the legal playing field between incumbent banks and aspiring new entrants. These rules would also help level the economic playing field by enabling payments entities to capture the economies of scale and network effects that currently flow only to conventional deposit-taking banks without first having to make costly and potentially duplicative investments in building basic network infrastructure.

In theory, leveling this playing field—and in particular removing banks as ubiquitous but essentially unnecessary middlemen—would help reduce the high costs of payments in jurisdictions like the United States. By eliminating this significant bottleneck, it would also pave the way for more competition from outside the conventional banking industry: including from the new breed of financial institutions and platforms looking to leverage their technological advantages to deliver better payments. And where the resulting technological innovations demonstrate real promise, the new governance framework would promote greater coordination between public and private sector stakeholders to ensure that this technology is incorporated into ongoing upgrades to our financial market infrastructure.

The third way that the blueprint would promote greater competition and innovation is by allowing institutions and platforms within the shadow monetary system to focus on what they do best: *payments*. In jurisdictions like the United States, these institutions and platforms currently face an unpalatable choice between obtaining a conventional bank charter, relying on banks—their principal competitors—for indirect access to core network infrastructure, or building their own payment networks entirely from scratch. All three choices put them at a distinct competitive disadvantage, whether because of the resulting regulatory burdens, the threat of exploitation, or the enormous economies of scale and network effects enjoyed by incumbent players. The payments charter notably solves all three problems. Most importantly, the charter is based on a regulatory, supervisory, and resolution framework that reflects the narrow business model of these institutions and platforms—specifically targeting the problem of bad money, but without imposing the types of intensive prudential regulation and supervision needed to address the unique problems stemming from the combination of money creation and financial intermediation.

This last point highlights one of the most important features of the proposed blueprint. The payments charter, open access and interoperability rules, and governance framework are all structured to reflect the comparative advantages of private enterprises and public actors. On the one hand, these pillars would enable a more diverse range of financial institutions and technology firms to conduct a multitude of experiments exploring the potential applications of cutting-edge technology to deliver better payments. On the other, they envision a steadfast role for government—with its unparalleled resources, freedom from liquidity and bankruptcy constraints, and wealth of experience as a prudential regulator and supervisor—in ensuring the credibility of their monetary commitments. This structure gives private enterprises the ability to move fast in pushing the technological frontier, but with an extremely low risk of breaking things at the heart of our monetary and financial systems.

FOR MICROPRUDENTIAL SAFETY AND SOUNDNESS

At present, the structure of the payment system in jurisdictions like the United States is extremely hierarchical. Residing at the apex of this hierarchy are central banks, which issue the ultimate settlement asset in the form of reserve balances. These reserve balances are held by conventional deposit-taking banks, which use them to settle their financial obligations toward one another. At the bottom of this hierarchy is then everybody else—those who can only participate in the system by opening a bank account, depositing money, and instructing their bank where to send it. The net result is a tiered payment system based on a complex network of credit relationships, where central banks issue monetary IOUs to banks, banks issue monetary IOUs to the platforms and institutions that populate the shadow monetary system, and the platforms and institutions issue monetary IOUs to their customers.

This tiered structure is the source of potentially significant credit risks. Importantly, these risks can flow both upstream and downstream, theoretically undermining the microprudential stability of not only banks but also the institutions and platforms that rely on them for access to the payment system. The failures of Silvergate Bank and Silicon Valley Bank (SVB) in March 2023 offer a powerful and timely illustration. Silvergate was an important part of the crypto ecosystem, providing bank accounts, processing payments, and offering other banking services to a wide range of crypto intermediaries. This role was reflected in the concentration of the bank's deposit base: with the vast majority of its deposits in some way connected to the crypto ecosystem.[31] Following the bankruptcy of FTX, one of Silvergate's most important customers, the bank suffered crypto-related withdrawals in excess of $8 billion, forcing it to prematurely liquidate many of its assets.[32] Together with the increased legal and regulatory scrutiny on both Silvergate and crypto in the wake of the FTX collapse, the resulting losses eventually forced the bank into voluntarily liquidation.[33]

If Silvergate is a story about how the shadow monetary system can destabilize conventional deposit-taking banks, SVB is a story about how bank failures can destabilize the shadow monetary system. On Friday, March 10, 2023, the FDIC and California Department of Financial Protection and Innovation announced that they were closing SVB, one of the country's largest banks, with immediate effect.[34] The next day, Circle, issuer of the popular USDC stablecoin, announced that it held approximately $3.3 billion of USDC's $40 billion in reserves in uninsured deposits with SVB. While Circle attempted to assure its customers that it would cover any losses, the value of USDC almost immediately plummeted, shedding its peg and eventually reaching a low of $0.8774 on the dollar.[35] For a time, USDC thus ceased performing one of the fundamental functions of money—maintaining a stable nominal value—for no other reason than its correspondent banking relationship with SVB. In the event, the emergency measures taken by the FDIC, Federal Reserve, and Treasury Department the following day helped stabilize the market, and the price of USDC quickly recovered. Nevertheless, the episode illustrates the inherent risks of forcing the entire payment system to run through conventional deposit-taking banks.

Together, the payments charter and open access rule would help reduce these latent credit risks. In terms of upstream risks, banks would no longer

31. See Matt Levine, "Silvergate Had a Crypto Bank Run," *Bloomberg* (March 2, 2023), https://www.bloomberg.com/opinion/articles/2023-03-02/silvergate-had-a-crypto-bank-run#xj4y7vzkg.

32. See Manya Saini, Niket Nishant, & Hannah Lang, "Silvergate Capital Shares Sink as Crypto-Related Deposits Plunge by $8 Billion," Reuters (January 5, 2023), https://www.reuters.com/technology/silvergate-capitals-crypto-related-deposits-plunge-fourth-quarter-2023-01-05/.

33. Silvergate Bank, "Silvergate Capital Corporation Announces Intent to Wind Down Operations and Voluntarily Liquidate Silvergate Bank," press release (March 8, 2023), https://ir.silvergate.com/news/news-details/2023/Silvergate-Capital-Corporation-Announces-Intent-to-Wind-Down-Operations-and-Voluntarily-Liquidate-Silvergate-Bank/default.aspx.

34. FDIC, "FDIC Creates Deposit Insurance National Bank of Santa Clara to Protect Insured Depositors of Silicon Valley Bank," press release (March 10, 2023), https://www.fdic.gov/news/press-releases/2023/pr23016.html.

35. See Arijit Sarkar, "USDC Depegs as Circle Confirms $3.3B Stuck with Silicon Valley Bank," *Cointelegraph* (March 11, 2023), https://cointelegraph.com/news/usdc-depegs-as-circle-confirms-3-3b-stuck-with-silicon-valley-bank.

be called upon to serve as the universal gatekeepers of the payment system, thereby removing them from the daisy chain of monetary IOUs and insulating them from the risk that the instability or failure of their customers might trigger destabilizing depositor runs. In terms of downstream risks, because chartered payments entities would have direct access to central bank reserve accounts and other financial market infrastructure, they would no longer be compelled to maintain correspondent banking relationships and take on the corresponding risk of bank failure. The proposed blueprint would thus flatten the existing hierarchy, reduce the number and size of outstanding credit exposures, and thereby enhance the microprudential stability of both banks themselves and the institutions and platforms of the shadow monetary system.

FOR THE RESILIENCE OF THE FINANCIAL SYSTEM

Finally, the blueprint would help bolster the resilience of the wider financial system. As a preliminary matter, enhanced microprudential stability would generate benefits at the macroprudential level, reducing the complex and often opaque web of credit exposures that often spread contagion. The creation of a stand-alone payments charter would also promote greater institutional diversity. Today, the seven largest banks in the United States have roughly the same stock of financial assets as all other US banks combined.[36] Not surprisingly, these are the same banks through which the vast majority of payments currently flow. The homogeneity of these institutions in terms of their business models, balance sheets, and regulation leaves them vulnerable to the same types of exogenous shocks. Their bundling of banking, money, payments, and other financial services also means that the impact of these shocks typically reverberates across the entire financial system and, too often, into the real economy. By creating a dedicated payments charter that does not functionally resemble these institutions, and is completely unconnected to them, the blueprint would go some distance toward reducing the impact of these shocks.

Greater diversity has another upshot: reducing the too-big-to-fail problem. As described in chapter 3, the too-big-to-fail problem reflects our

36. These fifteen banks collectively have approximately $13.4 trillion in assets; see "The 15 Largest Banks in the United States," Bankrate.com (March 14, 2023), https://www.bankrate.com /banking/biggest-banks-in-america/. This is compared against total assets of all commercial banks in the US of approximately $23.1 trillion; see Federal Reserve Board of Governors, Release H.8: Assets and Liabilities of Commercial Banks in the United States (March 31, 2023), https://www .federalreserve.gov/releases/h8/current/.

historical reliance on a handful of large banks as critical sources of financing, money, and payments. In jurisdictions like the United States, this problem is magnified by restrictions on access to basic financial market infrastructure that effectively make banks the only game in town. This deeply entrenched reliance creates the widespread expectation that policymakers will go beyond the financial safety net to provide these banks with extraordinary financial and other support during periods of severe institutional or systemic stress. This expectation then translates into lower funding costs, giving these too-big-to-fail banks yet another competitive advantage.

The blueprint is uniquely designed to ameliorate this problem. The principal rationale for the new payments charter, open access and interoperability rules, and governance framework is to support the emergence of a new breed of financial institutions and platforms capable of competing with banks in the realm of money and payments. The existence and success of these institutions and platforms would ensure greater substitutability, thereby reducing our structural reliance on a small number of large incumbents. By reducing this reliance, the blueprint would also reduce the probability that the failure of one or more systemically important banks, or more generalized banking crises, would trigger either widespread interruption to the payment system or broad-based contractions in the money supply. In effect, by severing the unstable link between banking, money, and payments, the blueprint would help ensure that the fate of our basic financial infrastructure is no longer firmly tied to the mast of risks taken within the conventional banking system.

No Free Lunches

The potential benefits of the proposed blueprint are substantial. Yet once again there is no such thing as a free lunch. The design and implementation of this blueprint would inevitably demand that policymakers confront a number of thorny challenges and trade-offs. It would also demand that they attempt to anticipate the potential unintended consequences of rewiring the intricate legal and institutional circuitry at the heart of our current systems of money and payments.

REGULATORY ARBITRAGE

An important threshold challenge, especially in the United States, is what to do with state money transmitter laws, the New York Bitlicense, and other legacy regulatory frameworks. In theory, having multiple state and federal regulators, each conducting different regulatory experiments, could prove to be a catalyst for competition and innovation. Yet in practice, the benefits of regulatory competition have often failed to materialize, in part because institutions and platforms are typically required to comply with the relevant regulatory frameworks in each and every state in which they do business. This jurisdictional overlap undercuts the incentives of regulators to experiment, while simultaneously increasing the temptation to free ride off the regulatory and supervisory frameworks of other states.

Even where regulatory competition does materialize, there is no guarantee that it will be socially desirable. Indeed, one might predict that—even after accounting for the benefits of the payments charter—some institutions and platforms would prefer to remain subject to the fragmented, inconsistent, but relatively lax requirements imposed by state money transmitter laws. After all, these laws typically allow them to invest customer funds in risky financial instruments, lend money to their affiliates, and otherwise profit from financial intermediation. This frames an important challenge. The existing US regulatory architecture effectively enables these institutions and platforms to have their cake and eat it too: permitting them to combine the issuance of monetary IOUs with financial intermediation, but without then subjecting them to the exquisitely tailored straitjacket of conventional bank regulation. The resulting threat of regulatory arbitrage poses risks for customer protection, for microprudential safety and soundness, for financial stability and, ultimately, for the success of the proposed blueprint.

Eliminating this threat would demand that Congress take three steps. The first step would be to replace the existing definition of a "deposit" under federal law with a broader and more functional one that brings the diverse and rapidly expanding universe of monetary IOUs within the federal regulatory perimeter.[37] In stark contrast to existing laws governing illegal deposit taking, regulators would then need to ensure that this perimeter is consistently and vigorously policed. The second step would be to clarify that, as a matter of law, institutions and platforms issuing these monetary IOUs have two—and only two—options: obtain either a conventional bank charter or a new payments charter. While these options could conceivably be expanded to include state-licensed institutions and platforms, they would need to be subject to

---

37. This definition could be based on the existing definitions of "money" and "monetary value" contained in state money transmitter laws. Morgan Ricks also provides a tractable functional definition; see Ricks, *The Money Problem*, chapter 9. See also Howell Jackson & Morgan Ricks, "Locating Stablecoins with the Regulatory Perimeter," Harvard Law School Forum on Corporate Governance (August 5, 2021), https://corpgov.law.harvard.edu/2021/08/05/locating-stablecoins -within-the-regulatory-perimeter/#8.

regulatory frameworks that closely mirror the core payments charter. Failing that, regulators would need to prohibit federally regulated banks and payments entities, along with state-chartered banks that are insured by the FDIC, from accepting transactional deposits traceable to customer funds from money transmitters, Bitlicense holders, and any other institutions and platforms that do not fall within the federal regulatory perimeter.[38]

These steps may seem dramatic—especially insofar as they would effectively unbank many existing state-licensed institutions. Yet they are ultimately what is necessary to eliminate the threat of regulatory arbitrage. They are also entirely consistent with the core logic of the no intermediation rule. Functionally speaking, if new financial institutions and platforms want to bundle financial intermediation with money and payments, there is absolutely no reason why they should not be regulated as banks. Conversely, if they are simply looking to offer money and payments, the no intermediation rule is a small price to pay in exchange for direct access to Fed master accounts and other financial market infrastructure, the ability to reduce their structural reliance on correspondent banking relationships, and the opportunity to leverage new technologies to compete with banks on a more level playing field.

MAKING PAYMENTS PAY

Without the tantalizing prospect of earning profits from financial intermediation, one might reasonably ask how chartered payments entities would be able to monetize their investments in the development of new payments technology. Generating interest income from the investment of customer funds—aka the float—is a business model as old as banking itself. Indeed, the ability to generate float income is often cited as one of the principal reasons why incumbent banks have been slow to invest in new payments technology. But times are rapidly changing. The emergence of new institutions and platforms, experimenting with new business models, reveal a broad spectrum of different ways to make payments pay.

At the narrow end of this spectrum are video game designers, social media and virtual reality platforms, and online subscription services that want their customers to be able to buy and sell virtual goods and services via

---

38. The primary reason why the third step is not simply to ban state-chartered nonbank financial institutions from issuing monetary IOUs is that, at least in the US, any such ban may not survive a constitutional challenge.

their proprietary portals. These payments can be denominated in existing sovereign currencies or in game-specific currencies, like Fortnite's V-Bucks, Minecraft's MineCoins, and Pokémon Go's PokéCoins. These small "in-app" payments are increasingly big business, with some estimates suggesting that customers already spend more than $80 billion a year on virtual goods and services sold through video games alone.[39] Outside the metaverse, similar business models are also being developed in the world of finance, where firms are exploring the possibility of offering dedicated trade and supply chain financing platforms that use their own "in-house" money.[40] And moving even farther along the spectrum, online marketplaces like China's Alibaba have long bundled money and payments with the ability to buy and sell a wide range of real-world products and services—everything from clothes, food, and home products to electronics, vehicle parts, and industrial machinery. These business models all share two things in common. First, they all aspire to use technology to disintermediate the conventional banking system. Second, they all seek to subsidize their investments in this technology, at least in part, through the prices they charge for other products and services.

At the other end of the spectrum are institutions with the ambition of creating monetary IOUs that can be used as a general-purpose medium of exchange. Since these institutions cannot tie the use of their monetary IOUs to specific products, services, or platforms, the opportunities for cross-subsidization are relatively limited. This leaves charging user fees as the most straightforward way for them to monetize their investments in new payments technology. In the United States, merchants are currently charged an average interchange fee of approximately 0.5 percent of the total transaction amount for small debit card payments. The corresponding figure for credit card payments is between 1.5 and 2.0 percent.[41] These fees are relatively high by international standards. In many cases, they also reflect a lower-quality service, with US customers often experiencing slower, less convenient, and less accessible payments. This gap suggests that there is scope for greater competition in terms of both the price and quality of payment services—two

39. See Anna Wiener, "Money in the Metaverse," *New Yorker* (January 4, 2022), https://www.newyorker.com/news/letter-from-silicon-valley/money-in-the-metaverse.

40. See, e.g., J.P. Morgan, "A New Era for Trade Finance: Technology, Innovation and the Drive for Efficiency" (2018), https://www.jpmorgan.com/content/dam/jpm/cib/complex/content/treasury-services/apac-trade-finance/pdf-0.pdf.

41. See Fumiko Hayashi & Sam Baird, "Credit and Debit Card Interchange Fees in Various Countries," Federal Reserve Bank of Kansas City 5 (August 2022).

fronts where we might expect new entrants to enjoy a sizable comparative advantage over incumbent banks.

IMPACT ON BANK STABILITY AND INTERMEDIATION

On the assumption that chartered payments entities can find ways to make payments pay, the next question is what impact this would have on the conventional banking system. There are two principal concerns. The first concern is that subjecting banks to more vigorous competition would undermine the stability of the banking system. There are essentially two variants of this concern. The first is that greater competition would siphon deposits away from banks, depriving them of what has historically been a relatively cheap and ample source of funding. The second is that the existence of truly credible substitutes for bank deposits, especially ones backed by the government's full faith and credit, would amplify the incentives of bank depositors to run at the first sign of trouble.

This first concern is valid but overstated. Nothing in this blueprint would prevent banks from competing for deposits by paying higher interest rates, designing better products and services, or offering these products and services to a wider universe of customers. To the contrary, this is precisely the type of welfare-enhancing competition that the blueprint is designed to encourage. In fact, the green shoots of competition have already started to emerge: witness, for example, the creation of the Regulated Liability Network, a blockchain-based programmable payments platform, by a consortium that includes many of the world's largest banks.[42] Nor does the blueprint do anything to undermine the existing financial safety net. As we have seen, this safety net exists to promote confidence in banks, prevent destabilizing runs, and protect depositors when illiquid banks cross over the threshold into insolvency. Viewed in this light, the safety net puts the conventional banking system in a far better position to undergo a competitive restructuring than just about any other industry.

The second concern is that greater competition for deposits, combined with the imposition of the no intermediation rule on payments entities, would decrease the total amount of capital that could be channeled into productive investments in the real economy.[43] While this objection is not

42. See Regulated Liability Network, white paper (November 15, 2022), https://regulatedliabilitynetwork.org/.

43. For articulations of this concern, see, e.g., Federal Reserve Board, "Money and Payments: The U.S. Dollar in the Age of Digital Transformation" (January 2022), https://www

without merit, it rests on three fundamentally contestable assumptions. The first assumption is that banks are the dominant source of investment capital and that any increase in their own financing costs would necessarily translate into more expensive loans and less investment. There is no doubt that banks play an important role in providing loans and other types of financing to households and businesses of all sizes. Yet, increasingly, banks are also facing stiff competition from fintech lenders, financing companies, and marketplace lending platforms. In some market segments—most notably US residential mortgages—these new entrants have already eclipsed banks as the primary sources of new financing.[44] In others—including lending to small businesses—they are rapidly gaining ground.[45] What this suggests is that a shift away from banks as the dominant providers of investment capital may already be well under way. If this is correct, this competition should make it harder for banks to pass on any increase in their financing costs. The resulting diversity of financing sources should also dampen the potential impact, if any, that greater competition for deposits might have on the availability of new investment capital.

The second assumption—grounded in the classical intermediation view of banking—is that banks need deposits in order to make new loans and other investments. The obvious problem with this assumption is that it fails to incorporate the important role that banks play in money creation. Specifically, while new deposits can certainly be transformed into new loans, new loans also create new deposits. As a result, new deposits are not strictly necessary as the raw material for the issuance of each and every new loan. This is not to suggest that greater competition for deposits would not have any impact whatsoever on financial intermediation. Ultimately, any significant decrease in aggregate demand for bank deposits would, in the complete absence of available substitutes, eventually be reflected in an increase in bank funding costs, along with a corresponding decrease in the supply of new bank loans. What it does suggest is that bank lending decisions are not

---

.federalreserve.gov/publications/files/money-and-payments-20220120.pdf, and Bank Policy Institute, "Confronting the Hard Truths and Easy Fictions of a CBDC," *Business Reporter* (September 23, 2021), https://www.business-reporter.co.uk/finance/confronting-the-hard-truths-and-easy-fictions-of-a-cbdc. While both examples relate to the impact on bank intermediation stemming from the introduction of a central bank digital currency, the introduction of payments entities would theoretically foster exactly the same type of competition for deposits.

44. See, e.g., Greg Buchak, Gregor Matvos, Tomasz Piskorski, & Amit Seru, "Fintech, Regulatory Arbitrage and the Rise of Shadow Banks," 130:3 Journal of Financial Economics 453 (2018).

45. See, e.g., Manasa Gopal & Philipp Schnabl, "The Rise of Finance Companies and FinTech Lenders in Small Business Lending," 35:11 Review of Financial Studies 4859 (2022).

solely a function of the immediate availability of deposit financing. This is especially true where banks can tap deep and highly liquid sources of wholesale funding as a substitute for bank deposits. For this reason, the intermediation view tends to overstate the risk that any changes in the demand for bank deposits would mechanically translate into fewer loans and lower levels of investment.

The third assumption is that the customer funds transferred to a chartered payments entity, and then held in a central bank reserve account, would be somehow immobilized and therefore incapable of being used to finance productive investments. This assumption reflects the view that central banks, in performance of their role as lenders of last resort, will only lend these reserve balances out to banks during periods of severe institutional and systemic instability.[46] Yet this is simply a policy choice. One could equally imagine making the choice to normalize this lending during periods of relative stability as both a counterweight to any deposit flight and as a vehicle for channeling these funds back into the financial system and real economy.[47] To be sure, this choice would come with its own challenges and trade-offs. But the point is not that this is necessarily the right choice for all jurisdictions, or in all states of the world. Rather, the point is that obstacles that may seem insurmountable are often simply a reflection of our failure to imagine the universe of available policy alternatives.

THE NEXT BIG THING

The final question is whether this blueprint would help pave the way for powerful platforms like Facebook, Twitter, Google, and Amazon to directly enter the payments industry—doubling down on their already massive economies of scale and network effects to further entrench themselves at the heart of the digital economy. Once again, this is an important point—especially in light of how privileged access to payment information can be used to build and entrench durable power in other markets.[48] Indeed, there is already a strong case for more robust enforcement of antitrust laws in

---

46. While less important, it also reflects the stigma sometimes attached to discount window borrowing; see chapter 2.

47. For a comprehensive proposal envisioning just such a policy choice, see Saule Omarova, "The People's Ledger: How to Democratize Money and Finance the Economy," 74 Vanderbilt Law Review 1231 (2021).

48. For a discussion, see Dan Awrey & Joshua Macey, "The Promise and Perils of Open Finance," 40:1 Yale Journal on Regulation 1 (2022).

many parts of the financial services industry. Yet the prospect that these already powerful platforms might pursue this strategy also demonstrates why open access and interoperability are so important. Over the long term, one of the most effective ways to prevent inefficient concentrations of market power is to remove structural barriers to competition, thereby reducing the costs of entry, promoting the emergence of new business models and technologies, and using the resulting threat of competition to constrain the monopolistic impulses of incumbent firms. Accordingly, while this blueprint is by no means sufficient to forever solve problems of market power, whether in finance or elsewhere, it is arguably necessary to ensure the longer-term dynamic efficiency of our intertwined systems of money and payments.

This analysis comes with one important caveat. The United States has long had a unique preoccupation with the separation of banking from commerce. This preoccupation is embedded deep within the structure of US banking law, including the prohibition against banks carrying on any business that is not necessary or incidental to the "business of banking"[49] and the group-level ownership and activity constraints imposed by the Bank Holding Company Act.[50] These prohibitions and constraints reflect the enduring concern that permitting banks to combine the business of banking with the same commercial activities as their customers would inevitably give them an unfair competitive advantage. Specifically, banks would be tempted to use their privileged access to capital and customer information to tilt the competitive landscape in favor of the enterprises in which they had an ownership stake.

Today, the historical rationale for the separation of banking and commerce may ring somewhat hollow. Not only do commercial enterprises enjoy a wealth of different avenues for raising capital, there is no single financial institution that enjoys anything resembling a dominant market position. Nevertheless, while US *capital* markets may be highly competitive, its *information* markets have become increasingly concentrated in the hands of a few large players: including, most notably, platforms like Facebook, Twitter, Google, and Amazon. Against this backdrop, permitting these same platforms to directly enter the payments industry—where their privileged access to customer information would give them yet another comparative advantage—would only serve to further entrench their growing market power. Accordingly, while the historical rationale for the separation of

49. See 12 U.S.C. § 24 (Seventh).
50. See 12 U.S.C. § 1841 et seq.

banking from commerce may no longer seem particularly persuasive, there may still be a compelling argument for separating *payments* from commerce.

THE ELEPHANT IN THE ROOM

Some may find it curious that we have made it to the conclusion of this book without touching upon what is by far the hottest topic in money and payments today: central bank digital currencies, or CBDCs. Indeed, the rise of the shadow monetary system has been one of the principal catalysts behind the growing interest, expressed by central banks around the world, in the prospect of developing and introducing CBDCs. In the past few years, this interest has yielded proposals that envision CBDCs of all shapes, sizes, and flavors. To date, a total of eleven countries have launched CBDCs, with another eighteen currently engaged in pilot projects.[51] Yet the prospect—however remote—of total government control over something so fundamental as our money has also given rise to important and predictable concerns around personal privacy, monetary policy transmission, and financial stability.[52] Reflecting these concerns, all eleven countries that have so far launched CBDCs have elected to adopt an *intermediated* model.[53] This model envisions a basic division of labor whereby banks and other financial institutions are responsible for administering accounts and clearing and settling payments between their own customers, but where payments between these institutions are settled on the balance sheets of central banks using conventional reserve balances.

If this model sounds familiar, it should. It's exactly the same system of money and payments that we have today. Importantly, it also shares the same basic structure as the proposed blueprint—just without the explicit

51. See Atlantic Council, Central Bank Digital Currency Tracker (April 7, 2023), https://www.atlanticcouncil.org/cbdctracker/.

52. For a more detailed description of these concerns, see, e.g., Christina Skinner, "Central Bank Digital Currency as New Public Money," 172 University of Pennsylvania Law Review (forthcoming); Toni Whited, Yufeng Wu, & Kairong Xiao, "Will Central Bank Digital Currency Disintermediate Banks?" IHS Working Paper No. 47 (January 13, 2023), https://papers.ssrn.com/sol3/papers.cfm?abstract_id=4112644; Rodney Garratt, Jiaheng Yu, & Haoxiang Zhu, "The Case for Convenience: How CBDC Design Choices Impact Monetary Policy Pass-Through," Bank for International Settlements Working Paper No. 1046 (November 2022); Daniel Sanches & Todd Keister, "Should Central Banks Issue Digital Currency?," Federal Reserve Bank of Philadelphia Working Paper No. 21-37 (November 2021), https://doi.org/10.21799/frbp.wp.2021.37; David Andolfatto, "Assessing the Impact of Central Bank Digital Currency on Private Banks," 131 Economic Journal 525 (February 2021).

53. Atlantic Council, CBDC Tracker.

emphasis on expanding access, promoting greater interoperability, or creating a new governance framework designed to coordinate future investments in financial market infrastructure. Ultimately, the term CBDC is little more than a marketing gimmick—a way for central banks to give the impression they're keeping pace with new technological advances. In reality, however, the design and implementation of a CBDC would demand that policymakers answer the exact same questions that we have explored throughout this book. How do we create good money? How do we promote cheap, fast, safe, convenient, and accessible payments? How do we design our laws and institutions to take advantage of new technology? And what potential challenges and trade-offs should we anticipate encountering along the way? If CBDCs are the elephant in the room, then we have been talking about elephants this entire time.

———

All of these challenges and concerns need to be taken seriously. Yet none of them are unresolvable. What's more, many of them reflect the narrow thinking that is the product of centuries of legal and institutional path dependence. Ultimately, if banks are no longer the only game in town, we need to come up with new rules, for all the new players, using new technology to play what is fundamentally a new game. This grounds one final point. Implementing this or any other blueprint will not only require changes to our laws and institutions. It will also demand new thinking about how finance works, about its role in society, and about how to harness this role in pursuit of social objectives. After all, it's *our* financial system, *our* money, and *our* payments. The only question is what we want to do with them—today, tomorrow, and beyond.

Final Settlement

The emergence and explosive growth of the shadow monetary system will almost inevitably force policymakers in the United States and elsewhere to confront some difficult choices. These choices include what policy objectives they want to achieve, which of these objectives to prioritize, and ultimately how to achieve them. Some argue that the overriding objective should be to protect the stability of the conventional banking system, regardless of the resulting impact on experimentation, competition, and innovation in the markets for money and payments. This is not an unreasonable view.

Yet we must also acknowledge that simply maintaining the status quo poses significant and growing risks for customers, for the safety and soundness of banks and other financial institutions, and for the stability of the financial system. Equally important, the emergence of the shadow monetary system represents a unique opportunity to finally break free from Tobin's dilemma by disentangling banking from money and payments. This chapter has laid out a blueprint for how to capitalize on this opportunity by redesigning our laws and institutions to eliminate bad money, harnessing new technology to deliver better payments, and arresting the destructive dynamics at the heart of Gresham's new law.

Conclusion

FOR ALL THE MONEY

> Money is, in some respects, like fire. It is a very excellent servant, but a
> terrible master.
>
> —P. T. BARNUM, PARAPHRASING FRANCIS BACON

Whether we like it or not, the forces of technological change are rapidly
transforming our financial system. And perhaps nowhere does this transformation present more opportunities, or pose more challenges, than in
the once relatively static but now increasingly dynamic world of money and
payments. The blueprint laid out in chapter 7 offers one possible way that
policymakers can respond to this change: redesigning our laws and institutions to promote greater monetary stability, while unleashing the forces of
experimentation, competition, and innovation to deliver better payments.
Yet, even if we think this blueprint is not the right way forward, this book has
illuminated a number of common themes that can help us better understand
the nature of the challenges we now face and, in the end, how to tackle them.

The iron law of money

The first theme—what we might call the iron law of money—is that the
ability of money to perform its dual functions as a reliable store of nominal
value and a widely accepted means of payment is always, and in a myriad of
ways, a function of the law. From *Foley v. Hill*, to state money transmitter
laws, to modern bank regulation and supervision, the law dictates the business models of the institutions and platforms that create and issue money.

The law also plays a variety of intertwined roles in establishing and maintaining the credibility of their monetary commitments. This is especially true of monetary IOUs, where the law determines which institutions and platforms enjoy the unique privileges and protections of the financial safety net and which must live and die in the shadow of bankruptcy.[1] Last but not least, the law regulates access to the basic financial market infrastructure that enables these IOUs to be transferred within electronic payment networks and thus widely circulated within the financial system and real economy.

To be clear, the law is not enough. As we have encountered throughout this book, the state of institutional and technological development clearly plays a key role in determining the types of assets that we use as money. Money is also a social construct; even a perfectly engineered monetary IOU will fail to satisfy our functional definition of money if people, businesses, and governments do not actually use and trust it as a reliable store of nominal value and a means of payment. Nevertheless, money is, always and everywhere, a legal phenomenon. Accordingly, if we want to make our money a more effective and equitable servant, the law is a good place to start.

More Monies, More Problems

A second important theme is that the injection of legal heterogeneity into the money supply introduces unique policy challenges. Once again, this is particularly true of monetary IOUs, where differences in the regulatory frameworks that govern institutions and platforms can have significant implications for the credibility of their monetary commitments. In good times, people and businesses may understandably be willing to overlook these differences. After all, if they didn't, the prices we pay for goods and services would vary depending on whether we were paying for them with bank deposits, PayPal balances, stablecoins, or some yet-to-be-imagined new species of monetary IOU. These people and businesses may not be accustomed to asking questions about these differences, lack the expertise to effectively interrogate the answers, or simply be lured by the cheapest, fastest, and

---

1. While not the subject of this book, the law also clearly supports and bounds systems based on *commodity* money. For example, both the UK gold standard under the Bank Charter Act of 1844 and the post–World War II gold exchange standard in the US were the product of sophisticated legal and regulatory frameworks. More generally, systems of commodity money rely heavily on both clear property rights and effective legal enforcement for their smooth and efficient operation. For a detailed discussion, see David Fox, *Property Rights in Money* (2008).

most convenient way of making payments. Whatever the reasons, the costs of conducting the necessary due diligence would almost inevitably generate enormous deadweight losses for society as we all invested the time and effort needed to successfully differentiate between, and accurately price, different types of money. This is why it's so important to engineer money that can be used and accepted, no questions asked.

The problem is that, in bad times, this legal heterogeneity can become a highly salient catalyst for collective action—driving these very same people and businesses to rapidly shift their savings into what they view as the safest monetary IOUs. It is precisely at this point that eliminating the need for costly due diligence morphs from a highly desirable feature into a potentially destabilizing bug. For having failed to ask questions about the credibility of their money in good times, the most rational thing for these people and businesses to do in bad times is to head for the exits—to withdraw first and ask questions later. These destructive dynamics have played out countless times in modern history—from the periodic banking panics of the nineteenth and early twentieth centuries, to the global financial crisis, to turmoil within US money markets during the early days of the COVID pandemic. These same dynamics are also at the root of Gresham's new law.

Viewed in this sobering light, the recent explosion in the universe of monetary IOUs represents a clear and present danger. If left unchecked, this growing heterogeneity poses mounting risks for customers, for banks and other financial institutions, and for the stability of the financial system. In theory, there are two ways to address these risks. The first is to completely eliminate the ability of new institutions and platforms to issue monetary IOUs, thus essentially doubling down on banks as the only game in town. The second is to give these institutions and platforms a single regulatory pathway—like the payments charter described in chapter 7—engineered solely for the purpose of ensuring that they issue good money. Importantly, while this framework need not formally resemble conventional bank regulation and supervision, it must ensure that any new monetary IOUs are effective functional substitutes for bank deposits. This helps frame a critical and, all too often, forgotten point. Whether it be state money transmitter laws, the New York Bitlicense, MiCA, or the stablecoin legislation currently winding its way through the US Congress, any regulatory framework that is not first and foremost designed to ensure functional equivalence across the entire universe of monetary IOUs will never fully address the core problem. Even in a world of many monies, there should only ever be one money.

Money versus Payments

A third, and critically important, theme is that we need to view the objectives, principal drivers, and key benchmarks of good money as fundamentally different from those of good payments. As we have seen, good money is the product of laws and institutions that enhance the credibility of our monetary IOUs, thus promoting their widespread use as a nominal store of value and means of payment. Good payments are then a product of the development and application of new technology, along with ongoing choices about network design and governance, which enable us to cheaply, quickly, safely, and conveniently send and receive money within the widest possible network of people, businesses, and governments. By the same token, the problems at the root of bad money are often the mirror image of those at the root of bad payments. Perhaps most importantly, while the problems of bad money are created and compounded by monetary heterogeneity, the problems of bad payments stem largely from the legally entrenched homogeneity that is a by-product of our current bundled system of banking, money, and payments.

There is no doubt that money and payments are inextricably connected. Indeed, it's almost impossible to talk about one without talking about the other. Yet, for far too long, our policy debates have essentially ignored that they are ultimately two inseparable but very different things: like tracks and trains, wires and electricity, water and pipes. As a result, we have frequently invested too much time and effort in the search for new and better money when what we really wanted was to deliver better payments. So long as we continue to view money and payments as representing a monolithic set of policy challenges, we are almost inevitably going to miss valuable opportunities to build a safer, more resilient, and more efficient system of money and payments.

A Level Legal Playing Field

One thing that good money and good payments do share in common is that they both greatly benefit from a level legal playing field. As we have already seen, good money requires a level playing field to eliminate any heterogeneity in the creditworthiness of different types of monetary IOUs, thus neutralizing the destabilizing dynamics of Gresham's new law. Meanwhile, good payments require a level playing field to eliminate barriers to new entry, thereby promoting ongoing investment in technological experimentation, competition, and innovation. This is not to say that the policy tools for leveling the playing field are the same in both spheres. Whereas good money demands functionally equivalent prudential regulation, good payments require open access and interoperability rules, along with a governance framework that balances competition and coordination in the development of financial market infrastructure. Nevertheless, over the longer term, creating and maintaining a level legal playing field is essential if we want our systems of money and payments to successfully weather financial shocks, harness new technology, and respond to the myriad of opportunities and challenges that the future no doubt holds.

As if the benefits of creating a level legal playing field were not enough to spur policymakers into action, they should also not lose sight of the potentially enormous costs generated by the current, and decidedly uneven, playing field. First and foremost, the financial safety net and restrictions on infrastructure access generate significant competitive distortions, forcing new institutions and platforms to choose between the exquisitely tailored straitjacket of conventional bank regulation and the strategic vulnerability associated with wholesale reliance on banks for indirect access to the networks at the heart of the modern payment system. In many cases, this choice results in destabilizing regulatory arbitrage, eroding basic customer protections and creating an opaque web of credit exposures that can become channels for the crystallization and transmission of systemic risk. Further compounding matters, by effectively forcing the entire payment system to run through banks, this tilted playing field only amplifies the too-big-too-fail problem. However policymakers want to look at it, the stakes are simply too high to continue to do nothing in the face of these critical and growing risks.

A Level Technological Playing Field

An important part of creating a level legal playing field is ensuring that the laws governing money and payments are technologically neutral. The evolutionary paths of finance and technology are deeply intertwined: with the invention of the telegraph, the computer, and the internet having been as critical to the development of modern finance as Wall Street, the venture capital industry, and global capital markets have been to the trajectory and pace of technological innovation. This is especially true in the world of payments, where the massive changes in the way we send and receive money over the past century have been almost entirely attributable to successive waves of technological development and adoption.

While governments have often played an influential role in this ongoing coevolution, they have until very recently followed a policy of technological neutrality. In broad terms, this means that policymakers have not sought to differentiate between financial institutions on the basis of which technologies they use or how they use them. After all, putting aside the obvious data security issues, a bank that stores its customer records in an old IBM mainframe is fundamentally no different than one that stores them in a cutting-edge Amazon-administered cloud. It also means that policymakers have refrained from fundamentally redesigning the regulatory frameworks that govern these institutions in response to technological shocks. Thus, for example, while the release of the Excel spreadsheet software application in 1985 was arguably one of the pivotal moments in the history of modern finance, it was not followed by any meaningful changes to financial sector regulation or supervision. And most importantly, this neutrality means that policymakers have not attempted to build entirely new regulatory frameworks around financial institutions simply because they happen to use a particular technology.

Unfortunately, it appears that policymakers have started to abandon this long-standing, if often implicit, policy of technological neutrality. Perhaps most notably, many of the new regulatory frameworks created in response to the rise of the shadow monetary system have explicitly and exclusively targeted financial institutions and platforms that use distributed ledger or blockchain technology. Examples include the New York Bitlicense, the EU's MiCA, and the raft of draft stablecoin bills released by the US House of Representatives.[2] Yet, if we take the dynamics driving Gresham's new law seriously, it is difficult to imagine a more misguided approach. Indeed, if the interwoven history of finance and technology teaches us anything, it's that change is the only real constant. Accordingly, unless we think that blockchain represents the terminus of centuries of technological innovation, these regulatory frameworks will ultimately have a very limited shelf life. More importantly, by singling out a specific and still largely unproven technology at the edge of today's technological frontier, these frameworks risk distorting the competitive landscape for decades to come.

---

2. See US House Financial Services Committee, Draft Stablecoin Bill, 118th Congress, 1st Session (April 15, 2023); Brendan Pedersen, "Draft Bill Lets Nonbanks Issue Stablecoins, Bans Algorithmic Coins for Two Years," *American Banker* (September 20, 2022).

The Challenge of Technological Governance

The importance of creating a level legal and technological playing field points us in the direction of one final theme. While competition can drive new innovation, it can also prevent the type of industry-wide coordination necessary to ensure that this innovation is successfully harnessed in pursuit of societal objectives. This suggests the need for active and ongoing public sector involvement in decisions about network design and the adoption of new technology in order to ensure that this innovation yields real, tangible, and universally accessible improvements to our systems of money and payments. This book has not sought to develop a detailed blueprint for this public-private governance structure; that is a project for another day. What it hopefully has demonstrated is *why* this governance structure is so urgently needed. Ultimately, the technological promise that has driven the emergence of the shadow monetary system will be completely wasted if the benefits do not flow to the growing number of people, businesses, and governments that ultimately use it. Like money, technology is an excellent servant, but a terrible master.

———

Together, these themes represent a baseline—a starting point for further discussion and debate about the future of money and payments. We don't all have to agree on what this future should look like, or how we should get there. Inevitably, none of us yet knows what challenges and opportunities the future holds. But if these themes drive home anything, it's that the future of money and payments is ours to imagine and, having imagined it, our collective responsibility to build.

BIBLIOGRAPHY

Official Sources

Atlantic Council, Central Bank Digital Currency Tracker (March 2023), https://www.atlanticcouncil.org/cbdctracker/.

Bank of England, Bankstats Tables A2.2.1—Components of M4 (tables VRJX, VQKT, VRJV, VWDO), https://www.bankofengland.co.uk/statistics/tables.

Bank for International Settlements, Payment, Clearing, and Settlement Statistics, https://www.bis.org/statistics/payment_stats.htm?m=3|16|385.

Basel Committee on Banking Supervision, "Basel III: Finalising Post-Crisis Reforms" (2017), https://www.bis.org/bcbs/publ/d424.pdf (articulating the Basel capital rules).

———, "Basel III: A Global Framework for More Resilient Banks and Banking Systems" (2011), https://www.bis.org/publ/bcbs189.pdf.

———, "Basel III: The Liquidity Coverage Ratio and Risk Monitoring Tools" (2013), https://www.bis.org/publ/bcbs238.htm.

———, "Report on Open Banking and Application Programming Interfaces" (November 2019).

Committee on Payments and Market Infrastructures, "Correspondent Banking," Bank for International Settlements (July 2016), https://www.bis.org/cpmi/publ/d147.pdf.

Conference of State Bank Supervisors, "Model Money Transmission Modernization Act" (January 6, 2022).

Darling, Alistair, "Statement of the Chancellor of the Exchequer on Financial Markets" (September 17, 2007).

Faster Payments Task Force, "The Path to Faster Payments: Final Report Part 2: A Call to Action" (July 2017), https://fasterpaymentstaskforce.org/wp-content/uploads/faster-payments-task-force-final-report-part-two.pdf.

FDIC (Federal Deposit Insurance Corporation), "Bank Failures and Assistance Data" (2022), https://banks.data.fdic.gov/explore/failures.

———, "A Brief History of Deposit Insurance in the United States" (1998), https://www.fdic.gov/bank/historical/brief/brhist.pdf.

———, *Crisis and Response, An FDIC History, 2008–2013* (2013).

———, "How America Banks: Household Use of Banking and Financial Services" (2019), https://www.fdic.gov/analysis/household-survey/.

———, Quarterly Bank Profile: First Quarter, Table II-A (2022), https://www.fdic.gov/analysis/quarterly-banking-profile/qbp/2022mar.

———, *Resolutions Handbook* (2014), https://www.fdic.gov/bank/historical/reshandbook/resolutions_handbook.pdf.

Federal Reserve Bank of Atlanta, 2021 Survey and Diary of Consumer Payment Choice (October 13, 2022), https://www.atlantafed.org/banking-and-payments/consumer-payments/survey-and-diary-of-consumer-payment-choice.

Federal Reserve Bank of St. Louis, FRED Economic Data, Currency Component of M1, (June 2020), https://fred.stlouisfed.org/series/CURRSL.

———, *Publications of the National Monetary Commission Series*, https://fraser.stlouisfed.org /series/1493.

Federal Reserve Board of Governors, "Assets and Liabilities of Commercial Banks in the United States," statistical release H.8 (March 31, 2023), https://www.federalreserve.gov/releases /h8/current/.

———, "Factors Affecting Reserve Balances, Federal Reserve," statistical release H.4.1 (July 4, 2007–December 29, 2010).

———, *Financial Stability Report* (November 2022), https://www.federalreserve.gov/publications /files/financial-stability-report-20221104.pdf.

———, *Financial Stability Report*, 27 (October 2023), file:///Users/aja288/Desktop/financial-stability-report-20231020.pdf.

———, "Money and Payments: The U.S. Dollar in the Age of Digital Transformation" (January 2022), https://www.federalreserve.gov/publications/files/money-and-payments -20220120.pdf.

———, "Money Stock and Debt Measures," statistical release H.6 (July 2023), https://www .federalreserve.gov/releases/h6.

Financial Stability Board, "Cross-Border Payments" (March 2023), https://www.fsb.org/work-of -the-fsb/financial-innovation-and-structural-change/cross-border-payments/.

———, "Decentralised Financial Technologies: Report on Financial Stability, Regulatory and Governance Implications" (June 6, 2019), https://www.fsb.org/wp-content/uploads /P060619.pdf.

———, "Evaluation of Too Big to Fail Reforms" (May 23, 2019), https://www.fsb.org/wp-content /uploads/P230519.pdf.

———, "Key Attributes of Effective Resolution Regimes for Financial Institutions" (2011).

———, "2021 Resolution Report: Glass Half-Full or Still Half-Empty?" (December 7, 2021).

Grey, Charles, "Letter from the Prime Minister and Chancellor to the Governor of the Bank of England" (November 12, 1857), Bank of England Archives G6/397.

Hamilton, Alexander, "Letter to Robert Morris" (April 30, 1781), https://founders.archives.gov /documents/Hamilton/01-02-02-1167.

International Association of Deposit Insurers, "Deposit Insurance Systems Worldwide" (April 9, 2022), https://www.iadi.org/en/about-iadi/deposit-insurance-systems/dis-worldwide/.

———, "IADI Annual Survey" (2021), https://www.iadi.org/en/research/data-warehouse /deposit-insurance-surveys/.

International Standards Organization, "Universal Financial Industry Message Scheme," https:// www.iso20022.org/about-iso-20022.

Investment Company Institute, "Money Market Fund Assets" (September 28, 2023), https://www .ici.org/research/stats/mmf.

National Credit Union Administration, Quarterly Credit Union Data Summary Q2–2023 (June 30, 2023), https://www.ncua.gov/files/publications/analysis/quarterly-data-summary -2023-Q2.pdf.

Plenderleith, Ian, "Review of the Bank of England's Provision of Emergency Liquidity Assistance in 2008–09," *Plenderleith Review* (2012).

UK Financial Services Authority, "FSA Announces FSCS Reforms to Ensure Faster Payouts and Boost Consumer Confidence" (July 24, 2009).

UK Treasury Committee, "The Run on the Rock," 2007–8 HC 56-I (2007).

US Department of the Treasury, *A Financial System That Creates Economic Opportunities: Nonbank Financials, Fintech, and Innovation* (2018).

———, Interagency Working Group for Treasury Market Surveillance, "Enhancing the Resilience of the U.S. Treasury Market: 2022 Staff Progress Report" (November 10, 2022), https://home.treasury.gov/system/files/136/2022-IAWG-Treasury-Report.pdf.

US National Monetary Commission, *Reports of the National Monetary Commission* (1909–1912), https://fraser.stlouisfed.org/series/publications-national-monetary-commission-series-1493.

US Office of Financial Research, OFR Short-Term Funding Monitor, "Repo Transaction Volumes by Venue" and "Tenor" (January 2023), https://www.financialresearch.gov/short-term-funding-monitor/.

Winters, Bill, "Review of the Bank of England's Framework for Providing Liquidity to the Banking System" (2012).

World Bank, "Business Enabling Environment: Alternative Existing Indicators for the Year 2020" (updated to September 30, 2021), https://www.worldbank.org/en/programs/business-enabling-environment/alternative-existing-indicators#3.

Secondary Sources

Acharya, Viral, Deniz Anginer, & Joseph Warburton, "The End of Market Discipline?: Investor Expectations of Implicit Government Guarantees" (May 1, 2016) (unpublished manuscript).

Adams, Robert, Paul Bauer, & Robin Sickles, "Scope and Scale Economies in Federal Reserve Payment Processing," Federal Reserve Bank of Cleveland Working Paper No. 02-13 (November 2002).

Admati, Anat, & Martin Hellwig, *The Bankers' New Clothes: What's Wrong with Banking and What to Do about It.* Princeton University Press, Princeton, NJ (2013).

Ahamed, Liaquat, *Lords of Finance: The Bankers Who Broke the World.* Penguin, New York (2009).

Alchian, Armen, "Why Money?," 9:1 Journal of Money, Credit and Banking 133 (1977).

Allen, Harold Don, "Canadian Tire Scrip," Numismatist 63 (2006).

Andolfatto, David, "Assessing the Impact of Central Bank Digital Currency on Private Banks," 131 Economic Journal 525 (February 2021).

Anson, Mike, David Bholat, Miao Kang, & Ryland Thomas, "The Bank of England as Lender of Last Resort: New Historical Evidence from Daily Transaction Data," Bank of England Staff Working Paper No. 691 (2017).

Areeda, Phillip, & Herbert Hovenkamp, *Antitrust Law: An Analysis of Antitrust Principles and Their Application.* Wolters Kluwer, Philadelphia (2017).

Armour, John, "Making Bank Resolution Credible," in Niamh Moloney et al. (eds,), *The Oxford Handbook of Financial Regulation.* Oxford University Press, Oxford, UK (2015).

Armour, John, Dan Awrey, Paul Davies, Luca Enriques, Jeff Gordon, Colin Mayer, & Jennifer Payne, *Principles of Financial Regulation.* Oxford University Press, Oxford, UK (2016).

Armour, John, & Jeffrey Gordon, "Systemic Harms and Shareholder Value," 6:1 Journal of Legal Analysis 35 (2014).

Arner, Douglas, Raphael Auer, & Jon Frost, "Stablecoins: Risks, Potential, and Regulation," Bank for International Settlements Working Paper No. 905 (November 2020).

Ausubel, Lawrence, "The Failure of Competition in the Credit Card Market," 81 American Economic Review 50 (1991).

Awrey, Dan, "Bad Money," 106:1 Cornell Law Review 1 (2020).

———, "Law and Finance in the Chinese Shadow Banking System," 48:1 Cornell International Law Journal 1 (2015).

———, "The Puzzling Divergence of the Lender of Last Resort Regimes in the US and UK," 45:3 Journal of Corporation Law 597 (2020).

Awrey, Dan, & Joshua Macey, *Open Access, Interoperability, and DTCC's Unexpected Path to Monopoly*, 132 Yale Law Journal 96 (2022).

———, *The Promise and Perils of Open Finance*, 40:1 Yale Journal on Regulation 1 (2022).

Awrey, Dan, & Kristin van Zwieten, "Mapping the Shadow Payment System," Swift Institute Research Paper No. 2019-001 (November 2019).

Bagchi, Amiya Kumar, "Transition from Indian to British Indian Systems of Money and Banking, 1800–1850," 19:3 Modern Asian Studies 501 (1985).

Bagehot, Walter, *Lombard Street: A Description of the Money Market* (1873).

Baring, Francis, *Observations on the Establishment of the Bank of England and on the Paper Circulation in the Country* (1797).

Michael Barr, Howell Jackson, & Margaret Tahyar, *Financial Regulation: Law & Policy*. Foundation Press, St. Paul, MN (2nd ed., 2018).

Bazot, Guillaume, "Financial Consumption and the Cost of Finance: Measuring Financial Efficiency in Europe (1950–2007)," 16:1 Journal of the European Economic Association 123 (2018).

Bech, Morten, & Bart Hobjin, "Technology Diffusion within Central Banking: The Case of Real Time Gross Settlement," 3 International Journal of Central Banking 147 (2007).

Bech, Morten, Yuuki Shimizu, & Paul Wong, "The Quest for Speed in Payments," in Bank for International Settlements (ed.), *BIS Quarterly Review: International Banking and Financial Market Developments*, 57–60 (2017), https://www.bis.org/publ/qtrpdf/r_qt1703.pdf.

Beijnen, Christine, & Wilco Bolt, "Size Matters: Economies of Scale in European Payments Processing," 33 Journal of Banking and Finance 203 (2009).

Bergier, Jean-Francois, "From the Fifteenth Century in Italy to the Sixteenth Century in Germany: A New Banking Concept?," in Centre for Medieval and Renaissance Studies, University of California, Los Angeles (ed.), *The Dawn of Medieval Banking*. Yale University Press, New Haven, CT (1979).

Bernanke, Ben, "Nonmonetary Effects of the Financial Crisis in the Propagation of the Great Depression," 73 American Economic Review 257 (1983).

———, "Origins and Mission of the Federal Reserve—the Gold Standard" (March 2012), https://www.federalreserve.gov/aboutthefed/educational-tools/lecture-series-origins-and-mission.htm.

———, "Statement Before the Financial Crisis Inquiry Commission" (September 2, 2010), http://www.federalreserve.gov/newsevents/testimony/bernanke20100902a).

Bernstein, Asaf, Eric Hughson, & Marc Weidenmier, "Identifying the Effects of a Lender of Last Resort on Financial Markets: Lessons from the Founding of the Fed," 98 Journal of Financial Economics 40 (2010).

Bignon, Vincent, Marc Flandreau, & Stefano Ugolini, "Bagehot for Beginners: The Making of Lender-of-Last-Resort Operations in the Mid-Nineteenth Century," 65 Economic History Review 580 (2012).

Bindseil, Ulrich, & George Pantelopoulos, "Toward the Holy Grail of Cross-Border Payments," European Central Bank Working Paper No. 2693 (August 2022).

Boissay, Frederic, Giulio Cornelli, Sebastian Doerr, & Jon Frost, "Blockchain Scalability and the Fragmentation of Crypto," Bank for International Settlements Bulletin No. 56 (June 7, 2022).

Bolt, Wilco, & David Humphrey, "Payment Network Scale Economies, SEPA, and Cash Replacement," 6 Review of Network Economics 453 (2007).

Bolton, Patrick, Tano Santos, & Jose Scheinkman, "Cream Skimming in Financial Markets," 71:2 Journal of Finance 709 (2016).

Brummer, Chris, "How International Financial Law Works (and How It Doesn't)," 99 Georgetown Law Journal 257 (2011).

Bruner, Robert, & Sean Carr, *The Panic of 1907: Lessons Learned from the Market's Perfect Storm*. John Wiley & Sons, Hoboken, NJ (2007).

Brunnermeier, Markus, & Lasse Pedersen, "Market Liquidity and Funding Liquidity," 22 Review of Financial Studies 2201 (2009).

Buchak, Greg, Gregor Matvos, Tomasz Piskorski, & Amit Seru, "Fintech, Regulatory Arbitrage and the Rise of Shadow Banks," 130:3 Journal of Financial Economics 453 (2018).

Burgon, John William, *The Life and Times of Thomas Gresham* (1839).

Burns, Helen, *The American Banking Community and the New Deal Banking Reforms, 1933–1935*. Praeger, Westport, CT (1974).

Calomiris, Charles, "Is the Discount Window Necessary? A Penn Central Perspective," 76:3 Federal Reserve Bank of St. Louis Review 31 (1994).

Calomiris, Charles, Marc Flandreau, & Luc Laeven, "Political Foundations of the Lender of Last Resort: A Global Historical Narrative," 28 Journal of Financial Intermediation 48 (2016).

Calomiris, Charles, & Charles Kahn, "The Efficiency of Self-Regulated Payments Systems: Learning from the Suffolk System," 28 Journal of Money, Credit and Banking 766 (1996).

Calomiris, Charles, & Eugene White, "The Origins of Federal Deposit Insurance," in Claudia Goldin & Gary Libecap (eds.), *The Regulated Economy: A Historical Approach to Political Economy*, 145. University of Chicago Press, Chicago (1994).

Cannon, James, *Clearing-House Methods and Practices* (1910).

Carlson, Mark, & David Wheelock, "The Lender of Last Resort: Lessons from the Fed's First 100 Years," Federal Reserve Bank of St. Louis Working Paper No. 202-056B (2013).

Carstens, Agustín, Stijn Claessens, Fernando Restoy, & Hyun Song Shin, "Regulating Big Techs in Finance," Bank for International Settlements Bulletin No. 45 (August 2, 2021).

Catalini, Christian, & Jai Massari, "Stablecoins and the Future of Money," *Harvard Business Review* (August 10, 2021).

Catterall, Ralph, *The Second Bank of the United States*. University of Chicago Press, Chicago (1903).

Cecchetti, Stephen, & Kermit Schoenholtz, "Why a Gold Standard Is a Very Bad Idea," Money & Banking blog (December 19, 2016), https://www.moneyandbanking.com/commentary/2016/12/14/why-a-gold-standard-is-a-very-bad-idea.

Chaddock, Robert, *The Safety Fund Banking System in New York, 1829–1866*, US Government Printing Office, Washington, DC (1910).

Chakravorti, Sujit, & Roberto Roson, "Platform Competition in Two-Sided Markets: The Case of Payment Networks," 5:1 Review of Network Economics 118 (2006).

Cheng, Linsun, *Banking in Modern China: Entrepreneurs, Professional Managers and the Development of Chinese Banks, 1897–1937*. Cambridge University Press, Cambridge, UK (2003).

Chorzempa, Martin, *The Cashless Revolution: China's Reinvention of Money and the End of America's Domination of Finance and Technology*. PublicAffairs, New York (2022).

Clapham, John, *The Bank of England: A History: Volume 1*. Macmillan, London (1944).

Cochrane, John, "Toward a Run-Free Financial System," in Martin Baily & John Taylor (eds.), *Across the Great Divide: New Perspectives on the Financial Crisis*. Hoover Institution Press, Palo Alto, CA (2014).

Collins, Michael, "The Bank of England as Lender of Last Resort, 1857–1878," 45 Economic History Review 145 (1992).

Conti-Brown, Peter, "The Fed Wants to Veto State Banking Authorities—but Is That Legal?," Brookings Center on Regulation on Markets (November 14, 2018).

Conti-Brown, Peter, & Sean Vanetta, *The Bankers' Thumb: A History of Bank Supervision in America* (forthcoming).

Cooke, C. N., *The Rise, Progress, and Present Condition of Banking in India* (1863).

Copeland, Adam, & Rodney Garratt, "Nonlinear Pricing and the Market for Settling Payments," 51:1 Journal of Money, Credit and Banking 195 (2019).

Crawcour, Sydney, "The Development of a Credit System in Seventeenth-Century Japan," 21:2 Journal of Economic History 342 (1961).

Cunningham, Colleen, Florian Ederer, & Song Ma, "Killer Acquisitions," 129 Journal of Political Economy 649 (2021).

Dahl, Drew, Andrew Meyer, & Michelle Clark Neeley, "Scale Matters: Community Banks and Compliance Costs," Federal Reserve Bank of St. Louis (July 14, 2016).

Davison, Lee, "Continental Illinois and 'Too Big to Fail,'" in *History of the Eighties—Lessons for the Future: An Examination of the Banking Crises of the 1980s and Early 1990s*. Federal Deposit Insurance Corporation, Washington, DC (1997).

Defina, Ryan, Bert Van Roosebeke, & Paul Manga, "E-Money and Deposit Insurance in Kenya," International Association of Deposit Insurers, Fintech Brief No. 6 (December 2021).

Demirguc-Kunt, Asli, & Leora Klapper, "Measuring Financial Inclusion: The Global Financial Inclusion Indicators," World Bank Policy Research Working Paper No. 6025 (2012).

Desai, Mihir, & Sumit Rajpal, "How 'Payment Banks' Could Prevent the Next Bank Collapse," Harvard Business Review (March 17, 2023).

Desan, Christine, *Making Money: Coin, Currency, and the Coming of Capitalism*. Oxford University Press, Oxford, UK (2015).

De Soete, Marijke, "Smart Card," Encyclopedia of Cryptography and Security, 1224 (2011).

Dhavalikar, Madhukar, "The Beginning of Coinage in India," 6:3 World Archeology 330 (1975).

Diamond, Douglas, & Philip Dybvig, "Bank Runs, Deposit Insurance, and Liquidity," 91 Journal of Political Economy 401 (1983).

Domanski, Dietrich, Richhild Moessner, & William Nelson, "Central Banks as Lender of Last Resort: Experiences during the 2007–2010 Crisis and Lessons for the Future," Federal Reserve Board Working Paper No. 2014-110 (2014).

D'Onfro, Danielle, "The New Bailments," 97 Washington Law Review 97 (2022).

Dowd, Kevin (ed.), *The Experience of Free Banking*. Routledge, Oxford, UK (1992).

———, "Models of Banking Instability: A Partial Review of the Literature," 6 Journal of Economic Surveys 107 (2002).

Duarte, Angelo, Jon Frost, Leonardo Gambacorta, Priscilla Koo Wilkens, & Hyun Song Shin, "Central Banks, the Monetary System, and Public Payment Infrastructures: Lessons from Brazil's Pix," Bank for International Settlements Bulletin No. 52 (March 23, 2022).

Dwyer, Gerald, Jr., "Wildcat Banking, Banking Panics, and Free Banking in the United States," Federal Reserve Bank of Atlanta Economic Review 1 (December 1996).

Eich, Stefan, *The Currency of Politics: A Political Theory of Money from Aristotle to Keynes*. Princeton University Press, Princeton, NJ (2022).

Eichengreen, Barry, *Exorbitant Privilege: The Rise and Fall of the Dollar and the Future of the International Monetary System*. Oxford University Press, Oxford, UK (2011).

———, *Globalizing Capital: A History of the International Monetary System*. Princeton University Press, Princeton, NJ (1998).

———, *Golden Fetters: The Gold Standard and the Great Depression*. Oxford University Press, Oxford, UK (1992).

Eichengreen, Barry, & Marc Flandreau, *The Gold Standard in Theory and History*. Routledge, Oxford, UK (1997).

Eidenmuller, Horst, "Comparative Corporate Insolvency Law," European Corporate Governance Institute Law Working Paper No. 319-206 (July 2017).

Ennis, Huberto, & David Price, "Understanding Discount Window Stigma," Federal Reserve Bank of Richmond Economic Brief No. 20-04 (April 2020).

Fama, Eugene, "Efficient Capital Markets: A Review of Theory and Empirical Work," 25 Journal of Finance 383 (1970).

Feinig, Jakob, *Moral Economies of Money: Politics and the Monetary Constitution of Society*. Stanford University Press, Palo Alto, CA (2022).

Feldman, Gerald, *The Great Disorder: Politics, Economics and Society in the German Inflation, 1914–1924*. Oxford University Press, Oxford, UK (1997).

Fetter, Frank, *Development of British Monetary Orthodoxy, 1797–1875*. Harvard University Press, Cambridge, MA (1965).

———, "Some Neglected Aspects of Gresham's Law," 46:3 Quarterly Journal of Economics 480 (1932).

Fisher, Irving, *100% Money*. Adelphi, New York (1936).

———, *The Purchasing Power of Money*. Augustus M. Kelley, New York (1911).

Flandreau, Marc, & Stefano Ugolini, "Where It All Began: Lending of Last Resort and the Bank of England during the Overend-Gurney Panic of 1866," Norges Bank Working Paper No. 2011-03 (2011).

Flannery, Mark, *The Economic Implications of an Electronic Money Transfer System*. Lexington Books, Lanham, MD (1973).

———, "Technology and Payments: Déjà vu All Over Again?," 28:4 Journal of Money, Credit and Banking 965 (1996).

Flood, Mark, "The Great Deposit Insurance Debate," in Dimitri Papadimitriou (ed.), *Stability in the Financial System*, 35. Springer, New York (1996).

Fox, David, "*Banks v. Whetson* (1596)" in Simon Douglas, Robin Hickey, & Emma Waring (eds.), *Landmark Cases in Property Law*. Bloomsbury, London (2015).

———, "Bona Fide Purchase and the Currency of Money," 55:3 Cambridge Law Journal 547 (1996).

———, *Property Rights in Money*. Oxford University Press, Oxford, UK (2008).

Friedman, Milton, *A Program for Monetary Stability*. Fordham University Press, New York (1963).

Friedman, Milton, & Anna Schwartz, *A Monetary History of the United States 1867–1960*. Princeton University Press, Princeton, NJ (rev. ed., 1971).

———, *Monetary Statistics of the United States: Estimates, Sources, Methods, and Data*. Columbia University Press, New York (1970).

Gandhi, Priyank, & Hanno Lustig, "Size Anomalies in U.S. Bank Stock Returns," 70 Journal of Finance 733 (2015).

Garratt, Rodney, Jiaheng Yu, & Haoxiang Zhu, "The Case for Convenience: How CBDC Design Choices Impact Monetary Policy Pass-Through," Bank for International Settlements Working Paper No. 1046 (November 2022).

Gelpern, Anna, & Erik Gerding, "Inside Safe Assets," 33 Yale Journal on Regulation 365 (2016).

Gennaioli, Nicola, Andrei Shleifer, & Robert Vishny, "Money Doctors," 70:1 Journal of Finance 91 (2015).

Geva, Benjamin, *Bank Collections and Payment Transactions: A Comparative Study of Legal Aspects*. Oxford University Press, Oxford, UK (2001).

———, "Bank Money: The Rise, Fall and Metamorphosis of the Transferrable Deposit," in David Fox & Wolfgang Ernst (eds), *Money in the Western Legal Tradition: Middle Ages to Bretton Woods*. Oxford University Press, Oxford, UK (2016).

———, *The Payment Order of Antiquity and the Middle Ages: A Legal History*, Hart Publishing, Oxford, UK (2011).

Gilbert, Alton, "Requiem for Regulation Q: What It Did and Why It Passed Away," 68 Federal Reserve Bank of St. Louis Review 22 (1986).

"The Giro, the Computer, and Checkless Banking," Federal Reserve Bank of Richmond Monthly Review 2 (April 1966).

Gleick, James, *The Information: A History, A Theory, A Flood*. Vintage Books, New York (2011).

Goldberg, Dror, *Easy Money: American Puritans and the Invention of Modern Currency*. University of Chicago Press, Chicago (2023).

Gopal, Manasa, & Philipp Schnabl, *The Rise of Finance Companies and FinTech Lenders in Small Business Lending*, 35:11 Review of Financial Studies 4859 (2022).

Gorton, Gary, "Clearinghouses and the Origin of Central Banking in the United States," 45 Journal of Economic History 277 (1985).

———, "Pricing Free Bank Notes," 44 Journal of Monetary Economics 33 (1999).

———, "Private Clearinghouses and the Origins of Central Banking," Federal Reserve Bank of Philadelphia Business Review 3 (1985).

Gorton, Gary, & Andrew Metrick, "The Federal Reserve and Panic Protection: The Roles of Financial Regulation and Lender of Last Resort," 27 Journal of Economic Perspectives 45 (2013).

———, "Securitized Banking and the Run on Repo," National Bureau of Economic Research Working Paper No. 15223 (August 2009).

———, *Slapped by the Invisible Hand: The Panic of 2007*. Oxford University Press, Oxford, UK (2010).

Gorton, Gary, & George Pennacchi, "Financial Intermediaries and Liquidity Creation," 45:1 Journal of Finance 49 (1990).

Gorton, Gary, Chase Ross, & Sharon Ross, "Making Money," National Bureau of Economic Research Working Paper No. 29710 (January 2022).

Gould, J. D., *The Great Debasement: Currency and the Economy in Mid-Tudor England*. Oxford University Press, Oxford, UK (1970).

Graeber, David, *Debt: The First 5,000 Years*. Melville House, Brooklyn, NY (2011).

Green, Peter, *Alexander to Actium: The Historical Evolution of the Hellenistic Age*. University of California Press, Berkeley (1993).

Greenacre, Jonathan, & Ross Buckley, "Using Trusts to Protect Mobile Money Customers," Singapore Journal of Legal Studies 59 (2014).

Greenwood, Robin, & David Scharfstein, "The Growth of Modern Finance," 27:2 Journal of Economic Perspectives 3 (2013).

Grewal, Paul, "Setting the Record Straight: Your Funds Are Safe at Coinbase—and Always Will Be," Coinbase blog post (June 1, 2022), https://www.coinbase.com/blog/setting-the-record -straight-your-funds-are-safe-at-coinbase-and-always-will-be.

Grossman, Richard, & Hugh Rockoff, "Fighting the Last War: Economists on the Lender of Last Resort," National Bureau of Economic Research Working Paper No. 20,832 (2015).

Hammond, Bray, *Banks and Politics in America from the Revolution to the Civil War*. Princeton University Press, Princeton, NJ (1957).

Han, Pengfei, & Zhu Wang, "Technology Adoption and Leapfrogging: Racing for Mobile Payments," Federal Reserve Bank of Richmond Working Paper No. 21-5 (August 30, 2022).

Hankey, Thomson, *The Principles of Banking, Its Utility and Economy; with Remarks on the Working and Management of the Bank of England* (1867).

Harfield, Henry, "Elements of Foreign Exchange Practice," 64:3 Harvard Law Review 436 (1951).

Hauser, Andrew, "Lender of Last Resort Operations during the Financial Crisis: Seven Practical Lessons from the United Kingdom," Bank for International Settlements Working Paper No. 79 (2014).

Hawtrey, Ralph, *The Art of Central Banking*. Routledge, Oxford, UK (1932).

Hayashi, Fumiko, & Sam Baird, "Credit and Debit Card Interchange Fees in Various Countries," Federal Reserve Bank of Kansas City 5 (August 2022 update), https://www.kansascityfed .org/Interchange%20Fees/documents/9021/CreditDebitCardInterchangeFeesVariousCou ntries_August2022Update.pdf.

Hicks, John, *Value and Capital*. Oxford University Press, Oxford, UK (2nd ed., 1946).

Hill, Julie, "Bank Access to Federal Reserve Accounts and Payment Systems," Yale Journal on Regulation (forthcoming).

———, "From Cannabis to Crypto: Federal Reserve Discretion in Payments," 109 Iowa Law Review 117 (2023).

Hockett, Robert, & Saule Omarova, "The Finance Franchise," 102 Cornell Law Review 1143 (2017).

Holden, J. Milnes, *The History of Negotiable Instruments in English Law*. Athlone Press, London (1955).

Holdsworth, John, "Lessons of State Banking before the Civil War," 30 Proceedings of the Academy of Political Science 23 (1971).

Holland, Steven A., & Mark Toma, "The Role of the Federal Reserve as 'Lender of Last Resort' and the Seasonal Fluctuation of Interest Rates," 23 Journal of Money, Credit and Banking 659 (1991).

Holmstrom, Bengt, "Understanding the Role of Debt in the Financial System," Bank for International Settlements Working Paper No. 479 (January 2015).

Horsefield, Keith, "The Beginnings of Paper Money in England," 6:1 Journal of European Economic History 117 (1977).

Huang, Yiping, & Tingting Ge, "Assessing China's Financial Reform: Changing Roles of the Repressive Financial Policies," 39:1 Cato Journal 65 (Winter 2019).

Hudson, Michael, "Reconstructing the Origins of Interest-Bearing Debt and the Logic of Clean Slates," in Michael Hudson & Marc Van de Mieroop (eds.), *Debt & Economic Renewal in the Ancient Near East*. CDL Press, Potomac, MD (2002).

Hughes, J.R.T., "The Commercial Crisis of 1957," 8 Oxford Economic Papers 194 (1956).

Humphrey, Thomas, "Lender of Last Resort: What It Is, Whence It Came, and Why the Fed Isn't It," 30 Cato Journal 333 (2010).

Innes, Mitchell, "What Is Money?," Banking Law Journal (May 1913).

Jack, William, "M-PESA Extends Its Reach," GSMA Mobile for Development blog post (April 5, 2012), https://www.gsma.com/mobilefordevelopment/country/kenya/m-pesa-extends-its-reach/.

Jack, William, & Tavneet Suri, "Risk Sharing and Transaction Costs: Evidence from Kenya's Mobile Money Revolution," 104:1 American Economic Review 183 (2014).

Jackin, Charles, & Sudipto Bhattacharya, "Distinguishing Panics from Information-Based Bank Runs: Welfare and Policy Implications," 96:3 Journal of Political Economy 568 (1998).

Jackson, Howell, & Morgan Ricks, "Locating Stablecoins with the Regulatory Perimeter," Harvard Law School Forum on Corporate Governance (August 5, 2021).

Jackson, Thomas, *Logic and Limits of Bankruptcy Law*. Harvard University Press, Cambridge, MA (1986).

Jackson, Thomas, & Douglas Baird, "Corporate Reorganizations and the Treatment of Diverse Ownership Interests: A Comment on Adequate Protection of Secured Creditors in Bankruptcy," 51 University of Chicago Law Review 97 (1984).

Jacobson, Daniel, Greg Brail, & Dan Woods, *APIs: A Strategy Guide*. O'Reilly Media, Sebastopol, CA (2012).

Jaremski, Matthew, "Bank-Specific Default Risk in the Pricing of Bank Note Discounts," 71 Journal of Economic History 950 (2011).

Jevons, Stanley, *Money and the Mechanism of Exchange* (1875).

Johnson, Kristin, "Decentralized Finance: Regulatory Cryptocurrency Exchanges," 62:6 William & Mary Law Review 1911 (2021).

Kahn, Alfred, *The Economics of Regulation*. MIT Press, Cambridge, MA (1988).

Kahneman, Daniel, & Amos Tversky, "Availability: A Heuristic for Judging Frequency and Probability," 5 Cognitive Psychology 207 (1973).

Kay, John, *Narrow Banking: The Reform of Banking Regulation.* Centre for the Study of Financial Innovation, London (2009).

Keynes, John Maynard, *The General Theory of Employment, Interest and Money.* Palgrave Macmillan, London (1936).

———, *A Treatise on Money.* Macmillan, London (1930).

Khan, Lina, "Amazon's Antitrust Paradox," 126 Yale Law Journal 710 (2017).

Killigrew, William, "A Proposal Shewing How This Nation May Be Vast Gainers by All the Sums of Money, Given to the Crown, without Lessening the Prerogative" (1690).

Kim, Jongchul, "How Modern Banking Originated: The London Goldsmith-Bankers' Institutionalisation of Trust," 53:6 Business History 939 (2011).

Kindleberger, Charles, *A Financial History of Western Europe.* Routledge, Oxford, UK (1984).

King, W.T.C., *History of the London Discount Market.* Routledge, Oxford, UK (1936).

Klein, Matthew, "Thoughts on Bank Bailouts," The Overshoot (March 13, 2023), https://theovershoot.co/p/thoughts-on-the-bank-bailouts.

Klemperer, Paul, "Network Goods (Theory)," in Steven Durlauf & Lawrence Blume (eds.), *The New Palgrave Dictionary of Economics.* Palgrave Macmillan, London (2nd ed., 2008).

Knapp, Georg, *The State Theory of Money.* Macmillan, London (1905).

Koning, J. P., "A Simpler and More Accurate Way to Teach Money to Students," American Institute for Economic Research (December 10, 2020), https://www.aier.org/article/a-simpler-and-more-accurate-way-to-teach-money-to-students/.

Lacker, Jeffrey, "Payment Economics and the Role of Central Banks," speech at the Bank of England Conference on Payments (May 20, 2005), https://tinyurl.com/58c7skx4.

Laibson, David, "Golden Eggs and Hyperbolic Discounting," 112:2 Quarterly Journal of Economics 443 (1997).

Lawson, William, *The History of Banking.* Richard Bentley, London (2nd ed., 1885).

Leibrandt, Gottfried, & Natasha de Teran, *The Payoff: How Changing the Way We Pay Changes Everything.* Elliott & Thompson, London (2021).

Levitin Adam, "Not Your Keys, Not Your Coins: Unpriced Credit Risk in Cryptocurrency," 101 Texas Law Review 877 (2023).

———, "Safe Banking: Finance and Democracy," 83 University of Chicago Law Review 357 (2016).

Li, William, Pablo Azar, David Larochelle, Phil Hill, & Andrew Lo, "Law Is Code: A Software Engineering Approach Analyzing the United States Code," 10 Journal of Business and Technology Law 297 (2015).

Liao, Gordon, & John Caramichael, "Stablecoins: Growth Potential and Impact on Banking," Federal Reserve Board of Governors, International Finance Discussion Paper No. 1334 (January 2022).

Lindert, Peter, "English Population, Wages, and Prices: 1541–1913," 15:4 Journal of Interdisciplinary History 609 (1985).

Litan, Robert, *What Should Banks Do?* Brookings Institution, Washington, DC (1987).

Lopez, Robert, "The Dawn of Medieval Banking," in Centre for Medieval and Renaissance Studies, University of California, Los Angeles (ed.), *The Dawn of Medieval Banking.* Yale University Press, New Haven, CT (1979).

Lowenstein, Roger, *America's Bank: The Epic Struggle to Create the Federal Reserve.* Penguin, New York (2015).

Lubben, Stephen, *The Law of Failure: A Tour through the Wilds of American Business Insolvency Law.* Cambridge University Press, Cambridge, UK (2018).

Macey, Jonathan, & Geoffrey Miller, "Double Liability of Bank Shareholders: History and Implications," 27 Wake Forest Law Review 31 (1992).

Macleod, Henry Dunning, *The Elements of Political Economy* (1858).

———, *The Theory of Credit* (2nd ed., 1894).

Malkiel, Burton, "The Efficient-Market Hypothesis and the Financial Crisis," in Alan Blinder et al. (eds.), *Rethinking the Financial Crisis*. Russell Sage Foundation, New York (2012).

———, "The Efficient Market Hypothesis and Its Critics," 17 Journal of Economic Perspectives 59 (2003).

Mankiw, Gregory, *Principles of Macroeconomics*. Dryden Press, Forth Worth, TX (1998).

Mann, Ronald, "Regulating Internet Payment Intermediaries," 82 Texas Law Review 681 (2003).

Mas, Ignacio, & Dan Radcliffe, "Mobile Payments Go Viral: M-PESA in Kenya," 32 Capco Institute Journal of Financial Transformation 169 (August 2011).

Massad, Tim, "Facebook's Libra 2.0: Why You Might Like It Even If You Can't Trust Facebook," Brookings Institution Studies in Economics (December 2021).

Matthews, Phillip, *The Bankers' Clearing House: What It Is and What It Does*. Pittman & Sons, London (1921).

Mayhew, N. J., "Population, Money Supply, and the Velocity of Circulation in England, 1300–1700," 48:2 Economic History Review 238 (1995).

McAndrews, James, "Network Issues and Payment Systems," Federal Reserve Bank of Philadelphia Business Review 15 (November/December 1997).

McCall, Brian, "How El Salvador Has Changed U.S. Law by a Bit: The Consequences for the UCC of Bitcoin Becoming Legal Tender," 74:3 Oklahoma Law Review 313 (2022).

McDowell, Daniel, *Bucking the Buck: US Financial Sanctions and the International Backlash against the Dollar*. Oxford University Press, Oxford, UK (2023).

McElderry, Andrea, *Shanghai Old-Style Banks 1800–1935: A Traditional Institution in a Changing Society*. Center for Chinese Studies, University of Michigan, Ann Arbor (1976).

McLeay, Michael, Amar Radia, & Ryland Thomas, "Money Creation in the Modern Economy," Bank of England Quarterly Bulletin (Q1 2014).

Melton, Frank, "Goldsmiths' Notes, 1654–1655," 6:1 Journal of the Society of Archivists 30 (1978).

Meltzer, Allan, *A History of the Federal Reserve, Volume 1: 1913–1951*. University of Chicago Press, Chicago (2004).

———, *A History of the Federal Reserve, Volume 2:1: 1951–1969*. University of Chicago Press, Chicago (2014).

———, *A History of the Federal Reserve, Volume 2:2: 1969–1986*. University of Chicago Press, Chicago (2014).

Menand, Lev, "Unappropriated Dollars: The Fed's Ad Hoc Lending Facilities and the Rules That Govern Them," Working Paper (May 22, 2020).

———, "Why Supervise Banks? The Foundations of the American Monetary Settlement," 74 Vanderbilt Law Review 951 (2021).

Menger, Karl, "On the Origin of Money," 2:6 Economic Journal 239 (1892).

Merton, Robert, *Social Theory and Social Structure*. Free Press, Glencoe, IL (1949).

Milkau, Udo, "The Advent of Machine Payments: The Right Way to Pay?," 12:4 Journal of Payment Strategy and Systems 293 (Winter 2018–2019).

Miller, A. C., "Responsibility for Federal Reserve Policies: 1927–1929," 25 American Economic Review 442 (1935).

Milne, Alistair, "What Is in It for Us? Network Effects and Bank Payment Innovation," 30:6 Journal of Banking and Finance 1613 (2006).

Minsky, Hyman, *Stabilizing an Unstable Economy*. McGraw-Hill, New York (1986).

Miron, Jeffrey, "Financial Panics, the Seasonality of the Nominal Interest Rate, and the Founding of the Fed," 76 American Economic Review 125 (1986).

Mitchell, D. M., "Mr. Fowle Pray Pay the Washwoman: The Trade of a London Goldsmith-Banker, 1660–1692," 23:1 Business and Economic History 27 (1994).

Moazzin, Ghassan, *Foreign Banks and Global Finance in Modern China.* Cambridge University Press, Cambridge, MA (2022).

Morrison, Alan, & Bill Wilhelm, *Investment Banking: Institutions, Politics, and Law.* Oxford University Press, Oxford, UK (2007).

Morrison, Ed, & Franklin Edwards, "Derivatives and the Bankruptcy Code: Why the Special Treatment?," 22 Yale Journal on Regulation 101 (2005).

Mueller, Reinhold, "The Role of Bank Money in Venice, 1300–1500," 3 Studi Veneziani 47 (1979).

———, *The Venetian Money Market: Banks, Panics, and the Public Debt, 1200–1500.* Johns Hopkins University Press, Baltimore, MD (1997).

Mundell, Robert, "Uses and Abuses of Gresham's Law in the History of Money," 2:2 Zagreb Journal of Economics 3 (1998).

Murphy, Antoin, "Money in an Economy without Banks: The Case of Ireland," 46:1 Manchester School 41 (1978).

"The New-Fashioned Goldsmiths," 2:2 Quarterly Journal of Economics 251 (1888).

Newman, John, "Anticompetitive Product Design in the New Economy," 39 Florida State University Law Review 681 (2012).

O'Brien, Dennis, "The Lender-of-Last-Resort Concept in Britain," 35 History of Political Economy 1 (2003).

Omarova, Saule, "The People's Ledger: How to Democratize Money and Finance the Economy," 74 Vanderbilt Law Review 1231 (2021).

Orbanes, Philip, *Monopoly: The World's Most Famous Game—and How It Got That Way.* Da Capo Press, Cambridge, MA (2006).

Pandy, Susan, "Developments in Open Banking and APIs: Where Does the U.S. Stand?," Federal Reserve Bank of Boston Brief (March 17, 2020), https://www.bostonfed.org/-/media/Documents/PaymentStrategies/Open-Banking-and-APIs-Brief.pdf.

Patterson, William, "A Brief Account of the Intended Bank of England" (1694).

Philippon, Thomas, "The Fintech Opportunity," National Bureau of Economic Research Working Paper No. 22476 (August 2016).

———, "Has the U.S. Finance Industry Become Less Efficient? On the Theory and Measurement of Financial Intermediation," 105:4 American Economic Review 1408 (2015).

Pistor, Katharina, *The Code of Capital: How the Law Creates Wealth and Inequality.* Princeton University Press, Princeton, NJ (2019).

Pomeranz, Kenneth, *The Great Divergence: China, Europe, and the Making of the Modern World Economy.* Princeton University Press, Princeton, NJ (2000).

Pozsar, Zoltan, Tobias Adrian, Adam Ashcraft, & Hayley Boesky, "Shadow Banking," 19 Federal Reserve Bank of New York Economic Policy Review 1 (2013).

Prakash, Satya, & Rajendra Singh, *Coinage in Ancient India.* Research Institute of Ancient Scientific Studies, New Delhi (1968).

Prasad, Eswar, *The Dollar Trap: How the U.S. Dollar Tightened Its Grip on Global Finance.* Princeton University Press, Princeton, NJ (2015).

Quinn, Stephen, "Balances and Goldsmith-Bankers: The Co-ordination and Control of Inter-Banker Debt Clearing in the Seventeenth Century," in David Mitchell (ed.), *Goldsmiths, Silversmiths, and Bankers.* Alan Sutton Publishing, Stroud, UK (1995).

Radcliffe, Dan, & Rodger Vorhies, "A Digital Pathway to Financial Inclusion," Bill and Melinda Gates Foundation (December 2012).

Reynolds, Robert, "A Business Affair in Genoa in the Year 1200: Banking, Bookkeeping, a Broker and a Lawsuit," in Enrico Besta (ed.), *Studi di Storia e Diritto in Onore di Enrico Besta per il xi anno del suo Insegnamento*. Giuffrè, Milan (1938).

Richards, David, *The Early History of Banking in England*. Routledge, Oxford, UK (1929).

Richards, R. D. "The Evolution of Paper Money in England," 41:3 Quarterly Journal of Economics 361 (1927).

Ricks, Morgan, *The Money Problem: Rethinking Financial Regulation*. University of Chicago Press, Chicago (2016).

Rockoff, Hugh, "The Free Banking Era: A Reexamination," 6 Journal of Money, Credit and Banking 141 (1974).

———, "It Is Always the Shadow Banks: The Regulatory Status of the Banks That Failed and Ignited America's Greatest Financial Panics," in Hugh Rockoff & Isao Suto (eds.), *Coping with Financial Crises: Some Lessons from Economic History*. Springer, New York (2018).

———, "New Evidence on Free Banking in the United States," 76 American Economic Review 866 (1985).

Roe, Mark, "The Derivatives Market's Payment Priorities as Financial Crisis Accelerator," 63 Stanford Law Review 539 (2011).

Rogers, James, *The Early History of the Law of Bills and Notes: A Study of the Origins of Anglo-American Commercial Law*. Cambridge University Press, Cambridge (1995).

Rolnick, Arthur, & Warren Weber, "The Causes of Free Bank Failures: A Detailed Examination," 14 Journal of Monetary Economics 267 (1984).

———, "Free Banking, Wildcat Banking and Shinplasters," 6 Federal Reserve Bank of Minneapolis Quarterly Review 10 (1982).

———, "Gresham's Law or Gresham's Fallacy?," 94:1 Journal of Political Economy 185 (1986).

———, "New Evidence on the Free Banking Era," 73 American Economic Review 1080 (1983).

Romer, Christina, & David Romer, "The Missing Transition Mechanism in the Monetary Explanation of the Great Depression," 103 American Economic Review 66 (2013).

Roover, Raymond de, "Early Accounting Problems of Foreign Exchange," 19:4 Accounting Review 381 (1944).

———, "New Interpretations of the History of Banking," in Julius Kirshner (ed.), *Business, Banking and Economic Thought in Late Medieval and Early Modern Europe: Selected Case Studies of Raymond de Roover*. Cambridge University Press, Cambridge, UK (1974).

Sanches, Daniel, & Todd Keister, "Should Central Banks Issue Digital Currency?," Federal Reserve Bank of Philadelphia Working Paper No. 21-37 (November 2021).

Schaps, David, "The Invention of Coinage in Lydia, in India, and in China," XIV International Economic History Congress (2006).

Scheidel, Walter, "The Monetary Systems of the Han and Roman Empires," Princeton-Stanford Working Papers on Classics No. 110505 (February 2008).

Schrepel, Thibault, "Predatory Innovation: The Definite Need for Legal Recognition," 21 SMU Science & Technology Law Review 19 (2017).

Scott, Susan, & Markos Zachariadis, *The Society for Worldwide Interbank Financial Telecommunication: Cooperative Governance for Network Innovation, Standards, and Community*. Routledge, Oxford, UK (2014).

Selgin, George, "Friday Flashback: The Folly That Is 'Local' Currency," Alt-M blog (January 6, 2017), https://www.alt-m.org/2017/01/06/the-folly-that-is-local-currency/.

———, "Gresham's Law," in Robert Whaples (ed.), EH.Net Encyclopedia (June 9, 2003), http://eh.net/encyclopedia/greshams-law/.

———, "Salvaging Gresham's Law: The Good, the Bad, and the Illegal," 28:4 Journal of Money, Credit and Banking 637 (1996).

———, "Ten Things Every Economist Should Know about the Gold Standard," Alt-M blog (June 4, 2015), https://www.alt-m.org/2015/06/04/ten-things-every-economist-should-know-about-the-gold-standard-2/#gold-supply-shocks.

———, "A Three-Pronged Blunder, or, What Money Is, and What It Isn't," Alt-M blog (October 27, 2021), https://www.cato.org/blog/three-pronged-blunder-or-what-money-what-it-isnt.

Shabsigh, Ghiath, Tanai Khiaonarong, & Harry Leinonen, "Distributed Ledger Technology Experiments in Payments and Settlements," International Monetary Fund FinTech Notes 20/01 (June 2020).

Shiller, Robert, "Indexed Units of Account: Theory and Assessment of Historical Experience," National Bureau of Economic Research Working Paper No. 6356 (January 1998).

Shleifer, Andrei, & Robert Vishny, "Fire Sales in Finance and Macroeconomics," 25:1 Journal of Economic Perspectives 29 (2011).

Simons, Henry, "A Positive Program for Laissez Faire: Some Proposals for a Liberal Economic Policy," in Harry Gideonse (ed.), *Public Policy Pamphlet No. 15*. University of Chicago Press, Chicago (1934).

Skinner, Christina, "Central Bank Digital Currency as New Public Money," 172 University of Pennsylvania Law Review (forthcoming).

Soramäki, Kimmo, Morten Bech, Jeffrey Arnold, Robert Glass, & Walter Beyeler, "The Topology of Interbank Payment Flows," Federal Reserve Bank of New York Staff Report No. 243 (March 2006).

Sprague, O. M., "History of Crises under the National Banking System," in *The National Banking System*. U.S. Government Printing Office, Washington, DC (1910).

Stango, Victor, "Pricing with Consumer Switching Costs: Evidence from the Credit Card Market," 50 Journal of Industrial Economics 475 (2002).

Statista, "Online Banking Penetration in Great Britain from 2007 to 2020" (August 2020), https://www.statista.com/statistics/286273/internet-banking-penetration-in-great-britain/.

Stigler Center for the Study of the Economy and the State, *Stigler Committee on Digital Platforms: Final Report* (2019).

Summers, Brian, "Private Coinage in America," 26:7 The Freeman 436 (1976).

Summers, Bruce, "The Payment System in a Market Economy," in Bruce Summers (ed.), *The Payment System: Design, Management, and Supervision*. International Monetary Fund, Washington, DC (1994).

Sumner, William, "A History of Banking in Leading Nations," 1 Journal of Commerce & Commercial Bulletin 4 (1896).

Sylla, Ricard, "Monetary Innovation in America," 42:1 Journal of Economic History 21 (1982).

Thornton, Henry, *An Enquiry into the Nature and Effects of the Paper Credit of Great Britain* (1802).

Timberlake, Richard Jr., *The Central Banking Role of Clearinghouse Associations*, 16 Journal of Money, Credit and Banking 1 (1984).

Tobin, James, *Financial Innovation and Deregulation in Perspective*, 3 Bank of Japan Monetary & Economic Studies 19 (1985).

Trivoli, George, *The Suffolk Bank: Study of a Free-Enterprise Clearing System* (1979).

van der Cruijsen, Carin, & Maaike Diepstraten, "Banking Products: You Can Take Them with You, So Why Don't You?," 52 Journal of Financial Services Research 123 (2017).

Van Loo, Rory, "Making Innovation More Competitive," 65 UCLA Law Review 232 (2018).

Walters, Raymond, Jr., "The Origins of the Second Bank of the United States," 53 Journal of Political Economy 115 (1945).

Warburg, Paul, "The Discount System in Europe: Report for the National Monetary Commission," S. Doc. No. 402 (1910).

White, Eugene, "Rescuing a SIFI, Halting a Panic: The Barings Crisis of 1890," Bank of England, Bank Underground blog (February 10, 2016), https://bankunderground.co.uk/2016/02/10/rescuing-a-sifi-halting-a-panic-the-barings-crisis-of-1890/.

White, Lawrence (ed.), *Free Banking, Volumes 1–3*. Cambridge University Press, Cambridge, UK (1993).

———, *Free Banking in Britain: Theory, Experience and Debate 1800–1845* (2nd ed. 1995).

———, *The Theory of Monetary Institutions*. Wiley-Blackwell, Oxford, UK (1999).

Whited, Toni, Yufeng Wu, & Kairong Xiao, "Will Central Bank Digital Currency Disintermediate Banks?" IHS Working Paper No. 47 (January 13, 2023), https://papers.ssrn.com/sol3/papers.cfm?abstract_id=4112644.

Whitney, D. R., *The Suffolk Bank* (1878).

Williamson, Oliver, "Transaction-Cost Economics: The Governance of Contractual Relations," 22:2 Journal of Law and Economics 233 (1979).

Wilson, James, *Capital, Currency, and Banking* (1847).

Wood, John, "Bagehot's Lender of Last Resort: A Hollow Hallowed Tradition," 7 Independent Review 343 (2003).

Wood, Philip, *Principles of International Insolvency*. Sweet & Maxwell, Oxford, UK (2007).

Yadav, Yesha, "The Failed Regulation of U.S. Treasury Markets," 121 Columbia Law Review 1173 (2021).

———, "Toward a Public-Private Oversight Model of Crypto Markets," Vanderbilt Law Research Paper No. 22-26 (2022).

Case Law

Alameda Research LLC, Voluntary Petition for Non-individuals Filing for Bankruptcy, Case 22–11066 (filed November 11, 2022).

Apple iPod iTunes Antitrust Litigation, 796 F. Supp. 2d 1137 (N.D. Cal 2011).

Beatty v. Guggenheim Exploration Co., 225 N.Y. 380 (1919).

Bretton v. Barrett, 74 ER 918 (1598).

Carr v. Carr, 35 ER 799 (1811).

Celsius Network LLC et al., U.S. Bankruptcy Court, S.D.N.Y., Case No 22-10964, Final Report of Shoba Pillay, Examiner (January 30, 2023).

Celsius Network LLC et al., U.S. Bankruptcy Court, S.D.N.Y., Case No. 22-10964, Memorandum Opinion and Order Regarding Ownership of Earn Account Assets (January 24, 2023).

Custodia Bank, Inc. v. Federal Reserve Board of Governors and the Federal Reserve Bank of Kansas City, Case 1:22-cv-00125-SWS (filed June 7, 2022).

Devaynes v. Noble, 35 ER 767 (1816).

Foley v. Hill, 2 HL 28 (1848).

FTX Trading Ltd., et al., Case No. 22-11-068, U.S. Bankruptcy Court for the District of Delaware, Affidavit of John Ray III (filed November 17, 2022).

FTX Trading Ltd., et al., Case No. 22-11-068, U.S. Bankruptcy Court for the District of Delaware, Motion of Debtors for Entry of an Order Modifying Certain Creditor List Requirements (filed November 14, 2022).

Higgs v. Holiday, Cro. Eliz. 746 (1600).

Lehman Bros. Holding Inc., 422 B.R. 407, 418 (U.S. Bankruptcy Court, S.D.N.Y., 2010).

Lehman Brothers International (Europe) (in Administration); Insolvency Act 1986 (2012), UKSC 6.

Masterwear Corp., 229 B.R. 301 (U.S. Bankruptcy Court, S.D.N.Y., 1999).

Miller v. Race, 97 ER 398 (1758).

Powder Co. v. Burkhardt, 97 U.S. 110 (1878).

Sims v. Bond, 110 ER 834 (1833).

Strum v. Boker et al., 150 U.S. 312 (1893).

TNB USA Inc. v. Federal Reserve Bank of New York, 2020 WL 1445806 (S.D.N.Y., March 25, 2020).

Newspapers and Magazines

Alpher, Stephen, & Danny Nelson, "Genesis' Crypto Lending Businesses File for Bankruptcy Protection," *CoinDesk* (January 20, 2023).

"APIs to Drive Banking-as-a-Service Growth in 2022," pymnts.com (February 8, 2022).

Asgari, Nikou, "'Nightmare': Collapse of Leading Crypto Lender Traps Investors," *Financial Times* (January 20, 2023).

Benoit, David, "Federal Reserve Wants Citigroup to Move Faster to Fix Problems with Its Risk Systems," *Wall Street Journal* (September 15, 2022).

Bobrowsky, Meghan, "Big Tech Seeks Its Next Fortune in the Metaverse," *Wall Street Journal* (November 9, 2021).

Business Week, "Deposit Insurance," (April 12, 1933).

Central Banking, "RBI to Give Some Non-banks Access to Payment Systems," (April 15, 2021).

China Banking News, "NetsUnion Clearing Corporation," (July 23, 2018), https://www.chinabankingnews.com/wiki/netsunion-clearing-corporation/.

Cross, Miriam, "Community Banks Find Right Fit with Smaller Core Providers," *American Banker* (August 17, 2022).

De, Nikhilesh, "FDIC Orders Crypto Exchange FTX US, 4 Others to Cease 'Misleading' Claims," *CoinDesk* (August 19, 2022).

Elder, Bryce, "Scenes from a Celsius Bankruptcy Report," FTAlphaville blog (January 30, 2023).

Elkins, Kathleen, "Why It Took the US So Long to Adopt the Credit Card Technology Europe Has Used for Years," *Business Insider* (September 27, 2015), https://www.businessinsider.com/why-it-took-the-us-so-long-to-adopt-emv-2015-9.

Farley, Peter, "Spotlight on Compliance Costs as Banks Get Down to Business with AI," *International Banker* (July 4, 2017).

Faux, Zeke, & Joe Light, "Celsius's 18% Yields on Crypto Are Tempting—and Drawing Scrutiny," *Bloomberg* (January 27, 2022).

Fintech News, "AliPay Is the Most Popular Digital Wallet in the World in 2022," (September 26, 2022).

Fujikawa, Megumi, "Some FTX Customers Can Withdraw Their Money—in Japan, at Least," *Wall Street Journal* (February 21, 2023).

Hiken, Asa, "Coinbase Takes Aim at US Financial System in New Campaign," *AdAge* (March 9, 2023).

Hill, Jeremy, "Coinbase Lets Users Know What a Bankruptcy Could Mean for Their Crypto," *Bloomberg News* (May 11, 2022).

Hirsch, Lauren, David Yaffe-Bellany, & Ephrat Livni, "BlockFi Files for Bankruptcy as FTX Fallout Spreads," *New York Times* (November 28, 2022).

"Is the US on the Verge of a Contactless Surge?," pymnts.com (June 6, 2019), https://www.pymnts.com/news/retail/2019/contactless-payments-tap-and-pay-mpos/.

Isaac, Mike, & Nathaniel Popper, "Facebook Plans Global Financial System Based on Cryptocurrency," *New York Times* (June 18, 2019).

Keoun, Bradley, & Phil Kuntz, "Wall Street Aristocracy Got 1.2 Trillion in Secret Loans," *Bloomberg News* (August 21, 2011).

Kharif, Olga, & Joanna Ossinger, "Crypto Lender Celsius Files for Bankruptcy after Cash Crunch," *Bloomberg News* (July 13, 2022).

Korin, Netta, "Blockchain Technology Can Make Micropayments Finally Functional," *Cointelegraph* (October 31, 2021).

Kury, Theordore, "Why Do Different Countries Have Different Electrical Plugs?," *The Conversation* (December 21, 2020).

Ledger Insights, "Australia's Wholesale CBDC Trial Allowed Access to Non-banks," (December 8, 2021).

Levine, Matt, "Silvergate Had a Crypto Bank Run," *Bloomberg News* (March 2, 2023).

Mashal, Mujib, & Hari Kumar, "Where Digital Payments, Even for a 10-Cent Chai, Are Colossal in Scale," *New York Times* (March 1, 2023).

McLannahan, Ben, "Bitcoin Exchange Mt Gox Files for Bankruptcy Protection," *Financial Times* (February 28, 2014).

McMillan, Robert, "The Inside Story of Mt. Gox, Bitcoin's $460 Million Disaster," *Wired* (March 3, 2014).

McMillan, Robert, & Cade Metz, "The Rise and Fall of the World's Largest Bitcoin Exchange" *Wired* (November 6, 2013).

Moeser, Michael, "Is Your Tech Agenda Set for Safety or Standout Growth?," *American Banker* (February 27, 2023).

Mongelli, Lorena, "Former Cop Recalls NYPD Arrest of Willie Sutton 60 Years Later," *New York Post* (February 12, 2012).

Muir, Martha, "Case for Blockchain in Financial Services Dented by Failures," *Financial Times* (December 22, 2022).

New York Times, "Wires Banks to Urge Veto of Glass Bill," (June 16, 1933).

Newar, Brian, "Voyager Digital Files for Chapter 11 Bankruptcy, Proposes Recovery Plan," *Cointelegraph* (July 6, 2022).

Noonan, Laura, "UK Regulator Attacks 'Unacceptable' Risk Posed by Payments Groups," *Financial Times* (March 16, 2023).

Osaka, Shannon, "Elon Musk Agrees to Open Parts of Tesla's Charging Network to Everyone," *Washington Post* (February 15, 2023).

Peck, Emily, & Matt Phillips, "As Crypto Crated, Gemini Talked to Customers about FDIC Insurance," *Axios* (January 30, 2023).

Pedersen, Brendan, "Draft Bill Lets Nonbanks Issue Stablecoins, Bans Algorithmic Coins for Two Years," *American Banker* (September 20, 2022).

Robertson, Katie, "Why Can't Americans Ditch Checks?," *Bloomberg Business* (July 26, 2017), https://www.bloomberg.com/news/articles/2017-07-26/why-can-t-americans-give-up-paper-checks.

Saini, Manya, Niket Nishant, & Hannah Lang, "Silvergate Capital Shares Sink as Crypto-Related Deposits Plunge by $8 Billion," Reuters (January 5, 2023).

Saks Frankel, Robin, "When Were Credit Cards Invented. The History of Credit Cards," *Forbes* (July 27, 2021), https://www.forbes.com/advisor/credit-cards/history-of-credit-cards/.

Sandor, Krisztian, & Ekin Genç, "The Fall of Terra: A Timeline of the Meteoric Rise and Crash of UST and LUNA," *CoinDesk* (December 22, 2022).

Sarkar, Arijit, "USDC Depegs as Circle Confirms $3.3B Stuck with Silicon Valley Bank," *Cointelegraph* (March 11, 2023).

Shubber, Kadhim, & Joshua Oliver, "Crypto Hedge Fund Three Arrows Fails to Meet Lender Margin Calls," *Financial Times* (June 16, 2022).

Stempel, Jonathan, "After 14 Years, Lehman Brothers' Brokerage Ends Liquidation," Reuters (September 28, 2022).

Thompson's Bank Note Reporter (February 19, 1846).

Times of London, "Important Resolution of the Bank of England," (October 16, 1847).

Times of London, "The Panic," (May 12, 1866).

Twain, Mark, "Pudd'nhead Wilson," *Century Magazine* (April 1894).

Uranaka, Taiga, & Yuki Hagiwara, "Japan Passes Stablecoin Bill That Enshrines Investor Protection," *Bloomberg News* (June 2, 2022).

Victor, Jon, "How the Push to Modernize Canada's Payment Systems Went Off the Rails," *The Logic* (March 17, 2022).

Wall Street Journal, "Reserve Suspends Interest Limits on Some Big Deposit Certificates," (June 24, 1970).

Wiener, Anna, "Money in the Metaverse," *New Yorker* (January 4, 2022).

Wildau, Gabriel, & Yizhen Jai, "Central Bank Takes Steps to Ensure Ant Financial and Tencent Do Not Grow Too Powerful," *Financial Times* (January 1, 2019).

Yaffe-Bellany, David, "FTX Assets Still Missing as Firm Begins Bankruptcy Process," *New York Times* (November 22, 2022).

INDEX

Page numbers in *italics* refer to figures and tables.

A NOTE ON THE TYPE

This book has been composed in Adobe Text and Gotham. Adobe Text, designed by Robert Slimbach for Adobe, bridges the gap between fifteenth- and sixteenth-century calligraphic and eighteenth-century Modern styles. Gotham, inspired by New York street signs, was designed by Tobias Frere-Jones for Hoefler & Co.